Sustainable Peace in Northeast Asia

Sustainable Peace in Northeast Asia

Yong-Shik Lee, Ph.D.

ANTHEM PRESS

Anthem Press
An imprint of Wimbledon Publishing Company
www.anthempress.com

This edition first published in UK and USA 2025
by ANTHEM PRESS
75–76 Blackfriars Road, London SE1 8HA, UK
or PO Box 9779, London SW19 7ZG, UK
and
244 Madison Ave #116, New York, NY 10016, USA

First published in the UK and USA by Anthem Press in 2023

British Library Cataloguing-in-Publication Data
A catalogue record for this book is available from the British Library.

Library of Congress Control Number: 2025935301
A catalog record for this book has been requested.

ISBN-13: 978-1-83999-608-5 (Pbk)
ISBN-10: 1-83999-608-0 (Pbk)

Cover Credit: Oleh Donets

This title is also available as an e-book.

In memory of all those who lived and died for peace
and who perished in Ukraine

ADVANCED REVIEWS

"The security environment in Northeast Asia is notoriously complex, but Y.S. Lee weaves a compelling introduction to it. A distinctive feature of the approach is to work through the perspectives of each of the relevant players, with a particular bonus in considering Mongolia's contributions. Professor Lee sees a long-term solution as requiring an institutional component; some kind of regional integration effort that would pull North Korea into the Asia-Pacific success story. He argues that building a rules-based order will hinge on where China's domestic politics is headed, but the US must also take diplomatic risks and lead on the economic issues. A useful introduction for both insiders to the region and those seeking an entry point."

Dr. Stephan Haggard, Lawrence and Sallye Krause
Distinguished Professor, School of Global Policy and
Strategy, University of California at San Diego

"Lee's volume is a balanced, penetrating, and up-to-date analysis of political, historical, military, and economic dynamics in Northeast Asia. It is comprehensive in scope, innovative in analytical orientation, rigorous in empirical investigation, and rich in policy implications. Departing from the traditional great power determinism, he adopts an 'inside-out' approach focusing on six individual countries (North Korea, China, South Korea, Japan, Russia, and Mongolia). Lee skillfully unravels hidden codes of regional dynamics and generates powerful policy implications for sustainable peace in Northeast Asia. Strongly recommended for scholars, policy-makers, and laymen who are interested in conflicts and peace in contemporary Northeast Asia."

Dr. Chung-in Moon, Professor Emeritus,
Yonsei University

"Professor Lee's book includes a chapter on Japan which comprehensively, accurately, and concisely describes Japan's political and economic history, its tense relationship with neighboring countries, and ways to resolve them. It is a must-read for researchers and students studying the subject. This book is an excellent introduction and a practical prescription for achieving peace in East Asia."

Dr. Hiroyuki Hoshiro, Professor, Institute of Social Science, University of Tokyo

"Dr. Yong-Shik Lee's new book 'Sustainable Peace in Northeast Asia' suggests innovative, in-depth and comprehensive analysis on the continuing geopolitical tension in Northeast Asia. His careful and thorough data-backed examination of the repercussions of the Korean unification to Northeast Asia gave me valuable academic insight for actual policy making in the Foreign Affair & Unification Committee. I am also truly inspired by Dr. Lee's anatomy of the influence of the external powers over the crisis, their political and economic objectives, their strategies and the dynamics that their engagement has created within Northeast Asia. This volume should be widely read not only among academics but policymakers as well."

Hon. Yongho Tae, Vice Chair of the Foreign Affair & Unification Committee of the National Assembly of the Republic of Korea, Former Deputy Ambassador of the Democratic People's Republic of Korea to the United Kingdom

"Dr. Lee's new book 'Sustainable Peace in Northeast Asia' is an interesting, innovative and multidisciplinary project. Cultural, historical, political economy, and geopolitical factors are closely integrated into the development of the book. The book is worth reading by scholars and students in international relationships, government officials focusing on Northeast Asia, and readers interested in politics and peace in this important and dynamic region."

Dr. Guanghua Yu, Professor of Law, University of Hong Kong

"Dr. Yong-Shik Lee's book 'Sustainable Peace in Northeast Asia' presents a new approach to the security issues in Northeast Asia. Many of us address these issues from a traditional perspective, focusing on current geo-political and military affairs. In contrast, Dr. Lee's book moves beyond the narrow confines of this traditional approach and performs a broader analysis of historical, political, economic, cultural and other factors that affect sustainable peace in the region. This innovative approach makes Dr. Lee's book a unique scholarly contribution and a must read for policymakers, academics, students, and all others sharing interests in the important question of sustaining peace in Northeast Asia."

Dr. Bayasgalan Sanallkhundev, Associate
Professor of International Relations and Public
Administration, National University of Mongolia

"Dr. Yong-Shik Lee is uniquely situated to engage in a thorough treatment of Northeast Asia as a legal academic, law and development expert, international law authority, law and economics specialist, diplomat, and multi-continent academic. The breadth and depth of his experience and knowledge provide insights that make 'Sustainable Peace in Northeast Asia' a must read for students, scholars, decision-makers, and policymakers. International relations literature tends to be dominated with large global theories, and area specialists often focus on one country as it relates to neighbors or on very specific issues. Dr. Lee is able to add a new perspective by examining China, North Korea, South Korea, Mongolia, and Japan from a regional and nation-specific perspective. Including the impacts of major global powers in regional alliances, diplomacy, trade, and investment provides a deeper understanding of the importance of Northeast Asia in the larger global landscape. By delivering a strong historical approach to situate modern positions, Dr. Lee allows a context-rich understanding of Northeast Asia that is not available elsewhere. The solid foundation makes his approach to potential solutions and strategies particularly helpful. Dr. Lee covers complex dynamics in an engaging and thought-provoking manner making 'Sustainable Peace in Northeast Asia' appealing read. 'Sustainable Peace in Northeast Asia' is a must-read and essential tool for anyone interested in Northeast Asia and larger global issues."

Dr. John Parsi, College of Law,
University of Nebraska

ABOUT THE AUTHOR

Yong-Shik Lee is a lawyer, economist, and international relations expert. He is currently the Director and Professorial Fellow of the Law and Development Institute. Lee has taught at leading universities throughout the United States, Europe, and Asia, including Cornell University, New York University, Emory University, Tulane University, University of Manchester, and University of Sydney. Prior to his academic career, Lee served as counsel for the Ministry of Foreign Affairs and Trade of the Republic of Korea. He graduated with a degree in economics with distinction from the University of California at Berkeley and received degrees in law with honors from the University of Cambridge (BA, MA, PhD). Author of *Law and Development: Theory and Practice* (2019, 2022), *Reclaiming Development in the World Trading System* (2006, 2009, 2016), and *Microtrade: A New System of Trade Toward Poverty Elimination* (2013), Lee has published over 120 scholarly articles, book volumes, chapters, and shorter notes with leading publishers in North America, Europe, and Asia.

CONTENTS

FIGURES

TABLES

LIST OF ABBREVIATIONS

AI	Artificial Intelligence
AUKUS	Australia–United Kingdom–United States alliance
CCP	Chinese Communist Party
CER	Chinese Eastern Railroad
COVID-19	Coronavirus Disease 2019
CRS	Congressional Research Service (United States)
CPTPP	Comprehensive and Progressive Agreement for Trans-Pacific Partnership
DMZ	Demilitarized Zone (Korea)
DRAM	Dynamic Random-Access Memory
EPB	Economic Planning Board (South Korea)
EU	European Union
EV	Electric Vehicle
FDI	Foreign Direct Investment
FTA	Free Trade Agreement
GATT	General Agreement on Tariffs and Trade
GDP	Gross Domestic Product
GNI	Gross National Income
IAEA	International Atomic Energy Agency
ICBM	Intercontinental Ballistic Missile
ICT	Information and Communication Technology
IMF	International Monetary Fund
IPEF	Indo-Pacific Economic Framework for Prosperity
IPR	Intellectual Property Right
IT	Information Technology
JMSDF	Japanese Maritime Self-Defense Force
KCIA	Korean Central Intelligence Agency
LDP	Liberal Democratic Party (Japan)
MFN	Most Favored Nation
MITI	Ministry of International Trade and Industry (Japan)
MPP	Mongolian People's Party

NAPCI	Northeast Asia Peace and Cooperation Initiative
NATO	North Atlantic Treaty Organization
NGO	Non-Governmental Organization
NPT	Treaty on the Non-Proliferation of Nuclear Weapons
OECD	Organisation for Economic Co-operation and Development
RCEP	Regional Comprehensive Economic Partnership
RTA	Regional Trade Agreement
SCAP	Supreme Commander for the Allied Powers
SDF	Self-Defense Force (Japan)
SEZ	Special Economic Zone
SME	Small- and Medium-Sized Enterprise
SOE	State-Owned Enterprise
THAAD	Terminal High Altitude Area Defense
TPP	Trans-Pacific Partnership
UB	Ulaanbaatar (Mongolia)
U.N.	United Nations
UNESCO	United Nations Educational, Scientific and Cultural Organization
UNCTAD	United Nations Conference on Trade and Development
U.S.	United States of America
WTO	World Trade Organization

FOREWORD

The strategic landscape in the Indo-Pacific region has devolved into a fraught set of conflict points, now stretching from the India-China border, through the South China Sea, the Taiwan Strait to the East China Sea. Yet no part of that arc is as complex as the Northeast Asian theatre, where the interests of six parties collide: the two Koreas, Japan, China, Russia and the United States. As U.S.-China relations have deteriorated, the Cold War divides that have been in place since the end of the Pacific War have hardened, with declining prospects of a negotiated settlement. China's struggle to define its global status and the war in Ukraine are now central drivers in this drama. But in the end, the Korean peninsula remains at its heart, precisely because it increasingly surfaces as a focal point for a broader array of competing interests. Those now include China's decision to cast its fate with Russia and the corresponding logic of tighter political, military and economic cooperation among the democracies: the United States, Japan and South Korea.

Y.S. Lee weaves an introduction to the current state of play. A distinctive feature of the approach is to work through the perspectives of each of the relevant players, with a particular bonus in considering Mongolia's contributions as well. Prof. Lee sees a long-term solution as requiring an institutional component—some kind of regional integration effort that would pull North Korea into the Asia-Pacific success story. He recognizes that building a rules-based order will hinge on where China's domestic politics is headed, but the U.S. must also take diplomatic risks and lead on the economic issues.

Prof. Lee's approach is anchored in realist fundamentals. China is clearly central to sustainable peace in Northeast Asia, and nothing will move unless Beijing comes to see it in its interest to make them move. Given China's massive political, economic, and military influence in the region, a more balanced, reconciliatory, and constructive engagement with the other Northeast Asian countries around the Korean peninsula is imperative to achieve a meaningful settlement. However, Lee's account acknowledges that the nature of China's foreign engagement is inseparable from its internal governance style. He outlines a classic liberal argument (and one with which I strongly agree): China's authoritarian turn is intimately connected with its more confrontational, aggressive, and coercive foreign policy, with Xi Jinping sitting as the architect of that approach. Unless there is some fundamental rethink of China's rise in Beijing, sustainable peace in Northeast Asia will remain elusive.

North Korea's nuclear ambitions represent a more immediate security risk for the region, and they too have an internal as well as external dynamic. Critics of the U.S., Japan and South Korea note that as a weak country facing much more capable rivals, it should come as no surprise that North Korea would seek the cheapest deterrent at its proposal: a missile-based nuclear capability. But the excesses to which the leadership has pushed this program suggests that its strategy is not just a bargaining chip to extract political and economic concessions; if so, the Six Party Talks would have achieved much more and negotiations would at some point have resumed. It is now probably too much to expect a hereditary regime to remake itself. But as China's earlier "peaceful rise" strategy suggests, it is certainly not impossible to combine a form of autocratic rule with an engaged and constructive foreign policy.

Each of the other players in the region—South Korea, Japan, the United States, Russia, and Mongolia—has unique historical, political, and economic contexts that Lee traces to national "codes": these rest on a complex combination of national characteristics, from the nature of postwar nationalism, to the level of economic development, and the extent of the embrace of liberal norms; as with China and North Korea, domestic political forces are given appropriate play.

The most intriguing and controversial component of Lee's book is his claim that the formation of an economic and political union in Northeast Asia, such as the European Union, will be a necessary institutional arrangement to ensure sustainable peace in the region. Without cross-cutting institutional and economic ties, the region will remain in its current rut. Prof. Lee is well aware that the lack of shared political values, economic disparities, and political and military tensions make the formation of such a union in the near future highly unlikely. But here is where the book makes it most important contribution: that without diplomacy, the chances of transcending the status quo are even more remote. Whether in the form of dialogues such as Ulaanbaatar Dialogue on Northeast Asia Security or cross-cutting initiatives such the China–Japan–South Korea initiative, which includes an FTA, steps must be found to cross the river to what Prof. Lee calls sustainable peace. The U.S. plays a crucial role in this regard, and must hold open the door for an alternative to the current impasse.

Stephan Haggard
Lawrence and Sallye Krause Distinguished Professor
School of Global Policy and Strategy
University of California at San Diego

PREFACE

Northeast Asia, a major region in Asia covering China, Korea (South and North Korea), Japan, Mongolia, and the Southeast corner of Russia, is economically one of the most vibrant areas in the world, with a rich array of economic opportunities. Yet, it is simultaneously one of the world's most politically and militarily unstable regions, creating a global security risk. This risk was made apparent by North Korea's nuclear crisis, which was followed by a series of its nuclear tests and ballistic missile launches from 2016 to 2017. Although the worst-case scenario may have been avoided by a summit meeting between the heads of South and North Korea on April 27, 2018, and another summit between the United States and North Korea on June 12, 2018, substantial uncertainty and the risk of a major military conflict remains.

Although less dramatic and visible to the outside world, other political and military tensions among constituent countries in Northeast Asia, with their deep historical origins dating back centuries, are also significant. These tensions have been demonstrated by persistent territorial disputes, lack of reconciliation on the question of war crimes during World War II, increasing disparities in political influence and military power among Northeast Asian countries as a result of China's ascension, and deepening uncertainty in the region due to the potential instability of North Korea (caused by its confrontations with South Korea and its allies, internal political issues, and economic problems). These problems carry with them the potential to destabilize Northeast Asia, the effects of which would have a substantial global impact.

This book examines the causes of these complex tensions in Northeast Asia and their underlying political, historic, military, and economic developments. It further discusses their political-economic implications for the world and explores possible solutions to build lasting peace in the region. This book offers a unique approach to these important issues by examining the perspectives of each constituent country in Northeast Asia: China, South and North Korea, Japan, and Mongolia, and their respective roles in the region. Major global powers, such as the United States and Russia, have also closely engaged in the political and economic affairs of the region through a network of alliances, diplomacy, trade, and investment. The book will discuss the influence of these external powers, their political and economic objectives in the region, their strategies, and the dynamics that their engagement has brought to the region. Russia's recent invasion of Ukraine also affects its engagement in Northeast Asia, as Russia had to withdraw its military resources from the region for deployment in its war effort in Ukraine, and several constituent states in the region, such as South Korea, Japan, and the United States, support Ukraine. Russia's political credibility has also been damaged in this region and beyond due to its globally condemned invasion.

Both South and North Korea have sought to unify the Korean peninsula for nearly eight decades. The Korean War (1950–1953) brought destruction and distrust between the two Koreas instead of the unification intended by the North at the beginning of the war. During several decades that followed, South and North Korea failed to build peace and trust between them. Although the prospect of Korean unification remains uncertain, the outcome of this process will have a substantial impact on the region. This book will also examine the justifications, feasibility, and regional effects of Korean unification. Lastly, this book discusses the role of Mongolia in the context of the power dynamics in Northeast Asia. This relatively small country, in terms of its population and economic size, has rarely been examined in such a context, and this book offers a discussion on its role.

It has been said that the nineteenth century was the European century, the twentieth century was led by the United States, and the twenty-first century will be the Asian century. The economic and political influence of Asia, particularly Northeast Asia, has grown substantially in recent decades, and this growing influence gives credence to this observation. Reflecting on the importance of the region, both the United States and Russia have been closely involved in the region. The escalating political tensions, associated with the rise of China, create a confrontational divide between China and the U.S. alliance, the effect of which goes well beyond the region. The nuclear issues in North Korea seem to have subsided after a series of summits but have not been permanently resolved, and they could erupt and develop into a major crisis again. These outstanding risks, which coexist with the massive economic opportunities in the region, call for new approaches and paradigms to achieve sustainable peace in Northeast Asia.

Y.S. Lee
Atlanta, Georgia
December 2022

ACKNOWLEDGMENTS

This book would not have been possible without dedicated support from my research assistants, colleagues, and many other individuals, all of whom cannot be listed in this limited space. I am grateful to my wife Hye Seong for her endearing support for my work and her kind understanding when I had to be away from family engagements to work on this book. I am indebted to leading scholars, Professors Stephan Haggard (University of California at San Diego), Moon Chung-In (Yonsei University), Yongho Tae (National Assembly, Republic of Korea), Guanghua Yu (University of Hong Kong), John Parsi (University of Nebraska), Salim Farrar (University of Sydney), Bayasgalan Sanallkhundev (National University of Mongolia), Hiroyuki Hoshiro (University of Tokyo), and Artyom Lukin (Far Eastern Federal University, Russia), for their insightful comments and constructive criticisms. I am thankful to my student assistants, including Thomas Oliver Flint, Andrew Smith, Skyler Martin, Kedric Ross, Max Robert Beal, Kate Billard, Matthew Bowling, Adam Xie, Inseok Jeong, Turner Jensen, Monica Vu, Sayeed Mohammad, Rachel Pearce, Matthew Dutton, Jamie Borscha, Jordan Cohen, Isabel Cheesman, John Clayes, Olivia Thiel, Philip Jeffry Abraham, and Aryka Klemme, for their research and editorial assistance. I also appreciate young Mongolian citizens Lkhagva Yesu, Saruul Khaliun, and Bill Guudei for participating in interviews for the book. I am also grateful to Georgia State University, the University of Nebraska, and Cornell University for providing research support for this book. Lastly, I am very appreciative of Anthem Press for its decision to publish this book. It would not have been possible to bring this book to the light of the day without the excellent work of its editorial staff and production team.

Chapter 1

INTRODUCTION

1.1 Northeast Asia: Economic and Strategic Importance

1.1.1 Economic rise of Northeast Asia

Northeast Asia, the region that encompasses China, Korea, Japan, Mongolia, and the southeast corner of Russia, is one of the world's most economically dynamic and strategically important regions.

Within 1,200 kilometers of Seoul, South Korea, a distance that can be covered by less than two hours of flight time, lie three national capitals that command over 20 percent of the world's population and nearly a quarter of the world's economy.[1] The region's economic importance is unquestionable: two of the world's three largest economies (China and Japan) and three of the world's 10 largest exporters (China, Japan, and South Korea) are located in this region.[2] By the end of World War II, Northeast Asia was among the poorest regions in the world; much of it laid in ruin as a result of the war's destruction. However, starting with the economic recovery of Japan in the 1950s, rapid economic development and successful industrialization of the constituent countries have turned this region into the world's premier economic powerhouse. North Korea, under its socialist economic system, showed rapid economic growth until the 1970s,[3] although it met economic struggles and has been on a decline since the 1990s. South Korea, with its successful economic development drive beginning in the 1960s, became an advanced, industrialized economy and a major trader by the 1990s. China, under Deng Xiaoping's leadership advocating the "socialist market economy," has also achieved phenomenal economic growth since the 1980s, becoming the second largest economy, next only to the United States, by 2010. Figures 1.2 and 1.3 illustrate the economic growth of Northeast Asian countries (China, Japan, and South Korea) vis-à-vis the United States.

The region is now known as the factory of the world and a bastion of new technologies and innovations. In the traditional manufacturing areas, such as steel, automobile, shipbuilding, electronics (including semiconductors), and chemical, Northeast Asian countries, particularly China, South

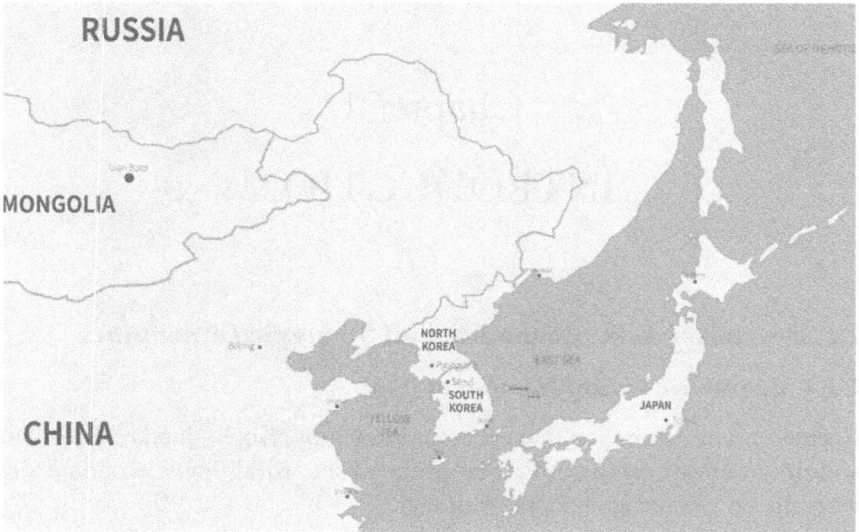

Figure 1.1 Map of Northeast Asia. (*Source*: Northeast Asia Countries Map, modified from https://www.alamy.com/northeast-asia-countries-map-editable-continental-map-of-country-image370477370.html)

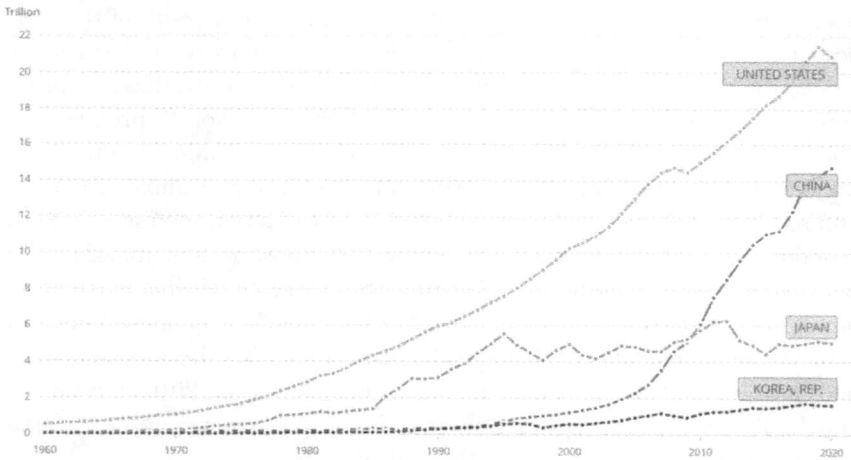

Figure 1.2 Gross domestic product of major Northeast Asian economies (1960–2020). (*Source*: World Bank, GDP (current US$) – China, Japan, Korea, Rep., United States)

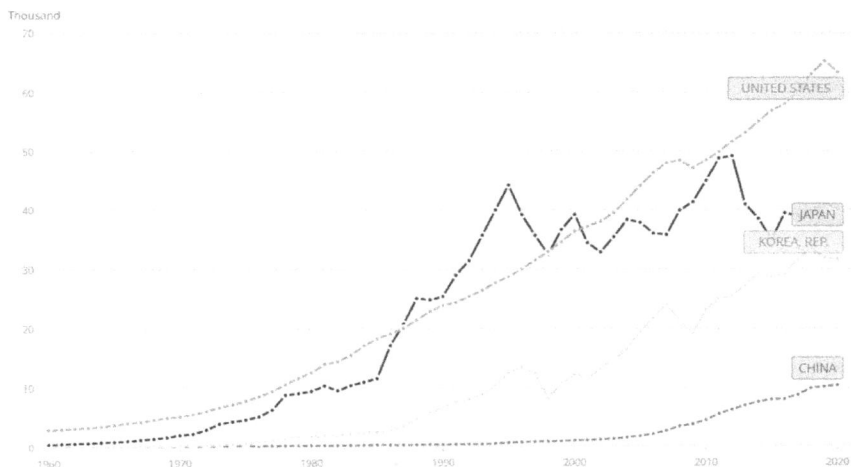

Figure 1.3 Gross domestic product per capita of major Northeast Asian economies (1960–2020). (*Source*: World Bank, GDP per capita (current US$) – China, Korea, Rep., Japan, United States)

Korea, and Japan, make up substantial shares of global production. By 2021, China, Japan, and South Korea produced over 61 percent of the world's steel supply,[4] over 44 percent of the world's automobiles,[5] and over 94 percent of all ships (in tonnage).[6] For electronics, Northeast Asia is home to the world's top five consumer electronics companies, as measured by revenue.[7] Northeast Asia is also an important region for semiconductor production: South Korea alone accounts for over 70 percent of the world's Dynamic Random-Access Memory (DRAM) production.[8] Northeast Asian countries are also major drivers of new technologies and industries, including artificial intelligence (AI), biotechnology, and information and communication technology (ICT). In 2021, China's ICT exports reached US$ 857 million.[9]

Northeast Asia has achieved rapid economic development over the past several decades and remains the fastest growing economic center, despite the worldwide pandemic (COVID-19) that slowed economic growth across the world.[10] In the pre-industrial era, Northeast Asian economies, including China, accounted for up to a third of the world economy.[11] The region lagged behind the West economically during the period of the Industrial Revolution, but successful industrialization and economic growth in the latter part of the twentieth century resulted in Northeast Asia becoming one of the world's three major economic areas, alongside North America and Europe. Northeast Asia, with three of the world's top 10 importers in the region (China, Japan, and South Korea), is also becoming the world's largest import market.[12] Thus, the continuing economic growth of the region will work as an engine for global economic growth.

1.1.2 Strategic importance of the region

Historically, Northeast Asia formed the frontline between the continental powers, which include Russia and China, and the Asian-Pacific maritime powers, which include the United States and Japan. Those who control Northeast Asia have enjoyed critical strategic advantages, as the region is the gateway to the Eurasian continent from the South and to the Pacific and Southeast Asia from the North. For this reason, imperial Japan first annexed Korea and occupied Northeast China (Manchuria) before it attempted to expand its empire across the entire Asian-Pacific region in the 1930s and 1940s. During the Cold War, communist Russia (formerly the Soviet Republic or the Soviet Union)[13] and China clashed with the United States in Northeast Asia, particularly in the Korean peninsula. Korea was divided into the South and North at the beginning of the Cold War conflict between the United States and Russia in the region. Communist attempts to expand in Northeast Asia culminated in the outbreak of the Korean War (1950–1953), in which 24 countries participated following the resolution of the United Nations Security Council.[14]

These strategic dynamics and the intense presence of global powers in the region indicate that maintaining peace in Northeast Asia will be essential to sustain global peace. As further discussed in Section 1.3, Northeast Asia, particularly the Korean peninsula, has undergone a massive military buildup over the past several decades, and the world's largest military forces, including the United States, China, and Russia, are maintaining strategic military forces in the region (although Russia recently withdrew substantial military resources from the region for its war effort in Ukraine). The Cold War may have ended, but political confrontations between Russia, China, and North Korea on one side and the United States, South Korea, and Japan on the other continue, with Mongolia trying to maintain its neutrality between the two groups. Increasing economic integration among these countries via international trade and investment[15] may work as a deterrent against all-out wars, but political tensions and the potential for military confrontations remain, due to unresolved critical issues. These issues include North Korea's nuclear ambitions; China's conduct in Xinjiang, Tibet, Hong Kong, and Taiwan, as well as its expansionary policies in the South and East China Seas; and Japan's decades-long rightward shift that has created political frictions with Korea and China, as further discussed in subsequent chapters.

Northeast Asia is also a theater for global powershift and rivalry between the United States and China. With its growing economic, industrial, and military capacities, China has challenged the global hegemony that the United States maintained for several decades.[16] In this rivalry, both the United States and China have vied for alliances and support from other constituent countries in Northeast Asia. The power struggle has put two major U.S. allies, South Korea and Japan, in sensitive positions, as their economies rely in substantial part on China's market,[17] and neither wants to undermine their own economic positions by provoking economic retaliation from China (*e.g.*, trade sanctions).[18] Nevertheless, the United States maintains a substantial military presence in both countries, and the possibility of a military conflict between the United States and China cannot be precluded given the history of confrontation between the two countries. The United States does not accept China's claims over the South and East China Seas and has also committed to protecting Taiwan from an invasion from China.[19] In the event of a conflict, the United States and China will likely attempt to geographically limit it to Taiwan and its surrounding seas, but U.S. allies outside the region could also be pulled into the conflict, sparking another war.

An example of this danger is well illustrated by the Korean War, which lasted for three years—from 1950 to 1953. This destructive war, waged by communist North Korea to unite the entire Korean peninsula under communist rule, claimed over 2.5 million lives.[20] Twenty-four countries—including South and North Korea, the United States, China, the United Kingdom, France, Canada, Australia, New Zealand, Greece, Turkey, Belgium, the Netherlands, Luxembourg, Thailand, the Philippines, South Africa, Ethiopia, and Columbia (combatants), as well as India, Sweden, Norway, Denmark, and Italy (noncombatant participants offering medical support)—participated in this war. The Korean War, which ceased in a stalemate, was contained to the Korean peninsula, but it could have exploded into a third world war, as the commander of the allied forces, General Douglas MacArthur, considered using nuclear bombs to halt the advance of Chinese forces during the war (although his plan could not be implemented due to his dismissal by President Truman).[21]

The economic importance of the region reinforces its strategic value. As discussed above, Northeast Asia has become a hub of industrial production, new technologies, trade, and investment. The rise of China, with increasing economic as well as political influence over the region and beyond, has alarmed the United States and its allies, which prompted the Obama administration to adopt policies with an eye toward a "pivot to Asia," as illustrated by its conclusion of the Trans-Pacific Partnership (TPP) negotiations in 2016 with 12 countries in the Asia Pacific region.[22] The subsequent Trump administration withdrew from the TPP, but the TPP survived without the participation of the United States.[23] China has also made efforts to reinforce its economic and trade ties with other Northeast Asian countries and has participated in two free trade agreements (FTAs), including the China–Japan–Korea tripartite FTA and the Regional Comprehensive Economic Partnership (RCEP) with 15 members, which represents a third of the world's population and accounts for 30 percent of the world's gross domestic product (GDP).[24]

Notably, two countries in the region, Mongolia and North Korea, have not participated in any of these FTAs. Mongolia is a member of the World Trade Organization (WTO) and has signed an Economic Partnership Agreement with Japan, but it has not participated in RCEP or the TPP. Due to its small economy (US$ 15.1 billion GDP as of 2021)[25] and low level of industrialization, the country is economically vulnerable to the influence of neighboring China, which is the largest importer of Mongolian exports and the largest investor in Mongolia. North Korea is another isolated country in the region. Its economic size (estimated US$ 28.1 billion GDP as of 2021) is larger than that of Mongolia, but its per capita income (estimated US$ 1,085 as of 2021) is among the lowest in the world. Due to the economic sanctions in place against North Korea, as further discussed in Chapter 2, the country is not in a position to pursue economic or trade agreements with another country. From an economic standpoint, these two countries remain in peripheral positions and do not have a significant economic presence in the region, despite their economic potential (*e.g.*, substantial mineral deposits).[26]

1.2 Historical Context

The current economic and political dynamics in Northeast Asia have a complex historical context. Northeast Asia is home to some of the world's oldest countries, such as China, Korea, and Japan, each with thousands of years of history. For ages, these countries have interacted with one another culturally, politically, and economically. The advancement of external powers, such as the United States and Russia, into Northeast Asia (since the nineteenth century) has further complicated the region's historical context. An understanding of this context is necessary to assess the present dynamics in the region. This section provides the relevant historical context.

1.2.1 *Pax China and its dissolution*

Northeast Asia was subject to the political and economic dominance of China until the late nineteenth century. The sheer size and capacity of China, with its vast territory, massive population, profound cultural heritage, and scale of economic resources unmatched by any other country in the region, allowed it to establish a dominant political influence over the region. Other nations that competed with China in the region have since perished. For example, the Manchurian state, which was established in the seventeenth century (Aisin Gurun or 後金, later the Qing Dynasty), conquered China, but the Manchurian conquerors were absorbed into the defeated China, and the Qing Dynasty became the last dynasty in China until its dissolution in 1912. For ages, the Chinese people considered their state to be the center of the world and reasoned that it should command all adjacent nations and states due to its superior civilization and mandate from the heavens (an idea referred to as "Sinocentrism").[27] From a historical perspective, the Roman Empire fell in Europe, but one created by the Chinese remained in East Asia.

However, the advancement of the Western powers in the nineteenth century shattered China's domination based on Sinocentrism. China's defeat in the Opium War (1839–1842) signaled the end of China's domination. Japan's subsequent victory in the Sino-Japanese War (1894–1895) vividly demonstrated China's decline, and it could no longer prevail in the region.[28] In contrast to Japan—which successfully modernized in the late nineteenth century by adopting Western technologies, reforming its state, and building modern industries and armed forces—China stagnated in these efforts. The demise of the Qing Dynasty in 1912 brought internal turmoil, civil wars, and foreign invasions. The new Chinese republic failed to establish control over China, and warlords claimed their own territories throughout China.[29] The Republic of China, under the leadership of Chiang Kai-shek, began to prevail over the warlords, but the subsequent Japanese invasion and strife with the communists put China through decades of political turmoil and destruction.[30]

The dissolution of China's dominance did not, however, lead to the colonization of China. The colonial powers, including Britain, France, and Germany, as well as Russia and later Japan, established their own enclaves and spheres of influence within China, but unlike India and the Southeast Asian nations that became colonies of the Western powers, the Qing Dynasty retained its sovereignty until its demise in 1912 and preserved most of its territory. The succeeding Chinese republic reestablished its sovereignty across all of China except for Mongolia, which the Qing Dynasty had conquered by the mid-eighteenth century. In 1921, Mongolia established its government with the support of the Russians.[31] Chinese leaders initially resisted the independence of Mongolia but formally approved its independence in 1945. However, Inner Mongolia, which was closer to China, could not achieve independence and remained a part of China. Korea, which was under China's political influence for centuries, became briefly autonomous after the first Sino-Japanese War but was colonized by Japan in 1910.[32]

1.2.2 *Rise of Japan, war, and destruction*

Another important historical context is the rise of Japan as a modern and ambitious expansionary state in the late nineteenth century. Japan, a Pacific island state some 200 kilometers southeast of the Korean peninsula, histori-cally occupied a relatively peripheral position in the region and held limited political and economic influence over Northeast Asia. However, its signifi-cance as a nation has radically increased since it successfully modernized by adopting Western technologies and modern state systems through the process of political reform called "the Meiji Restoration," which began in 1868.[33] The new Japanese government consolidated political power by replacing its tra-ditional governance system (that afforded regional lords political autonomy) with a modern bureaucracy.[34] By the end of the nineteenth century, Japan built substantial industrial capabilities and armed forces, as demonstrated by its victory over China in the first Sino-Japanese War.

Japan sought territorial expansion beyond its islands and deployed its military power in Northeast Asia. As a result of the first Sino-Japanese War, Japan acquired Taiwan from China. Japan also prevailed in the subsequent Russo-Japanese War (1904–1905) despite contrary expectations and drove Russia away from Northeast China.[35] The United States approved Japan's occupation of Korea in the Taft-Katsura Agreement in 1905,[36] and Japan for-cibly annexed Korea in 1910. Japan's territorial aggression did not stop with Taiwan and Korea. The Japanese military invaded Manchuria in 1931 and created a puppet state, Manchukuo (滿洲國), under Japanese control.[37] In 1937, Japan invaded mainland China, starting the Second Sino-Japanese War.[38] China's nationalists and communists formed a joint resistance against the Japanese invasion, and the Japanese military, despite initial victories in major battles, could not defeat the joint Chinese forces in the prolonged war.

Japan's warfare in China was atrocious.[39] The Japanese military com-mitted massacres of civilian populations (*e.g.*, 300,000 deaths in the Nanjing Massacre of 1937) as well as other human rights violations, such as the sex-ual enslavement of so-called "comfort women" endorsed by the military.[40] Western powers, including the United States, pressed Japan to withdraw its armed forces from China by imposing economic sanctions, including export bans on oil and steel scraps to Japan.[41] In 1941, Japan started a war with the United States, without finishing its ongoing war in China, by bombing the U.S. Pacific fleet stationed at Pearl Harbor. Much of Northeast Asia was destroyed by the war. Chinese cities and towns were demolished, and tens of millions of Chinese lost their lives. Japan began to lose the war in the Pacific by the summer of 1942, and the Japanese islands were obliterated by aerial bombings, including two nuclear bombings in Hiroshima and Nagasaki, in

1945. The Korean peninsula escaped the carnage of the war as it was not used as a battlefield, but hundreds of thousands of the Korean population were mobilized for Japanese war efforts as laborers and soldiers and died or were wounded under harsh conditions.[42]

1.2.3 Communist China, the Korean War, and economic development

China prevailed in the war against Japan in 1945, but a civil war subsequently broke out between China's nationalists and communists.[43] The communists defeated the nationalists under the leadership of Mao Zedong and established the People's Republic of China in 1949.[44] The defeated nationalists did not surrender to the new communist state but escaped to Taiwan, which had been retaken by China from Japan.[45] The nationalists formed a government in Taiwan, which still stands today. During World War II, the Soviet military repelled the Japanese from Northeast China.[46] The Soviets withdrew from Northeast China after the war but retained their territory in the northeast corner of the region.[47] This meant that much of Northeast Asia, except for South Korea and Japan, fell under communist rule, which resulted in alliances among China, the Soviet Union, and North Korea on one end and the United States, South Korea, and Japan on the other. The structure of these two alliances remains in place, even after the end of the Cold War.

After World War II, the Korean peninsula was occupied by the United States in the South and the Soviet Union in the North, and it was eventually divided into South and North Korea. The subsequent Korean War, waged by the communist North, destroyed most of the country, leaving millions of casualties.[48] China entered the war when North Korean forces were driven back north by allied forces. China's involvement in the Korean War foreshadowed the decades-long confrontation between the United States and China that would follow. The Korean War ceased in a stalemate in 1953, without a formal peace treaty, and the war changed the political and security apparatus of the region for decades to come. First, the bloody war created strong animosity between the two Koreas, which made it impossible for them to have any meaningful economic or political relations for several decades. Serious hostilities remain on both sides of the most heavily guarded border in the world. Second, the United States and South Korea signed a mutual defense treaty under which U.S. armed forces are stationed in South Korea permanently, and this alliance has created a significant strategic and security impact on all countries in the region. Third, the participants of the war realized, based on the war experience, that another war in the Korean peninsula could escalate into another world war, which would be disastrous to all stakeholders in the region. This realization has made all nations in the region tread cautiously. Although there have been hundreds of provocations and small skirmishes across the border between the two Koreas, these incidents have not developed into an all-out war since the armistice of the Korean War in 1953.

In the Korean War, China may have stopped the United States and its allies from defeating North Korea and brought the war to a stalemate, but it did not pose a substantial economic, technological, or military threat to the United States for decades. Instead, China went through economic, social, and political turmoil until the late 1970s. China's trouble began with an economic disaster caused by catastrophic economic initiatives, such as the Great Leap Forward Movement (1958–1962).[49] The unrealistic goal of turning China's agrarian countryside into a base for its industrial revolution caused disasters and severe food shortages, which claimed tens of millions of Chinese lives due to starvation.[50] China and the Soviet Union also had a dispute over what Mao perceived to be revisionist policies adopted by the Soviet Premier Nikita Khrushchev to reform its economy in the late 1950s.[51] Mao's response to this revisionism was the Cultural Revolution (1966–1976), which aimed to eliminate the remaining capitalist elements in Chinese society.[52] The revolution led to widespread violence that lasted for years and destroyed much of China's cultural and intellectual foundations.[53]

Another defining moment in Northeast Asian history is China's economic reform in 1978, pronounced by the pragmatic leader Deng Xiaoping, which ended the nation's prolonged state of economic stagnation and political turmoil. The reform led to a change in the global and regional economic— and later military—balance by transforming China's economy and rapidly increasing its industrial and technological capacities. In the 1960s and 1970s, Japan and South Korea achieved phenomenal economic development (see Figures 1.2 and 1.3), and China joined the economic success by adopting market mechanisms in its economy while maintaining its communist rule (often referred to as "the socialist market economy").[54] Credit for China's economic transformation should be given to its leadership. While Russia's poorly planned economic reform after the fall of the Soviet Union led to an economic crisis during the 1990s, China's more careful and gradual reform has proven successful, rapidly growing its economy and lifting hundreds of millions of Chinese out of absolute poverty.[55] By the beginning of the twenty-first century, China became a major economic and industrial power with a global reach. Its economic success has also generated substantial resources for its military buildup. As discussed in Section 1.3 below, China's military capabilities are now among the largest in the world, challenging the U.S. position in the region.

1.2.4 Underlying currents

Several distinct "currents" shape the relevant context surrounding the question of sustainable peace in Northeast Asia. First is the powershift and rivalry between the United States and China, which traces back to the military confrontations in the Korean War seven decades ago. Because of its relative economic and technological regression, China did not pose a real threat to the economic, political, and military hegemony of the United States for most of the twentieth century. However, this has changed due to China's successful economic development since the 1980s. Rapid economic development has provided China with economic, technological, and military resources and capabilities that challenge the United States. The United States has responded to its challenges by adopting measures to restrain imports from China,[56] limiting the transfer of sensitive technologies to China, and reinforcing its network of alliances against China (*e.g.*, the Australia–United Kingdom–United States alliance or "AUKUS").

Second is the collective memory shared by the Chinese and Koreans of foreign invasions, wars (including civil wars), and the destruction of their countries. These collective memories encourage political leaders to take nationalist stances against those who are perceived to be external threats (*e.g.*, the United States for the Chinese) and to use this sentiment to rally their supporters and consolidate their powerbases. Collective memories have formed a supportive basis for Chinese President Xi Jinping's attempts to reinforce his executive power. Xi has weakened the collective governance that Deng Xiaoping tried to institutionalize, and he has consolidated his powers.[57] The widespread sense of nationalism, shared by the Chinese populace, which originated from these collective memories, also provides popular support for Xi's hardline policies against Hong Kong, Tibet, Xinjiang, and Taiwan.[58] Koreans' collective memories of the deprivation and destruction of the war enabled the South Korean government to rally Korean citizens toward economic development from the 1960s to 1980s.[59] Memories of Japan's oppressive colonial rule over South Korea (1910–1945) also create popular animosity and resistance to Japan for its unapologetic attitude about the atrocities committed against Koreans during Japan's colonial rule, which include the oppression of political freedoms, forced labor during the war, and forced sexual slavery ("comfort women"). As will be further discussed in Chapter 5, memories of these atrocities continue to generate lasting political tensions between the two countries.

Third is the contest between the pull toward China (due to its unmatched economic opportunities) on the one hand and the resistance against China (to preserve national autonomy and independence) on the other. In the past, countries in the region could not find an adequate counterweight against the dominance of China, so they recognized China's supremacy in the region, and China, in return, preserved their autonomy. However, Sinocentrism,[60] which formed the ideological basis for such relationships, remains alive among Chinese officials. Sinocentrism provides a justification for the attitude and tendency of the Chinese government to treat smaller adjacent countries as junior partners, which, in turn, provokes anti-Chinese sentiment and resistance in those countries.[61] Other Northeast Asian countries, such as South Korea, Japan, and Mongolia, seek a counterweight against China to maintain their autonomy and independence, which provides politically fertile ground for the United States, currently the only nation that could be a feasible economic, political, and military counterweight to China, to form alliances in the region.

1.3 Military and Political Tensions in the Region

1.3.1 Military buildup and regional alliances

As discussed at the outset, substantial military and political tensions coexist with economic dynamism in Northeast Asia. Northeast Asia is among the most militarized regions in the world. The world's largest military powers, the United States, Russia, and China have maintained a military presence in Northeast Asia since World War II. Both North Korea and South Korea also maintain massive military forces in the Korean peninsula, comprised of thousands of artillery pieces, tanks, armored vehicles, and missiles (with various ranges and capabilities), hundreds of fighter planes, bombers, and warships ready on both sides of the narrow border between the two Koreas. The United States also maintains a sizable army, air force, and naval force stationed in South Korea and Japan, which could be reinforced by additional forces, dispatched from the United States in a time of crisis. Figure 1.4 illustrates the massive military outlay in the region (subject to the changes in Russia's military deployment since the outbreak of the Russia—Ukraine war in 2022).

These massive military forces are operational under military alliances. The United States commits to protecting South Korea and Japan under defense treaties with both countries. There is also a defense treaty between China and North Korea. Russia does not have a defense treaty with China or North Korea, but Russia and China have conducted joint military exercises, which suggests that the armed forces of both countries can operate jointly when necessary. As for North Korea, China's armed forces can enter into a war for the protection of North Korea under the terms of its defense treaty.[62]

	Tanks	Combat jets	Warships	Submarines
United States	2,645	1,574	124	67
Russia	2,927	1,172	32	49
China	6,150	2,475	60	59
South Korea	2,074	601	26	19
North Korea	4,060	545	2	71
Japan	579	514	45	22

Source: SIPRI/AFP

2021 active personnel

Military spending in $ billion,
( ) = Number of personnel

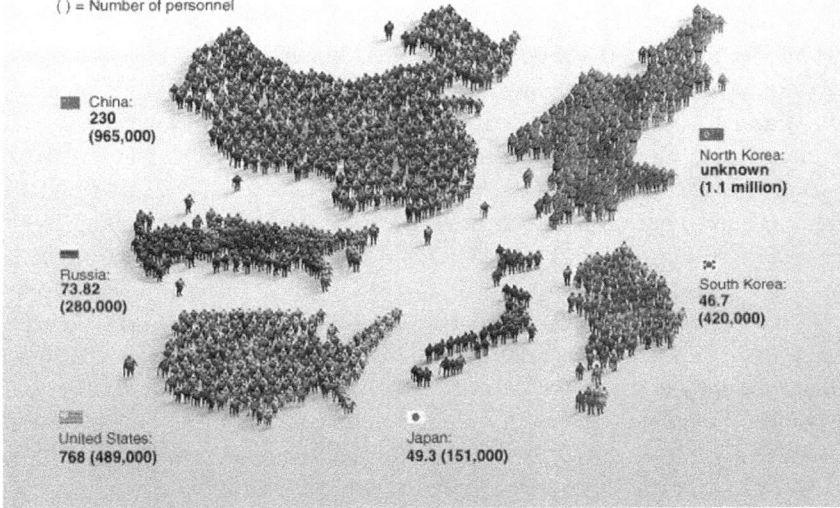

China:
230
(965,000)

North Korea:
unknown
(1.1 million)

Russia:
73.82
(280,000)

South Korea:
46.7
(420,000)

United States:
768 (489,000)

Japan:
49.3 (151,000)

Figure 1.4 Military deployment in Northeast Asia. (*Source*: International Institute for Strategic Studies, *Military balance in Northeast Asia*, 2022)

Despite the absence of any treaty obligation, Russia might also support China and North Korea should there be a military crisis (subject to its weakened military capacity due to its military deployment in Ukraine), as the Soviet air force (unofficially) participated in the Korean War.[63]

The Korean War has not officially ended—the United States, North Korea, and China signed an armistice, but not a peace treaty. Numerous military skirmishes have taken place on the border between the two Koreas, including artillery attacks by North Korean forces on Yeonpyeong Island in 2010, which resulted in civilian casualties.[64] Considering the heavy military concentration around the 250-kilometer border, these types of military provocations have the potential to trigger an all-out war although they have managed to avoid such escalation since the armistice of the Korean War. North Korea also launched commando attacks, including an operation to assassinate the South Korean president in 1968,[65] but such attacks have subsided in recent decades, as South Korea has repelled them and reinforced its border patrols. The growing economic gaps between South and North Korea have resulted in significant disparities in the economic and technological resources that could be devoted to military buildups. As a result, South Korean military forces are expected to repel attacks by North Korea (unless they are nuclear attacks),[66] which is a primary reason that North Korea has reduced its military operations against South Korea.

With the growing gaps in military capacities between the two Koreas, North Korea embarked on a nuclear buildup to level the playing field, as further discussed in the following chapter. North Korea's nuclear buildup does not have support from any other country, including its traditional allies, China and Russia.[67] The United States, South Korea, and Japan have condemned North Korea's nuclear buildup and imposed heavy economic sanctions against North Korea (through United Nations resolutions and by their own measures), but these efforts have not been successful in stopping North Korea's nuclear program. Both China and Russia, North Korea's traditional allies, have also objected to North Korea's nuclear program, but China's economic sanctions against North Korea have been limited, and China has not stopped supplying essential goods, such as gasoline, to North Korea.[68] The economic sanctions against North Korea, known to be the heaviest ever imposed on a single country, have undoubtedly strained the North Korean economy a great deal, but the country has survived and continued with its nuclear program.[69]

1.3.2 Continuing political tensions

North Korea's nuclear and long-range ballistic missile programs have heightened tensions between the United States and North Korea in recent years. In November 2017, North Korea announced the development of new missiles that put all of the United States within striking distance.[70] The United States considered this announcement a direct threat and, in turn, warned that it was prepared to launch a preemptory strike on North Korea to prevent a nuclear attack on the continental United States.[71] Threats of nuclear attacks were exchanged publicly between the United States and North Korea until the heads of South and North Korea met in April 2018, and the representatives of North Korea and the United States met at the Singapore summit in June 2018.[72] In those meetings, North Korea agreed to "denuclearize" the Korean peninsula, but the subsequent United States–North Korea summit in Hanoi, Vietnam, failed to produce any specific agreement on denuclearization.[73] Although North Korea has performed no additional nuclear tests as of December 2022, it resumed a number of missile launches, and the issue remains without resolution. The economic sanctions on North Korea are still in place, and the North Korean government has not given up its nuclear program.

Another major political tension exists between the United States and China. China's expansionary policy in the South and East China Seas and its conduct in Xinjiang, Tibet, and Hong Kong, which undermine the human and civil rights of residents in these provinces, have raised objections from the United States and its allies.[74] Chinese President Xi Jinping has sought to consolidate his political powers and showcase his leadership by reinforcing Beijing's control in those places over local and international objections.[75] Another Chinese initiative, the Made in China 2025 Plan, which aimed to dominate in key technologies, was perceived by the United States as a direct challenge to its economic and industrial superiority and provoked the United States to adopt restrictive trade measures (increased tariffs) against Chinese exports.[76] Questions arise as to whether these trade measures are in compliance with international trade law that binds WTO member states (hence "WTO law") such as the United States and China,[77] but the Biden administration has not withdrawn the measures.

China has also threatened military action against Taiwan should it decide to pursue independence, and the United States, in response, has reaffirmed its protection of Taiwan.[78] China's conduct in Xinjiang, Tibet, and Hong Kong, including arrests and the arbitrary detainment of local residents (*e.g.*, over one million Muslims in Xinjiang),[79] has been a subject of international attention and criticism. The United States has spoken out against China's oppressive treatment of Hong Kong and has also expressed its intentions to raise genocide issues in Xinjiang in talks between them.[80] China has rejected U.S. charges and claimed that the United States is unduly interfering in China's internal affairs.[81] It is unlikely that the United States–China dispute over Hong Kong, Xinjiang, or Tibet will develop into a military conflict in the foreseeable future, but such a possibility cannot necessarily be precluded in the case of Taiwan. As discussed earlier, the U.S. alliance with countries outside the region, such as Britain, Australia, and New Zealand, could be brought to bear against China (as implied by a visit of HMS Queen Elizabeth, a British aircraft carrier, to South Korea and Japan in 2021),[82] although their participation in a possible conflict over Taiwan is uncertain.

Another continuing tension, which was also introduced in the preceding discussion, is one between South Korea and Japan. South Korea and Japan are close economic and trade partners and are also U.S. allies, but these two countries have never formed a military alliance, as substantial political tensions over the issues of Japan's colonial rule of Korea from 1910 to 1945 remain. South Korea and Japan normalized their diplomatic relations in 1965.[83] Under the 1965 agreement, Japan made payments to South Korea as compensation for its colonial rule,[84] but Japan has been criticized for failing to admit its legal responsibilities for the atrocities it committed on the Korean people, particularly during World War II. As cited earlier, such atrocities include sexual slavery (the "comfort women") committed by the Japanese military and the forcible wartime recruitment of Korean laborers who were compelled to work under harsh conditions.[85] Exacerbating these tensions, Japan imposed economic pressure on Korea by tightening its export approval process for certain key materials required by Korean companies for their production of semiconductors.[86] Its measures, which lasted from August 2019 to July 2023, were widely perceived to be an act of retaliation against the Korean Supreme Court's decision ordering the responsible Japanese companies to pay reparations to Koreans who were subject to forced labor during the war.[87]

As further discussed in Chapter 5, there has been a rightward shift in Japanese politics over the past two decades, and the right-wing Japanese government has escalated tensions with South Korea to secure support from its conservative constituencies.[88] Such an escalation has been shown, for example, in the territorial dispute between South Korea and Japan over the Dokdo Islands.[89] The Dokdo Islands are essentially two small rocks located in the East Sea, approximately equidistant from the Korean peninsula and the Japanese islands. These islands have been under South Korea's territorial control since its independence, but Japan has claimed that these islands are its own and that they are being illegally occupied by South Korea.[90] The Japanese government has reinforced its claims to these islands, sending patrol boats near the islands some 440 times over the past 5 years.[91] The dispute over the Dokdo Islands has been an unsettling element of South Korean–Japanese relations, as many Koreans consider Japan's invasion of Korea to have begun with the occupation of these islands five years before the Japanese annexed Korea in 1910.[92] Japan's claim to the Dokdo Islands reminds Koreans of Japan's colonial aggression. Japan also has continual territorial disputes with China and Russia, over the Senkaku (Diaoyu) Islands and the Kuril Islands, respectively,[93] constantly raising political tensions in its relations vis-à-vis these two countries.

This introductory chapter has surveyed the economic and strategic importance of Northeast Asia, its historical context, and the military and political tensions in the region. As discussed above, the region is economically vital but also politically volatile with a risk of military conflict. The massive military buildup in the region, ironically, has deterred the outbreak of a major military conflict that would likely result in devastating outcomes for all parties, including a potential nuclear disaster. After all, four out of the seven countries present in Northeast Asia—the United States, Russia, China, and North Korea—have nuclear arsenals. South Korea and Japan are also capable of developing their own nuclear weapons, particularly if they see signs of a weakening commitment on the part of the United States to protect them against nuclear attacks.[94] There is a common interest in the region to share in vibrant economic opportunities and reduce potentially devastating military and political tensions. The following chapters will explore possible pathways toward achieving these objectives in consideration of the unique political, economic, and historical conditions of each of these constituent countries.

Chapter 2

THE HERITAGE FROM THE COLD WAR—NORTH KOREA AND THE NUCLEAR CRISIS

2.1 Causes of the Nuclear Crisis: Political and Economic Issues

2.1.1 North Korea's nuclear drive

North Korea's nuclear ambition is one of the most concerning military developments in Northeast Asia and beyond. North Korea is not the only country that has developed nuclear weapons outside the NPT (Treaty on the Non-Proliferation of Nuclear Weapons)—India, Pakistan, and Israel have not accepted the NPT and have developed their own nuclear weapons. Regardless, the continuing hostility between North Korea and the West renders North Korea's nuclear development particularly alarming. On October 9, 2006, North Korea announced its first nuclear test.[95] North Korea has since developed and tested intercontinental ballistic missiles (ICBMs) capable of delivering nuclear warheads to the continental United States.[96] While other countries—India, Pakistan, and Israel—have secured nuclear capabilities rather quietly, North Korea has openly threatened to use its nuclear weapons against the United States and South Korea.[97] Analysts have estimated that North Korea has more than 60 nuclear weapons and could develop around 200 nuclear weapons and stockpile hundreds of ballistic missiles by 2027.[98] North Korea's nuclear ambitions have altered the balance of military power in Northeast Asia and the security landscape of the region, creating substantial political and economic ramifications.

North Korea's nuclear development traces back to the mid-1950s, shortly after the Korean War.[99] North Korea had the uranium deposits to develop nuclear weapons, but it lacked the technology. In 1956, North Korea signed an agreement on nuclear research with the Soviet Union, and North Korean scientists received training in nuclear technologies in Russia.[100] In September 1959, the Soviet Union also agreed to help North Korea establish a nuclear research center.[101] That same year, North Korea also signed a nuclear coop-eration agreement with China.[102] In 1965, the Soviet Union sold North Korea a small two- to four-megawatt research reactor, which North Korea began operating near Yongbyon in 1967.[103] In the 1970s, however, conciliatory international developments such as the non-proliferation treaty between the United States and the Soviet Union made it more difficult for North Korea to obtain foreign assistance to build nuclear weapons.[104] North Korea felt little urgency to develop its nuclear capabilities, though, because it perceived lit-tle or no threat from South Korea,[105] which was then focusing on economic development. Interestingly, North Korea proposed a joint nuclear program to South Korea in the 1970s, although South Korea did not accept.[106] In the 1980s, North Korea realized its nuclear program lagged behind South Korea's (which had an extensive non-military nuclear program) and intensi-fied its nuclear research.[107] In 1985, the Soviet Union and North Korea agreed to build four nuclear power plants in North Korea (perhaps as a reward to North Korea for signing the NPT that same year).[108]

A critical development took place in 1993, in what commentators describe today as the first North Korean nuclear crisis; North Korea refused to com-ply with a request from the International Atomic Energy Agency (IAEA) to conduct special inspections of two unregistered sites that were suspected to be nuclear waste dump facilities.[109] The country subsequently announced its withdrawal from the NPT on March 12, 1993. By 1994, North Korea had produced as much as 10 kilograms of plutonium, enough for one or two crude nuclear weapons.[110] North Korea's withdrawal from the NPT heightened international tensions and prompted efforts to stop North Korea's nuclear drive. The United States, through its 1994 Geneva Agreed Framework with North Korea, agreed to provide North Korea with economic and techni-cal support to build light water reactors to generate electricity in return for demolishing its existing reactors that had the potential for military use.[111] Stakeholders in Northeast Asia, including South and North Korea, the United States, Japan, China, and Russia, also organized the Six Party Talks in 2003 and sought to address the nuclear crisis.[112] However, these agreements and talks eventually collapsed and ultimately failed to prevent North Korea from developing nuclear weapons.

North Korea conducted its first nuclear test in 2006 following its 2005 announcement that it was in the process of developing atomic bombs.[113] North Korea conducted five additional tests in 2009, 2013, 2016, and 2017 (with two tests conducted in 2016). North Korea's fifth test, in September 2016, had an estimated yield of between 15 and 30 kilotons, which is compa-rable to the explosive yields of the two nuclear bombs dropped on Hiroshima and Nagasaki in 1945. North Korea also claimed it tested a hydrogen bomb in 2017.[114] Along with its nuclear program, North Korea has simultaneously been developing long-range missiles that can deliver nuclear warheads. In 2016, North Korea claimed that it successfully created a nuclear warhead design for use on ballistic missiles.[115] North Korea also tested ICBMs, which it claims could reach the continental United States, although there is debate over whether North Korea actually overcame the technical challenges of pairing a nuclear warhead to an ICBM.[116] Despite this controversy, North Korean leader Kim Jong-Un announced in 2017, following North Korea's sixth nuclear test and the test launch of a Hwasong-15 ICBM, that North Korea had "completed the state nuclear force."[117]

2.1.2 *Questionable security justifications*

North Korea has paid a heavy price for its nuclear ambitions. Since 2006, the country has faced severe economic sanctions imposed by the United Nations Security Council,[118] which have been supported not only by North Korea's adversaries such as the United States, South Korea, and Japan but also by its traditional allies such as China and Russia.[119] In addition to the United Nations Security Council's economic sanctions, several countries, including Australia, the United States, South Korea, and Japan, have imposed their own sanctions against North Korea for conducting nuclear and missile tests. The economic sanctions have escalated in severity as North Korea has continued with its nuclear and missile tests. The first U.N. Security Council economic sanction in 2006 prohibited exporting some military supplies and luxury goods to North Korea, but the subsequent sanctions, such as the ones passed in 2013, 2016, and 2017, imposed severe restrictions on money transfers (aimed at excluding North Korea from the international financial system), banned its major exports such as coal, limited exports of oil and petroleum products to North Korea, and required the repatriation of all North Korean nationals earning income abroad.[120]

North Korea may have survived these economic sanctions,[121] but the sanctions have imposed a substantial strain on North Korea's economy. Regardless, North Korea continues with its nuclear and missile programs. A question arises as to why North Korea is so persistently continuing its ballistic missile and nuclear programs under enormous international pressure when it is facing no apparent immediate security threat. There was indeed a time when Kim Jong-Un appeared to share a commitment to denuclearize the Korean peninsula during a historic meeting with then-U.S. President Donald Trump in 2018.[122] However, negotiations between the two countries have been unsuccessful, and Kim reaffirmed to the Worker's Party Congress in 2020 that North Korea would remain a "responsible nuclear weapons state" and that it would only pursue talks with the United States concerning "arms control" rather than denuclearization.[123] North Korea recently hardened its position: its leader, Kim Jong-Un, declared that North Korea will not "negotiate" or use nuclear weapons as a "bargaining chip."[124] At the time of this writing, there is no evidence to suggest that North Korea is reconsidering its nuclear programs despite clear international consensus against them.

It is questionable what drives North Korea to continue with its costly nuclear and missile programs. Among the countries in Northeast Asia, China, Russia, and the United States are nuclear powers. Japan and South Korea are under the "nuclear umbrella" offered by the United States through their military alliances with the United States. This means that North Korea's nuclear capability is unlikely to secure it a superior military or political position in the region. Thus, it is necessary to consider other reasons or motivations that make this expensive project somehow worthwhile for the North Korean regime. This subsection and the next inquire into North Korea's motivations to pursue nuclear weapons, despite the immediate economic cost and the strong international objections that it faces. These motivations are complex but revolve primarily around protecting the security of the North Korean regime and promoting North Korea's long-term economic and political interests.[125]

As for security motivations, North Korea possesses a massive military force in terms of soldiers (over one million), tanks, artillery, fighter planes, and warships. However, much of its military equipment is outdated—some developed in the 1950s and 1960s—and the country lacks the financial resources and technology to replace them with updated equipment. Additionally, North Korea is facing the world's most robust military force: the allied forces of the United States and South Korea possessing superior strike capabilities and the financial resources to sustain warfare. North Korea has not formed a comparable military alliance with its traditional allies, China and Russia, and there is no guarantee that either country would actually defend North Korea in the event of a military conflict.[126] This arguably puts North Korea in an unfavorable security environment, even if South Korea or the United States does not pose an immediate threat.

Given this challenging security environment and the increasing gaps between conventional military powers, securing nuclear capabilities would be an attractive option for North Korea.[127] Having nuclear capabilities could be a game changer for North Korea. With the 2017 test of its ICBM system that can deliver nuclear warheads, North Korea claims that it possesses a credible nuclear deterrent.[128] North Korea's diminishing confidence in China as a reliable ally has also reinforced its security concerns.[129] China has made clear that it supports North Korea's denuclearization and has endorsed international sanctions imposed on the country.[130] Despite China's lax enforcement of those sanctions, China's objection to a nuclear North Korea has undermined the confidence of North Korean policymakers, who see China as an unreliable ally unwilling to defend the North if it were attacked by the United States or its allies.[131] This eroded confidence further drives North Korea to pursue a nuclear deterrent because Pyongyang is concerned about the possibility of facing an invasion on its own.[132]

However, questions remain as to whether North Korea's security concerns justify its nuclear drive. Since the armistice of the Korean War in 1953, there have been thousands of border incidents, small-scale military incursions, and infiltrations between South and North Korea.[133] However, these incidents have been waged mostly by North Korea, and the North has not seen major military aggression by South Korea or the United States over the past seven decades. It is questionable whether any country in the region poses a credible security threat to North Korea. Even without the use of nuclear weapons, an all-out war and a full-scale invasion of North Korea would likely cause mass casualties and a substantial economic loss, making an invasion by South Korea or the United States unlikely. Nuclear weapons are also not a deterrent to all military incursions or to domestic uprisings—nuclear weapons cannot prevent small-scale military incursions or large-scale military exercises by South Korea and the United States, which North Korea has critically labeled as "dangerous."[134] Another potential danger to the security of the North Korean regime is not external but internal; substantial discontent among the North Korean population, who are suffering from economic deprivation and political oppression, could lead to a revolt. Section 2.2 examines some of these issues.

2.1.3 Economic and political motivations

As discussed earlier, North Korea's nuclear ambitions have led to international economic sanctions, which strain the North Korean economy. Ironically, North Korea's nuclear weapons programs, through a negotiated reduction thereof, could create an economic opportunity for North Korea. North Korea has gone through an economic disaster since the 1990s: after the collapse of the Soviet Union, North Korea faced a major famine that devastated its economy and caused widespread suffering and starvation.[135] Due to the collapse of the Soviet bloc and the continuation of North Korea's internal economic problems—such as military overspending—North Korea could neither secure external economic assistance nor find internal solutions for its plight. The substantial international sanctions have only compounded North Korea's economic problems.[136]

The North Korean regime could use its nuclear weapons development as a potentially valuable bargaining chip for economic aid (despite its recent denial otherwise).[137] Global powers, such as the United States, and North Korea's neighbors, such as South Korea and Japan, have an interest in seeing North Korea's nuclear programs removed, and Pyongyang, well aware of their concerns, has consistently sought to extract major economic rewards in exchange for concessions.[138] This strategy of "nuclear extortion" has yielded billions of dollars in foreign aid from South Korea, the United States, Japan, and China over the past few decades.[139] This economic motivation for weapons development has become magnified over the past year, with the North Korean economy contracting by as much as 8.5 percent in 2020 and trade with China declining by roughly 80 percent.[140] In addition, the border entry-ban imposed by the North Korean government to control the spread of COVID-19 has had a devastating impact on the already weakened North Korean economy, increasing its need for economic aid.

Despite North Korea's needs, such economic extractions now have limits. The United States and its allies are most likely to grant North Korea economic incentives in exchange only for substantial reductions in or the total removal of North Korea's nuclear programs and current nuclear facilities. However, there is no indication that the North Korean regime will accept complete or substantial denuclearization. Despite the talks with South Korea and the United States, the North still sees the possession of nuclear weapons as an essential element of its survival strategy.[141] Pyongyang may instead wish to negotiate "arms control" instead of full disarmament,[142] but it is unlikely for the international community to accept North Korea as a nuclear state and embark on such negotiations in exchange for economic incentives. Even so, Kim Jong-Un seems to believe that if North Korea remains firm on its right to possess nuclear weapons, the international community will eventually capitulate and accept North Korea's nuclear status without maintaining sanctions.[143] While it has happened with other countries, such as India, such an accommodation for North Korea is unlikely considering the strong international concern about the risk presented by its nuclear capability, their distrust of the oppressive Kim regime, and the precarious security environment of the Korean peninsula it generates.

The preceding discussion has revealed the limits of the security justifications and economic arguments for North Korea's nuclear drive. Perhaps the strongest motivation is a political one. North Korea's status as a nuclear weapons state has been codified in the country's constitution since its second nuclear test in 2012, signifying its importance.[144] Since the 1990s, North Korea has undergone a series of economic disasters. In contrast, its southern counterpart, once economically and militarily inferior to the North, has prospered and economically developed beyond recognition,[145] even joining the ranks of the world's affluent countries in the Organisation for Economic Co-operation and Development (OECD) in 1996. Some have observed that a prosperous South Korea could "absorb" North Korea in the event of unification,[146] which raises concerns over North Korea's national integrity and future sustainability. North Korea has pursued nuclear weapons and a world-class military as a means to restore its lost prestige and garner domestic support despite its economic difficulties.[147] The possession of nuclear weapons makes a country appear stronger domestically, which helps to establish the legitimacy of the current regime and prevent the emergence of discontent about the regime.[148]

The North Korean regime has also highlighted the importance of its nuclear weapons program in the context of its national identity and culture. North Korea's state ideology is constructed around the notion of *Juche*, which refers to "self-reliance," and is understood as a paradigm of fierce national independence.[149] Throughout the Cold War era, North Korea, under the leadership of Kim Il-Sung, sought assistance from other communist states on the development of nuclear weapons, citing the perceived unfairness of the United States' large nuclear stockpiles contrasted with Pyongyang's meager military resources.[150] Throughout the 1970s and 1980s, *Juche* became increasingly codified as a controlling principle of North Korea's constitution and national existence.[151] As *Juche* became more significant to North Korea's cultural and political identity, Kim Il-Sung highlighted the significance of nuclear weapons in ensuring national self-defense and political self-determination. He argued that North Korea's status as a nuclear state would place it on a more equal footing with more powerful adversaries like the United States.[152]

When Kim Il-Sung died in 1994, his successor, Kim Jong-Il, further emphasized the centrality of *Juche* to North Korea's national identity and culture.[153] Kim integrated the development of nuclear weapons into the national narrative of *Juche*, making nuclear weapons a powerful symbol of North Korean strength that would promote a sense of pride and prestige among its people.[154] While sparse sociological evidence regarding North Korean culture suggests that the cultural impact of *Juche* is concentrated among elites in North Korea, this narrative also exerts a strong influence on skeptical citizens, pushing them to publicly accept the legitimacy of the regime even if they harbor private doubts.[155] Thus, the entwinement of *Juche* with North Korea's nuclear program exerts a potent cultural force that supports the development of nuclear weapons.[156] According to this narrative, the development of nuclear weapons is not just a military buildup but an essential political process to secure and demonstrate national identity and independence.

In addition to its national identity and culture, North Korea's nuclear buildup also serves a more pragmatic political need, as is common with many authoritarian countries. North Korea relies substantially on its military, not only to defend itself from outside security threats but also to keep the country in order. North Korea's official policies ("Seon-Goon-Jeong-Chi" or "Military First") evidence the prioritization of its military. Prioritizing nuclear weapons development has helped to shore up support for North Korea's present leader, Kim Jong-Un, among members of the North Korean military because it ensures high military budgets and promotes morale among North Korean soldiers.[157] Maintaining support for the military also prevents the possibility of military leaders attempting a coup.[158] This political strategy (focusing on maintaining military support) has been especially crucial for Kim Jong-Un, who came into power while still young and inexperienced and who has therefore felt the need to prove himself as a strong and competent leader.[159] The nuclear buildup, despite the strong objections it has drawn from the international community, has been a fitting way for Kim to show his strong leadership to the military as well as the general public.

Lastly, North Korea's nuclear weapons program also affords the North Korean regime a degree of influence over the international political arena, particularly in South Korea.[160] Even if North Korea's nuclear capabilities alone are unlikely to extract concessions in the future (although it worked in the past) without substantial reductions or removal of its nuclear programs and facilities, it is effective at discouraging South Korea from pressing North Korea on political issues, such as its widespread human rights violations.[161] South Korea, without nuclear weapons of its own, relies on the U.S. nuclear umbrella and has substantial vulnerability vis-à-vis North Korea. This vulnerability raises caution and tends to put the country on defense. Observers have reported North Korea's attempt to influence South Korean elections in 2022.[162] North Korea has sought to use the bargaining power associated with its nuclear program to influence the outcome of those elections.[163] Specifically, North Korea has sought to ensure that South Korea remains under the control of its progressive faction, which has historically been more willing to make concessions and provide aid to the North.[164] However, South Korean voters elected the conservative party candidate Yoon Seok-Yeol as the president in the 2022 election.

The preceding discussion has examined North Korea's nuclear drive, the most acute security issue in Northeast Asia. Throughout the 2016–2017 crisis, confrontations between the United States and North Korea were intense, with the heads of the world's strongest country, the United States, and of the world's most unpredictable country, North Korea, publicly exchanging nuclear threats. Since the 2018 Singapore accord between the United States and North Korea, a nuclear crisis has not recurred, but North Korea has not substantially reduced or removed its nuclear weapons programs. The tension between South and North Korea remains, with threats repeatedly made by North Korea to use its nuclear weapons.[165] The tension between the two Koreas could intensify because South Korea's conservative faction won back control of the government in the 2022 presidential election. Further, North Korea's nuclear drive is expected to continue into the foreseeable future, diminishing the prospect of sustainable peace and stability in the region and beyond. The following section examines North Korea's historical, political, and economic contexts, in which the country has become the uniquely authoritarian and hereditary regime it is today, seeking to possess nuclear weapons despite enormous domestic sacrifices and international objections. Discussion begins with the division of Korea in 1945.

2.2 The Cold War and North Korea

2.2.1 Establishment of North Korea and the Korean War

Korea is one of the very few "divided" countries that still exists today. The division of the Korean peninsula along the 38th parallel was caused in part by the post–World War II conflicts between the United States–led West and the Soviet-led communist bloc. The United States allowed the Soviets to occupy North Korea, initially to disarm the Japanese army stationed in the North, but the Soviet Union did not leave Korea without creating a communist government under Soviet control. The Soviets believed it was necessary to create a government in Korea loyal to the Soviet Union because it likened the Korean peninsula to Poland in Eastern Europe and reasoned that Korea could be used as a springboard to attack Russia.[166] Thus, the Soviet military government in North Korea (1945–1948) rejected the idea of establishing one Korean government under the guidance of the United Nations, which would likely become a pro-West country.[167] Despite the Soviets' concern, the United States, which was then occupying South Korea, would not allow for the establishment of a pro-Soviet communist country in control of the entire Korean peninsula. With the uncompromising standoff continuing between the United States and the Soviet Union, each planning to set up a Korean government loyal to its own bloc, the division of Korea was inevitable.

In 1948, after three years of military rule in South and North Korea by the United States and the Soviet Union, respectively, two separate Korean governments were established: one in South Korea under the blessing of the United Nations and the other in the North under the direction of the Soviet Union. North Korea, led by Kim Il-Sung, implemented communist policies such as land confiscation and nationalization of productive facilities and infra-structure built by the Japanese during their colonial occupation of Korea.[168] The government also adopted a Soviet-style system of planned economy and controlled industries under state planning.[169] The North put a significant amount of resources (some 20 percent of the first People's Committee budget) into education, propaganda, and culture to strengthen its communist rule.[170] North Korea also set up intense policing and a system of surveillance of the populace to increase governmental control over the population.[171] Those who were treated with hostility by the communist government or who did not see much of a future in the communist North, such as landowners and busines-sowners, fled to the South in large numbers (an estimated 500,000 people),[172] reinforcing the ideological divide between the South and North.

Kim Il-Sung, then North Korea's leader, did not stop with the establish-ment of a communist country in the North under Soviet direction. He wanted to "unite" all of Korea under his control and asked for Soviet support to arm North Korean forces.[173] Then Premier of the Soviet Union, Joseph Stalin, who wanted to see the entire Korean peninsula incorporated into one communist bloc, gave support. Kim also gained support from the newly-established com-munist China.[174] With full support from the Soviet Union and assistance from China, Kim Il-Sung launched military attacks on South Korea on June 25, 1950, with forces that were better armed, equipped, and prepared than their South Korean counterparts.[175] The United States considered this attack a communist invasion under Stalin's order. "The attack upon Korea," U.S. President Harry Truman said, "makes it plain beyond all doubt that commu-nism has passed beyond the use of subversion to conquer independent nations and will now use armed invasion."[176] Historian Carl Berger, agreeing with this sentiment, also posited that North Korea's attack was Moscow's first step toward dominating all of East Asia.[177]

The Korean War (1950–1953) shaped much of the political landscape in Northeast Asia for the next several decades. The war resulted in casualties of combatants and civilians in the millions and destroyed key infrastructure in both the South and North, causing enormous economic loss. According to a study, about 600 thousand housing units, 46.9 percent of railroad infra-structure, 1,656 roads (a total of 500 kilometers in length), and 1,453 bridges (totaling 49 kilometers) were destroyed during the war.[178] By August 1951, 44 percent of factory buildings and 42 percent of production facilities laid in ruins, and nearly 80 percent of power plants were also destroyed.[179] In this three-year war, Koreans suffered immeasurably, lost families and homes, and witnessed countless cases of torture and murder committed in the name of safeguarding political ideologies. Through the war, the South and North became bitter enemies, and intense hostility remained for decades to follow.

The war stopped with a draw and a cease fire, with new borders set close to the old, and the South and North have yet to sign a peace treaty. The hardened hostility was not confined to the Korean peninsula but extended across Northeast Asia. A commentator observed that the Korean War was a turning point in the extension of the Cold War to Asia and strengthened U.S. commitments to the region, enhancing support for Taiwan, South Korea, and the French and non-communist elements in Southeast Asia.[180]

The Korean War also provided Kim Il-Sung with an opportunity to consolidate his political power and control in North Korea. Kim eliminated his potential rivals and crushed opposition during and after the war, becoming North Korea's first absolute ruler who stayed in power until he died in 1994.[181] Kim consolidated his powers and rallied North Koreans around their hostile sentiments about South Korea and the United States, whom they believed were responsible for the destruction of North Korea during the war. Having witnessed the United States' massive firepower during the war, North Korea also diverted substantial resources to build and maintain its military forces, taxing its limited resources and manpower. The root cause of North Korea's costly military buildup can therefore likely be traced to the Korean War. As discussed in the preceding section, the North Korean regime considers building nuclear weapons an essential means of protecting its security interests against South Korea and the United States, both of whom possess substantially superior conventional military forces.

2.2.2 Cold War confrontations and the decline of the North Korean economy

The Korean War was a turning point in the development of the Cold War and intensified confrontations between the West and the Eastern communist bloc. The Korean War had a significant impact on the public's perception of the dangers of communism and the resulting risk of war. For instance, according to Professor Robert Jervis, most U.S. officials in the 1940s reportedly had "a mixed, incoherent, view of the danger of war," and "Russia was regarded as threatening and expansionist but also weak and cautious."[182] However, following the Korean War, public opinion shifted from viewing Russia as a mix of cautious and intimidating to predominately considering Russia an expansionist threat.[183] The U.S. Senate observed that the Korean War indicated communists were willing to resort to armed aggression whenever they believed they could prevail, even at the risk of starting a third world war.[184] Public concerns about communism remained heightened throughout the Cold War (1945–1991), and both the West and the communist bloc consolidated and strengthened their militaries and economic support from their "allies."[185]

Ironically, North Korea benefited from these Cold War confrontations. After the Korean War, it received substantial economic support from the communist bloc, particularly from the Soviet Union. North Korea received raw materials, machinery, and technical assistance from other communist countries, including the Soviet Union, Eastern Germany, Poland, and Czechoslovakia.[186] With this support, North Korea was able to rebuild itself and its economy from the rubble of the Korean War. South Korea also received substantial economic support from the United States (equivalent to US$ 47 billion by the early 1970s), but throughout the 1950s and the 1960s, the fast-growing North Korean economy surpassed its southern counterpart. Table 2.1 depicts North Korea's impressive economic growth during these periods.

North Korea implemented a socialist planned economy and mobilized the resources necessary for a rapidly growing economy.[187] By the 1960s, North Korea had built an industrial economy, capable of providing its population with the necessities of life. In 1965, a leading Cambridge economist, Joan Robinson, described North Korea's economic success as the "Korean Miracle."[188] It was indeed a significant success at a time when socialist economic experiments elsewhere, such as China's Great Leap Forward Movement, had brought disastrous outcomes, including tragic starvation and sharp economic declines.[189] It is questionable how communist economies, such as the North Korean economy, disallowing private incentives for production (*e.g.*, profit), could achieve economic development. Recently developed (by the author), the "New General Theory of Economic Development" explains that government mobilization of resources can lead to the successful initiation of economic development, even without private corporations and a capitalist market, and shows that North Korea was an example of such success.[190]

However, this success was not sustainable. North Korea's industrial potential, based on state-driven resource mobilization, technical and resource support from its communist partners, and the pre-war infrastructure built by Japan, was exhausted by the early 1970s. North Korea's economy started to

Table 2.1 Average annual growth rates of North Korea (1946–1960).

	1946		1949		1953		1956		1960
National income	100	(27.8)	209	(–7.6)	145	(30.0)	319	(20.4)	683
Gross industrial product	100	(49.9)	337	(–10.5)	216	(41.0)	605	(36.6)	2105

(average annual growth percentage rate in parentheses)
(*Source*: Hong Taek Jeon, "Economic Growth of North Korea: 1945–1995" (북한의 경제발전: 1945–1995), Journal of Economic Development (경제개발연구), Vol. 1, 1995)

decline in the 1980s and faced a state of collapse in the 1990s.[191] The reasons for this failure included chronic inefficiencies associated with bureaucratic control of the economy, which hampered innovation, excessive military spending, the loss of economic partners from the collapse of the communist bloc, and economic sanctions from the West, particularly trade and investment bans from the United States.[192] While South Korea also adopted state-led economic development policies, such as the government planning on scarce resource allocations and industrial development, the government allowed private corporations, such as Samsung and Hyundai, to play a key role in the economy. These private corporations were the main producers and innovators who engaged in competition with both domestic and foreign corporations, improving the overall efficiency of the economy.

By contrast, North Korea did not permit individuals to form and own corporations. Without private corporations, North Korea failed to sustain the level of innovation necessary to improve the competitiveness of its industries and the efficiency of its economy. Its hostile relationship with the West, particularly the United States, created a substantial barrier to trade and investment. After the collapse of the communist bloc, the North Korean economy became isolated, whereas South Korea continued to achieve a high level of economic growth and industrial development, primarily through international trade and investment.[193] Since the 1980s, North Korea has initiated economic reforms, including admission of select foreign investments and authorization of corporations to exercise a degree of managerial control and retain certain profits. However, the attempted reforms failed to reverse its economic downturn—without repairing its relations with other major economies such as the United States and Japan, North Korea could not attract foreign investments at the level required to substantially enhance its domestic industries and employment.[194]

By 1996, the economic and industrial gaps between the two Koreas had increased beyond comparison: South Korea's GDP reached US$ 610.17 billion[195] while North Korea's GDP was estimated at US$ 21 billion.[196] It became clear that South Korea's once inferior economy had far surpassed North Korea's economy and industry, and North Korea faced devastating starvation and sharp economic declines. The large economic gap between the two Koreas also created a significant gap in conventional military strengths. While South Korea continued to improve and modernize its military, North Korea did not have the economic resources or technological capabilities to update its outdated and obsolete military equipment. These increasingly large economic and military gaps drove North Korean leaders to resort to relatively inexpensive means to close these gaps, such as the development of nuclear weapons. However, as discussed earlier, North Korea's nuclear weapons development has heightened tensions with the West, and this, in turn, has created a more unfavorable economic environment for North Korea that will only further increase its gaps with South Korea.

2.2.3 The Kim Dynasty Post–Cold War

By the time the Cold War was over, North Korea was facing both political and economic crises. The political crisis was caused by the sudden death of North Korea's absolute ruler, Kim Il-Sung, in 1994.[197] Despite his notoriety, Kim Il-Sung was one of the most influential figures in modern Korean history. Kim rose to power in 1945 with support from the Soviet Union, formed the North Korean government in 1948, and started the Korean War by invading South Korea in 1950.[198] Kim survived the Korean War, preserved his power through the elimination of his political opponents and tight control of the populace,[199] and sustained himself as an unchallenged ruler for nearly five decades. His sudden death created speculation about the uncertain future of North Korea.[200] South and North Korea had previously agreed to a historic first summit meeting, which could have been a turning point for Korean history, but Kim died only weeks before the planned summit with the South Korean president.

Shortly after Kim's death, North Korea faced the worst famine in its history, which resulted in at least 340,000 deaths.[201] Hundreds of thousands fled the country, mostly to China, in search of food and basic necessities. North Korea appeared to be on the brink of collapse. The communist bloc was dismantled, leaving no country to support North Korea when it had yet to normalize its relationships with the United States and the rest of the West, and it did not have an opportunity to seek support elsewhere. Nevertheless, North Korea escaped from total collapse. Kim Jong-Il, Kim Il-Sung's eldest son and successor, maintained control of North Korea until his death in 2011 in a manner similar to his father's: through the brutal control of the populace and elimination of his potential opponents. Kim Jong-Il prioritized and favored the military to protect his power base.[202] North Korea also received substantial economic support from South Korea totaling 3.37 trillion won (approximately US$ 2.6 billion) between 1995 and 2020,[203] an amount South Korea accelerated after the first summit between Kim and then South Korean President Kim Dae-Joong in 2000.

In 2011, Kim Jong-Il died of a heart attack.[204] After his death, his son, Kim Jong-Un, became his successor, regressing North Korea from a republic to a hereditary dynasty. Kim Jong-Un followed the path of his father and grandfather by consolidating his power. He eliminated his potential rivals, even killing his uncle Jang Seong-Taek and his half-brother Kim Jong-Nam.[205]

Kim Jong-Un, despite his young age (known to be born in 1984), proved to be no less ruthless a leader than his father and grandfather. He pushed the nation's nuclear weapons program over widespread objections from the international community, incurring unprecedented economic sanctions against his country. South Korea's 19th president, Moon Jae-In (2017–2022), adopted an appeasement policy toward the North, meeting with Kim Jong-Un and attempting to help North Korea improve its relations with the United States. However, the talks between North Korea and the United States failed to reach an agreement on specific denuclearization measures. Kim Jong-Un has since returned to his original position—maintaining and further developing nuclear weapons.[206] With Kim's resolve and his control over nuclear weapons development, the nuclear crisis is yet to be resolved.

The Kim regime has proven to be sturdy through three generations. It has survived three decades of the post–Cold War era while most former communist bloc countries have been transformed into democracies based on civil representation. As further discussed in the following section, the Kim Dynasty's Stalin-style control remains intact. When the regime required a means to maintain its control and to protect itself against the liberalizing world in the post–Cold War era, it chose to pursue nuclear weapons development. North Korea has declared that it has completed its nuclear weapons program and claims to have the capacity to strike the continental United States with nuclear force. This capability not only represents the country's military autonomy but also has become a symbol of the country's military prestige and the regime's resolve to maintain its power and control. The North Korean regime has integrated its nuclear weapons into the Kim Dynasty's core security apparatus, making it unlikely the regime will give up its nuclear weapons in the foreseeable future.[207] Thus, the nuclear crisis may re-emerge, as long as the Kim regime stays in power.

There lies an irreconcilable reality. Kim Jong-Un has expressed his desire to improve North Korea's economy for its citizens, undertaking a series of economic reforms aimed at improving economic efficiency.[208] For example, Kim has allowed the proliferation of marketplaces and sought to increase foreign investments.[209] Efforts have also been made to improve industries, including tourism. However, the economic sanctions in place, as well as the border blockade that the North Korean government imposed due to COVID-19, have put an extreme strain on North Korea's economy and have undermined Kim Jong-Un's early reform efforts. There are also systemic barriers to economic development. The autocratic nature of Kim's regime, which is preserved by exercising tight control over the populace through threats of imprisonment, torture, and execution,[210] is a fundamental and insurmountable barrier to economic development. Economic development requires open access to information, innovation, and economic freedoms,[211] all of which have been restricted under Kim's regime. The following section examines this irreconcilable reality faced by North Korea.

2.3 North Korea's Irreconcilable Reality

2.3.1 Economic development in isolation?

North Koreans have gone through substantial deprivation since the 1990s. As discussed earlier, the famine in the late 1990s claimed the lives of hundreds of thousands.[212] Another hundreds of thousands fled the country for economic reasons (many, over 33,800, fled to South Korea).[213] Figure 2.1 illustrates the declining state of North Korea's economy since the 1990s.

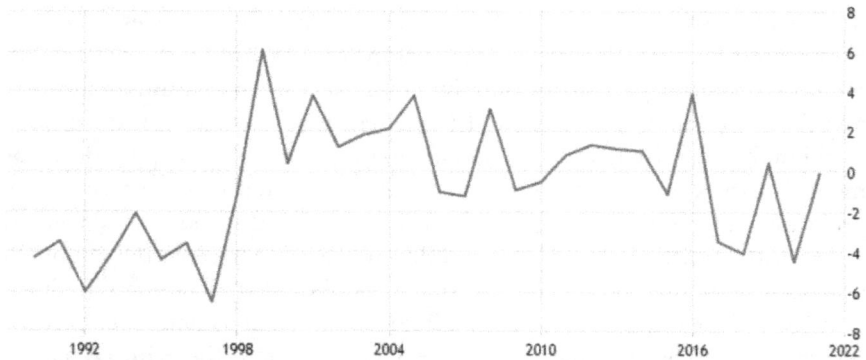

Figure 2.1 Annual GDP growth rates of North Korea (1990–2021) (unit: percent). (*Source*: Bank of Korea)

Facing the risk of total economic collapse, the North Korean regime inevitably prioritized economic development. In a 2016 speech, Kim Jong-Un outlined a five-year economic plan, setting forth policies to facilitate both traditional industries (*e.g.*, metal and railways) and innovative industries (*e.g.*, renewable energy sources, including hydropower, geothermal, and solar).[214] Kim Jong-Un expressed his desire to engage more with the international economy through international trade.[215] The 8th Congress of Korean Workers' Party in 2021 reiterated the country's prioritization of economic development. The Congress stressed the need to "stabilize the economy amidst an extremely harsh environment and be self-sufficient in the economic sector."[216] Despite this emphasis, North Korea did not make significant economic achievements in 2021 and has not met its five-year economic goals.[217]

The conflict between North Korea's need for economic development on the one hand and its pursuit of nuclear weapons and control of the populace on the other is irreconcilable. The primary hindrance to North Korea's economic development is the plethora of economic sanctions that were imposed in response to North Korea's nuclear tests and ballistic missile launches. In 2017, the United States proposed to reinforce sanctions and impose its own maximum-pressure policy.[218] The reinforced sanctions (such as United Nations Security Council Resolution 2371) were supported by China and Russia—North Korea's traditional allies—and prohibit North Korea from exporting major items such as coal, iron, lead, and seafood.[219] The sanctions also impose restrictions on North Korea's access to foreign financial services, creating major barriers to North Korea's access to international trade. This result is the opposite of the outcome Kim Jong-Un sought in his 2016 speech: more engagement with the international economy and trade.[220]

In addition to the economic sanctions, North Korea's internal governance system has also proven to be a significant impediment to its economic development. North Korea has adopted some elements of a market economy, including the allowance of marketplaces throughout the country. However, economic freedom in North Korea remains limited. For example, individuals are not authorized to form corporations. North Korea achieved substantial economic growth until the 1960s, primarily through the state-led mobilization of resources and industrialization, but the lack of for-profit private corporations and the continued control of the economy by inefficient bureaucracies' impeded innovation, which is an essential component of economic development.[221] Thus, the regression of the North Korean economy—the stagnation of the North Korean economy in the 1970s, the economic decline in the 1980s, and the crisis in the 1990s—reflects structural problems impeding sustainable economic development in North Korea.

Economic development, although a stated priority of Kim Jong-Un, is not actually prioritized by Kim over what he thinks is required to protect his regime, such as nuclear weapons and state control over the economy. As further discussed in this section, the Kim regime has become a hereditary dynasty, requiring nothing less than absolute obedience and compliance from every North Korean. As a result, there is no higher state priority than protecting and preserving the Kim regime, and North Korea will pursue nuclear weapons as long as they are deemed necessary to achieve this goal, even if it provokes crushing economic sanctions and diminishes prospects for North Korea's economic development. For this same reason, Kim is unlikely to reduce the regime's control over the populace or its restrictions on individual freedoms in the near future. North Korea's economic development will thus be limited to the extent possible while still maintaining its existing policies that protect the regime.

2.3.2 Nuclear development vs. denuclearization

North Korea's inconsistent position on denuclearizing the Korean peninsula also reflects this seemingly irreconcilable dilemma. After acute political tensions and the exchange of nuclear threats between the heads of the United States and North Korea in late 2017, Kim Jong-Un changed his position in hopes of economic support from the West. Kim agreed to denuclearize the Korean peninsula at the summit between South and North Korea in April 2018 and again at the summit between the United States and North Korea in June 2018.[222] Before the summit with South Korean President Moon Jae-In, Kim Jong-Un halted the testing of all nuclear weapons and ICBMs in light of the successes achieved to date. Kim Jong-Un declared that North Korea had already "perfected" its nuclear forces, with the capacity to mass produce nuclear warheads and missiles, and possessed a powerful deterrent against the United States, which did not require further testing.[223] Demonstrating its willingness to proceed with denuclearization, North Korea shut down its nuclear test site ("Pyunggye-ri") and even blew up the tunnels it used for its nuclear tests in the presence of the international press.[224]

However, the subsequent Hanoi summit in 2019 failed to produce an agreement, due to disagreements between North Korea and the United States. North Korea was reportedly prepared to shut down the Yongbyon nuclear facility, a symbolic site for North Korea's nuclear development, in return for corresponding concessions on the part of the United States, such as relief from sanctions. However, such a gesture was insufficient for South Korea and the United States because they expected complete denuclearization in return for their concessions.[225] It is not altogether clear whether North Korea was willing to concede to complete denuclearization, even in return for full relief of sanctions and economic aid. Experts hold negative views on this. For example, the director of (U.S.) National Intelligence stated in his 2019 threat assessment to Congress that "North Korea is unlikely to give up all of its nuclear weapons and production capabilities, even as it seeks to negotiate partial denuclearization steps to obtain key US and international concessions."[226] Given the enormous sacrifices made by North Koreans to develop nuclear weapons, it will be difficult for Kim Jong-Un to give up North Korea's nuclear arsenal completely, even for considerable economic aid and relief of sanctions.

The U.S. intelligence community's 2022 annual threat assessment reached a similar conclusion.[227] According to political commentators Alexander Ward and Quint Forgey, Kim Jong-Un views nuclear weapons and ICBMs as "the ultimate guarantor of his totalitarian and autocratic rule of North Korea and believes that over time he will gain international acceptance as a nuclear power."[228] North Korea's previous declaration of denuclearization cannot be reconciled with its political need to retain nuclear weapons although the Kim regime may have been willing to give up *some* of its nuclear weapons and nuclear facilities in return for relief from sanctions and economic aid. The United States and the international community are, however, unlikely to relieve economic sanctions imposed on North Korea only for the partial removal of its nuclear weapons and facilities. It would also be difficult for the North Korean regime to have confidence that the United States and South Korea would guarantee its security and continue providing economic aid once North Korea removed all of its nuclear weapons and facilities.

Regardless of feasibility, North Korea is likely to pursue economic development and its nuclear weapons program simultaneously. Despite its internal rhetoric, North Korea could still entertain the possibility of denuclearization in return for the relief of sanctions and economic aid, despite its recent announcement that it will not negotiate.[229] The United States, South Korea, and North Korea all share an interest in maintaining stability in the region for their own internal political needs; thus, continued dialogue may be as useful to North Korea as it is to the United States and South Korea. North Korea seems more likely to engage in such a proposal if it is made by the United States. North Korea recently turned down the South Korean president's proposal for economic aid in return for denuclearization.[230] North Korea seems to believe the United States has a controlling influence over South Korea, so for North Korea, any agreement on the nuclear issue needs to be conducted between the United States and North Korea.

Despite its utility, it is unclear whether the United States would be willing to embark on such negotiations with North Korea, as shown by its retraction from the Hanoi summit, when it is aware of North Korea's intent to retain its nuclear capacity.[231] The status quo—North Korea's continuing nuclear weapons program and the international community's denial of North Korea as a legitimate nuclear nation—is likely to continue without any breakthrough on either side. The United States' massive nuclear arsenal and its continuing commitment to protect its allies in the region, including South Korea and Japan, will deter North Korea's potential use of nuclear weapons, but it does not preclude the possibility of a miscalculation by North Korea, such as a limited use or threat of its nuclear capabilities to elicit concessions (despite the recent U.S. announcement that there is no scenario in which the Kim regime will survive after deploying its nuclear weapon).[232] Kim Jong-Un has already warned that he is ready to use nuclear weapons in the case of military conflicts with the United States and South Korea and that he could preemptively use nuclear weapons if threatened,[233] which signifies the continued danger.

2.3.3 Preservation of the absolute regime in the twenty-first century

North Korea's costly pursuit of nuclear weapons, its oppressive control of its populace coupled with strong restrictions on individual freedom, and its internal governance structure impeding economic development (such as bureaucratic control over its economy) are designed and implemented to protect the Kim regime. According to a commentator, the regime survival model is the best explanation for North Korea's seemingly erratic and inconsistent actions.[234] This is unlike the post–Cold War development in China where the socialist governance system was preserved but was not implemented solely to protect a particular regime. Since the late 1970s, China's national leadership has changed regularly, and the country has been able to focus on economic development with significant success as further discussed in Chapter 3. Authoritarian regimes and dictatorships exist in other parts of the world today, but no other country that has had a hereditary dynasty for three generations has declared itself to be a republic.

One of the factors that explains North Korea's unique hereditary control is its isolation from the West. When the North Korean government was formed in 1945, its southern border was blocked by South Korea and the United States, and restrictions on travel were reinforced after the Korean War. Its northern borders were shared by the authoritarian countries of China and Russia, but there is no direct route to any Western countries. Throughout history, North Koreans have never experienced a liberal democracy. After the fall of the Joseon Dynasty (조선왕조), which lasted six centuries, Koreans went through oppressive Japanese colonial rule. By the time the North Korean government was set up, the replacement of its foreign ruler with a domestic leader, such as Kim Il-Sung, would have been a welcome change to many, if not all, North Koreans. When Kim Il-Sung's son and grandson subsequently succeeded as North Korea's rulers, many North Koreans accepted succession, which was an observed tradition in the old dynasty under Confucian rule.[235] This development contrasts with the political development of South Korea where a democratic form of governance was constructed under U.S. influence.

Other factors that explain North Korea's hereditary succession are cultural and political. North Korea declares itself to be a socialist republic, not a hereditary kingdom. While it supports socialist ideals, rather than feudalistic heredity, the country is under Confucian influence, which has dominated Korea for over six centuries.[236] There is also an argument that North Korean elites have used Confucianism to solidify and systemize the Kim regime's rule.[237] In this discourse, the regime used Confucian virtues, such as loyalty and filial piety, to justify the Kim family's hereditary rule,[238] although family succession is neither an ideal nor a tradition of a socialist state. North Korea's political ideology, *Juche*, also supports absolute rule by the Kim family. In the *Juche* ideology, the head of the party (Su-ryong) is not just a political leader who can come and go but is rather the core brain of the socialist revolution who cannot be replaced.[239] From this perspective, the people's unity and loyalty to the Su-ryong has paramount importance, and its successive nature is not an impediment to realizing the ideal society under the *Juche* ideology.

The reality in North Korea, however, has not been a harmonious rule by their benevolent leader based on the unity and loyalty of the people. Any political opponents to North Korea's leaders have been brutally put down, detained, and executed.[240] To prevent political challenges, the Kim regime has created a country with severe restrictions on the political freedoms of the populace. North Koreans do not enjoy the freedom of travel, speech, assembly, or religion,[241] which are considered unbreachable fundamental rights in most other countries. Political dissidents, or anyone who is suspected of being disloyal to the regime, are arrested without a warrant, subject to extended detainment, torture, and even execution after a summary trial.[242] Political dissidents and their families, who escape execution, are detained in one of several large-scale concentration camps, each of which houses up to 50,000 people. The detainees are subject to forced labor, deprivation of adequate food, clothes, and housing, torture, and execution.[243] North Korea also implements the world's tightest monitoring system of its population; each North Korean citizen is required to report suspicious activities, including disloyal comments, of fellow citizens to authorities.[244]

North Korea also organizes all citizens, including young children, into closely-managed groups, including the Children's Alliance and the Youth Alliance, that continuously instill loyalty to the regime and hostility to the United States and its allies.[245] Decades of this indoctrination and absence of information from the outside world—North Korean citizens, except for a very small elite group, do not have access to the internet—have created a mass populace that is loyal to the Kim regime, which is a reason that a large-scale public resistance to the regime is unlikely. Despite all of this control, North Koreans, particularly the younger generations, have started to access information and entertainment programs from the outside world, such as South Korean pop music and television dramas, which are smuggled in on mobile devices such as flash drives. Fearing this inflow of outside information, Kim Jong-Un ordered his government to "stamp out" the cultural invasion.[246] Those who have accessed information from the outside may well harbor hostility toward the oppressive Kim regime, particularly if they know that their southern neighbors, South Koreans, enjoy freedom and economic prosperity.

This is likely why the North Korean government is vigilant about cutting off outside influences on its people.

However, it will be increasingly challenging for the Kim regime to preserve its absolute rule in the twenty-first century digital age where completely blocking information and communication from the general population is no longer feasible. Millions of North Koreans reportedly own cellular phones (albeit without connection to the internet).[247] North Korea's nuclear capabilities are a visible threat to sustainable peace in the region, but a less obvious and more fundamental threat is the existence of a country in Northeast Asia that is willing to forcibly cut off information and communication to its own population, restrict fundamental rights with threats of detainment, torture, and execution, and risk a nuclear war to preserve its regime. Even in the unlikely event that North Korea agreed to offer considerable concessions, such as substantially reducing its nuclear weapons and facilities, it would not be feasible for other free countries in the region to pursue peace and co-prosperity with a country that runs large-scale concentration camps where hundreds of thousands of its own people are subject to forced labor, torture, and execution. Public opinion in these free countries would not tolerate such an atrocity. In fact, the very existence of the current North Korean regime, so long as it maintains its extremely oppressive governance practices and structures, is an enduring threat to sustainable peace in Northeast Asia.

Chapter 3

THE NEW ASIAN PARADIGM OR RETURN TO THE OLD ASIA—RISE OF CHINA AND ITS ROLE IN THE REGION

3.1 The Rise of China: From a Historical Perspective

3.1.1 China and Northeast Asia in a historical context

Throughout history, China has maintained a dominant presence in Northeast Asia. Its size, massive population,[248] unmatched resources, and profound cultural influence have largely defined the political, economic, and social dynamics of Northeast Asia. China went through a turbulent time since the mid-nineteenth century, enduring foreign invasions, a civil war, economic deprivation, and the destructive Cultural Revolution. However, since the late 1970s, China has undertaken economic reforms and achieved remarkable economic development, providing significant economic opportunities for all of the other constituent countries in Northeast Asia. China's successful economic development has also strengthened its global and regional political influence to the extent that its policies now have a profound impact on political, economic, and military dynamics in Northeast Asia. This chapter examines whether the rise of China in recent decades will lead to a new political paradigm for the region and how its political governance influences sustainable peace in Northeast Asia. The first part of the chapter discusses its historical context.

China's history reveals several important characteristics: continued expansion of its territorial, political, and cultural parameters; extraordinary capacity to endure foreign rule (when invaded and conquered); influence over foreign rulers and the ability to assimilate foreign conquerors; sustained domination through a combination of warfare and appeasement; and a strong drive to unify the Chinese states (when divided). Other great powers have shown some of these characteristics; for example, the United States underwent a civil war after disallowing the South to secede in 1861.[249] However, in the case of China, these factors have worked to reinforce and sustain its control in the region. China's history demonstrates its immense expansion: an early Chinese state, the Zhou (周) Dynasty (1046 BC–256 BC), occupied a smaller part of present-day China as shown in Figure 3.1.

The Zhou Dynasty maintained a feudal system that allowed regional rulers' substantial political autonomy and was split into several autonomous states.[250] One of such autonomous states, the Qin Dynasty (秦, 9th century BC–206 BC), conquered the other Chinese states, creating the first Chinese Empire in 221 BC.

While the Qin's unification of China marks the beginning of China's history as East Asia's dominant power, it took another several centuries before China prevailed over Northeast Asia. Unlike Europe though, where no state unified Europe after the fall of the Roman Empire, several subsequent Chinese dynasties, such as the Han (漢, 202 BC–AD 220), Sui (隋, 581–619), Tang (唐, 618–907), Song (宋, 960–1279), and Ming (明, 1368–1644), "united" China

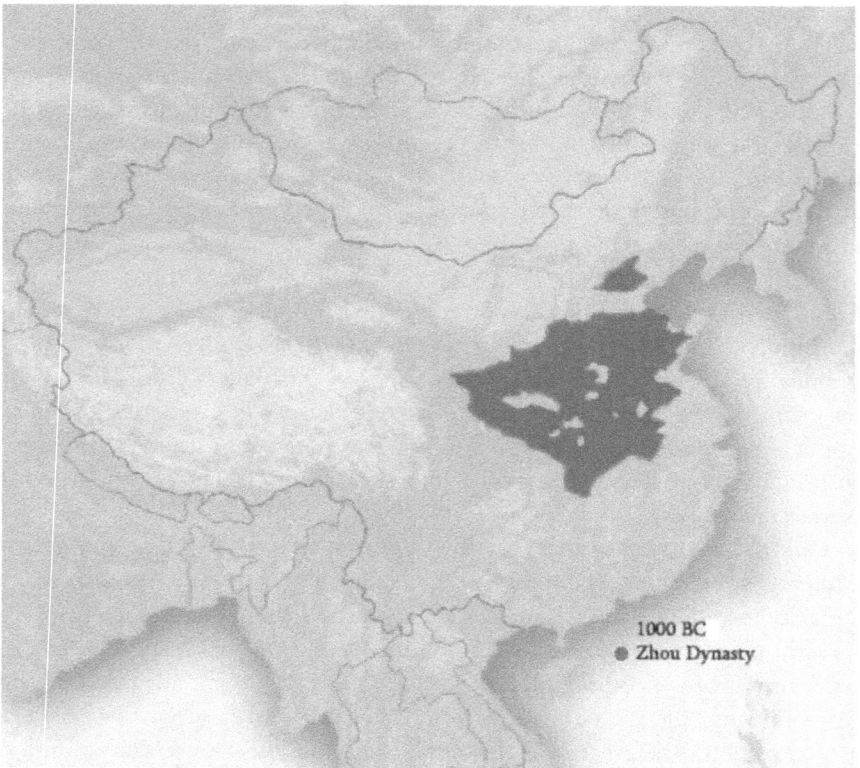

1000 BC
● Zhou Dynasty

Figure 3.1 Territory of Zhou Dynasty (1000 BC). (*Source*: History and Commercial Atlas of China, Harvard University Press)

after periods of division and separation. These shifts often entailed political, military, and diplomatic struggles. Warfare from both regional Chinese states and non-Chinese northern tribes threatened unification. The northern tribes, such as the Xiongnu (匈奴), exerted considerable pressure on the dynasties that united China. The Qin Dynasty erected the Great Wall to fend off the invasion of the northern tribes while the Han Dynasty paid tributes to prevent the tribes' invasions.[251] Despite these efforts, China did not always successfully defend itself. The Mongols and the Manchu tribes conquered China and set up their own dynasties in the heart of China, most notably as the Yuan Dynasty (元, 1271–1368) and the Qing Dynasty (清, 1636–1912, ruled China from 1644).

Extraordinarily, these foreign conquerors were assimilated into China over time. Both the Yuan and Qing Dynasties effectively became Chinese dynasties by adopting the Chinese bureaucracy and governance system and accepted Chinese ideologies such as Confucianism.[252] The new emperors and the ruling classes may have been the conquering tribes (e.g., the Mongols and the Manchus), but they operated within the centuries-old Chinese political, cultural, and economic apparatus.[253] The Chinese conquered their conquerors without waging a battle. By the time the Yuan Dynasty fell to the rising Ming Dynasty, the remaining Mongol elites fled north, maintaining their statehood (Northern Yuan or 北元). When the Qing Dynasty fell in 1912, many of the Manchu tribes had lost their identities and assimilated into China. The influence of Chinese civilization was powerful enough to dissolve the national identities of those who once invaded and conquered China. Historians Walter Meserve and Ruth Meserve observed that "whenever the barbarian hordes swept over China and assumed leadership, China maintained that unique amoeba-like ability to absorb whatever was foreign until it eventually became Chinese."[254]

Before the Yuan and Qing Dynasties, the Chinese had absorbed several once autonomous adjacent nations. While these nations became part of China through conquest and assimilation, the Chinese never lost their own identity. The presently independent nations in Northeast Asia, including Korea and Japan, also fell under China's strong political and cultural influence, albeit after considerable struggle. For example, the Chinese Empires (e.g., the Sui and the Tang) and the northern Korean Kingdom (Goguryeo or 고구려) fought bloody wars for several decades in the late sixth and seventh centuries. The Sui Dynasty experienced massive defeats during its Korea campaigns (598–614), which exhausted its resources and led to its fall.[255] The Sino-Korea struggle eventually ended with the fall of the Korean Kingdom of Goguryeo in 668.[256] Goguryeo was succeeded by another Korean state, Balhae (발해, 698–926), but Korea and China have maintained a peaceful relationship since then. Both Korea and Japan adopted Chinese culture while maintaining their own national identities. In Korea, Chinese Confucianism (朱子學) formed the central political and social ideology.[257] By the end of the fourteenth century, China had become a dominant political, military, and economic power in Northeast Asia.

3.1.2 Historical turmoil and China's transformation

Until the end of the eighteenth century, China was an unchallenged hegemon in Northeast Asia. The Qing Dynasty was one of the world's most powerful states with the largest economy in the world (making up over one-third of the world's GDP)[258] and had a powerful military that stopped Russian forces in 1685.[259] At the height of the Qing Dynasty, it ruled Manchu (presently China's northeast territory), Mongolia, Xinjiang, and Tibet, and mainland China—occupying a massive territory even larger than today's China. However, China started to decline in the first half of the nineteenth century. Excessive financial expenditures, due to costly military campaigns under Emperor Qianlong and internal corruption, began to take a toll.[260] Despite its massive appearance, China was also stagnant in industrial development, technological innovation, and trade expansion, while the West was transforming itself through the advancement of industry and science. These different trajectories between China and the West would result in considerable gaps in industrial capacity and military power by the nineteenth century.

China's humiliating defeat in the Opium War at the hands of the British (1839–1842) revealed China's vulnerability. The British sought to export opium from India into China to make up for their chronic trade deficit with China.[261] When the Chinese imperial government attempted to enforce its ban on opium imports, the British government retaliated by deploying its naval forces, starting the war.[262] The British secured a decisive victory over Qing forces by virtue of their superior weaponry and military technology. Britain forced China to sign the Treaty of Nanjing in 1842, which provided British citizens with immunity from Chinese law, expanded the number of Chinese ports open to international trade, and gave control of Hong Kong to the British.[263] The Treaty signaled the end of China's unchallenged superiority in East Asia and exposed its weaknesses in technology and military power. The concessions made by the imperial Qing government opened the floodgates to further expansion by European imperial powers—French and German settlements soon followed after the British.[264]

The advancement of Western powers was not the only concern for the Qing government. Racial and ethnic tensions erupted—particularly between the ruling-class Manchus and the Han Chinese, the majority ethnic group in China.[265] The Taiping Rebellion (太平天國之亂, 1850–1864), led by a Han Chinese named Hong Xiuquan, sought to eradicate the Manchus as an enemy ethnic group and create a new "ideal" nation.[266] Although the Qing government eventually crushed the rebellion, the conflict claimed millions of Chinese lives and undermined the authority and legitimacy of the Qing Empire. Additionally, China experienced another decisive defeat against the British and French in the Second Opium War (1856–1860).[267] British and French forces invaded Beijing, the capital of the Qing Dynasty, and destroyed imperial buildings such as the Old Summer Palace. The internal turmoil and China's continued defeat in the wars against the West raised a sense of crisis in the Qing government and prompted reform-minded government officials—including Zeng Guofan, Li Hongzhang, and Zuo Zongtang—to initiate a series of reforms in China, including initiatives to build modern industries and military forces.

These reform-minded officials carried out the Self-Strengthening Movement (洋務運動, 1861–1894), but it failed to transform China into a modern nation as the Meiji Restoration did for Japan. Unlike its Japanese counterpart, the reform movement did not challenge the Confucian ideology that reigned over Chinese politics and society for centuries and failed to make broader institutional and educational reforms necessary for modernization.[268] The reformers sought to adopt the instrumental utility of Western technologies but not the broader cultural and ideological apparatuses of democracy, the rule of law, or science-based approaches that made Western industrial innovations and development possible. The inherent limits of China's reform became apparent when it was defeated again in the war against Japan in 1894.[269] Corruption and lack of training made China's military ill-prepared for the war, and this defeat marked China's loss of control over Northeast Asia. China's centuries-old superiority in Northeast Asia had dissipated, and others, such as Russia and Japan, began to expand their influence.

The Xinhai Revolution (辛亥革命, 1911–1912)[270] overthrew the Qing Dynasty and established the Republic of China, initiating China's transformation into a modern republic. The revolution also signaled the beginning of a period of decades-long turmoil. Those who led the revolution, such as Sun Won, failed to take power, and members of the old political factions, such as Yuan Shikai, took leadership positions and were unprepared to lead a modern nation. The lack of effective political leadership plunged China into decades of internal conflicts and regional control by warlords.[271] China's turmoil deepened. Nationalist leader Chiang Kai-shek's military campaigns to "unite" China under the Nationalist Party (中國國民黨), the rise of communism under the leadership of Mao Zedong, and the Japanese invasion of China in the 1930s tore the country apart, claiming tens of millions of lives and destroying much of the country.[272] Facing these challenges, particularly the Japanese invasion, the Chinese forged a national identity—mirroring the modern example of Ukraine, whose citizens have reinforced their national identity by resisting Russia's military invasion in 2022. By the end of World War II, China had been substantially transformed from an old empire ruled by a domestic or foreign hereditary ruler (*e.g.*, the Manchus) to a modern nation-state that was solidly a republic—although it was not yet clear whether the new republic would be a liberal democracy or a socialist/communist regime.

3.1.3 Economic development and rise of China

The end of World War II in 1945 did not bring an end to China's turmoil; a civil war between the nationalists and the communists soon broke out.[273] The nationalists initially held military superiority, but the communists, who had gained support from local populations, turned the tide of the war and defeated the nationalists.[274] The Chinese Communist Party (中國共產黨 or "CCP") occupied mainland China and established the People's Republic of China in 1949.[275] The defeated Nationalist Party fled to Taiwan where it formed its own government that remains today.[276] China, under communist rule, adopted economic policies such as the Great Leap Forward Movement (1958–1962), which brought economic devastation instead of prosperity.[277] The Chinese leadership was concerned about the regression of China's industry and economy vis-à-vis the West and pushed through plans to create industrial bases in China's agrarian countryside. It was a catastrophic disaster, causing serious food shortages and starvation that cost the lives of up to 45 million people.[278] The subsequent Cultural Revolution (1966–1976), which had begun in the aftermath of the disastrous economic initiatives, sought to eliminate the capitalist elements in society and inflicted further damage to the economy.[279]

After Mao Zedong's death in 1976, China shifted its direction under Deng Xiaoping's leadership. Unlike his predecessors, Deng was prepared to implement pragmatic policies at home after learning from the success of the West, even if it meant a departure from traditional communist economic policies.[280] Adopting this pragmatism, China began liberalizing segments of its economy and allowed markets to operate.[281] China adopted a gradual approach, establishing Special Economic Zones (SEZs) in several coastal areas where foreign companies were allowed to invest and trade while the government maintained control over their influence and growth.[282] Labeled the "socialist market economy," the government has maintained control over the economy while allowing markets to operate.[283] This approach resembles the economic development policies of other successful East Asian countries, such as South Korea, Taiwan, and Singapore, which are market economies that have also adopted strong state-led economic growth policies.[284] Unlike North Korea, which did not allow markets or private corporations to operate, China and these other successful East Asian countries adopted both, albeit under strong government leadership. As explained by the New General Theory of Economic Development, markets and corporations *sustained* successful economic development in these countries.[285]

China, like the other successful East Asian countries, focused on export promotion as a means of achieving economic development.[286] Deng introduced several reform measures to decentralize international trade under government control through his "reform and open door policy."[287] These measures included extending "trading rights," which had been exclusively vested with the state, liberalizing import and export prices, introducing tariff and non-tariff trade measures compliant with international practices, devaluing the Chinese currency (Renminbi) to promote exports, providing incentives for foreign investment, and allowing trade by foreign-funded firms.[288] The government still controlled much of the economy, but these reforms introduced substantial market elements by allowing some private sector autonomy in international trade.[289] China's export-led growth policy had optimal timing as global trade and investment was expanding rapidly. China's lower labor costs and market potential attracted foreign companies and investments, which provided China with capital, technology, managerial expertise, and employment opportunities.[290]

China's economic development policy was phenomenal—its economy grew nearly 10 percent annually, lifting more people (some 600 million) out of extreme poverty than at any other time and place in history.[291] By the time China joined the WTO in 2001, the country, which once lost tens of millions of its people due to starvation, had become a solidly middle-income country. China also began to improve market access for imports as a part of its accession commitments to the WTO.[292] The market access measures included reductions in tariffs and nontariff barriers, extension of trading rights to both foreign and domestic firms, greater market access (in the areas of telecommunications, banking, and insurance), grants of direct distribution rights within China, and protection of intellectual property rights.[293] These measures meant both greater export opportunities for other countries and more choices for Chinese consumers. In addition, China agreed to substantial "transparency commitments," such as publishing trade-related laws, regulations, and other measures.[294] China extended this transparency obligation to its rule-making process, creating positive implications for developing the rule of law.

China's success in economic development has led to its political rise on the international plane. China became the second largest economy in the world in 2010 (second only to the United States) and the world's largest trader in

2013. With the aforementioned measures to increase market access, it has become the largest export market for Northeast Asian countries, including South Korea and Japan, creating substantial political leverage for it vis-à-vis these other countries. The impact of China's successful economic development is not limited to alleviating poverty for its population, but it has created industrial power that can compete and even prevail over its Western counterparts. China's massive production capacity in major industrial areas has made the country the "world's factory."[295] China's increased industrial capacity also means that competing industries in other countries, such as the United States, face increasing difficulties in competing against Chinese exporters, causing large trade deficits.[296] In addition, China's advancement in strategic industrial areas, such as semiconductors, has alarmed the United States, for fear of losing its competitive edge.[297] The economic rise of China has also transformed its military power. As a result of substantial investment, China's military capacity is larger than every other country except the United States, signifying China's rise as a global power.

3.2 Economic Opportunities and Political Tensions

3.2.1 China as the world's factory to the world's market

As a result of its phenomenal economic development, China has become the largest manufacturing country in the world. In 2019, China made up 28.7 percent of the total global manufacturing output, which was greater than the manufacturing output of the United States (16.8 percent) and Japan (7.5 percent) combined.[298] China has been labeled the world's factory, a position once occupied by great Western powers, such as Britain in the nineteenth century and the United States in the twentieth century. These countries' superior manufacturing capacity had been transformed into their military superiority and political hegemony on the international plane. Mao Zedong unsuccessfully tried to replicate that path by industrializing and expanding China's manufacturing capacity in the 1950s through failed initiatives such as the Great Leap Forward Movement.[299] China's new approach beginning in the 1980s—adopting more market-friendly economic development initiatives—has been far more successful and has expanded China's manufacturing capacity dramatically. China increased its manufacturing output (value added in current US$) from US$ 622 billion in 2004 to US$ 4.87 trillion in 2021, nearly eight times in less than two decades.[300] When China announced its economic reform in 1978, its manufacturing output was a mere US$ 77 billion (estimated).[301]

Foreign investors have contributed to China's exceptional increase in manufacturing capacity. Since China began to accept foreign investments in the

1980s, hundreds of thousands of foreign companies have invested in China, built factories within its borders, and produced products for both export and domestic markets.[302] Several factors favorable to manufacturing have attracted foreign investors, including an abundance of low-cost labor, availability of utilities (*e.g.,* electricity and water), transportation systems (*e.g.,* roads and ports), government support for manufacturing and foreign investments (*e.g.,* low taxes and regulatory support for investments), robust supply chains and a raw materials ecosystem supporting manufacturing, and China's successful entry into the WTO in 2001 (which facilitated exports of manufactured products from China).[303] As a result, China's foreign direct investment (FDI) inflow increased from US$ 1.43 billion in 1984 to US$ 173.5 billion in 2021.[304] The role of foreign-invested companies in China's manufacturing has been significant; they make up less than 3 percent of Chinese companies but reportedly contribute to one-quarter of the industrial output and 50 percent of China's international trade.[305]

China's phenomenal increase in manufacturing capacity has correlated with large increases in its exports. Figure 3.2 illustrates China's rapid increase in exports in recent decades, particularly since joining the WTO in 2001.

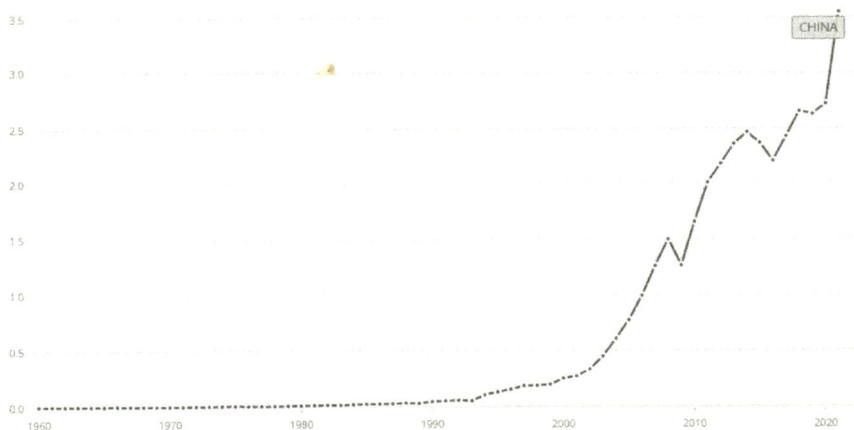

Figure 3.2 Export growth of China (1960–2021) (unit US$ trillion). (*Source*: World Bank, Exports of goods and services (current US$)—China)

This export expansion has drawn some of the world's largest producers (*e.g.,* Apple, Johnson & Johnson, and IKEA) to China, providing enormous economic opportunities, which has, in turn, caused job losses and declines in manufacturing elsewhere, including in advanced countries such as the United States. The relocation of production facilities to China and other low-wage countries has caused former industrial hubs in the United States, such as the large area from the Great Lakes to the upper Midwest (termed "the Rust Belt") to lose manufacturing industries.[306] The resulting economic and social decline in these areas has brewed widespread concern about offshore production. This concern has led political leaders in the affected areas to pursue "reshoring" policies that encourage and incentivize home production rather than offshore production, although reliance on the global supply chain seems to limit the effectiveness of such efforts.[307]

China has also expanded its demand for imports. China's export-led economic growth policy required large amounts of parts, processed materials, and machinery to function. In earlier years, such products were not available domestically, but China began to produce them as its manufacturing sector developed. On account of successful economic development, China's rising per capita income (from US$ 194 in 1980 to US$ 12,556 in 2021)[308] also meant that demand for foreign consumer goods would increase. As a result, China has become the world's second largest importer, making up 11.5 percent of the world's merchandise imports in 2020 (next only to the United States which makes up 13.5 percent).[309] China's expanding import market has provided significant export opportunities for other countries, particularly the major exporting countries in Northeast Asia such as South Korea and Japan. In fact, China provides the largest export market for all the other countries in the region—South and North Korea, Japan, Mongolia, and Russia—and the third largest market for the United States.[310] As a result, China has become both the market and factory of the world and is positioned to provide economic opportunities for the rest of the world, including Northeast Asia.

3.2.2 *The socialist market economy in the global context*

Since the 1980s, China's approach to economic development has been predicated on its socialist market economy. Under this strategy, China has adopted some free-market mechanisms while maintaining its communist rule. This blended policy has led to exceptional economic success.[311] It is seemingly a self-contradictory proposition, though—communist ideals mandate equal distribution of wealth and prohibit private ownership of property, including production facilities. On the contrary, market economies allow private property ownership and encourage competitive market players to profit from their efforts, accepting the resulting gaps in income and wealth. Today, China exhibits one of the largest gaps in income and wealth among major countries, and it seems that the communist ideals of equal wealth distribution have disappeared, despite the CCP still officially proclaiming them.[312] What does remain is the command structure of the communist rule over the economy. Although private firms now produce and sell on the markets without instructions under government plans, the government may still instruct domestic firms on specific economic transactions with or without an official mandate, as further illustrated below.

The Chinese economic governance structure (socialist market economy), in which the government exercises substantial control over the economy, has posed global problems. For example, the Chinese government has shown a willingness to use its influence over trade as a means to fulfill its political objectives outside the mandate of WTO law (international trade law).[313] In 2017, the United States deployed a high-altitude missile defense system (Terminal High Altitude Area Defense or "THAAD") in South Korea to counteract potential missile attacks from North Korea.[314] China objected to this deployment, alleging that the THAAD's radar coverage included the eastern part of China. In response, China adopted a series of restrictive trade measures against South Korea. China restricted trade in several areas, including tourism (banning the sales of Korea tour packages on an unofficial government mandate), entertainment (suspending the sales and distribution of entertainment programs), retail stores (shutting down "Lotte" retail stores in China), and certain goods originating in Korea (reducing the number of baby formula products sold in China).[315] Most of the measures were unannounced and implemented through unofficial government instructions, breaching the rules of WTO law prohibiting discrimination against goods and services imported from another WTO member country.[316]

In this case, China utilized trade restrictions to influence South Korea's acceptance of the THAAD system's deployment, which China alleged would pose a security risk.[317] However, China never declared or admitted that adopting such measures was necessary to protect its security interests. If these measures had been necessary to protect essential national security interests, the measures would have been justified under WTO law (GATT Article XXI). Thus, the unannounced nature of China's restrictions suggests that it was not convinced of the legitimacy of these measures under the rules of international trade. Yet, the Chinese government implemented these trade restrictions through its influence over private firms. This case illustrates how China's seemingly contradictory "socialist market economy" and the government's resulting economic control can interfere unjustly with international trade and investment. As a result of this incident, one Korean company, Lotte, alone incurred a financial loss of US$ 1.7 billion. Furthermore, several Korean conglomerates, including Lotte, Samsung, LG, and Posco, either left or downsized their operations in China and sought new places for their investments, such as Vietnam, adversely affecting local economies and employment in China.[318]

Another important aspect of China's socialist market economy is the presence of a large number of state-owned enterprises (SOEs). China is known to have more than 150,000 SOEs owned by various levels of government. SOEs accounted for over 60 percent of China's market capitalization in 2019 and generated 40 percent of China's GDP in 2020.[319] SOEs are, in some sense, an embodiment of the socialist ideals in the economy. Some of the largest SOEs employ hundreds of thousands of workers and provide housing, schools, and hospitals for them,[320] creating living communities, not just workplaces, for large portions of the population. SOEs dominate strategic sectors (including petroleum, electricity, communications, railway, and banking), and receive preferential treatment from the government.[321] In the global context, SOEs, which enjoy considerable cost advantages due to government subsidies and other preferences, raise concerns for China's trade partners. Competing industries in other countries, which are not owned by the government and do not receive such government support, are at a competitive disadvantage vis-à-vis Chinese SOEs. Also, the government control over SOEs means that China may implement government mandates through its domestic and international business activities.[322]

China's socialist market economy, by design and practice, has not given confidence to its trade partners on the compatibility of its trade practices to free-market economies. As a result, China's trade partners have been reluctant to recognize China's market economy status, which would accord the country certain regulatory advantages under WTO law, such as anti-dumping assessments.[323] Reflecting this concern, Sandy Levin, the leading Democrat on the U.S. House Ways and Means Committee, stated that China has "acted like a non-market economy in so many respects with their state-owned companies, with subsidies, with dumping...."[324] Former United States Trade Representative Robert Lighthizer also opined in his testimony before Congress that any decision to label China a "market economy" would have "cataclysmic" consequences for the WTO.[325] In addition to the United States, the European Union also expressed concerns about granting China market economy status.[326] China's behavior with South Korea during the cited THAAD deployment controversy also indicates that the government's political objectives, rather than market mechanisms, have been used to determine China's trade practices. Such uncontrolled state influence over the economy is expected to continue in the absence of an independent judiciary that provides checks against the administration.

3.2.3 Political tensions with the other countries in the region

China's economic rise has provided the Chinese government with resources to expand its military and restore its political influence. This exertion of power has generated tension between China and other countries in the region. Some of these political tensions concern regional issues, while others, such as tensions with the United States, concern global hegemony and China's challenge to the global order (set by the West in the twentieth century).[327] These tensions also reflect the region's political and ideological divide—the United States maintains close economic ties and military alliances with South Korea and Japan, advocating liberal democracy, while China has maintained military and economic cooperation with Russia and North Korea, exercising authoritarian rule. These two groups of countries were adversaries in the Korean War, although Japan and Russia did not formally participate. The Korean War ceased in 1953 without a peace treaty, but South Korea and Japan remained supportive of the United States' global and regional military and economic initiatives. Russia and North Korea began collaborating with China against the United States, creating tension between the two groups.[328]

The rivalry between China and the United States, which generates substantial political tension, extends beyond the boundaries of Northeast Asia. As a result of its rapid economic development, China is in a position to challenge the industrial, economic, military, and political dominance of the West, which the United States leads. In response to this challenge, the United States has adopted policies to suppress China's economic and military advances. On the economic front, the United States has adopted trade restrictions, such as a 25 percent tariff increase on a broad range of products imported from China.[329] The United States accused China of widespread, state-sponsored intellectual property rights (IPRs) piracy and illegitimate acquisition of sensitive information.[330] The United States has also adopted measures to prevent the dissemination of high-end technologies to China and even banned China's information technology (IT) enterprises, such as Huawei, with the aid of its allies including Japan.[331] In response, China has retaliated against the U.S. tariff measures with increased tariffs on imports from the United States.[332] China has also criticized the U.S. action against Huawei and pressured U.S. allies, such as South Korea, not to participate in the Huawei ban.[333]

On the military front, China has been expanding its naval capacity and activities in the Asia Pacific, challenging the position of the United States. A Congressional Research Service (CRS) report has observed:

China's navy is viewed as posing a major challenge to the U.S. Navy's ability to achieve and maintain wartime control of blue-water ocean areas in the Western Pacific—the first such challenge the U.S. Navy has faced since the end of the Cold War. China's navy forms a key element of a Chinese challenge to the long-standing status of the United States as the leading military power in the Western Pacific.[334]

The gaps in military technology between the United States and China are closing, with China building new aircraft carriers, supersonic anti-ship missiles, and stealth jet fighters—all posing threats to the U.S. military in the region.[335] The United States has responded by increasing its naval presence and its activities in the South and East China Seas. The United States also maintains large-scale military bases in South Korea and Japan, which can be used against China in case of a potential military conflict, although the United States has not declared that it will involve either country in a potential conflict with China.

China has political tensions with other countries in the region. It has imposed political and economic pressure on South Korea for its military and economic cooperation with the United States. As discussed above, China adopted restrictive trade measures against Korea when it approved the U.S. deployment of the THAAD system in South Korea.[336] China has also "warned" South Korea against cooperating with the United States in its effort to exclude China from the global semiconductor supply chain.[337] Chinese leadership appears to share a perception that Korea was once subordinate to China,[338] a viewpoint that most Koreans would find objectionable. It adopts policies that tend to undermine Korea's political and historical autonomy, including a project many Koreans see as China's attempt to rewrite Northeast Asian history. This "Northeast Project" (東北工程), which China's Academy of Social Sciences conducted with the support of the Chinese government, asserts that the Korean Kingdom of Goguryeo that once dominated this region was merely a regional government of China.[339] This project has created substantial political tensions between the two countries, resulting in a diplomatic protest by South Korea.[340] The project ended in 2007, but Korea's concerns about China's expansionism remain.[341]

Tensions between China and Japan have also grown in recent decades. The substantial anti-Japanese sentiment is derived from Japanese aggression and the resulting atrocities from the Second Sino-Japanese War (1937–1945), the territorial dispute over the Senkaku (Diaoyudao) Islands, and Japan's support for U.S. economic and military policies against China. Anti-Chinese sentiment has also increased in Japan due to concerns about China's aggression toward its neighboring countries and the adverse impacts it has on Japan. According to a 2016 report, only 11 percent of the Japanese have a positive view of China, and merely 14 percent of the Chinese expressed a positive view of Japan.[342] The territorial dispute over the Senkaku Islands, which caused massive demonstrations and violations against the Japanese in China, has not been resolved to date.[343] Both governments are cautious about escalating adverse public sentiment and political tension on account of the important economic interdependence between the two countries. China is presently

Japan's largest trade partner, and Japan is the second largest trade partner for China, next only to the United States.[344] Despite these efforts, political tensions have again been heightened due to Japan's exclusion of Huawei and ZTE, the Chinese IT firms, from government contracts in line with the U.S. policy cited above.[345]

China's relations with its old communist comrades—Russia, North Korea, and Mongolia—were known to be friendly and cooperative, but historical developments have shown substantial political tension. In 1969, China engaged in an armed conflict with Russia over a border dispute.[346] The conflict did not develop into a full-scale war, but hostility remained afterward.[347] While these two countries now maintain cooperative relations, at times forming a common stance against the United States, they are also cautious about each other's increasing influence. For example, China refused to supply arms to support Russia in the Ukraine War.[348] As for North Korea, the Kim regime has become increasingly reliant on China for economic support and trade while economic sanctions against North Korea intensify. However, China's support for North Korea has been measured—China does not support North Korea's nuclear ambitions and also approved the U.N. economic sanctions against North Korea.[349] Commentators have observed a significant degree of disbelief and tension between the two countries.[350] As for Mongolia, the country has trodden carefully to ensure survival and maintain independence from China and Russia (despite their pressure to shed its independence and join their anti-western platform).[351]

3.3 Toward a New Asian Paradigm? Creating a Sustainable Power Balance in the Region

3.3.1 Revival of Sinocentrism?

Since the 1980s, China's economic and political rise has changed the economic, political, and military landscape of Northeast Asia. China once dominated the region economically and politically, and scholars have inquired whether China's rise signals the region's return to Sinocentrism.[352] Sinocentrism refers to the Chinese political ideology that the Chinese state is the center of the world due to its superior civilization and (perceived) mandate from the heavens. Thus, the ideology professes that China should command all adjacent nations and states.[353] As discussed, Sinocentrism formed the central ideology for China's political governance for several centuries until the West diminished its power in the nineteenth century. As archaic as this notion sounds in the twenty-first century, China's apparent shift from its focus on economic development (advocated by Deng Xiaoping) to coercive political and military expansion (reinforced under Xi Jinping's leadership) raises concerns over the revival of Sinocentrism although the Chinese government has not officially proclaimed it.[354]

China's recent conduct appears to signal progress toward its revival. On August 9, 2022, China's foreign minister Wang Yi, while in talks with South Korea's foreign minister during a 30th-anniversary commemoration of the establishment of diplomacy between South Korea and China, reportedly demanded a "five-point commitment" from South Korea. The proposal includes mutual commitments to "independence regardless of external interference"; "upholding good neighborliness and friendship while accommodating each other's major concerns"; "openness and win-win cooperation, and stable and unimpeded industrial and supply chains"; "equality, mutual respect, and non-interference in each other's internal affairs"; and "multilateralism and the purposes and principles of the UN Charter."[355] The Chinese government described this "commitment" as "the greatest common denominator of the will of the two peoples and the inevitable trend of the times." However, many Koreans perceived the demand for "commitment" as disrespecting Korea's sovereign rights and as a condescending guideline that warns against the pursuit of a strategic alliance with the United States.[356]

Whether or not the five-point demand is intended as a guideline for South Korea or was devised to portray Korea as subordinate to China, the revival of Sinocentrism is unfeasible. Sinocentrism prevailed in Northeast Asia until the mid-nineteenth century because of the region's acceptance of the Chinese-originated Confucian order. Confucianism—which upholds the hierarchical and "harmonious" orders in family, society, and among nations—justified China's political and cultural dominance in the region (as the region's most "advanced" country).[357] However, in the process of modernization during the nineteenth and twentieth centuries, Confucianism was replaced with other modern ideologies such as democracy and equal sovereignty among states. Even in China, where Confucianism originated, it was challenged and condemned, particularly during the Cultural Revolution.[358] Without an ideology, such as Confucianism, justifying China's rule in the region, the revival of Sinocentrism will not have any ideological support. China's communist rule and so-called socialist market economy are not followed by any other country in the region, except perhaps North Korea (communist rule), and cannot provide ideological support for the revival of Sinocentrism.

Furthermore, China's economic and military powers, although vast in size, are insufficient for the revival of Sinocentrism. Other countries in Northeast Asia, such as South Korea and Japan, have smaller economies and militaries than China, but they are supported by economic coalitions with the West, such as FTAs (free trade agreements).[359] They also hold a military alliance with the United States. These networks of global economic and military cooperation do not allow for the domination China once enjoyed in the region, which is necessary to revive Sinocentrism. It is notable that the West's global domination from the late nineteenth century through the twentieth century was facilitated by the combination of its superior military and economic powers. The stronghold was also aided by superior technology, scientific knowledge, mass production capabilities, and ideologies of universal appeal, such as liberal democracy and the rule of law (although the latter was not applied in many of the West's colonies). China's advancements in science, technology, and production capacity are remarkable, but they have not allowed absolute superiority over other countries in the region.[360]

Sinocentrism may nevertheless function as a psychological tendency among Chinese officials in their treatment of smaller countries. At a regional security meeting in Hanoi in July 2010, Yang Jiechi, China's then foreign minister, shocked the audience with his remark that "China is a big country and other countries are small countries, and that's just a fact."[361] Political commentator Gordon Chang observed that this derogatory sentence sums up how Beijing views the world.[362] Despite what high-level Chinese officials such as Yang may expect, the "smaller" countries in the region are not likely to accept such a subordinate position to China. In its approach to other countries, Beijing may overlook the historical strength of these countries' resolve to stay independent and autonomous. The Han Chinese may have been successful in assimilating over ethnic groups, many of whom were once autonomous, by absorbing them into China. Yet, the remaining independent countries in the region, such as Korea, Japan, and Mongolia, have maintained their autonomy for thousands of years, withstanding enormous pressure from China when it dominated Northeast Asia. Thus, it is unlikely for these countries to accept China's supremacy and assume subordinate positions when they can rely on economic coalitions and military alliances with the West. As a result, Sinocentrism is not likely to become a feasible working order in Northeast Asia.

3.3.2 Continuation of the status quo

If Sinocentrism is unlikely to be a working paradigm for Northeast Asia, a continuation of the status quo might be another possibility. The status quo is a "confrontational balance" between China, North Korea, and Russia on the one hand and the United States, Japan, and South Korea on the other. The confrontational balance refers to a state of political standoff with a possibility of military conflict, while both sides actively continue to trade and invest with each other. It differs from the twentieth-century Cold War, as there is currently a tremendous volume of international trade and investment activities between China and the other side. This relationship creates significant mutual economic reliance (*e.g.*, approximately 1.8 million jobs in the United States reportedly supported by exports to China),[363] which did not exist during the Cold War, at least not to any comparable degree. Contrasting the Cold War, either side is unlikely to wage an all-out war. There has been concern over the possibility of a military conflict between the United States and China over Taiwan. Some commentators observe its occurrence is unlikely in the near future,[364] but even if it happens, both countries will likely try to geographically limit such a conflict to Taiwan and its surrounding seas.

Despite the cited differences from the Cold War, the status quo is confrontational and unstable. For the three decades following the 1980s, China focused on economic development, expanding economic relationships with other countries and increasing international trade and investment. The outcome, as discussed in the preceding sections,[365] was an unprecedented success in economic development. This success lifted hundreds of millions of Chinese out of absolute poverty and lifted hundreds of millions more to the middle class. Chinese leaders during this time—Deng Xiaoping (1978–1989), Jiang Zemin (1989–2003), and Hu Jintao (2003–2013)—devoted themselves to Chinese economic development and tried to maintain cooperative relationships with other countries, including the United States. In 2005, China signified its emphasis on foreign relations through its first strategic dialogue with the United States.[366] During this period, China largely respected Hong Kong's autonomy, invited the head of Taiwan's Nationalist Party to China to improve the Sino-Taiwan relationship, provided public health insurance to all Chinese citizens, and hosted the 2008 Summer Olympic Games in Beijing.[367] The CCP's standing committee, comprised of nine standing members, formed a collective leadership during this period, offering more collaborative governance than other common dictatorships ruled by one person.[368]

Xi Jinping's emergence as China's leader has changed the status quo. Unlike his predecessors, Xi has consolidated his powers by weakening the standing committee and removing presidential term limits. Xi has also advocated for the need for stronger and more effective leadership to realize the "Chinese Dream," which he described as the "great rejuvenation of the Chinese nation."[369] When Xi first mentioned the plan in 2012, it was unclear how he would implement the Dream, but his actions over the last decade revealed its controversial trajectory.[370] Economically, it meant direct challenges to the economic and technological superiority of the West. The Made in China 2025 Plan aims for China's domination in several high-technology areas, including IT, robotics, pharmaceuticals, and new energy vehicles.[371]

China has also rapidly increased the capacity of its military forces, which are poised to threaten U.S. fleets in the Pacific and have raised concerns for its neighboring countries.[372] Politically, the Chinese government violently suppressed Hong Kong's pro-democracy movements, breaching its commitment to Hong Kong's autonomy.[373] Moreover, China declared an intent to push unification with Taiwan using military force as necessary.[374] China also persecuted Muslims in Xinjiang, arbitrarily detaining over one million of them and dissidents elsewhere.[375]

Xi's aggressive moves in and outside China have put the United States and its allies on alert. The United States has responded to China's industrial ambitions, such as the Made in China 2025 initiative, with extensive trade measures, substantially raising tariffs on a broad range of Chinese imports.[376] As discussed earlier, the United States and its allies have banned China's leading IT companies, such as Huawei, for security concerns and have also taken actions to exclude China from supply chains in strategic areas like semiconductors.[377] The Biden administration, which vowed to adjust Trump administration policies in several areas, has maintained its predecessor's economic stance against China, including tariffs. On the military front, the United States and its allies have joined forces to check China's advances in the Pacific. The United States increased its naval activities in the Pacific, denying China's control over the South and East China Seas, and announced its commitment to protecting Taiwan against any Chinese military attack in the future.[378] On the political front, the United States and its allies have criticized China's actions in Hong Kong, Xinjiang, and Tibet, and pressured China by publicly invoking human rights violations.[379]

China's economic, military, and political challenges and the cited responses mean instability and confrontation for Northeast Asia. Significant mutual economic dependency between China and other countries in Northeast Asia (including the United States), coupled with nuclear capabilities, may not render an all-out war likely. Nonetheless, the continuing political standoff, the regional military buildup with the resulting risk of military conflict, and the supply chain exclusions are not conducive to continuing peace in the long term. The peace and stability of Northeast Asia is also intimately connected to global economic and political development, and the global competition and rivalry between the United States and China affects economic and political dynamics in the region. Concerns about China may not necessarily be based on its economic and industrial expansion but on the critical risk that it poses to global stability when a single political leader, such as Xi, controls such vast economic, industrial, and military powers without democratic accountability. A sustainable political order and balance of power cannot be drawn from the status quo.

3.3.3 *The power balance from within*

The preceding discussion has revealed that the confrontational checks and standoffs, which are characteristics of the status quo, do not generate an order that facilitates sustainable peace in Northeast Asia. China alone does not control the outcome of peace and war in the region. However, considering its size, economic capacity, industrial advancement, and massive military, China's actions have a crucial effect. China's rise, particularly over the last decade, has raised concerns for the region (and beyond) due to the authoritarian nature of its governance and decision-making process, which a single leader, Xi Jinping, increasingly controls without democratic accountability. Accountability tends to deter decisions that have drastic effects, such as the decision to impose lockdowns on major Chinese cities, such as Shanghai, due to the spread of the Coronavirus Omicron variant. It is well known that this decision was influenced by Xi Jinping's personal insistence rather than the recommendation of experts.[380] This unrealistic zero-coronavirus policy, which has adversely affected both China's domestic economy and the global economy,[381] may not have been pushed forward if a more deliberative decision-making process was in place.[382]

Democracy does not guarantee better decision-making. Some of the decisions made by former U.S. President Donald Trump, such as withdrawing from the Paris Climate Agreement and the Trans-Pacific Partnership Agreement,[383] appear to be regressive, disregarding the well-founded consensus for environmental protection and free trade expansion (of which the United States has been the driving force). Imperfect as it may be, as reflected by these decisions of a democratically elected president, the democratic governance system nevertheless enables institutional checks against power. For example, in November 2018, the White House suspended the press credentials of a journalist for sharing a testy exchange with President Trump. However, the U.S. District Court ordered the White House, the world's most prestigious powerhouse, to reinstate the press pass for the journalist.[384] In another example, which concerns sustainable peace on the international level, a top U.S. commander stated that he would resist an order from President Trump for a nuclear strike if it were "illegal."[385] Under the U.S. Constitution, the president is the commander in chief of the U.S. armed forces, but the commander emphasized that even the president's order was not above the law, which is a key tenet of democratic governance.

The above-cited strength of democratic governance does not imply that China should have implemented a Western-style democracy from the beginning. As discussed in the preceding sections, China underwent serious economic deprivation in the 1950s and 1960s, resulting in tens of millions of deaths caused by starvation. Understandably, overcoming crushing poverty was a priority for China and several other Asian countries after World War II. Successful East Asian countries, including South Korea, Taiwan, Singapore, and later China, have achieved unprecedented economic development, overcoming abject poverty.[386] Notably, all of these countries adopted authoritarian governance during periods of economic development. In the course of economic development, unpopular decisions need to be made in the interest of long-term progress, such as mandating long work hours for laborers and allowing the availability of savings for industrial investment rather than immediate disbursement.[387] In South Korea, for example, the government did not allow banks to provide home mortgage loans until the 1980s to secure all available funds for industrial pursuit.[388] These policies may have been necessary to pursue long-term economic development where available funds were extremely limited, but such measures would not likely create political popularity. Notably, it would be difficult, if not entirely impossible, for elected democracies to implement such unpopular policies for economic development.

China mobilized resources for economic development under authoritarian rule as other successful developing countries in East Asia had done. As a result, China has achieved economic development while overcoming poverty and moving beyond, firmly placing itself among middle-income countries.[389] The question is whether its authoritarian governance system still serves the interests of modern-day, middle-income China. Other successful East Asian countries, such as South Korea and Taiwan, began a shift toward democracy in the 1980s, when they had achieved middle-income country status.[390] Unfortunately, as seen above, the undeliberated one-person rule is more likely to generate decisions that may impose drastically negative effects, and it does not serve the interests of sustainable peace. As Xi Jinping has consolidated his powers and weakened the party's standing committee, China's economic and military policies have become more aggressive and confrontational, as demonstrated by China's announced economic challenges to the West (*e.g.*, Made in China 2025 Plan), trade retaliations against South Korea, Japan, and other countries over political issues (*e.g.*, U.S. deployment of the THAAD system in South Korea),[391] increased scrutiny over domestic private corporations (*e.g.*, Alibaba, a Chinese e-commerce company),[392] military threats to Taiwan and other countries, and the violent suppression of pro-democracy movements in Hong Kong.

Chinese policies threaten stability and freedom both within China and beyond its borders. None of the other countries in Northeast Asia would be powerful enough to stand against China alone. Thus, Northeast Asian countries constantly look to bring in the United States, the only other country that can offer a counterbalance against China, to keep it in check and create a power balance in the region. As Kenneth Waltz articulated, states that endeavor to survive pursue the balance of power,[393] and this pursuit explains the expansion of military and economic alliances (*e.g.*, the Chip 4 Alliance) between the United States and other countries, such as South Korea and Japan. Consequently, the confrontational status quo will continue, as discussed above, and will not benefit the long-term interests of China or any other country in the region. External forces, such as the United States, cannot change the status quo or create sustainable peace in Northeast Asia. To achieve sustainable peace, change must come from within China: a more deliberative Chinese leadership is likely to advance more balanced and temperate foreign policies.[394] When China possessed such leadership before Xi Jinping, it enjoyed more cooperative foreign relationships, attained stronger economic performance, and achieved stability and less confrontation within China and Northeast Asia.[395] Reforming the Chinese governance system is key to creating a political environment that supports sustainable peace in the region.

In addition, improving regional autonomy within China may also facilitate a political environment conducive to peace and stability in Northeast Asia. A government's power is correlated to the number of resources at its disposal. China's central government controls a massive amount of resources unmatched by any other country in Northeast Asia. These resources include extensive manpower from the world's largest population (as of 2022), financial resources secured by the world's second largest government revenues (US$ 3.20 trillion as of 2021),[396] advanced technological assets, strong administrative networks, and formidable military holdings.[397] Massive central government resource control, coupled with unchecked power to pronounce unitary decisions, enables the central government to adopt sweeping policies, such as the above-cited zero-coronavirus policy (with no exit plan, which caused the proliferation of coronavirus infections after its abrupt discontinuation). This policy held no regard for the regions in China or other countries affected by its implementation and has had a substantial negative impact on global trade and investment.[398]

Reallocating power and resources between China's central and regional governments will reduce the risk of negative policy decisions. For example, suppose that the Shanghai Municipal Government, instead of the central government, had possessed the authority to make its own lockdown decisions. In that case, the outcome for Shanghai and the global economy may have been different. The effect of such regional autonomy has been illustrated through the Trump administration. During his presidency, Trump discussed the possibility of a federal quarantine in the tri-state area of New York, New Jersey, and Connecticut.[399] State governors objected to the proposed quarantine, and the New York State governor commented that "[the imposition of the federal quarantine] would be a declaration of war on states. A federal declaration of war."[400] Likewise, the autonomous regional authority in China can combat objectionable central government policies. Regional autonomy will provide deterrence to the unchecked power of the central government, which will, in turn, prevent it from undermining stability and peace within the country and beyond.

Lastly, on the reallocation of power within China, securing an independent judiciary is necessary to create checks against illegal government decisions and practices.[401] The Chinese Constitution declares the independence of China's judiciary. Article 126 of the Constitution provides, "The people's courts exercise judicial power *independently*, in accordance with the provisions of law, and not subject to interference by any administrative organ, public organization or individual" (emphasis added).[402] However, judicial independence is not honored in practice. A report by the Congressional–Executive Commission on China notes various external and systemic interferences with the Chinese judiciary. Such interference includes the CCP's influence on judicial decisions, supervision by the people's congresses, and the procuratorate over the work of judges and the courts.[403] Supervisors may call for the reconsideration of cases, which weakens judicial independence.[404] The report recommends a constitutional amendment to remove the supervision of the people's congresses and the procuratorate over the judiciary.[405]

In summary, Chinese governance reform, which improves the power balance within China, is necessary to achieve sustainable peace in Northeast Asia. The proposed reform includes building a deliberative governance system away from the one-person rule, improving regional autonomy through reallocating central powers and resources, and securing judicial independence through a constitutional amendment. China's massive size and extensive national capacity limits the effectiveness of external pressures to change the status quo in Northeast Asia, although such pressure might temporarily keep China in check. Thus, a lasting solution should be found elsewhere. As discussed, the cited reforms are necessary to improve the power balance within China and ultimately to transform the confrontational status quo and achieve sustainable peace in Northeast Asia. The negative ramifications of one-person rule for regional and global peace have been made vividly clear by the recent developments in Ukraine. The absence of deliberative central governance, the concentration of power in the central administration, and the weak Russian judiciary failed to prevent Vladimir Putin from waging war against Ukraine. Russia's authoritarian rule has severely undermined peace and stability in the region. China's authoritarian governance carries the same risk for China and Northeast Asia, calling for reforms proposed in this chapter.

Chapter 4

A NEW BALANCER IN THE REGION? SOUTH KOREA AT THE CROSSROADS

4.1 South Korea: Center or Periphery?

4.1.1 The role of Korea in Northeast Asia: A historical perspective

Historically, united Korea played the role of a regional balancer in Northeast Asia. Since the tenth century, the Korean states such as Goryeo (고려, 918–1392) and Joseon (조선, 1392–1910) had cultural, economic, political, and military engagements with the adjacent powers, including Chinese dynasties, the northern tribes—the Jurchens (Manchus), Khitans, and Mongols—and the Japanese. The Korean states deterred other powers from fully conquering Northeast Asia. For example, the Khitans occupied northern China in the tenth century and subsequently invaded Korea.[406] In 1019, Korea defeated the Khitans (then the strongest military force in Northeast Asia) and destroyed much of their military in historic warfare, preventing their further invasion into China and creating a balance of power in the region.[407] For another example, Japan invaded Korea in 1592 with an ambition to conquer China.[408] After a seven-year-long war, Korea repelled the Japanese invaders with the help of a Chinese expeditionary force, thereby stopping Japan's advance into mainland China and once again maintaining the balance of power in the region.[409]

Korea ceased acting as a regional deterrent when the Qing Empire defeated it in 1637. For the first time in Korean history, the King of Korea formally surrendered to the foreign invader and swore obedience to the Qing.[410] The Joseon Dynasty internally recovered from this defeat, continuing for another two centuries, but Korea lost its military influence in the region. Without Korea as a regional deterrent, the buffer between China and Japan disappeared. Japan waged war against China in 1894 and again in 1937, putting Northeast Asia through years of destructive war.[411] After World War II,

Korea was divided into the communist North and the capitalist South, which led to the outbreak of the Korean War.[412] South Korea was at the forefront of East-West confrontations and helped to stop the spread of communism by defending itself from the communist North. The war may have ceased in 1953, but South Korea's struggle with communism did not; for decades, the country withstood continued pressure from North Korea, including numerous military incursions and infiltrations.[413]

Politically, Korea supported a political hierarchy in Northeast Asia described as Sinocentrism. For example, both Goryeo and Joseon Dynasties accepted the "appointment" of their kings from the Chinese dynasties (although it was largely a formality) in recognition of their superior position in the Northeast Asian political order.[414] In turn, Korea treated certain tribes sharing borders with Korea—such as the Jurchens and Japanese (Tsushima) islanders—as its subordinate subjects, accepted their tributes, and allowed trade to support their livelihood.[415] To protect this political order and maintain regional stability, the Joseon Dynasty undertook expeditions against the Tsushima Islanders and Jurchens in the fourteenth and fifteenth centuries, respectively.[416] However, after its defeat in the war with the Qing Dynasty in 1637, Korea lost its balancing role in the Northeast Asian political order. Manchus (formerly Jurchens) were no longer subordinate to Korea, as they had been in the fifteenth century, and they instead became a dominant power in Northeast Asia by the seventeenth century. The Tsushima islanders, once semi-autonomous, assimilated into the central Japanese Shogunate regime rather than Korea's. Korea continued to maintain its political autonomy while recognizing Qing's superiority, but by the seventeenth century, its political role was limited to its borders, and the country functioned as a mere peripheral power in the region.

Korea has also played a unique cultural role in Northeast Asia. Since the Joseon Dynasty adopted Confucianism as its founding ideology for the nation, Korea became a bastion of Confucianism in Northeast Asia. Confucian virtues, such as loyalty (忠) and filial piety (孝), became the ethical values upheld by Koreans.[417] The influence of Korean Confucianism reached beyond its borders, inspiring Japanese scholars such as Yamazaki Ansai (1619–1682), who suggested that the famous Korean Confucianist, T'oegye, was on par with Zhu Xi (朱子), the founder of the new Chinese Confucianism (朱子學) in the twelfth century.[418] While Confucianism was weakened in Japan during its modernization and in China amid the Cultural Revolution, Korea maintained its cultural emphasis on Confucianism throughout the twentieth century through public education and campaigns.[419] A commentator found Confucianism ingrained in almost every aspect of Korean culture in modern times.[420]

Lastly, Korea played an economic role in the region due primarily to political rather than commercial necessities. Korea traded with the northern tribes such as the Jurchens and the Tsushima islanders who needed to import necessities (*e.g.,* food) from Korea.[421] They had invaded Korean borders and shores in search of necessities, such as food. Korea was able to reduce their incursions by allowing them to meet their economic needs through trade.[422] Korea also traded with China, initially through official channels formally sanctioned by both governments.[423] However, such official trade was used to offer tributes to China and receive return gifts without extensive economic and commercial impact on either country. Private trade outside the official channels increased over time, but its commercial impact remained limited. Korea was an agrarian country with limited manufacturing capacity; thus, the economic impact of trade on the national economy was not extensive. It was not until the early twentieth century that Korea's trade expanded substantially, mostly due to increased imports of manufactured products from Japan (which needed an outlet for their increased quantity of manufactured products after industrialization).[424] Korea's increased trade in this period did not have much of an impact on the Northeast Asian economy, showing its peripheral economic position in the region.

4.1.2 A regional power: Strength and vulnerability

As discussed earlier, Korea's position in Northeast Asia deteriorated after its defeat to the Qing Dynasty in the seventeenth century, but it has increased its political and economic influence since the second half of the twentieth century. As a result of phenomenal economic development since the 1960s, the country transformed itself from a periphery with political and economic vulnerabilities to a regional power with substantial political influence, industrial and financial resources, and military capability. As of 2021, South Korea was the world's tenth largest economy (next to China and Japan in Northeast Asia),[425] the sixth largest manufacturing country (larger than France and the United Kingdom),[426] the eighth largest trading country,[427] and the sixth leading military power.[428] While South Korea is a smaller economy than China and Japan, its military, equipped with the latest technology, provides substantial deterrence to potential threats in the region. The U.S. News and World Report has also rated South Korea as the world's sixth most powerful country (next only to China in Northeast Asia).[429] South Korea, by any measure, has become a regional power with a strong economic and military presence in Northeast Asia.

South Korea has displayed its economic and industrial strengths in traditional and strategic industrial areas such as steel, chemical, shipbuilding, electronics, semiconductors, information technology, and electric vehicle (EV) batteries.[430] Every country in Northeast Asia, as well as the United States and Russia, has sought economic cooperation and collaboration with South Korea. South Korea is a leading trade partner for Northeast Asian countries, supplying essential products for their economies and industries such as semiconductors, machinery, chemical products, intermediate materials, and electrical and electronic equipment.[431] South Korea's economic capacity has also been viewed as a means to facilitate reconciliation with North Korea. South Korea is capable of offering substantial economic support to North Korea to meet its pressing economic needs.[432] In fact, South and North Korea had jointly operated a manufacturing production facility in the North Korean city of Kaeseong ("Kaeseong Industrial Complex")[433] until 2016, when the South Korean government closed it over the concerns associated with North Korea's nuclear and missile tests. Economic cooperation between South and North Korea has not resumed due to the unresolved nuclear issue.

Another source of South Korea's strength is its military alliance with the United States. As discussed above, South Korea is currently a leading military power, although it does not possess nuclear weapons. South Korea's military alliance with the United States has greatly reinforced its military deterrence. The United States maintains its largest overseas military base in South Korea (Camp Humphreys hosting over 35,000 military and civilian personnel),[434] and it operates a joint military command in South Korea.[435] The two countries regularly convene large-scale, joint military exercises.[436] South Korea depended on the United States for security from the North at the beginning of the alliance,[437] but this relationship transformed over the years as South Korea's military and economic capacities radically increased. The transformation represents South Korea's increased independence from the United States regarding security concerns, but without sacrificing the mutually beneficial alliance.[438] However, the U.S. military presence in South Korea still deters North Korean aggression and profoundly influences the security landscape in Northeast Asia, raising concerns for China.[439]

Nonetheless, South Korea's successful economic and industrial development has not completely removed its vulnerabilities. Ironically, it has instead created some. South Korea's economic engine is exports, which have made up a considerable portion of its economy—the percentage of GDP made up by exports in goods and services reached 41.7 percent in 2021, much higher than its counterparts in the region such as China (20 percent) and Japan (15.6 percent).[440] South Korea is one of the world's most export-dependent industrialized nations.[441] This export dependency creates economic vulnerability. First, South Korea imports raw materials, such as crude oil and minerals, processes them into intermediate or final products, and exports them into the world market. Thus, the Korean economy is vulnerable to external shocks. For example, unprecedented trade deficits continued for several months in 2022 while the war in Ukraine affected the supply and prices of raw materials.[442] Beyond economic factors, political considerations also affect exports,[443] and the latter's sensitivity to political influence adds vulnerability—countries reliant on exports may find it necessary to accept the importer's political demands or face negative economic consequences after non-compliance. As discussed in the preceding chapter, China's trade retaliation in the aftermath of the THAAD deployment is an example. The U.S. pressure on Korea to join its "Chip 4 Alliance" is another.[444]

South Korea's deepest vulnerability is the division of Korea itself and the existence of a hostile, now nuclear-armed North Korea. South Korea's economic and political center, Seoul, is only 45 kilometers away from the demilitarized zone ("DMZ") bordering North Korea, well within the artillery range from North Korea. The nuclear and missile threats from North Korea are critical. South Korea is a signatory of the NPT and must rely on the United States to provide nuclear deterrence against the North. However, South Korea has no control over this deterrence, and U.S. scholars Jennifer Lind and Daryl G. Press have argued that South Korea should build its own nuclear weapons.[445] In addition to North Korea's nuclear threat, other issues associated with the division of Korea have also been costly, adding significant vulnerability. Every year, South Korea has to spend large amounts of financial resources, manpower, and political assets on maintaining military readiness and domestic security against possible threats from the North. As a part of this cost, South Korea has undergone diplomatic warfare against the North in Africa, Southeast Asia, and elsewhere for several decades.[446] North Korean agents and operatives overseas have worked against South Korean interests and security. For example, North Korean agents bombed the South Korean government delegation in Rangoon, Myanmar, on October 9, 1983, killing 21 members of the delegation including cabinet ministers,[447] demonstrating, rather dramatically, the extent of South Korea's vulnerability under the division.

4.1.3 South Korea as a regional "balancer"?

South Korea, a regional power in Northeast Asia, has both strengths and vulnerabilities as discussed above. The country may not be powerful enough to prevail over other major countries in the region, such as China and Japan, but it has sought to meet its interests and contribute to sustaining peace in the region by acting as a "balancer" among the contesting powers. The idea of the "balancer" originated from former South Korean President Roh

Moo-Hyun (2003–2008).[448] He envisioned South Korea, with its newfound economic and industrial strengths, as a "business hub" for the region, which would solidify the region's economic integration and strengthen diplomatic relations.[449] Roh also saw an opportunity for South Korea to serve as an ombudsman or a mediator in conflict among the powers in the region.[450] International relations scholar Emanuel Pastreich observed that Roh's vision for a more "assertive" South Korean role in international affairs appealed to South Koreans, with many recognizing "the validity of a bridge-building role for Korea at a time when economic integration with China and Japan present great challenges."[451]

   If South Korea should be successful in this role, it would enhance regional stability. However, Roh's vision encountered substantial resistance, particularly from the United States, which viewed his vision as an attempt to distance itself from the U.S. security umbrella in the Pacific and move closer to China.[452] To the United States, his vision meant less reliance by Koreans on the U.S.–Korea alliance, and the less reliance would mean weakened U.S. influence in the region without any corresponding diminution in other powers' influence (China and Russia).[453] The United States was also concerned that his vision (a stronger Korea) would weaken its ability to directly control the North Korean nuclear threat—a cost the Bush administration found unacceptable.[454] Additionally, South Korea planned support for North Korea's economic development and accommodated its needs to act as a balancer of the region. The United States objected to Seoul's plan and viewed it as running "afoul of a new U.S. determination to keep regional relations under its firm control."[455] Facing objection from the United States, Roh's vision to position South Korea as a balancer in the region was largely stalled.

   Since Roh advocated his vision in 2005, the political, economic, and security environment of Northeast Asia has undergone a substantial transformation.[456] China's economic, industrial, and military powers have significantly increased under the ambitious leader Xi Jinping who pronounced his vision for the "great revival of the Chinese nation."[457] As a result, the rivalry between Washington and Beijing has intensified, resulting in trade disputes, military tensions, and political strife between the two countries. North Korea has also stepped up its nuclear weapons program and developed ICBMs capable of delivering nuclear warheads to the continental United States.[458] The nationalist right-wing faction has prevailed in Japanese politics, creating tensions with neighboring countries, such as South Korea. The position of the United States has not substantially improved in Northeast Asia although it has maintained alliances with South Korea and Japan. The changed economic, political, and security landscape of Northeast Asia seems to render the previous U.S. position to "keep regional relations under its firm control" no longer tenable and requires a more concerted approach with other regional stakeholders.

South Korea may have a role in this concerted approach. The country stands primarily on the side of the United States and Japan (rather than China and Russia) due to its military alliance and security concerns. However, South Korea's historical, cultural, political, and economic ties with the other countries in Northeast Asia and its enhanced economic, industrial, and military capabilities place it in a unique position that enables collaboration across the region. Yet, it is not clear whether South Korea will be able to mediate and facilitate reconciliation among the contesting powers. For example, former South Korean President Moon Jae-In attempted to mediate between North Korea and the United States on nuclear issues.[459] However, his administration failed to identify the intentions of the North Korean regime and respond to the changing security environment after North Korea's advancement of its nuclear technology.[460] This failure has had negative repercussions, with the United States and North Korea beginning to distrust the South Korean government. Tensions between South Korea and the United States arose over the disagreement about North Korea's intentions on nuclear development,[461] and the North Korean leaders blamed President Moon for the failure, deteriorating the North-South relationship.[462]

There is a historical precedent for a country playing the "balancing" role sought by South Korea—Britain demonstrated its role as a regional balancer in the eighteenth and nineteenth centuries. Britain was also a trading nation, driving much of its wealth and diplomatic influence from trade similar to present-day South Korea. Against greater European powers such as France and Austria, Britain sought to maintain the balance of power by supporting lesser powers (*e.g.*, Prussia against Austria) and preventing the domination of Europe by a single nation (*e.g.*, Napoleonic France).[463] However, a fundamental difference exists between Britain in that era and South Korea in the present day. Britain may not have been all-powerful over the other European countries—Michael Sheehan pointed out Britain's economic and military weaknesses compared to the other European powers[464]—but the gaps between Britain and other European powers were nowhere close to those between South Korea and China (nearly ten times in terms of GDP) or South Korea and Japan (nearly three times).[465]

Also, France and Austria may have been great European powers, but their relative economic and military powers (vis-à-vis other powers in Europe) were not comparable to those of China in Northeast Asia today. In other words, South Korea is facing much larger powers than the countries that Britain had to face in Europe, with smaller endowments than Britain possessed at the time in relative terms. In the nineteenth century, Britain's Industrial Revolution elevated it to the position of the world's factory, and given its economic and naval supremacy, Britain was able to maintain the balance of power in Europe.[466] Despite its substantial economic, industrial, and military powers, South Korea lacks such superior endowments to implement its vision vis-à-vis the other powers in Northeast Asia. Nonetheless, the country's phenomenal economic development and successful democratization, achieved over significant challenges, offers another vision of inspiration relevant to regional peace and co-prosperity. The following section discusses South Korea's "long and winding road" to prosperity over the past several decades.

4.2 The Long and Winding Road: From Poverty to Prosperity

4.2.1 Colonial exploitation, war, and prosperity

The first half of the twentieth century was probably the most treacherous period for Korea in its long history. Japan dominated Korea economically, politically, and militarily (although there was no official war between the two countries *per se*) after its victory over China and Russia in armed conflicts in 1895 and 1905, respectively. Japan deprived Korea of its diplomatic sovereignty and made her Japan's protectorate in 1905.[467] In 1910, Japan forcibly annexed and colonized Korea.[468] Koreans lost their country to a foreign state for the first time in Korean history. The Joseon Dynasty (the "Korean Empire" from 1897 to 1910) had undergone a series of reforms toward the end of the nineteenth century to modernize the country, but adverse factors such as internal corruption, political strife between the reformists and the conservatists, and Japan's expansionary move toward the Korean peninsula undermined its effort.[469] Resistant Koreans initiated armed resistance against the Japanese colonial authorities, but the Japanese authorities suppressed them, and survivors moved to Manchuria and Russia to continue their resistance.[470]

In colonized Korea, Japan implemented exploitive colonial policies for over three decades (1910–1945). For example, from 1910 to 1918, the Japanese colonial government adopted a land-survey ordinance that compelled landowners to report the size and location of their land.[471] Farmers who failed to report were deprived of their land; farmlands and forests jointly owned by a village or a family were also expropriated and sold inexpensively to the Japanese.[472] Koreans suffered from the consequence of this policy—many moved to the woods and tried to survive by slash-and-burn tillage, while others went to Manchuria and Japan in search of work.[473] The Japanese built modern infrastructure in Korea, such as railways, roads, and ports,[474] but their primary purpose was to support Japanese commerce and exploit resources in Korea. Economic development and industrialization proceeded in Korea under Japanese occupation: between 1939 and 1941, the manufacturing sector represented 29 percent of Korea's total economic production.[475] The share of Korea's primary industries—agriculture, fishing, and forestry—decreased from 84.6 percent of total economic production to 49.6 percent, demonstrating the rise of industrialization during the Japanese occupation.[476]

However, Koreans benefited little from the economic development. The Japanese owned virtually all industries in Korea and suppressed the emergence of Korean entrepreneurs. As of 1942, Korean capital constituted only 1.5 percent of the total capital invested in Korean industries. Banking practices unfavorable to Koreans, such as discriminatory loan practices, suppressed the growth of Korean capital (for example, Korean entrepreneurs were charged interest rates substantially higher—up to 25 percent higher—than their Japanese counterparts).[477] An increasing proportion of Korean farmers became sharecroppers or migrated to Japan or Manchuria as a result of the Japanese takeover of farmland.[478] Food deprivation became prevalent in Korea: between 1932 and 1936, per capita consumption of rice in Korea declined to half the level consumed between 1912 and 1916, as greater quantities of Korean rice were exported to Japan.[479] The Japanese colonial government imported coarse grains from Manchuria to supplement the Korean food supply, but per capita consumption of food grains in 1944 was still 35 percent below that of 1912 to 1916.[480] The Japanese exploitation of Korea intensified during World War II: hundreds of thousands of Koreans were drafted to work in mines, factories, and military bases and to fight for Japan on war fronts.[481] Additionally, the Japanese forced tens of thousands of Korean women to provide sexual services (as "comfort women") for the military.[482] After its defeat in World War II, Japan was forced to leave Korea, but the newly liberated Korea was scarred by economic deprivation and human suffering after 35 years of exploitative Japanese colonial rule.

The subsequent division of Korea and the outbreak of the Korean War devastated the weak Korean economy. The Japanese had built industrial installations, such as factories and power plants, mostly in resource-rich North Korea, as part of the Japanese program of economic self-sufficiency and war preparations.[483] This meant that after the division, South Korea did not have access to the manufacturing sites in the North. South Korea also relied on the supply of electricity from the North, but in May 1948, North Korea turned off the electric power supply to South Korea, causing devastation to the South.[484] The Korean War (1950–1953) destroyed much of Korea's infrastructure and production facilities and caused millions of casualties.[485] After the War, South Koreans began to rebuild their destroyed country with aid from the United States.[486] However, foreign aid also caused the South Korean economy to become aid-dependent. A substantial part of the aid was comprised of foodstuff, which suppressed agricultural prices and distorted farmers' incentives, causing a decrease in rice production from 14.7 million Sok (approximately 2.4 million tons) in 1949 to 12.8 million Sok (2 million tons) in 1956.[487] In addition to the reduction of agricultural production, the overall South Korean economy also stagnated as U.S. aid decreased toward the end of the 1950s, with a majority of South Koreans remaining in poverty.[488]

South Korea's first republic (1948–1960) ended with a civil revolution in April 1960, and its brief second republic (1960–1961) with a military coup in May 1961.[489] South Korea's military regime under the leadership of Park Jung-Hee adopted state-led economic development policies emphasizing exports and industrialization.[490] South Korea's economic development was an unprecedented success. By 1962, when President Park initiated the first five-year economic development plan, South Korea was among the poorest countries in the world, with per capita income of a mere US$ 120 and its economy based on primary industries—*e.g.*, agriculture and fishery—with low productivity.[491] By 1996, when South Korea completed its seventh five-year economic development plan, it had become a high-income, industrialized economy with global enterprises, including Samsung, Hyundai, LG, and SK, that prevailed in the world market with cutting-edge technologies.[492] Its per capita income rose to over US$ 13,000, and South Korea joined the OECD in 1996.[493] Within a generation, South Korea transformed itself from a country suffering from abject poverty to one that enjoyed economic prosperity. Today South Korea is the highest paid nation in Northeast Asia (with an average wage of US$ 42,747 as of 2021, higher than Japan's average wage of US$ 39,711).[494]

4.2.2 Process of economic development

South Korea's successful economic development resulted from an extraordinary national endeavor against all odds. In the early 1960s, Korea exhibited many of the characteristics shared by developing countries today, including low per-capita income reflecting prevalent poverty, an economy relying heavily on primary non-manufacturing industries, low levels of technology and entrepreneurship in society, insufficient capital, a poor endowment of natural resources, over-population in a relatively small territory, internal political instability, and external threats to its security from North Korea.[495] South Korea has successfully overcome these unfavorable conditions, and its economy progressed from relying on less-productive primary industries to an advanced economy by the mid-1990s, based on large industrial capacity generating high per-capita income.[496] The Korean economic development process is unique, as it exhibits all major stages of economic development in a mere three decades, which is considerably shorter than the periods of development for most other developed countries.

South Korea had clear development objectives since the beginning of its development era: mainly to overcome the prevalent poverty affecting the vast majority of its population.[497] South Korea set out to achieve this main objective by growing its economy and developing industries to generate employment and income. South Korea considered exports essential for industrial development to overcome the constraints of its small domestic market. As a result, the total value of exports and the share of exports in the country's gross domestic product (GDP) increased simultaneously, as displayed in Table 4.1.

The South Korean government also developed and implemented the Five-Year Economic Development Plans from 1962 to 1996 (the period of South Korea's rapid economic development) setting specific development targets at the time.

South Korea legislated specific statutes empowering the government to support exports and industries. The General Theory of Law and Development, developed by the author, explains that regulatory design, regulatory compliance, and the quality of implementation affect the effectiveness of law for development.[498] In the areas of export promotion and industrial promotion, the South Korean government effectively implemented well-designed laws, as listed below, securing strong public compliance with them. To promote exports, the government adopted statutes such as the Act on Temporary Measures for the Grant of Export Subsidies (1961), the Export Promotion Act (1962) (which was replaced by the Trade Transactions Act of 1967), and the Tax Exemption and Reduction Control Act (1965) that authorized the government to grant tax reductions for the profits generated by exports. These statutes aimed to ensure timely payment of subsidies contingent upon exports ("export subsidies"), prioritize the allocation of scarce foreign reserves for the

Table 4.1 Export expansion and exports/GDP of South Korea (1962–1996).

Year	Real GDP Growth Rate (percent)	Goods Export Values (US$ billion)	Exports of Goods and Services/GDP (percent)
1962–1966	8.0	1	7.7
1967–1971	9.7	3	13.7
1972–1976	8.0	22	27.8
1977–1981	6.2	77	31.5
1982–1986	8.7	141	34.4
1987–1991	9.4	307	32.3
1992–1996	7.3	510	28.7

(*Source*: Yong-Shik Lee, *Reclaiming Development in the World Trading System*, 2d ed., 2016)

Table 4.2 Five-year economic development plans of South Korea (1962–1996).

1st (1962–1966)	2nd (1967–1971)	3rd (1972–1976)
• Promote import-substitute industries • Build petroleum and fertilizer plants • Transition to export-oriented policy (1964)	• Expand export bases • Strengthen international competitiveness of light industries • Produce industrial raw materials • Introduce and adopt new technologies	• Promote heavy and chemical industries • Promote science and technology • Increase exports
4th (1977–1981)	**5th (1982–1986)**	**6th (1987–1991)**
• Attain the status of world's major (advanced) economy • Rationalize industrial structure • Build key plants	• Promote best quality and precision in products • Export plant facilities • Support private enterprises to develop production technologies	• Promote world-class industries • Promote aviation industry • Expand overseas industrial investments
7th (1992–1996)		
• Enhance the competitiveness of corporations • Promote social equity and balanced development • Support internationalization and develop foundations for the unification of the two Koreas		

(*Source*: Yong-Shik Lee *et al.* (eds.), *Law and Development Perspective on International Trade Law*, 2011)

purchase of raw materials to produce export products, and permit only those traders with strong export performance to engage in the lucrative import business.[499]

For industrial promotion, the South Korean government implemented statutes such as the Act on Temporary Measures for Textile Industrial Facilities (1967); the Acts on Promotion of Mechanical Industries (1967), Shipbuilding Industries (1967), Electronic Industries (1969), Petrochemical Industries (1970), and Steel Industries (1970); the Act on Refining Service of Non-Ferrous Metals (1971); and the Act on the Promotion of the Modernization of Textile Industries (1979).[500] These statutes authorized the government to adopt measures of support for the designated industries. The government measures included tax incentives, preferential loans (or policy loans, whose terms, such as interest rates, were more favorable than the prevailing commercial terms), subsidy grants, tariff rebates, import control, and overseas loan guarantees.[501] The South Korean government provided support to businesses on a conditional basis: businesses were required to show market performance to receive continuing support from the government. The government rewarded strong performers with continuing support and let go of weak performers. South Korea's economic development was essentially a partnership between the private sector and the government.

Another key to South Korea's success was flexibility and adaptability in implementing economic development policies. The government determined its export promotion and industrial development goals in accordance with available resources, technology, and industrial experiences at the time. At the beginning of Korea's economic development process in the early 1960s, when Korea lacked capital and technology, the government focused on labor-intensive industries, such as textile and clothing, as these products did not require large capital or technological resources for production. The industries endeavored to export these products to generate income and then used income from exports to finance industrial development. Export promotion was inseparable from industrial development in South Korea. The industrial experience through manufacturing, the accumulation of capital, and the development of technology during the initial period of successful economic development enabled South Korea to transition into more advanced and potentially more profitable industries, such as the heavy and chemical industries in the 1970s and electronics in the 1980s. The government support also focused on these areas during the respective periods.[502]

South Korea shifted its economic development policy in the 1980s; after two decades of successful economic development, Korea had become a middle-income country with a robust private sector, and its economy had become technology based. The South Korean government adjusted its policies to meet this change, reducing government control over the economy and supporting the private sector as a whole, rather than specific industries.[503] The government also replaced the statutes that provided industry-specific support with the Manufacturing Industry Development Act in 1986 (replaced by the Industrial Development Act in 1999), granting more selective assistance to industries based on a need to improve their efficiency through restructuring or reorganization.[504] The transition accelerated through the 1990s. The abolishment of the Economic Planning Board (EPB) in 1994—which had been the government's control center for economic development by planning and implementing economic development policies since 1961—signaled the transition of one era (where the government led economic development with public resources) to a new era (where the private sector began to prevail in the economy).

By the mid-1990s, South Korea had met its economic development objectives—economic growth, industrial development, and relief of poverty. The World Bank has described South Korea as "one of the few countries that has successfully transformed itself from a low-income to a high-income economy and a global leader in innovation and technology."[505] Economic indicators support this observation and demonstrate the magnitude of success; Korea's per capita income (measured by per capita gross national income or per capita GNI) increased by 111 times between 1962 and 1996.[506] Korea's unemployment rate also decreased from an estimated 35 percent in 1961 to just 2.4 percent in 1990.[507] The value of its exports also increased by 510 times.[508] South Korea achieved inclusive growth: in the 1990s, its income distribution was better than in some of the most advanced countries, including the United States.[509] When Korea's seventh and final five-year economic development plan was completed in 1996, the country had become a world-class industrial economy and a world-leading trader, generating high incomes for a majority of its citizens. South Korea also became a home for innovative multinational corporations, such as Samsung, Hyundai, LG, and SK, today's global leaders in the production of semiconductors, home electronics, IT devices, automobiles, ships, and chemicals.

4.2.3 A vibrant democracy

South Korea is a vibrant democracy, one of the very few countries that has achieved both economic development and democratization simultaneously.[510] While Japan is also a parliamentary democracy, its democratic governance was established after World War II under heavy U.S. influence after industrialization in the late nineteenth and early twentieth centuries. Mongolia also practices elective democracy, but it is still a developing economy. China, North Korea, and Russia are considered authoritarian regimes rather than liberal democracies. For much of South Korea's period of rapid economic development, South Korea also remained under an authoritarian regime. Park Jung-Hee, who rose to power through a military coup in 1961, was elected as South Korea's president in the election in 1963, and he suspended the constitution in 1972, thereby limiting the voting rights of Korean citizens (e.g., removing their voting rights to directly elect their presidents).[511] The previous Rhee administration, ousted by the April Revolution in 1960, also undermined democratic governance through illegitimate constitutional amendments and election fraud.[512]

South Korea's road to democracy was treacherous. South Korea's first republic (1948–1960) adopted an American-style presidential system, but democratic governance was not embedded in society. For centuries, Korea was under the Confucian tradition, which emphasizes a vertical hierarchy; the Japanese colonial rule further instilled the duty to obey authorities (rather than democratic practices) in the minds of Koreans through education and harsh punishment for noncompliance. During Japanese rule, Koreans were deprived of the freedoms of speech, association, the press, and assembly, which was inconsistent with democratic governance.[513] The first Korean republic affirmed these fundamental civil rights under the constitution, but the South Korean government, under its first president, Rhee Seung-Man, amended the constitution in breach of the procedural mandate (*e.g.,* the 1954 constitutional amendment was without sufficient votes for the amendment proposal). President Rhee's government also mobilized the police and gangsters to suppress its opposition and committed nationwide election fraud while failing to develop the economy and relieve poverty.[514] Students protested against the election fraud committed in March 1960. The brutal police response and the resulting casualties provoked widespread anger among Korean citizens, and the protest turned into a revolution that ousted the Rhee government in April 1960.[515]

Korea's April Revolution was the first revolution that ended an authoritarian regime in a newly independent country after World War II. The movement inspired freedom-seeking people worldwide and marked the beginning of postwar student movements such as China's student protest in Tiananmen Square in 1989.[516] The second Korean republic, established after the revolution, was democratic but was short-lived. General Park Jung-Hee led a coup against the government in May 1961 and set up a military government.[517] Park promised to restore a civil government, but he breached his commitment by running for the presidency. He was elected as the South Korean president in the 1963 election. The third republic (1963–1972) adopted a democratic constitution, but President Park, as his predecessor had done, also pushed for a constitutional amendment to extend his presidential term beyond the two-term limit.[518] Government security agencies such as the Korean Central Intelligence Agency (KCIA) were mobilized to suppress opposition, and Park was able to extend his presidential term.[519]

Park suspended the constitution in 1972 and proposed a series of constitutional amendments (named the "October Restoration"), limiting civil liberties such as the freedom of speech and citizens' voting rights.[520] The administration tried to justify these amendments by citing the uncertain and unstable international environment, such as the withdrawal of the United States from Vietnam in 1973 and the subsequent communist victory of North Vietnam.

According to the government, these developments justified the consolidation of powers in the hands of the president to protect the nation and promote economic development without setbacks. However, many Koreans did not approve of them and resisted the government under severe and often violent oppression by the administration (including "emergency measures" that limited dissent and restricted civil freedoms).[521] The Park administration's relationship with Washington also came under pressure when liberal U.S. President Jimmy Carter voiced objection to his authoritarian rule.[522]

There was a brief window of opportunity to restore democracy when the head of the KCIA assassinated Park Jung-Hee in 1979, but it was closed by the subsequent military rebellion under the leadership of General Chun Doo Hwan. The government, secured by Chun and his allies, extended martial law and violently suppressed the civil protest in Kwangju in May 1980, causing thousands of casualties ("Kwangju Massacre").[523] Student protests continued throughout Chun's regime (1980–1987), often subject to harsh treatment by the authorities. In June 1987, students and citizens, provoked by the police killing students, held massive protests against the authoritarian government.[524] The regime finally conceded and agreed to amend the constitution mandating a general presidential election.[525] This 1987 amendment, which marked a new era for South Korea's democracy, set a constitutional framework for political governance in South Korea that remains unchanged today. Under this constitution, South Korea's two opposition leaders, Kim Young-Sam and Kim Dae-Joong (2000 Nobel Peace Laureate), were elected as presidents in 1992 and 1997, respectively. They continued democratic reform such as restoring the regional government elections that had been abolished under the Park regime.[526]

South Korean democracy has continued to progress under the 1987 constitutional framework. Seven presidents have been elected under this constitution and served the country. The process of democratization has also encouraged the proliferation of civil societies advocating a broad range of agendas, such as labor rights, the environment, gender equality, civil rights, Korean unification, and animal rights.[527] The rule of law has also been reinforced through the development of an independent judiciary and the establishment of a separate constitutional court to conduct constitutional reviews of laws.[528] South Korea today is a vibrant democracy based on the rule of law. In 2022, the World Population Review classified South Korea as a "full democracy" (ranking above the United States which was rated as a "flawed democracy").[529] As for the rule of law, the World Justice Report (2022) has ranked South Korea 19th out of 140 countries, above both the United States (26th) and France (21st).[530] Notably, South Korean politics recently went through a crisis when its 18th president, Park Geun-Hye, was impeached and removed from office in 2017, and its 17th president, Lee Myung-Bak, was criminally convicted and imprisoned in 2018. Arguably, both incidents demonstrate the strength of Korea's democracy and its rule of law, rather than its weaknesses.

4.3 South Korea at the Crossroads: Challenges and Prospects

4.3.1 Economic challenges

After successfully developing its economy for three-and-a-half decades, South Korea faced a major economic crisis in 1997. Although South Korea constantly experienced challenges during its economic development, such as the oil crises in 1973 and 1979,[531] the 1997 crisis posed an unprecedented threat to its economy. The financial crisis was caused by the over-leveraging of major South Korean corporations. In the course of rapid economic development, South Korean companies made aggressive investments for growth and maintained a high debt-to-equity ratio to meet their financial needs.[532] Some major South Korean companies started to collapse in the 1990s, and the government, seeking to reduce government control in the economy, did not bail them out. Foreign lenders, who lost confidence in the viability of the Korean economy, also declined to extend loans.[533] Consequently, South Korea faced a critical shortage of foreign exchanges, which led to the 1997 financial crisis.[534] The South Korean government had also adopted a misguided policy that elevated the value of the Korean currency for political reasons. The adjustment resulted in a massive, US$ 23 billion trade deficit in 1996, weakening the South Korean economy.[535]

The government could not resolve this crisis and subsequently requested a bailout from the International Monetary Fund (IMF). In return for the requested bailout, the IMF demanded neoliberal changes in South Korea's economic policies, which reduced the role of the state in the economy to a further extent than the government had already implemented. The IMF also imposed stringent austerity measures to reduce debts, including a rapid increase in interest rates.[536] South Korea had no choice but to accept the IMF's demands to avoid a national default. The IMF's demands were inconsistent with decades of economic management and practices in South Korea; many firms had routinely operated with short-term loans on a rolling basis. The outcome was an economic catastrophe. The measures imposed by the IMF caused over 3,000 companies to fail and millions of people to lose jobs. South Korea recovered from the crisis relatively quickly (only one year after the outbreak of the crisis),[537] aided by rapid export expansion due to favorable foreign exchange rates. The Korean economy recovered from the crisis, but the impact of the crisis still lingers; the IMF's policy demands, such as a radical increase in interest rates, reduced investments and lowered economic growth, from which South Korea has never recovered to pre-crisis levels.[538]

Another structural challenge to South Korea's economy is over-dependency on a small number of conglomerates ("chaebol"), which survived the 1997 financial crisis (while other smaller corporations failed).[539] As of 2021, the revenues of the top 10 conglomerates, including Samsung, SK, Hyundai, LG, Lotte, Hanwha, and GS, were equivalent to 58.3 percent of South Korea's GDP.[540] Samsung alone generated revenue equivalent to 18.4 percent of GDP in 2021.[541] The government has facilitated the growth of chaebols and supported them since the 1960s through various means such as tax breaks, subsidies (including policy loans and loan guarantees), favorable exchange rates for exports, and import controls in efforts to facilitate economic development and industrialization. The economic concentration and control by these conglomerates has exacerbated economic disparity in South Korea, as demonstrated by the change of the Gini coefficient from the range of 0.28–0.29 in the 1990s to the range of 0.33–0.38 in the 2010s (a lower Gini coefficient represents a better income distribution).[542] While these conglomerates' revenues make up a significant share in the Korean economy, their contributions to employment are minimal: only 3.8 percent of all employment in South Korea. Thus, economic dependency on the conglomerates presents a challenge for the South Korean economy as these conglomerates' performance has a critical impact on the national economy.

The growing productivity gaps between a few large enterprises and many small- and medium-sized enterprises (SMEs) raise another economic challenge. The labor productivity of SMEs was 53.8 percent of large enterprises in 1988, and it has since fallen below 30 percent.[543] While SMEs account for 99.9 percent of all enterprises and provide for 81.3 percent of all employment,[544] their low productivity has reduced employment opportunities (particularly for young people), increased income gaps among Korean populations, and slowed overall economic growth over the years.[545] The government has supported SMEs through public funds and credit guarantees, which amounts to the second largest among the OECD countries (at 3.8 percent of GDP in 2016).[546] However, the government policy frameworks for SMEs are incoherent, inconsistent, and ineffective.[547] The government policies focus on protecting SMEs across the board rather than facilitating the growth of SMEs showing market performance or strong potential.[548] By contrast, large enterprises are subject to stringent government regulations,[549] and this policy has discouraged the growth of SMEs and has provided incentives for SMEs to remain "small" so that they can continue to obtain government support and avoid stricter government regulations.[550]

The weakening multilateral trading system under the auspices of the WTO is also a significant concern as South Korea relies on exports for its economy. The increasing global rivalry between Beijing and Washington has put South Korea in a challenging position. While South Korea is not able to give up its largest export market—China—it also cannot ignore the pressure from the United States to join its supply block against China, such as the Chip 4 Alliance.[551] The Biden administration has announced a policy to push for the manufacture of strategically important products such as semiconductors, electric vehicles, and EV batteries within the United States.[552] These products are essential exports for South Korea. South Korean manufacturers are under pressure to build manufacturing sites in the United States to secure the U.S. market at the expense of their domestic investments. Professor Moon Chung-In (former advisor to Korean President Moon Jae-In) has expressed concern that transferring so much of Korea's capital and technology to the United States could "hollow out" Korea's high-tech industry.[553] Some of these U.S. policies, such as its recently announced tax breaks for domestic EV production, may also breach international trade law.[554] However, the WTO is not expected to provide an effective remedy because the United States has blocked all appointments to the WTO Appellate Body since 2016, rendering the WTO appellate process unfunctional.[555]

4.3.2 Political challenges

South Korea is also facing political challenges, which affect its ability to handle international affairs. One of these challenges is a decades-long confrontation between the conservative, pro-capitalist, anti-communist faction (보수 우파) and the progressive faction (진보좌파), which is more sympathetic to social causes, such as economic equality, labor rights, and reconciliation and unification between South and North Korea.[556] It is not unusual to observe political divisions between conservative and progressive factions in any given country.[557] However, in South Korea, the confrontation and distrust between the two factions is deeply embedded in politics such that any bipartisan collaboration and cooperation has become increasingly difficult.[558] While such confrontational polarization is not unique to South Korea,[559] the divisive confrontation in South Korean politics is deeper. These factions, particularly the hardliners, have criticized each other for siding with foreign powers that once oppressed Korea (the progressive faction often criticizes the conservative as pro-Japan, and the latter attacks the former as pro-China).[560]

Another political challenge in South Korean society is the persistence of Confucian order—social hierarchy based on age and social status—despite political democratization since the late 1980s. A recent development in South

Korean politics demonstrates this problem. In June 2021, South Korea's conservative People Power Party (국민의힘), then Korea's largest opposition party, elected the youngest head of a major political party in South Korean history, Lee Jun-Seok, at 36 years old.[561] Lee endeavored to transform the party and initiated a series of reforms, such as selecting the party's spokesmen through rounds of open competition and introducing a qualifying examination for candidates for local political offices.[562] Lee's merit-based initiatives gained support from younger generations (many in their 20s and 30s), who had never supported the conservative party. As a result, the party won the presidential election in March 2022 and the local elections in June 2022.[563] The party had not won an election since its previous president Park Geun-Hye was impeached in 2017. Lee came aboard and led election campaigns with attractive policy proposals and creative approaches.

However, shortly after Lee assumed party leadership, the old party establishment began to attack and criticize Lee on dubious grounds. The old establishment criticized him for what by Western standards would be quite trivial or even irrelevant, such as the frequency of his media interviews, the tone of his remarks, and the spontaneity of his response to criticism. They essentially criticized him for failing to appear "mature enough" in his role as the party's head.[564] Despite his important achievements—winning major elections for the party that had lost every major election since the 2017 impeachment—Lee did not fill the role of a good "Confucian leader" with calm, courteous, virtuous, and mature mannerisms (although his attackers have never used the term "Confucian"). Korean media described Lee's election as the party leader as ushering Korean politics into a new era,[565] but many of his critics appeared unable to psychologically accept a party leader who was years younger than themselves, no matter what his achievements—leading victories in two major elections, including the presidential election—may have been.

Critical attacks on Lee proceeded shortly after his party won local elections in June 2022. The party's ethics (disciplinary) committee, headed by Lee Yang-Hee, announced its decision to suspend Lee's party membership for six months. It is not clear whether the ethics committee, whose chair is appointed by the party leader, has the authority to discipline an elected party leader. Regardless, this unprecedented decision against party leadership was made on an unproven claim that Lee had tried to "conceal" evidence for his alleged sexual misconduct. The decision had the effect of suspending Lee's role as party leader.[566] South Korean President Yoon Seok-Yeol, a former prosecutor, was known to disfavor Lee, and senior party members moved to displace Lee by forming an emergency committee that would replace party leadership to satisfy President Yoon.[567] This is another example of an old Confucian tradition—punishing those who appear to be disloyal to the head of the state,[568] although other political considerations—such as the party establishment's desire to secure and control the party's nomination of candidates for the next general election and to prevent Lee from reforming the nomination process that may risk their nominations—also influenced its decision.

The clash between the call for modern democracy and the outdated Confucian tradition represents a political challenge in South Korea. In October 2022, the party's ethics committee suspended Lee's party membership for an additional year. The decision was on account of his application for a court injunction against the party's decision to form a new emergency committee (which was his legal right) and his "offensive and critical comments" against other party members (which should be protected under the freedom of speech). Ironically these are the rights that ethics committee chair Lee Yang-Hee once set out to protect as a former special rapporteur of the United Nations—the United Nations Human Rights Covenant clearly protects these rights.[569] The questionable process of Lee's expulsion from the ruling party's leadership raises an inquiry as to whether democracy and the rule of law are firmly rooted in Korean society (notwithstanding that the country's formal political process and governance system might be classified as a democracy).[570]

This gap explains the generational divide in South Korea; younger generations do not favor old Confucian mandates such as unquestioned loyalty to the leader, an emphasis on appearance ("courtesy") over substance, and discriminatory treatment according to age and social status.[571] As Lee was being ousted, many young supporters withdrew or suspended their support for President Yoon, resulting in one of the lowest presidential approval ratings in South Korean history.[572] His ratings have since improved,[573] but without support from young generations, it is questionable whether he will secure the solid majority support necessary to undertake influential diplomatic roles as well as the domestic reforms he set out to achieve (*e.g.*, labor reform). Hierarchical Confucian practice did not stop with Lee's expulsion from party leadership. His party, now South Korea's ruling party, has changed rules for the election of its new party leader to ensure the election of a pro-president candidate rather than a potential candidate (like Yoo Seung-Min) who has popular support but is known to be critical of President Yoon.[574]

Lastly, the prevalence of populism and fandom politics presents another political challenge for South Korea. Populism and resulting populist policies are a problem not only for South Korea but many other countries. For example, both the Trump and Biden administrations made large cash disbursements during the pandemic, which, in turn, caused the highest inflation in decades in the United States.[575] In South Korea, massive fandoms have formed in conservative and progressive factions supporting influential politicians. As a result, political leaders adopt policies to satisfy their own fandoms instead of national interests, such as unproductive and costly cash disbursements.[576] Fandom politics is not conducive to working democracy. Fierce attacks on political opponents—waged by fandoms—only deepen the already contentious political environment and create a political culture that entertains and encourages attacks and counterattacks rather than careful deliberation and collaboration across political factions.[577] Political processes controlled by populism and fandom politics are likely to deepen partisan confrontations, waste taxpayer money, and fail to deliver effective solutions to complex problems in society.[578] South Korea needs inclusive and effective political leadership to overcome its divisive bipolarism and present broadly acceptable solutions that effectively address pressing national agendas, including economic polarization and stagnation, decreasing population, international trade and investment problems, and national security.

4.3.3 The question of unification

The division of the Korean peninsula and the continuing conflict between South and North Korea has become the most serious and apparent threat to sustainable peace in Northeast Asia. This threat was vividly demonstrated by the outbreak of the Korean War, which destroyed much of Korea and caused millions of casualties (among Koreans, Americans, and Chinese). After the war, hundreds of military operations, skirmishes, and incursions, executed mostly by North Korea,[579] claimed hundreds of additional lives, and the North Korean government kidnapped thousands more in the course of South and North Korean confrontations.[580] As mentioned earlier, the United States maintains its largest military base in South Korea, primarily to defend South Korea from North Korean aggression.[581] A high degree of tension is continuing: on October 9, 2022, North Korea announced that its air force launched 150 military planes in response to a United States–South Korean joint military exercise, demonstrating North Korea's resolve to use a military response to any perceived threat.[582] Throughout 2022, North Korea launched more than 90 cruise and ballistic missiles, some of which are capable of delivering nuclear warheads, in shows of force.[583] The 2018 and 2019 summits (between South Korea and North Korea and between the United States and North Korea) did not reduce the tension in the Korean peninsula or the risk of war.

However, South and North Korean relations have not been solely a confrontational standoff. Since the first South-North dialogue in 1971, both governments have continued dialogues, resulting in agreements, reunions of families separated by the division, sports and cultural exchanges, and economic aid (from South Korea). South and North Korea simultaneously attained full U.N. membership in 1991, which can also be viewed as a step toward a peaceful Korean peninsula.[584] Despite these efforts, however, the two Koreas have failed to establish a peaceful relationship. The most important cause of this failure was North Korea's continuing ambition to occupy and rule South Korea under its communist leadership. Despite the failure of the Korean War, North Korean leader Kim Il-Sung did not abandon his plans to occupy the South. Kim reportedly prepared to invade South Korea in 1965[585] and sent commandos to assassinate the South Korean president in 1968.[586] The prospect of the North occupying South Korea has become increasingly unfeasible as the economic and military gaps between the two Koreas have radically increased since the 1980s, and the military alliance between the United States and South Korea has remained strong. Regardless, as recently as 2014, the North Korean leader threatened to wage a "grand war" to reunite Korea.[587]

Threats from the nuclear North persist. Peaceful unification of the Korean peninsula would be the best way to remove all of these threats. Absent unification, the North's nuclear threats could be developed into a full-scale war that might transcend the Korean peninsula—for example, during the Korean War, General MacArthur proposed to attack China.[588] The unification of Korea is a common national objective shared by both South and North Korea. Korea had been a united state for over 1,300 years, and it is ironic that Korea was divided in 1945 as a result of the war waged by Japan. The constitutions of both Koreas stipulate this objective,[589] and their governments have also agreed to pursue unification by peaceful means. On July 4, 1972, South and North Korea issued their first joint statement to set out the key principles for the unification of Korea,[590] including the goal for the unification to be achieved "independently, without depending on foreign powers and without foreign interference," "through peaceful means, without resorting to the use of force against each other," and "a great national unity" to be sought "transcending differences in ideas, ideologies, and systems."[591] The 1991 Inter-Korean Basic Agreement also affirms these principles and defines the South-North relationship as "a special interim relationship stemming from the process towards reunification."[592]

Both governments have also proposed more specific frameworks for unification. In 1994, South Korea proposed a unitary state model based on liberal democracy and the market economy, to be achieved through the following three stages: (1) the first stage of reconciliation and cooperation; (2) the second stage of the Korean Commonwealth (a union of two Korean states); and (3) the final stage of unified Korea (one nation, one state).[593] By contrast, North Korea prefers a looser form of unification and proposes to create a federation of two separate Korean states, preserving each Korea's statehood after the unification (one nation, two states).[594] The unitary state model proposed by South Korea could be considered advantageous to South Korea with its larger population (over 51 million compared to North Korea's population of 25.9 million) and greater economic endowments. The North Korean model, which preserves political autonomy for each Korea, would be conducive to the preservation of the North Korean regime after the proposed unification.

Despite a series of declarations, agreements, and proposals toward unification, the feasibility of Korean unification remains unclear. Over five decades have passed since the 1972 Communiqué, but the two Koreas have not even begun the first stage, which is to build reconciliation and cooperation.[595] Only a small number of South Koreans have visited North Korea, and even fewer North Koreans have ever visited the South[596] as there are no regular exchanges between the two Koreas. They maintain the world's most heavily guarded border with no regular traffic between the South and North. The sporadic shifts between confrontation and pause characterize the South-North relationship: short periods of reconciliation following some agreements and meetings are abruptly ended by bursts of discontent and hostility, as recently demonstrated by North Korea blowing up the Inter-Korean Liaison Office in 2020 over its discontent with the South Korean response to South Korean civilians flying balloons containing flyers and small amounts of cash to the North.[597] There is a reason for the North Korean regime to interrupt short periods of relative peace with erratic behavior. From the perspective of North Korean leadership, the peaceful unification of Korea will likely invite the economic domination of South Koreans over the entire Korean peninsula and will almost certainly undermine their absolute rule in the North. Such a possibility would be an unwelcome risk, despite their rhetorical support for unification.

South Koreans also share concerns about the proposed unification. For example, there is a growing concern about "the cost of unification" due to the enormous economic gaps between the two Koreas.[598] The estimated cost of unification ranges widely from tens of billions of dollars to over a trillion dollars,[599] most of which will have to be assumed by the wealthier South. There could also be a substantial social cost associated with the integration of the two groups of very different Korean populations separated for nearly eight decades. Demonstrating the potential cost, North Korean refugees—reaching over 33,800—reportedly experience cultural and economic difficulties when integrating into South Korean society.[600] Despite the costs, Korean unification would be necessary to ensure long-term survival for the Koreans. Despite the U.S. commitment, there is no guarantee that the current United States–South Korean alliance will last permanently—former U.S. Presidents Jimmy Carter and Donald Trump both considered withdrawing U.S. troops from South Korea.[601] Given the massive economic and military powers of China and the continuing tensions with Japan, a divided Korea is inherently vulnerable and will not be conducive to the long-term security of Koreans. Arguably, unification is the only permanent solution to remedy this vulnerability and ensure lasting security for the Korean people.

Despite considerable challenges, both South and North Korea maintain their national objective of unification. Korean unification would be an important step toward sustainable peace in Northeast Asia. Historically, Northeast Asia maintained stability when Korea was united and robust. As discussed earlier, united and militarily-prepared Goryeo repelled the invasions from the Khitans in the tenth and eleventh centuries and prevented them from conquering China, thereby maintaining the balance of power in Northeast Asia.[602] United Joseon, despite internal issues, defended itself and Northeast Asia from the Japanese invasion in the sixteenth century.[603] By contrast, a weakened Korea in the late nineteenth century could not stop the Japanese colonial occupation, and using occupied Korea as the base, Japan subsequently invaded Northeast Asia and mainland China, putting the entire Northeast Asian continent in the flames of the war. A peacefully united Korea would once again function as a point of balance to sustain peace in the region. The proposed unification is also a permanent solution to the nuclear threats from the current North Korean regime, which not only threaten peace in the Korean peninsula but undermine the political and economic stability of Northeast Asia.

There is a caveat though. It is questionable whether South Korea could pursue political integration with North Korea, while it continues committing serious human rights violations (*e.g.*, public execution, concentration camps for political prisoners and their families, and torture and unlawful detainment),[604] if North Korea is to maintain its own political autonomy in the process of unification. The South Korean public is unlikely to tolerate the proposed political integration with North Korea continually committing extreme human rights violations. This dilemma may require an adjustment of the Inter-Korean Basic Agreement. The principle of "no interference with internal affairs" (article 2 of the Inter-Korean Basic Agreement) may have been feasible in the 1990s, but the strengthened requirements for human rights in the twenty-first century may not allow for "no interference" given the extent of human rights abuses in North Korea. To pursue unification between the two Koreas, a new inter-Korean agreement that highlights the importance of human rights and mandates compliance with them might be necessary—although it is questionable whether the North Korean regime will acknowledge the issue and agree to such a commitment.

Chapter 5

A POWER WITH RISING CONCERNS: ESCALATION OF TENSIONS BETWEEN JAPAN AND ITS NEIGHBORS

5.1 A Restored Power

5.1.1 Economic restoration: From defeat in World War II to success in the global market

By the end of World War II, much of Japan had been destroyed. While the allied forces did not invade the main Japanese islands during the war, heavy U.S. bombing destroyed cities, villages, and much of its infrastructure. According to a Japanese government report on war damages, Japan lost 25 percent of its buildings and structures, 33 percent of its urban housing, 34 percent of its industrial machines, 81 percent of its commercial ships, 16 percent of its telegraph, telephone, and water supplies, 11 percent of its electricity and gas supplies, and 10 percent of its railroad and other land transportation.[605] Over two million Japanese citizens also died during the war, while survivors suffered through food shortages and inflation.[606] Economic production sharply decreased because of this war destruction. Figure 5.1 illustrates the low Japanese production of food, textiles, steel, and machinery in 1946 compared to its pre-war production.

The Japanese economy has gradually recovered since 1946. To foster recovery, the Supreme Commander for the Allied Powers (SCAP)[607] initiated land reform in occupied Japan. Before the war, approximately two-thirds of the Japanese farmers did not own land. The SCAP's policy transferred land ownership to the farmers and improved farm tenancy practices.[608] The reform was successful: the percentage of owner-operated cultivated land increased from 54 percent to 90 percent by 1950[609] (although the land reform had only a limited impact on agricultural production).[610] An economically more significant development was the outbreak of the Korean War in 1950. The destructive war was a tragic event for the Koreans, but it provided Japan with decisive momentum for economic recovery. Due to its proximity to the

(1935 = 100)

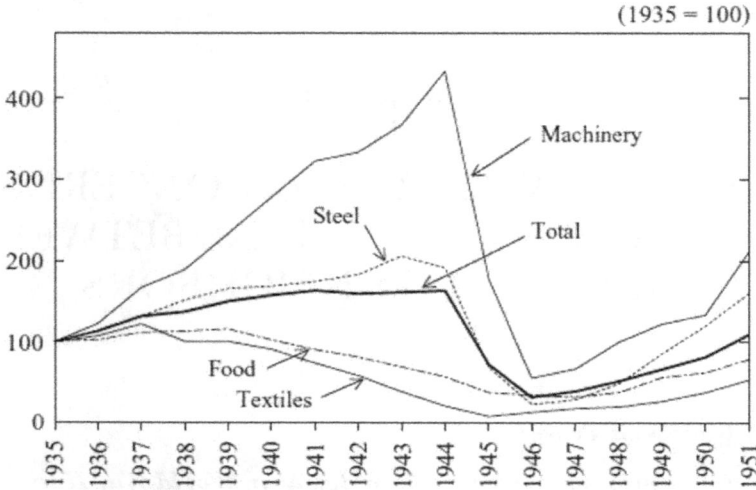

Figure 5.1 Industrial production index (Japan, 1935–1951). (*Source*: Management and Coordination Agency, Historical Statistics of Japan, Vol. 2, 1988)

Table 5.1 Gross domestic product of Japan (1960–1995).

Year	GDP (in billions of US$)
1960	44.3
1970	212.6
1980	1,110
1990	3,130
1995	5,500

(*Source*: World Bank, GDP (current US$)—Japan)

Korean peninsula, Japan served as the supply base for U.N. forces, and money poured into the Japanese economy for supplies from Japanese producers. As a result, production increased by nearly 70 percent during the war—as much as US$ 590 million in 1951 and over US$ 800 million in 1952 and 1953 (which amounted to 60 to 70 percent of its exports at the time) was pumped into the Japanese economy.[611] Thanks to this wartime economic boom, the Japanese economy recovered to its pre–World War II level by 1952.[612]

The Japanese economy continued to grow—an increase of 2.8 to 4.8 times every decade as shown in Table 5.1.

Capital accumulation and a long-term rise in labor productivity drove Japan's economic growth. On account of this rapid growth, Japan became the world's second largest economy in 1968, next only to the United States.

In 1995, Japan's GDP per capita was among the highest in the world (over 50 percent higher than that of the United States) and 6 of the world's 10 largest companies (including the 4 largest) were Japanese.[613] Japan's successful economic growth is accompanied by sharp increases in exports. The Japanese government supported domestic producers with tax breaks, subsidies, preferential financing, and trade protection while encouraging exports to expand the output further.[614] The economic gains from successful exports fueled the growth of Japanese firms and the economy, which, in turn, further boosted exports. Japan's exports increased rapidly, as illustrated in Table 5.2.

Major Japanese companies, including Toyota, Sony, Mitsubishi, Hitachi, and Toshiba, led exports and prevailed in world markets in major product areas, including electronics, automobiles, ships, machinery, chemicals, processed materials, and mechanical parts. Since the 1985 Plaza accord—which increased the value of the Japanese currency yen vis-à-vis the U.S. dollar— the focus of the Japanese economy has shifted to the domestic market.[615]

The Japanese government played an essential role in Japan's economic development. The SCAP envisioned economic reform consistent with a demilitarized and democratic Japan by dissolving the large Japanese conglomerates (財閥 or "zaibatsu"), which supported the war efforts, but Japan pursued government-led economic development policies for decades. During the postwar reconstruction period between 1945 and 1960, the government directly regulated the activities of the private sector through price and ration controls and priority production for certain key materials.[616] Additionally, between 1960 and 1973, the government provided support for specific key industries through industrial facilitation measures, such as tax benefits, subsidies, preferential financing, and trade protection as cited above.[617] Finally, between 1973 and the 1990s, the Japanese government shifted its industrial policy approach toward adopting "soft" measures for industrial support, such as administrative guidance and state-facilitated industry research coordination associations.[618] The autonomy of the private sector increased after the shift, but the influence of the government ministries, such as the Ministry of International Trade and Industry (MITI) and the Ministry of Finance, remained strong in the Japanese economy.

Table 5.2 Export expansion of Japan (1970–2000).

Year	1970	1980	1990	2000
Unit (US$ in billions)	22	145.1	320.2	519.9

(*Source*: World Bank, Exports of goods and services (current US$)—Japan)

The government's economic development initiative is not the only reason for Japan's economic success. (Some argue that Japan's successful economic growth occurred *in spite of* the nation's inefficient industrial policies.) Japan possessed endowments that are conducive to economic development, such as an educated workforce, a high rate of savings and investments, and its ability to import and adopt foreign technology.[619] Japan suffered from a lack of natural resources, relatively limited land space historically resulting in food shortages, and trauma from the war. However, it successfully overcame these constraints by building a world-class manufacturing capacity through innovation, which led to a substantial increase in exports that dominated world markets in key product areas (such as electronics, automobiles, and ships). The postwar Japanese economic success was due to its success in the global market as explained above. The export-driven economic development model is also found in other successful East Asian economies, such as South Korea, Taiwan, Hong Kong, Singapore, and China.

Since the mid-1990s, however, the Japanese economy has experienced decades of downturn. The economic shock resulting from its real estate bubble burst in the mid-1990s and subsequent policy failures (such as the consumption tax hike in 1997) caused negative growth for years, ending the long period of growth and prosperity of the postwar Japanese economy.[620] During the financial crisis, the Japanese banking sector was plagued by nonperforming loans.[621] Yet, the Japanese government failed to undertake necessary financial reforms due to political considerations.[622] Alarmed by the financial crisis, many Japanese businesses started to operate conservatively and became cautious about expanding investment for new facilities and innovations.[623] Concerned about their uncertain economic future, households also did not increase consumption.[624] Insufficient investment and stagnant consumption demand plunged the Japanese economy into a decades-long recession. The Japanese economy has not regained vitality (except, perhaps, for a few years between 2013 and 2019). As a result, Japan's per capita income in 2021 was US$ 42,620—lower than its 1996 per capita income of US$ 43,940 (in current value)—showing the stagnation of the Japanese economy.[625]

5.1.2 *Political reform and rearmament*

Prewar Japan was an authoritarian regime under the Meiji Constitution (1889–1947). This Constitution established the Japanese monarchy under a deity emperor and was founded upon notions of divine rule.[626] Scholars have argued that these notions fueled the nationalistic attitudes that caused Japan's military aggression toward other countries.[627] Thus, when the United States occupied Japan in 1945, it began replacing, or substantially revising, the Meiji Constitution to turn Japan into a demilitarized and democratized state.[628] The SCAP initially took an indirect approach to accomplish this—it left the Japanese government mostly intact and coordinated with the Japanese government to implement its directives. However, when the Japanese government failed to produce a new constitution to its satisfaction, the SCAP developed one itself and presented it to the Japanese government for review.[629] This new constitution was premised on three key principles identified in the Potsdam Declaration: popular sovereignty, pacifism, and human rights.[630] The Japanese government adopted the new constitution, which went into effect in May 1947.[631]

The most notable feature of the new Japanese constitution was the renouncement of war and the threat or use of force as means of settling an international dispute.[632] The constitution also removed the authoritarian element of prewar Japanese political governance: under the new system, the emperor no longer held political power. He remained a figure-head of the nation, but the postwar constitution established the people of Japan, rather than the emperor, as the source of sovereign power.[633] The constitution instilled in Japanese law several U.S. legal traditions, including recognition of various civil rights and liberties, civilian (rather than military) control of the government, and judicial review.[634] While U.S. constitutionalism influenced the stipulation of constitutional rights in the Japanese constitution, the European parliamentary structure influenced the government structure. The Japanese central government is composed of a bicameral legislature whose members are directly elected by the public,[635] and a prime minister forms the government and leads the nation.[636]

The public has supported the 1947 Constitution since its enactment. However, the conservative faction of Japanese politics (日本右翼) remained discontent and advocated for its revision. The conservatives criticized the constitution, primarily for its clauses mandating disarmament and the limited role of the emperor.[637] Despite its discontent, the faction could not obtain a two-thirds majority in both houses of the parliament, which must be ratified by a majority vote in a national referendum to amend the constitution.[638] Another important feature of postwar Japanese governance is the political dominance of the conservative Liberal Democratic Party (自由民主党 or "LDP") for over six decades.[639] The LDP's platform centered on economic growth and Japan's return to the international community.[640] Other political factions have also appeared on the political scene, such as the Japan Socialist Party (日本社会党, which advocated against national rearmament and voiced support for the Chinese government)[641] and the Japanese Communist Party (日本共産党, which rose to relative prominence in the 1970s),[642] but the LDP's domination characterizes postwar Japanese politics. The LDP's long reign in Japanese politics reflects the conservative nature of Japanese society and contrasts with other democracies in the region—such as South Korea, where there have been more frequent shifts of administration between the conservative and progressive parties.

Following the brief period of demilitarization, rearmament became a noticeable phenomenon in postwar Japan and affected the military landscape in Northeast Asia. The SCAP dissolved the Japanese Imperial Army and Navy after the war, but the outbreak of the Korean War caused a shift of the policy. The Japanese government created a 75,000 troop-strong National Police Reserve, which was expanded and became the National Safety Forces in 1952 and the Self-Defense Force (自衛隊 or "SDF") in 1954.[643] Japan's SDF has grown over time. The continuing growth of the SDF seems to be contradictory to the demilitarization policy but can be understood in the context of Japan's security relationship with the United States.[644] In the aftermath of World War II, the United States assumed sole responsibility for Japan's national defense.[645] When the Cold War ended and the United States reduced its troops from the region, the Chinese and North Korean militaries continued to grow, which stirred security concerns among the Japanese public who realized that the U.S. support might be wavering.[646] The growth of the SDF reflects this concern. Today, the SDF is one of the world's largest and highest-funded military forces, commanding over 260,000 armed forces personnel.[647] In 2020, Japan recorded the world's ninth-largest annual military expenditure of US$ 54.1 billion,[648] equivalent to 1.1 percent of the nation's GDP. The Japanese government has recently announced "doubling" its military budget.[649]

Over the years, the SDF has not only grown in size but also increased the scope of its operations and cooperation with the United States. During the Cold War, the Japanese Maritime Self-Defense Force (海上自衛隊 or "JMSDF") supported the U.S. Navy in the Pacific on missions such as mine-sweeping, anti-submarine warfare, and offensive submarine warfare to keep the Soviet Navy in check.[650] After the Cold War, the JMSDF also cooperated with the U.S. Navy to counter China's naval build-up in the Pacific. However, critics have expressed concerns that such military cooperation, mandated in formal agreements such as the revised 1997 Guidelines for Japan–U.S. Defense Cooperation, constitutes further rearmament in contravention of Article 9 of the Japanese Constitution, which prohibits the use of force as means to settle international disputes.[651] Critics such as Professor Tomoyuki Sasaki have also argued that the SDF's expanded role beyond self-defense, such as its participation in the U.N. peacekeeping missions abroad, is inconsistent with Article 9.[652] Japan's increasing military role in the region has also raised concerns among its neighbors, including South Korea, which experienced invasion and occupation by the Japanese military forces[653]—although some say it is unlikely that Japan's military buildup, proceeding under the strong influence of the United States, would pose a threat to Northeast Asia in the near future as it did in the 1930s.[654]

5.1.3 A Pacific power

Japan is a solid pacific power with global economic influence. Despite its defeat in World War II and the destruction from the war, Japan became one of the most prosperous countries in the twentieth century. Japan is one of the very few countries outside the West that successfully industrialized and escaped colonization by the West. Despite its small territorial and population size (a little over 1 percent of the world's land mass and less than 2 percent of the world population), Japan created the world's second largest economy (1968–2009), led technological innovations, and dominated the world markets for decades. Qualities such as a strong work ethic, respect for order, and robust public education explain Japan's extraordinary success.[655] Despite the rise of China since the 1980s and Japan's economic stagnation since the 1990s, Japan's standing in the Asia-Pacific remains solid, maintaining the world's third largest economy (after China since 2010) and possessing a world-class military (the strength of which has been evaluated as the fifth by Global Firepower).[656] Japan's enduring alliance with the United States also reinforces its regional position.

However, despite the nation's prominent economic presence in the world, Japan has not achieved a proportionate degree of political influence since the end of World War II. The unique imbalance between its economic and political influence has been caused, at least in part, by the strong political influence of the United States in postwar Japan. The United States was Japan's sole occupier after the war, and under the dominant U.S influence, which continued after the occupation, Japan's postwar foreign policies aligned with U.S. interests.[657] This dependency reduced Japan's autonomous diplomatic space despite Japan regaining its sovereignty in 1952.[658] Besides the U.S. influence, the postwar Japanese leadership also tried to limit its international presence to economic activities and to avoid anything appearing as political or military interventions.[659] Considering the remaining hostility and resentment about the Japanese invasion in World War II, Japan's focus on economic affairs and avoidance of political or military confrontation has been considered a safe course of action.[660] Japan contributed to economic development in Asia by expanding its economic aid—from 1974 to 1984, Japan's aid increased by 380 percent, with two-thirds of the aid going to Asia and the Pacific.[661] Japanese investments have also been conducive to industrial development in Asia-Pacific countries.[662]

However, the United States became increasingly discontent with Japan's policy focusing on economic affairs. The United States, which suffered through massive budget and trade deficits in the 1980s, pressured Japan to assume higher military responsibility in the region and boost its military spending.[663] As a pacific power, Japan had to balance between its preference for economic focus and the need to accommodate demands from the United States to assume an increased military role in Northeast Asia. However, it needed to do so without disrupting its relationship with the other neighboring countries, such as South Korea and China, which were weary of Japan's growing military influence. In the 1990s following the Cold War, Japan was at the peak of its economic influence and had the political space to define its role in Northeast Asia. Japan could have set out the terms of its relationships with the other countries in the region to rebuild confidence and bring reconciliation beyond the economic sphere. This approach may have restored the region's political confidence in Japan and reduced Japan's dependency on the United States for national security by improving its ties and collaborations with other countries in Northeast Asia. However, the Japanese government did not show such leadership, perhaps justifying Professor Roger Brown's use of the term "the economic giant-political pigmy" to describe the anomaly.[664]

Japan's progressive political faction (Japan Socialist Party), briefly in power (1994–1996), had a deeper interest in regional reconciliation than its conservative counterpart but started to lose power in Japanese politics in the late 1990s.[665] Japan's diplomatic approach started to change as the right-wing faction began to dominate Japanese politics at the turn of the century. The Japanese government replaced its apologetic tone in diplomacy with a more assertive one vis-à-vis the other countries in the region that it once invaded. For example, as further discussed in the following section, Japan has ongoing territorial conflicts with adjacent countries, including South Korea, China, and Russia. The Japanese government has voiced its territorial claims more aggressively in recent years, intensifying tension with its neighboring countries.[666] The political motive of this shift may have been to consolidate its hardline supporters and reinforce its powerbase, but it has had the negative effect of escalating tensions with the other countries in Northeast Asia.[667] Japan's failure to resolve issues associated with its past war crimes and offenses has also weakened its political influence and credibility in the region, increasing, rather than bridging, the gaps between its global economic power and political influence.[668]

Unlike Germany—which successfully recovered from the political and economic wounds of World War II through repentance and reparations and rose to become a European leader by gaining confidence from the other European countries it once had invaded[669]—Japan's political leadership failed to settle the issues with the other countries in Northeast Asia that were victimized during the war. This inability represents Japan's limit as a pacific power: an economic powerhouse but without international political leadership and vision. Japan's stature as a prominent pacific power may have been better demonstrated in other areas, such as its cultural display through the international boom of Japanese music, fashion, and entertainment throughout Asia and beyond in the 1990s.[670] Japan also made significant contributions to literature and science (as demonstrated by 25 Nobel laureates Japan produced up to 2021). Yet another area where the world may see Japan's capacity as a pacific power is its military. Japan possesses a leading military capacity, particularly in its naval force, and has sufficient resources, including 10.5 metric tons of weapons-grade plutonium, to improve its military capacity even further.[671] The increasing military threats from China and North Korea may justify Japan's military buildup; however, its rearmament raises concerns for the other countries in the region, escalating an arms race in Northeast Asia.[672]

Japan being a pacific power, a vital element of the political dynamics affecting sustainable peace in Northeast Asia is Japan's political relationships with the neighboring powers, South Korea, China, and Russia. Several issues that predate World War II have strained Japan's political relationships with these countries. These issues include territorial disputes, disagreements over the past war crimes committed by Japan during World War II, and the discrepancy between Japan's political aspirations and the strength of its political leadership in Northeast Asia. There is also a potential that some of these conflicts may escalate—although no armed conflict has arisen from these tensions, political tensions and disputes between Japan and these other countries have not been conducive to sustaining peace in the region. The following section discusses why these political tensions exist and explores possible pathways to relieve them.

5.2 Escalation of Political Tensions with Neighbors

5.2.1 A friend or foe? Continuing disagreements with South Korea

Japan's relationship with South Korea has been strained by memories of Japanese oppression, notably the atrocities committed by Japanese authorities during Japan's colonial occupation of Korea from 1910 to 1945. Japan's unapologetic attitude toward these incidents has also aggravated the wound.[673] (The Japanese government offered "apologies" for its conduct in Korea, but these apologies were undermined by the derogatory comments made by Japanese high-level officials and politicians toward Korea and Koreans.)

Japan's position on the incidents during colonial occupation, which include forced labor during World War II, is that proper compensation has already been made under its agreement with South Korea in 1965.[674] Under the terms of this 1965 agreement, Japan paid the South Korean government 108 billion yen, the equivalent of US$ 300 million, as a full and final settlement. However, the South Korean government believes the treaty does not bar individual victims from demanding reparations from the culpable Japanese entities, including private corporations.[675]

Tension over this disagreement climaxed in July 2019 when the Japanese government announced the exclusion of South Korea from its approved export list for exporting materials and items that Japan considers "strategic." This list includes three key items—photo resists, hydrogen fluoride, and fluorinated polyimides—all of which are essential to South Korea's most important export product: semiconductors.[676] This exclusion meant that the export of these items to South Korea would be subject to more stringent, case-by-case approval, threatening to substantially delay the export process or even prevent the export of these essential items altogether.[677] South Korean semiconductor producers rely substantially on the Japanese to supply these items,[678] which means that this exclusion may cause significant economic disruption to South Korea.[679] The Japanese government justified these measures by citing security concerns over the exportation of such items, but it is widely believed they were in retaliation to the decision of Korea's Supreme Court ordering Japanese companies to provide compensation for the Korean individuals who were forced to work for them during World War II.[680] After the announcement of this exclusion, anti-Japanese sentiment swept throughout South Korea, resulting in widespread boycotts of Japanese products. Koreans perceived this measure as yet another Japanese attempt to subjugate Koreans to meet Japanese political demands.[681]

Economic rivalry is another source of tension between these two countries. Over the years, South Korea has rapidly closed the existing economic gap between itself and Japan. According to a World Bank report, Japan's per capita GNI was over five times higher than South Korea's in 1962.[682] That gap was reduced to three times by 1996, and it was further closed to 18 percent as of 2021.[683] South Korea's average wage is already higher than Japan's.[684] Due to its successful industrial and economic development, South Korea has become a significant competitor to Japan in important product categories that Japan once dominated, such as home electronics, automobiles, and semiconductors.[685] Accordingly, the previously cited export measure may also have had an economic objective: to keep South Korea in check. South Korean manufacturers, such as Samsung, had been planning to expand their production into new areas, such as the next generation of systems semiconductors, which use new production technologies requiring materials from Japan.[686] Because South Korean semiconductor manufacturers rely on Japan for their supply of these items, finding alternative suppliers might be difficult, if not impossible.[687]

Yet another source of tension between South Korea and Japan is a territorial dispute. Both countries have claimed the Dokdo Islands (also called "Liancourt Rocks" or "Takeshima Islands"), located in the East Sea (see Figure 5.2), as their own territory.

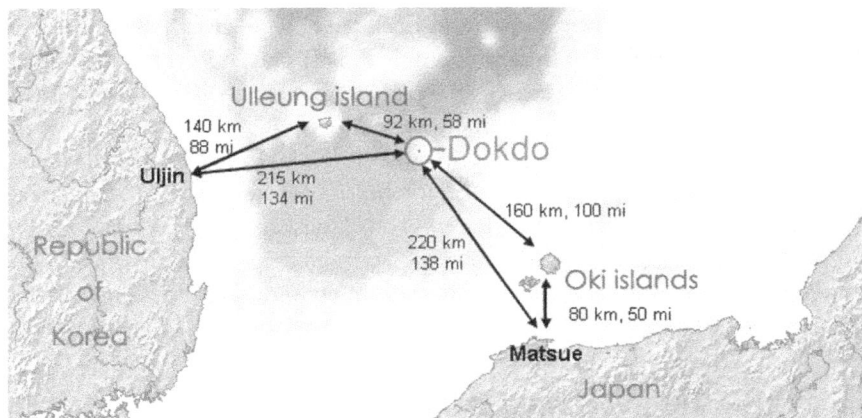

Figure 5.2 Location of the Dokdo Islands. (*Source*: Historical facts about Korea's Dokdo Islands)

This dispute dates back several decades. In 1900, the Korean Empire (1897–1910) decreed that it annexed the Dokdo Islands as a territory of Korea—but five years later, Japan, recognizing the islands' strategic importance, declared that it was annexing the islands as a territory of Japan.[688] Since 1953, the Dokdo Islands have been under South Korea's occupation, but Japan has not relinquished its territorial claim. This dispute has been a continual source of tension between the two countries. For South Koreans, Japan's claim to the Dokdo Islands reminds them of Japanese imperial expansion in the early 1900s, which led to the colonial occupation of the entire Korean peninsula.[689] For Japan, the adjacent ocean area that it would control by acquiring the Dokdo Islands has become economically important.[690] This dispute over the Dokdo Islands is likely to continue with the potential for conflict.[691] South Korean and Japanese coastal guard patrol ships have had standoffs near the Dokdo Islands, and Japan's new defense plan has implicated the possible involvement of the SDF in future disputes over the Dokdo Islands.[692]

The Korea–Japan relationship is a complex one. It has lasted for two millennia, with a long history of cultural, political, and economic exchanges.

Despite the cited disagreements, these two countries share cultural traits (such as respect for order and community values), economic achievements through successful industrialization and international trade, and political democratization under U.S. influence. The Koreans and Japanese have created two of the most economically advanced, technologically innovative democratic states in Northeast Asia. South Korea and Japan continue to have dynamic exchanges, as demonstrated by the millions of individuals traveling between the nations each year.[693] South Korea and Japan are important economic partners as evidenced by robust trade between them—South Korea is the third largest market for Japan, and Japan is the fifth largest for South Korea. Both countries also share security interests against North Korea and China and participate in the security framework led by the United States (although they are not formally military allies). However, the lack of consensus between the two countries on the atrocities of colonial times has constantly strained their relationship (although the current Yoon administration seems to have adopted an appeasement policy toward Japan under U.S. influence). This issue requires a new approach and a paradigm change, which will be further discussed in Section 5.3.

5.2.2 Political tensions with China

Sino-Japanese relations have gone through dramatic changes over the last century.[694] Japan, as an island nation, consistently sought to occupy the Asian continent to secure resources and new territories, first by annexing Korea in 1910, occupying Manchuria in 1932, and then invading China in 1937. Japan's attempts to acquire continental Asia ultimately failed with its defeat in World War II, which led to the U.S. occupation of Japan. After the war, Japan normalized its relationship with China in 1972.[695] However, the atrocities that Japan committed during the Sino-Japanese War (1937–1945), including tens of millions of civilian casualties and massacres committed by the Japanese military, have led to substantial anti-Japanese sentiment in China, which continues to strain the Sino-Japanese relationship.[696] Additionally, the postwar political and security landscape in Northeast Asia has placed certain restraints on Japan concerning its relationships with China. Japan's military alliance with the United States, the increasing rivalry between the United States and China, and Japan's support of U.S. positions in East Asia have reduced the political space that Japan has with respect to China, making it difficult for Japan to move beyond the strategic parameters set by the United States in the region.[697]

China's economic and military rise is another source of concern for Japan, which has, in turn, created a degree of political tension between the two countries. China's rapid economic development has threatened Japan's economic position in recent decades, and China surpassed the Japanese economy in size when it became the second largest economy in 2010. As of 2021, China's GDP was over 3.5 times larger than that of Japan, and that gap is expected to grow in the coming years.[698] China has rapidly increased its competitiveness in product areas where Japan used to dominate, including machinery.[699] China's military rise is an even more serious concern for Japan. Japan has a vital interest in securing its sea lanes in the South China Sea for the supply of resources essential to its survival. About 80 percent of Japan's energy imports and much of its trade travel through the South China Sea.[700] China currently possesses a larger naval force than Japan. China has recently increased its military activities in the South China Sea.[701] In response, Japan has been shifting its military posture toward southwestern Japan, notably toward Okinawa and the remote islands near Taiwan, creating the potential for conflict with China.[702]

The two countries also have a territorial dispute over the Senkaku (Diaoyu) Islands. These islands comprise eight small islets, with a total land size of approximately seven square kilometers and a location about 170 kilometers east of Taiwan (see Figure 5.3). China claims it discovered and has owned the

Figure 5.3 Location of the Senkaku Islands. (*Source*: Location of the Senkaku Islands, modified from https://en.wikipedia.org/wiki/Senkaku_Islands_dispute#/media/File:Senkaku_Diaoyu_Tiaoyu_Islands.png)

islands since the fourteenth century, whereas Japan claims to have annexed the islands in 1895 and controlled them until the end of World War II.[703] After the war, the United States administered the Senkaku Islands and the other islands in the Ryukyu Islands until they were returned to Japan in 1972.[704] Interestingly, the United States initially showed a somewhat ambiguous attitude about the conflicting territorial claims to the Senkaku Islands. The U.S. administration originally stated, "The U.S. passes no judgment as to conflicting claims over any portion of [the Senkaku Islands], which should be settled directly by the parties concerned."[705] More recently, however, the United States has changed its tone and began to express support for Japan's sovereignty over the Islands, swaying away from its traditional position of neutrality over the territorial claim.[706]

The area's economic importance has invigorated the dispute over the Senkaku Islands. A 1968 survey conducted under the authority of the United Nations Economic Commission for Asia and the Far East reported the possibility of substantial energy (oil) deposits in the areas surrounding the Senkaku Islands.[707] By 1969, as many as 4,000 applications for drilling rights had been filed with the regional government of Okinawa Prefecture, and by September 1970, the number of applications increased to 25,000.[708] After the discovery of oil, Japan started negotiating with the United States to reclaim its sovereign control over the islands, which had been under U.S. administration.[709] China and Taiwan, which had not shown much interest in the islands, also began to make territorial claims.[710] The Japanese government eventually decided to suspend the development of the oil deposits around the islands to avoid a potential conflict when China and Taiwan expressed territorial interests in the islands. Nevertheless, the enormous oil deposits—estimated at about 100 billion barrels (sufficient to provide Japan with energy sources for several decades)—renders it difficult for either Japan or China to relinquish its territorial claim to the islands.

The East China Sea has been a stage for the growing political tensions between China and Japan. China has been expanding its influence over the East China Sea with its naval power, and the areas surrounding the Senkaku Islands have become a contested space between China and Japan.[711] The two countries have additional disputes in the East China Sea, including over maritime boundaries and hydrocarbon resources.[712] In 2008, they agreed to facilitate joint exploration of hydrocarbon resources in the East China Sea, but the intensified dispute over the Senkaku Islands in 2010 put an end to that agreement.[713] The United States and Japan share common interests in keeping China in check in the South and East China Seas to protect vital sea lanes and contain China's expansion.[714] The presence of the dominant U.S. military forces may have contained tensions in the past,[715] but the region today shows different dynamics as China seeks to challenge U.S. dominance in the Asian-Pacific by increasing its naval presence in the South and East China Seas. As a part of the U.S. security apparatus in the Asia-Pacific, Japan has become increasingly inseparable from the U.S.-led military pressure against China. Japan has, in turn, faced political resistance from China, most recently through China's warning to Japan not to join forces with the United States in confronting China on disputes involving Taiwan.[716]

5.2.3 Territorial disputes with Russia

The treacherous Russo-Japanese relationship in the twentieth century affected power dynamics in Northeast Asia and shaped much of the political landscape throughout the region. Once a periphery nation located at the southeast end of Northeast Asia, Japan rose to the position of a regional hegemon through its military victory over Russia in 1905.[717] The outcome of that war changed power dynamics and territorial arrangements in Northeast Asia. Under the terms of the Treaty of Portsmouth, Russia recognized the Japanese sphere of influence over Korea and agreed not to "obstruct or interfere with measures for guidance, protection and control which the Imperial Government of Japan may find necessary to take in Korea."[718] As a result, Japan was able to annex Korea in 1910 without resistance from other powers in the region. Russia also agreed to evacuate Manchuria, which Russia had occupied, as well as to cede the southern half of Sakhalin Island to Japan.[719] That cessation of part of Sakhalin Island marked the beginning of territorial disputes between Russia and Japan.

Sakhalin Island is an island adjacent to the northeastern shores of Manchuria (Khabarovsk Krai) located between the East Sea (to the west) and the Sea of Okhotsk (to the east). The southern tip of the Island is only 40 kilometers north of Japan's most northern island, Hokkaido. It is a sizable island with an area of 72,500 square kilometers.[720] The island has substantial oil and gas deposits, coal mines, forests, and maritime resources such as fish and other seafood supplies around the coast.[721] China had limited control over the island since the Yuan Dynasty[722] until the Russians and Japanese reached the island and agreed to share control in 1855.[723] Continuous friction forced the Japanese to concede sovereignty over the island to Russia in 1875 in return for the Kuril Islands.[724] Since then, the Russo-Japanese strife over control of the island continued for decades. During the Russo-Japanese War, Japan occupied the entire Sakhalin Island but only annexed its southern half under the Treaty of Portsmouth.[725] Japan occupied again the entire island after the Russian Revolution but withdrew from the northern part of the island in 1925.[726] The Soviet Union invaded and occupied the southern half of the island toward the end of World War II.[727] The Russo-Japanese dispute over the island finally ended when Japan relinquished its territorial claim in the 1951 San Francisco Peace Treaty.[728]

The Russo-Japanese territorial dispute over Sakhalin Island may have ended in 1951, but another territorial dispute continues over the four southernmost Kuril Islands, namely Iturup (Etorofu), Kunashir, Shikotan, and Habomai, all of which are located off the northern shores of Hokkaido (see Figure 5.4).[729] Under the terms of the San Francisco Peace Treaty, Japan renounced all right, title, and claim to the Kuril Islands,[730] but it has been disputed whether these four islands were included in the Kuril Islands that Japan renounced. The Japanese government claims that these islands are distinct from the relinquished Kurils whereas Russia considers them to have been included.[731] The treaty itself does not adequately specify what is encompassed in the term Kuril Islands. The Soviet Union did not sign the San Francisco Peace Treaty, but the Soviets and Japanese signed, instead, a joint declaration in 1956, which failed to clarify which of them would have sovereign control over the disputed islands.[732] Since the end of World War II, the disputed four islands have been under Russia's administration.

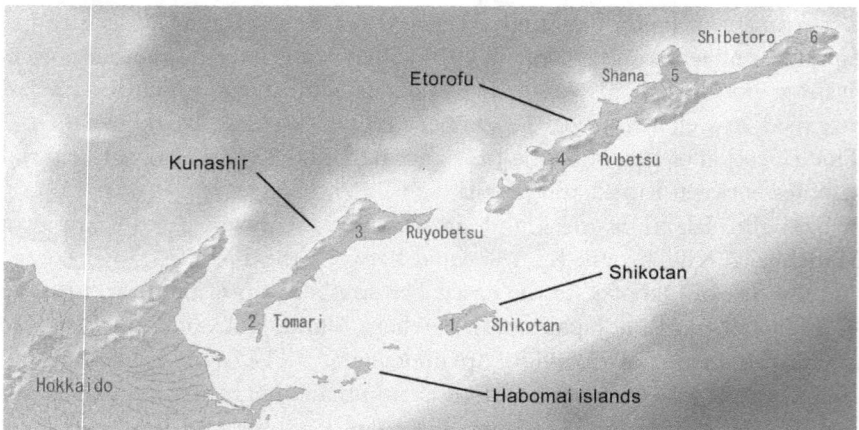

Figure 5.4 Location of the disputed Kuril Islands. (*Source*: Location of the Senkaku Islands, modified from https://en.wikipedia.org/wiki/Kuril_Islands_dispute#/media/File:Kuril-Islands-Northern-Territories-of-Japan-Map.png)

Russia has attempted to resolve the dispute by offering to return two disputed islands (Shikotan and the Habomais) in exchange for Japan's renouncement of the other two islands (Iturup and Kunashir), but Japan has not accepted this proposal.[733] Russia also allowed Japanese citizens to visit the Kuril Islands without a visa and Japanese fishermen to catch fish in Russia's claimed exclusive economic zone around the islands. However, these concessions have recently been withdrawn or suspended in response to Japan's participation in the international sanctions against Russia over the Ukraine War.[734] The state of the dispute also reflects a long-standing political divide in Northeast Asia. The United States supports Japan's claim to the four islands—the U.S. ambassador to Japan, Rahm Emanuel, has stated, "The United States supports Japan on the issue of the Northern Territories and has recognized Japanese sovereignty over the four disputed islands since the 1950s."[735] By contrast, China supports Russia's position, as demonstrated by China's joint naval drills with Russia near the disputed islands over Japanese protests.[736] The increasing rivalry between the United States and China, each supporting Japan and Russia in the dispute, is likely to exacerbate, rather than resolve, the problem.

The close proximity of the disputed islands to mainland Japan raises security concerns for Japan. According to a report, Russia has increased its military presence on the islands in recent years by placing military barracks, airstrips, surface-to-air missile batteries, and anti-ship missile battalions.[737] Some of these installations are located as close as 16 kilometers to Hokkaido, and the missile systems on the disputed islands have a range of hundreds of kilometers with the capacity to strike most ships coming into or sailing around Hokkaido.[738] In addition to these installations, Russia reportedly deployed an estimated 3,500 troops to the islands in 2018.[739] This dispute over the Kuril Islands and Russia's militarization presents a higher risk to Japan's security than the risks associated with Japan's territorial disputes with South Korea and China; the locations of the islands disputed with South Korea and China (the Dokdo Islands and the Senkaku Islands) are much further away from mainland Japan and thus do not raise as direct a security problem to Japan. In contrast, Russia's strategic military assets stationed in the disputed Kuril Islands pose a direct threat to Japan's security. This security risk, as well as the diplomatic impasse caused by the dispute—such as the failure to enter into a peace treaty with Russia for nearly eight decades after World War II—calls for a reevaluation of Japan's approach to the disputed islands, which is further discussed in the following section.

5.3 Toward Sustainable Peace: Call for Closure and a New Approach

5.3.1 The need for closure: Ending historical disputes

Japan's continuous historical disputes with South Korea and China are an unsettling factor in postwar Northeast Asia, creating a barrier to intraregional collaboration toward sustainable peace. As for its historical disputes with South Korea, Japan's position that its 1965 Treaty with South Korea conclusively settled all issues arising from Japan's colonial occupation is untenable for the following reason. The treaty may have foreclosed the South Korean government from making further demands for reparation to the Japanese government,[740] but it does not bar individual victims from doing so and certainly does not erase the painful memories that Koreans still harbor about the atrocities committed by Japanese authorities.[741] Although nearly eight decades have passed since the end of World War II, the Japanese government has not yet been successful in reconciling with its neighbors over historical disputes. On the contrary, high-level Japanese officials have at times made provocative comments justifying Japan's inhumane conduct during its colonial occupation of Korea.[742] These comments have typically been made for suspect domestic political reasons to mobilize right-wing support for the government. Unsurprisingly, these comments have exacerbated, rather than resolved, those disputes.[743]

Thus, it is necessary to bring closure to these disputes and open a passage for reconciliation to achieve sustainable peace in the region. This requires some common ground between Korea and Japan to understand the past. First, the process of Japan's forcible annexation of Korea in 1910 and the nature of Japan's colonial rule need to be clarified and understood by both governments. The postwar reconciliation of Europe has been made possible by Germany's clear condemnation of the Nazi regime and its unequivocal commitments to compensate for the harm that the Nazis inflicted on victims and prevent a recurrence.[744] Likewise, a similar level of commitment from Japan would be necessary to achieve reconciliation in Northeast Asia. Japan's annexation of Korea in 1910, which had been completed under duress of Japan's military presence, would be invalid under international law today.[745] Japan's forcible annexation of Korea remains a traumatic historical memory for Koreans who had never lost their national sovereignty until then. The Japanese government can begin to bring closure by admitting the coercive and illegitimate nature of Japan's annexation of Korea in 1910.

Next, to resolve the historical dispute, both governments must affirm the coercive nature of Japan's colonial rule of Korea. Although all colonial occupations during the nineteenth and twentieth centuries encompass an inherent degree of brutality, coercion, and exploitation,[746] Japan's colonial rule of Korea is different for the following reasons. First, while most other colonial powers ruled peoples outside their own cultural sphere, often located in different continents such as Africa, South Asia, and Latin America, Japan occupied and colonized Korea, which had existed alongside it as a neighboring state for two millennia and shared a long history of cultural, political, and economic exchanges. Because Koreans had long considered the Japanese to be cultural, political, and economic counterparts and neighbors, it was deeply troubling to see them suddenly emerge as colonial masters, which, in turn, created an unprecedented hierarchy between the two peoples.[747] Secondly, Japan, through its colonial rule, not only exploited the Koreans and their resources but also sought to eliminate their cultural and national identities to an extent not commonly observed by the colonial occupations of other powers. International relations scholars David Hundt and Roland Bleiker observed:

> The Japanese colonial administration tried everything possible to eradicate Korean identity-to the point that schools were not allowed to teach Korean history, culture, or language. Koreans were forced to adopt Japanese names and to worship at Shinto shrines, thus affirming their fealty to the Japanese emperor.[748]

There is an argument that Japan's colonial rule helped to develop Korea into a modern, capitalist nation by building infrastructure (*e.g.*, manufacturing facilities and railways), school systems, judicial courts, and modern central and local administrations.[749] While there may be some truth in this argument, it is clear that Japan's colonial buildup in Korea was primarily to exploit the nation for the benefit of the Japanese empire rather than the welfare of the Koreans.[750] Japan's exploitation of Korea climaxed during World War II when Japanese authorities forcibly recruited Korean laborers for Japanese war efforts, Korean soldiers for the Japanese military, and Korean women to serve Japanese soldiers sexually on war fronts.[751] The forcible recruitment of Korean women is an unprecedented crime against humanity, as confirmed by the Human Rights Commission of the United Nations, the United States State Department, and numerous other national and intergovernmental agencies around the world.[752] Even so, the Japanese government has been unwilling to admit these atrocities (aside from its more reconciliatory attitude in the 1990s).[753] Thus, it would not be possible to bring closure without a change of attitude and perception on the part of the Japanese government.

Japan's historical dispute with China has been continuous for several decades, forming a root of discontent between the two countries.[754] One of the most debated historical issues between China and Japan is the Nanjing Massacre, which occurred during the Second Sino-Japanese War. In 1937, Japanese forces occupied Nanjing, then the capital of China, and slaughtered between 260,000 and 350,000 Chinese civilians, in addition to raping between 20,000 and 80,000 Chinese women.[755] The Nanjing Massacre was an unprecedented wartime massacre in modern times, but some conservative Japanese politicians and scholars have denied or downplayed the existence of the massacre.[756] In a joint study by China and Japan in 2010, Japan admitted that the murder of non-combatant civilians in Nanjing was undeniable.[757] However, in 2015, the Japanese government submitted a statement of opinion to the United Nations Educational, Scientific and Cultural Organization (UNESCO), citing the views of individuals who were known to deny the occurrence of the massacre.[758] Although concern has arisen in Japan that such a statement might create the impression that the Japanese government supports the views of Nanjing Massacre denialists, this concern did not change the conduct of the Japanese government.[759]

The Japanese government has shown a similar attitude of denial toward Japan's other war crimes such as the comfort women issue discussed above.[760] The Japanese government has responded defensively to questions of its war crimes and the atrocities committed during its colonial rule, denying their occurrence altogether in some instances (such as denying evidence of the coercive recruitment of comfort women by Japanese authorities) and downplaying the extent of their harm in other instances (such as with statements suggesting the number of deaths during the Nanjing Massacre does not amount to 300,000). Whether such responses may have been the result of pressure from Japan's conservative factions (who deny the occurrence of the war crimes) or by its motivation to avoid international embarrassment and potential legal liabilities, Japan's response to the historical disputes with China and South Korea has not brought closure to these decades-long disputes. The continuation of these disputes does not serve Japan's security interests, which require reconciliation and cooperation with its neighboring countries, nor does it serve the region's interest in long-term stability. This impasse requires a paradigm change and a new approach on the part of Japan, which will be further discussed in the final subsection of this chapter.

5.3.2 Controversy over the proposed constitutional amendment

Another important issue that may redefine Japan's political and military role in Northeast Asia is the proposed amendment to the Japanese constitution. As discussed earlier, the Japanese constitution stipulates the renouncement of war and the threat or use of force to settle international disputes. Article 9 of the constitution reads:

Aspiring sincerely to an international peace based on justice and order, the Japanese people forever renounce war as a sovereign right of the nation and the threat or use of force as means of settling international disputes. In order to accomplish the aim of the preceding paragraph, land, sea, and air forces, as well as other war potential, will never be maintained. The right of belligerency of the state will not be recognized.[761]

Japan's conservative political factions have been discontent about Article 9 since its inception and have unsuccessfully sought to revise it.[762] The current security environment in Northeast Asia, which includes the rising nuclear threat from North Korea and intensifying military tensions with China, reinforces the view that Japan needs to play a more active military role in the region.[763] Japan's late prime minister Shinzo Abe echoed this view in a statement to the Japanese parliament in 2017, asserting "the security environment now surrounding Japan is the most severe in post-war history" and expressing his "firm conviction that . . . discussions on constitutional reform will be able to move forward."[764] In addition to the attempt to revise Article 9, efforts have also been made to reinterpret Article 9 to allow for "collective self-defense," a doctrine allowing for the protection of an ally in the event of an attack. The Japanese government formally adopted this reinterpretation in 2014.[765] In December 2022, the Japanese government also announced its decision to authorize strikes on enemy bases in the event of an attack on Japan or a friendly nation.[766] This new strategy is, arguably, a subversion of Article 9 prohibiting the use of force because it expands the parameters of Japan's self-defense beyond the constitutional limit.

Both China and South Korea have expressed concern about these developments.[767] Both nations, having experienced invasion and occupation by the Japanese imperialist state in the twentieth century, still harbor memories of Japan's invasion and view Japan's military expansion as concerning given its unapologetic attitude about its past aggression.[768] Despite these concerns, another full-scale Japanese invasion beyond a localized conflict is unlikely due to the current military readiness of both countries: China is currently ranked as the world's third strongest military and South Korea as the world's sixth.[769] The Japanese public seems to be divided on revising Article 9; according to a 2022 survey, 50 percent of the respondents supported revision while 48 percent did not.[770] Despite the long passage of time since the end of World War II, memories of the destruction of war and the massive loss of life are vivid among the Japanese.[771] Japan's conservative factions have been pushing for the revision of Article 9, hoping to transform Japan into a "normal" country (as opposed to a pacifist postwar country)[772] with a full right to engage in war if necessary. It is unclear whether the Japanese public will be ready to accept such a change in the foreseeable future, although a limited adjustment to Article 9, such as the clarification of the legal status of the SDF therein, might be possible.[773]

The United States, on the other hand, has been supportive of Japan's increased military role in Northeast Asia. The United States supports Japan's adoption of collective self-defense under Article 9 and has also recognized Japan's right to amend the article altogether.[774] For the United States, defending its allies in Northeast Asia and protecting its interests in the region against the rising military threats from China and North Korea requires significant financial expenditure and the substantial deployment of its military assets.[775] For these reasons, the United States has been demanding its allies increase their financial and military contributions.[776] From the U.S. perspective, Japan's adoption of collective self-defense or its renouncement of Article 9 would be a welcome event regardless of any concerns that it may raise with its ally, South Korea, or its adversary, China.[777] It would enable the Japanese government to increase its military contribution to defending the region against potential enemies. This U.S. position is expected to continue into the foreseeable future, as the United States does not perceive Japan's increased military capacity as a threat but as an asset for the United States–Japan alliance, which will advance U.S. interests in the region.

Amendment of Japan's constitution should be approached with caution. A commentator has opined that there are implicit limits on the amendment of the Japanese constitution and that Article 9 may be constructively unamendable.[778] Regardless of the constitutional debate, postwar Japan has prospered under the current constitutional arrangement, including the current version of Article 9. Additionally, the alliance with the United States has allowed Japan to focus on economic development and avoid potentially dangerous military engagements with other players in the region. However, the significant financial and military burden on the United States for the defense of its allies and its own interests in Northeast Asia, as well as the change of the security environment caused by the rise of China and the nuclear threat posed by North Korea, may necessitate Japan's increased role in defense of the region. Japan's military expansion has been met with significant concerns from the countries that experienced invasion and occupation by Japan during the last century, including China and South Korea. Their concerns are amplified by Japan's unapologetic attitude toward its past war crimes, and they are unlikely to welcome Japan's constitutional amendment unless they see a fundamental change in Japan's approach to these issues.[779]

5.3.3 Call for a new approach

Japan's current impasse on historical issues and its continuous tension with neighboring countries calls for a new approach. Germany's success with reconciliation offers a lesson. At the end of World War II, Germany was in a similar state as Japan: the country laid in ruins, with much of its infrastructure destroyed by the war and over seven million Germans dead.[780] Similarly, as Tokyo lost hundreds of thousands of civilian lives from aerial bombing, the population of Cologne dropped from 750,000 to just 32,000.[781] From the ashes of the war, both Germany and Japan successfully restored their economies; they had achieved unprecedented economic prosperity within their respective histories by the 1960s. In addition to this economic success, Germany has regained the trust and confidence of the neighboring European countries that it invaded during the war and has become a European leader and the lynchpin of the European Union (EU).[782] According to a report, Germany ranked first in a poll on international popularity, with 60 percent of the international community rating it positively.[783] Conversely, Japan has failed to gain a comparable degree of trust and confidence from its neighboring countries, likely an outcome of its continued dispute of historical issues, which have sustained intraregional tensions for decades.

These different outcomes derive from the differing approaches of the two countries. As former German chancellor Angela Merkel explained, Germany rehabilitated its international reputation following the war by reconciling with Nazi victims and acknowledging the atrocities her country had committed.[784] By contrast, Japan has been unwilling to admit to the atrocities it committed during World War II, as evidenced by its downplaying them (in the case of the Nanjing Massacre) and citing the lack of documentary evidence (in the case of the comfort women).[785] While the Japanese government remains unwilling to recognize its past war crimes and atrocities, revisionists supported by the Japanese right-wing factions have distorted this tragic part of history, further traumatizing the victims and their families. A notable example of this is the publicized argument of Harvard law professor John Ramseyer, who has published a provocative argument that the comfort women were prostitutes under contract and they had never been forcibly recruited or coerced into sexual servitude by Japanese authorities.[786] Thousands of scholars, including Nobel laureates, have protested against this distortion. Professor Alexis Dudden has pointed out that Ramseyer ignored the extensive literature by Japanese, Chinese, Korean, and Anglophone authors, as well as the documentary record detailing the Japanese military's wartime system of military sexual slavery.[787] Ramseyer's argument is flatly wrong, against the facts established by the thorough investigations of numerous national and international organizations, including the United Nations Human Rights Commission.[788] Japan's silence on the fallacy of his argument constituted a missed opportunity for the Japanese government to be forthright and truthful about its history; the German government would have condemned such a publicized falsehood and corrected it if it had denied controversial Nazi war crimes.[789]

Japan's unrepenting attitude has also affected reparations with the victims. Germany was proactive about the reparations issue. The German government reached out to Israel and made a reparations agreement on September 10, 1952, which was 13 years earlier than the agreement that Japan entered into with South Korea.[790] Despite Germany's first reparations payment to the Israeli state occurring in 1953 and its final payment in 1965, it continues to make payments to individuals to this day.[791] By the end of 2008, Germany had provided 66 billion Euros in all forms of compensation.[792] Japan's payments to its victims (termed payments because, unlike Germany, Japan has never used the term reparation) have been minuscule compared to Germany's. Japan paid the Korean government in Japanese yen equivalent of US$ 300 million in 1965, but it has long rejected claims from individual Korean and Chinese victims. The Japanese government still maintains that this compensation issue was settled by the 1965 Treaty on Basic Relations between South Korea and Japan and the Joint Communiqué of the Government of Japan and the Government of the People's Republic of China in 1972.[793] Because the Joint Communiqué waives Japan's war reparations, no payment in war reparations has been made to China. Equally concerning is Japan's lack of school education about the atrocities that Japan committed during World War II. Conversely, Germany educates future generations on its war crimes so that lessons from history will not be forgotten.[794] All of these factors affected the trust and confidence of Japan's neighboring countries in the postwar period.

A new approach, which may offer a solution to Japan's current impasse and help to gain trust from its neighboring countries, is found in the 1993 Kono Statement, a statement by Japan's Chief Cabinet Secretary Kono Yohei:

> We shall face squarely the historical facts as described above instead of evading them, and take them to heart as lessons of history. We hereby reiterate our firm determination never to repeat the same mistake by forever engraving such issues in our memories through the study and teaching of history.[795]

Ironically, Germany, not Japan, implemented the commitment stipulated in the Kono Statement and successfully gained the trust and confidence of its neighbors. This, in turn, elevated Germany's position from a country defeated in a war and accused of having committed atrocious war crimes to one of Europe's most influential leaders. As a country that possesses even greater economic resources than Germany, Japan has coveted such a position in Northeast Asia and beyond. Japan has "demonstrated that it has the determination, willingness and capacity to take on further responsibility as a permanent member in a reformed [U.N. Security] Council."[796] However, for over 10 years since its declaration, Japan has not been able to win this leader-ship position, due particularly to objections raised by China and South Korea over Japan's lack of repentance about its past war crimes.[797] Japan is unlikely to overcome such objections unless it gains the trust and confidence of its neighbors as Germany has done. This failure indicates that it would be in Japan's interest to reconsider its current approach to these disputes and adopt a new approach such as the one that Germany has successfully implemented.

Japan could also adopt a more flexible approach to territorial disputes with its neighboring countries. On the question of the Dokdo Islands, South Korea exercises complete territorial control over the islands, and Japan does not have a strong claim that will overcome South Korea's sovereign rights.[798] Regardless of the legal debate, it is unlikely that South Korea's possession of the Dokdo Islands will change in the foreseeable future. Japan's periodi-cal announcement of its claim to these islands has only provoked anti-Jap-anese sentiment among Koreans, as this claim reminds Koreans of Japan's aggression and occupation of Korea in the last century.[799] It will be advisable to reconsider the wisdom of its current policy to maintain its claim to the Dokdo Islands at the expense of reconciliation with South Korea. As for the Senkaku Islands, Japan has exercised territorial control. Even if Japan does not renounce its sovereignty over the islands, it can nevertheless entertain reconciliatory measures to alleviate tensions such as sharing the substantial energy and maritime resources in the adjacent areas, which is an important factor underlying the territorial dispute. Finally, concerning the disputed four Kuril Islands currently occupied by Russia, Russia has previously offered to concede two of the four disputed islands to Japan.[800] According to a report, 46 percent of Japanese citizens favor an initial return of the two islands.[801] Thus, acceptance of this proposal may initiate a settlement of the issue.

The above-proposed measures are not one-sided concessions that would be imposed upon Japan against its interests. On the contrary, the continuation of territorial disputes with its neighboring countries is not in the security interest of Japan, nor does it serve Japan's long-term political interest, particularly if Japan aspires to take a leadership role in the international community.[802] It would be reasonable to conclude that Germany would not be the European leader it is today if it had engaged in territorial disputes with its neighbors, such as Poland, France, and Austria, as Japan has for several decades. As long as Japan continues to assert its claim to the Dokdo Islands, Koreans who still remember Japan's aggression and occupation of the Korean peninsula will find it difficult to trust Japan. Japan's dispute over the Senkaku Islands with China remains an unsettling factor that adds instability to the East China Sea. Japan's dispute over the Kurils may induce Russia to increase its military presence on the islands (perhaps not immediately due to the war in Ukraine), which would be a direct security threat to mainland Japan.[803] Thus, it would be in Japan's interest to seek permanent solutions to these territorial disputes, such as the options discussed above.

Japan's reconciliation with its neighboring countries is important to sustain peace in Northeast Asia. These current historical and territorial disputes limit intraregional security collaborations and could also progress into localized conflicts although full-scale armed conflicts between Japan and these other countries remain unlikely. Japan may not have complete autonomy to determine its position on security issues due to its dependence on the United States–Japan alliance, but that does not mean that it should increase its vulnerability by aggravating other countries in the region through these continuous tensions. Japan's security interests would be reinforced by gaining the trust and confidence of other countries in the region. Japan's diminished political capital due to these disputes will only increase the country's dependency on its alliance with the United States, and it would be a step in the wrong direction away from being a "normal country" such as rehabilitated Germany, which is supported by the rest of Europe.

Chapter 6

INSIDERS FROM THE OUTSIDE: THE UNITED STATES AND RUSSIA

6.1 Historical Context: "Insiders from the Outside"

6.1.1 The emergence of the United States in Northeast Asia

The United States and Russia are "outsiders" in Northeast Asia because most or all of their territory is located outside the region. The United States holds no territory in Northeast Asia although it has Guam and the Saipan Islands in the Western Pacific. Russia has held territory along the eastern shores of Northeast Asia (Khabarovsk Krai and Primorsky Krai) and above the Amur River (Amur Oblast) since the late nineteenth century although most of its vast territory and population are located outside Northeast Asia. Yet, both are also "insiders" because they have exercised a massive influence in the region, particularly since the end of World War II, shaping the region's political and economic landscape. The United States and the Soviet Union, Imperial Russia's successor, became the two most important countries leading the capitalist free world and the communist bloc, respectively, and forming their own alliances in Northeast Asia. This chapter discusses these countries' engagements in Northeast Asia and their profound impact on war and conflicts in the region, beginning with the United States.

The United States, which was still in the process of its own national development throughout the nineteenth century, was a relative late-comer to Asia, initially focusing on missionary operations in China and elsewhere.[804] However, commercial interests drove the United States to follow the path of other European powers by seeking economic privileges from China.[805] The United States signed the Treaty of Wanghia with China in 1844 and secured concessions mirroring those gained by Britain through its treaty with China two years earlier (the Treaty of Nanjing). The treaty included the granting of extraterritoriality—the idea that foreigners operating in China would only be subject to the laws of their home countries.[806] It also stipulated fixed tariffs on trade, opened ports for American traders, and conferred rights to build churches and hospitals therein.[807] The United States also received most-favored-nation (MFN) status, which accorded the United States the same beneficial treatment China gave to other European powers.[808] Thus, the United States could reap the benefits of Europe's exploitation of China while still being seen as the least aggressive Western power. Because the United States did not take initiatives against China, Chinese officials viewed Americans as less of a threat.[809]

The United States may have followed other European powers in its engagement with China, but it took its own initiative with Japan. The United States successfully opened formal relations with Japan in 1854, on a mission led by Commodore Matthew C. Perry.[810] The United States adopted the same gunboat diplomacy as Britain. Perry used a show of naval force although it did not amount to a full-scale invasion, to pressure Japanese leaders into accepting U.S. demands for trade.[811] Japan subsequently opened ports for American traders and acknowledged U.S. jurisdiction over the prosecution of Americans in Japan,[812] following the patterns of similarly unequal treaties signed between China and the European powers in the nineteenth century. The United States also attempted to open Korea, which, like Japan, had maintained self-imposed isolation from Western powers before Perry's expedition. The U.S. expedition to Korea in 1871 did not achieve this goal, but a decade later, when Korea decided to open its economy to the West, the United States was the first Western country to sign a peace and commerce treaty with Korea.[813] The treaty with Korea included provisions granting MFN treatment to American traders, fixed tariffs, and extraterritoriality, just as its treaty with Japan, thereby protecting U.S. interests in Korea.[814]

The United States significantly increased its presence and influence in Northeast Asia throughout the nineteenth and early twentieth centuries. In the Russo-Japanese War (1904–1905), the United States mediated the Treaty of Portsmouth between Russia and Japan. Then U.S. President Theodore Roosevelt tried to prevent Germany and France from interfering with the war, signaling that the United States was no longer a minor power in Northeast Asia.[815] The United States maintained a friendly stance toward Japan—Roosevelt had notified Germany and France that he would support Japan promptly should these countries interfere.[816] The United States also supported Japan with its move to occupy Korea after the Russo-Japanese War, reneging on its prior commitment to Korea under its 1882 treaty with it.[817] The Taft-Katsura Agreement in 1905 between the United States and Japan approved the latter's occupation of Korea.[818] The United States did not realize that supporting Japan's occupation of Korea and its colonial expansion into Northeast Asia would eventually collide with U.S. interests in the region.

Japan's occupation of Manchuria in 1932 and its superior regional position raised concerns about potential adverse ramifications for U.S. trade and commercial interests.[819] The United States did not initially consider those interests vital enough to take action to deter Japan's aggression and risk its relationship with Japan.[820] This ambivalent attitude changed as the Sino-Japanese conflict deepened throughout the 1930s and 1940s. In 1940, the United States increased aid to China and restricted its supply of materials to Japan, including oil, steel, iron, and other commodities needed for Japanese war efforts.[821] Japan showed a hostile response by signing the Tripartite Pact with Germany and Italy in 1940. The two countries failed to reach a diplomatic solution, and the failure of negotiations meant that a war between them was imminent.[822] The war began in December 1941 when Japanese naval forces bombed the U.S. naval fleet at Pearl Harbor.[823] Japan was initially successful with its Pacific campaign, but its initial success could not be sustained due to its strategic errors, inferior production capacity, and weaker resources vis-à-vis the United States. When the United States prevailed in World War II after a complete victory over Japan in the Pacific, it emerged as a dominant power in Northeast Asia.

6.1.2 Russia's advance to Northeast Asia

The development of the Russian state in the late sixteenth century led to Russia's expansion into Siberia and Northeast Asia.[824] Russia initially expanded through conquering Siberia's indigenous population, and lucrative fur trade subsequently drove colonization of the eastern territory.[825] In the early 1600s, Russia sought to establish contacts with the Ming Dynasty to secure a market for Siberian furs in Beijing.[826] Russia encountered the Manchus (who would later found the Qing Dynasty) in the 1640s as the Russians expanded their colonization along the Amur River in Manchuria.[827] Low-level conflicts ensued between the Manchus and the Russian colonists in the Amur region, but the Russians established a channel for their fur trade with Beijing.[828] Those trade relations came under threat in the 1670s when local tribes in the Amur region began to choose sides between Russia and the rising Qing Empire, and border raids became common.[829] After negotiations, the Qing agreed on its northeastern border with Russia and codified it in the Treaty of Nerchinsk in 1689. By this treaty, the Qing Dynasty was successful in keeping the Russians out of the Amur region in exchange for trading rights.[830]

By the 1720s, Russia became an empire under the rule of Peter the Great and extended its territory to the Pacific Ocean. In 1727, the Russian Empire and the Qing Dynasty signed the Treaty of Kyakhta, clarifying the Qing's northwestern border with Russia and terms of their trade.[831] By that time, Russia had also found new economic resources in Siberia in addition to lucrative fur—large deposits of iron and other precious metals.[832] Russia increased mining in Siberia, eventually transforming itself from a net importer into Europe's largest iron exporter.[833] The conquest of Siberia and the advancement to the East had become an integral part of Russia's identity and national mission, as each was seen as cementing Russia's role as a powerful empire with a massive and rich territory.[834] With permanent territory in Siberia and the Far East, and substantial economic and political interests therein, Russia was no longer just a European power but a Euro-Pacific power. In line with this observation, historian Dr. Mikhail Nosov described Russia as an essentially bi-continental state, with at least 20 percent of its population comprised of Asians (compared to a little over 6 percent of the Asian population in the United States).[835]

In 1858, nearly 160 years after the Treaty of Nerchinsk, the Russian Empire again attempted to establish settlements in the Amur River region.[836] The Qing Dynasty had been weakened by its defeat in the Opium War against Britain (1839–1842) and was unable to defend its northeastern border. Russia took advantage of the weakened Qing and signed the Treaty of Aigun in 1858 and the Treaty of Beijing (or Convention of Peking) in 1860, giving Russia territorial control over large swaths of Manchuria. The treaty established the Amur River as the formal border between Russia and China, leaving substantial territory alongside the eastern shore of Manchuria and north of the Amur River (Khabarovsk Krai and Primorsky Krai) to Russia.[837] As a result, Russia could build a port open to the Pacific, Vladivostok, in its newly acquired territory. Russia did not stop with this territorial acquisition. In the 1890s, Russia began to expand further south into Manchuria, along with its development of the Chinese Eastern Railroad (CER), an extension of the Trans-Siberian railroad. Stations along the railway became hubs for Russian settlements, even when those stations were located in Chinese territory. Russia did not formally annex additional territory, but Russian policymakers saw the railroad as the centerpiece of a plan to spur Russia's industrial development and attract international capital, especially in Siberia's less economically-developed region.[838]

Russia's expansion into Manchuria was met with competition from Japan, which was also expanding into Manchuria from the south. Japan took control of the Liaodong Peninsula (located in the southwest corner of Manchuria) from China during the 1894 Sino-Japanese War. Concerned about Japan's expansion in the region, European powers—France, Germany, and Russia—pressured Japan to return the Liaodong Peninsula to China.[839] Russia was heavily involved in the negotiations, eventually leading to Japan's relinquishment of the peninsula. In 1897, Russia built the Port Arthur fortress in the Liaodong Peninsula and based its Pacific Fleet in the port.[840] It also built new cities such as Harbin.[841] Manchuria was increasingly under Russian influence although it was still formally Chinese territory. Russia also started to have considerable influence over Korea, in part because the Korean King exiled himself to the Russian legation in search of security from the Japanese forces stationed in Korea (following the tragic murder of the Korean Queen by the Japanese).[842] The rising tensions between Russia and Japan led to the outbreak of the Russo-Japanese War (1904–1905). The United States and Britain supported Japan. Despite expectations otherwise, Japan defeated Russia in the war. Following the war, Japan dominated southern Manchuria, including the Liaodong Peninsula.[843]

The outbreak of World War I and the subsequent Russian Revolution (1917–1923) plunged Russia into years of turmoil.[844] The Soviet Union, which succeeded Imperial Russia, regained control of its Far East territories, but Japan occupied all of Chinese Manchuria by 1932 (see Figure 6.1).[845] In 1939, the Soviet Union and Japan clashed in the battles of Khalkhin Gol on the

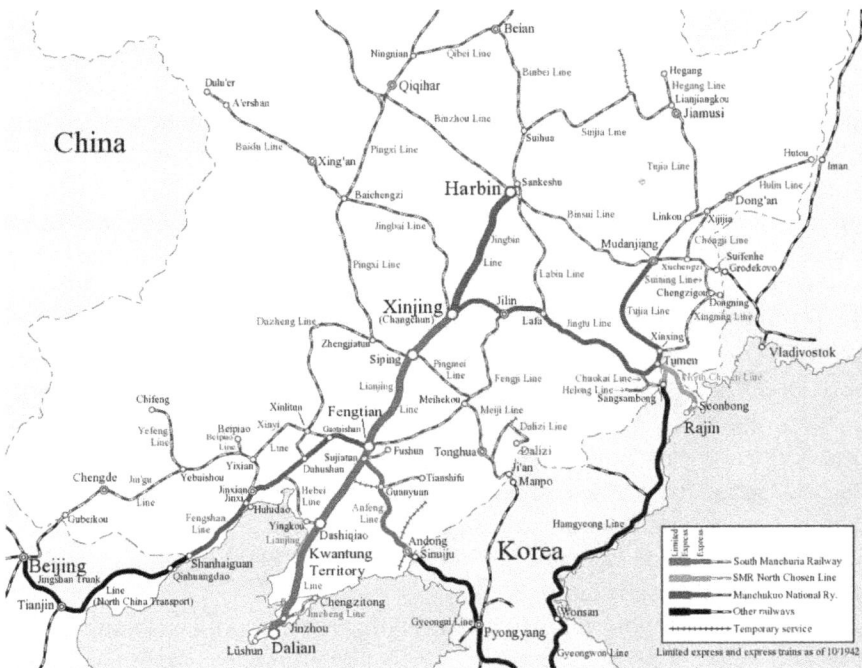

Figure 6.1 Map of Manchuria (1945). (*Source*: Manchukuo Rail Network, modified from https://commons.wikimedia.org/wiki/File:Manchukuo_Railmap_en.png#/media/File:Manchukuo_Railmap_en.png)

border between Mongolia and Manchuria. Soviet forces under the command of Georgy Zhukov decisively defeated Japanese forces, pushing the Japanese out of Mongolia.[846] Although the Soviet Union and Japan signed a neutrality pact in 1941,[847] just months before Japan attacked the U.S. naval fleet at Pearl Harbor, Soviet forces nevertheless attacked the weakened Japanese forces stationed in Manchuria in August 1945.[848] The depleted Japanese forces in Manchuria were no match for the more experienced, better-equipped Soviet forces. By the end of that month, Soviet forces occupied all of Manchuria, and the Japanese forces surrendered.[849] Soviet forces also entered the Korean peninsula and occupied the northern half of the peninsula by early September. Four decades after their defeat in the Russo-Japanese War, the Russians once again occupied all of Manchuria and beyond, which Imperial Russia had never done. After the war, the Soviet Union allowed the Chinese Communist Party to take over Manchuria, thereby assisting the latter in the Chinese Civil War (1946–1949).

6.1.3 United States and Russia: From outsiders to insiders

By the end of World War II, the United States and the Soviet Union had become the most powerful forces in Northeast Asia. The United States occupied war-defeated Japan and the southern half of the Korean peninsula (below the 38th parallel), which was to become South Korea (Republic of Korea) in 1948.[850] Soviet forces eliminated the weakened Japanese forces stationed in Manchuria within a few weeks in August 1945 and occupied all of Manchuria and the northern part of the Korean peninsula, which would become North Korea (People's Democratic Republic of Korea).[851] A century before, both countries had been relatively minor powers in the region, merely following the precedents of other European powers (in the case of the United States) and trying to negotiate with still powerful China (in the case of Russia)—until its defeat by the British. These two nations mostly remained "outsiders" in the mid-nineteenth century, with a limited role in the region, although their influence grew during the second half of the nineteenth century. In the postwar period, the United States and the Soviet Union supplanted the role of their older European counterparts—they did not only occupy Northeast Asia but also became the region's "insiders," shaping Northeast Asia's political, military, and economic landscape.

The United States became the architect of postwar South Korea and Japan. The U.S. military set up a government in South Korea, a nation newly liberated from Japanese colonial rule in 1945, and governed there until 1948.[852] The SCAP governed Japan indirectly until 1952.[853] In postwar South Korea and Japan, U.S. political influence was profound; both countries adopted liberal democracies based on free elections, civil liberties, and the rule of law with an independent judiciary—all key tenets of U.S. democracy. Political developments in postwar South Korea and Japan included changes to the Japanese constitution, which stripped political power from the Japanese emperor and renounced war, as well as the election of Dr. Rhee Seung-Man, who was educated in the United States and supported by the U.S. military government, as the first South Korean president. These political developments meant the birth of two pro-American, democratic states in Northeast Asia, demonstrating the strong political influence of the United States.

On the economic front, South Korea and Japan adopted capitalist market economies, with only supplementary roles for their governments. The United States supported the economic recovery of Japan and South Korea after World War II and the Korean War, respectively, and their continued economic development. The United States provided both economies with access to its vast domestic market—the largest export market in the world—which was essential to the economic development of both countries that adopted export-driven economic development policies.[854] In addition to its market, the United States supplied technology and capital investments for producers and entrepreneurs in both countries.[855] The United States has maintained strong economic influence in the region. For example, Northeast Asian countries affected by the 1997 Asian financial crisis, such as South Korea, adopted measures to overcome the crisis in close consultation with the United States. The United States has a crucial influence on international organizations, such as the IMF, that addressed the crisis.[856]

The United States also designed and operated the security apparatus in Northeast Asia.[857] U.S. participation in the Korean War deterred China-supported North Korea from uniting the Korean peninsula under communist rule, changing the political and security landscape in the Korean peninsula permanently. The United States, under the terms of its military alliance with South Korea, guaranteed South Korea's security by stationing battle-ready forces in South Korea for several decades.[858] The United States has also maintained military forces in Japan, forming a strong military bloc against North Korea and its allies (China and Russia). In the 1970s, however, the United States made an important shift in its approach to the region, primarily driven by the Vietnam War. It reinforced diplomatic influence over China and reduced the potential for another costly war. In February 1972, U.S. President Richard Nixon made a historic visit to China, which led to the normalization of the Sino-American relationship by 1979.[859] The United States also assisted China with its economic development efforts, initiated by its economic reform in 1978.[860] The United States admitted large quantities of Chinese exports into the U.S. market (just as it did for South Korean and

Japanese exporters), provided capital investments, and allowed technology transfers.[361]

Russia became another regional "insider." After it acquired the Far East territory in the nineteenth century, Russia became a permanent fixture in Northeast Asia's political and military landscape. Russia had a profound influence over other Northeast Asian countries, particularly through the spread of communism.[362] The Russians were closely involved in the development of the communist regime in China.[363] The Russians also supported the establishment of the Mongolian government in the 1920s and ensured that China recognized its independence.[364] After World War II, Soviet forces occupied the northern half of the Korean peninsula and facilitated the establishment of the communist government in North Korea.[365] The Soviets also supported North Korea in its invasion of South Korea to unite the Korean peninsula under communist rule although Soviet forces did not formally participate in the war.[366] In the postwar period, the Soviet ideology (communism), bureaucracy, technology, and industrial methodology continued to influence the political, economic, and industrial development of other communist countries in the region, including China, North Korea, and Mongolia.[367]

Russia had become an important player and influential insider in Northeast Asia at the end of World War II, but its regional leadership started to decline in the 1960s. Rising nationalism in China began to deter unquestioned acceptance of Russian leadership. It was of little consequence that Russia had sent thousands of engineers and laborers, as well as massive quantities of machinery and tools, to build a network of modern industrial plants across China in the 1950s.[368] Mao Zedong's 1958 statement reflects this sentiment—China would learn from the Soviet experience but take a selective approach to applying its experience.[369] In the fall of 1959, Mao denounced Russian leadership by stating that "it was intolerable to allow foreign Communist parties to meddle in Chinese Communist Party affairs."[370] Mao also became increasingly dissatisfied with the policies of Nikita Khrushchev, the Soviet Premier, such as reducing aid to China and promoting détente with the United States.[371] Mao distrusted Khrushchev for adopting what he considered a revisionist approach not strictly adhering to the Marxist-Lenin tradition.[372] Tensions between Russia and China culminated in an armed border conflict in 1969, demonstrating a major rift in their communist alliance.[373] After Mao's death, the ideological rivalry between the two countries, which was the primary source of tension, disappeared, and both governments adopted a more reconciliatory approach, which remains today.[374] In 2003, Russia was invited to participate in the Six Party Talks (which included South and North Korea, the United States, China, and Japan) to resolve North Korea's nuclear crisis. The Russian participation demonstrates its continuing position as a regional insider.[375]

6.2 Continued Engagement: Sustained Economic, Political, and Military Presence

6.2.1 The United States as a leading power in the region

Nearly eight decades after the end of World War II, the United States remains a leading power in Northeast Asia, with profound political and economic influence over the region.[876] In the 1950s, the United States signed bilateral defense treaties with South Korea and Japan, providing security guarantees for both countries.[877] With bilateral military alliances with the United States in place, the South Korean and Japanese governments developed their defense policies and strategies in conjunction with U.S. defense policies.[878] The U.S. military presence in Northeast Asia has affected not only the defense policies of South Korea and Japan but has also led to military buildups in North Korea, China, and Russia. The massive superiority of U.S. military forces (and later South Korean forces) has influenced North Korea's nuclear buildup.[879] China has also reinforced its military power in recent decades in preparation for potential conflicts with U.S. forces.[880] Russia has also sought to increase its military assets in Northeast Asia.[881]

The United States has a massive military outlay in Northeast Asia. It maintains 53,000 troops in Japan and 26,000 troops in South Korea.[882] The U.S. 7th Fleet, which operates in the Western Pacific, is the largest of the U.S. Navy's forward-deployed fleets under the command of the U.S. Pacific Fleet.[883] The 7th Fleet has long maintained naval dominance in the region,[884] deploying 50 to 70 ships and submarines, 2 aircraft carriers, 150 aircraft, and over 27,000 sailors and marines.[885] At times of crisis, the 7th Fleet joins forces with the Japanese Maritime Self-Defense Force and the South Korean Navy. The entire U.S. Pacific Fleet, consisting of approximately 200 ships, including 5 aircraft carrier strike groups, 1,100 aircraft, and 2 Marine Expeditionary Forces (including 86,000 personnel and 640 aircraft), supports U.S. forces stationed in Northeast Asia.[886] In addition, the U.S. Pacific Air Forces, comprising 46,000 airmen and more than 420 aircraft, will also provide operational support.[887] Although the United States has not maintained a nuclear arsenal in Northeast Asia since the 1990s, the U.S. government has clarified that it is willing to use its arsenal if its allies in the region were threatened by nuclear weapons.[888]

The United States also exerts strong political influence in Northeast Asia. The United States had a profound influence on the governments in postwar South Korea and Japan—both countries adopted American-style liberal democracies based on free elections and the rule of law. U.S. political influence has continued over the years.[889] For example, the United States pressured South Korea's authoritarian regimes in the 1970s and the 1980s to return to democracy.[890] It also demanded Japan pay forward some of the U.S. aid it received by increasing its own aid to other East Asian countries, including South Korea.[891] Japan's payment to South Korea, in turn, helped to normalize relationships between the two countries—South Korea and Japan did not have formal diplomatic relations for nearly two decades after World War II.[892] China's rising influence since the 1980s and the growing nationalism in South Korea and Japan have prevented the United States from attaining full political control in the region. Nevertheless, the United States has recently demonstrated its continuing political influence by initiating the Chip 4 Alliance against China with South Korea (preliminarily) and Japan.[893]

The United States has extended its political influence beyond South Korea and Japan by spreading its political ideals. Since the United States formalized its diplomatic relationship with China in the 1970s, the ideals of American democracy have influenced students and intellectuals in China. Tens of thousands of Chinese students, researchers, and scholars have visited the United States annually, been exposed to American values, and returned to China. This influence culminated in the student demands during the 1989 Tiananmen Square protests. Protestors demanded greater government accountability, constitutional due process, democratic reform, freedom of speech, and freedom of the press—all essential tenets of American democracy.[894] Although the Chinese government and military crushed the protests, leaving hundreds of casualties, American political values continue to influence China, particularly in Hong Kong where protests against the Chinese Communist Party and pro-democracy movements have taken place in recent years.[895] In the recent protests against China's zero-coronavirus policy, some demonstrators have also demanded a free election, which may have been inspired by American democracy.[896]

The United States is also a leading economic power in the region. The United States has provided its consumer market, technology, and investments for South Korea, Japan, and China throughout the periods of their economic development.[897] These countries have also relied on U.S. technologies, materials, and equipment to produce their key products, such as semiconductors (although they have also developed their own technologies and equipment).[898] The United States is also among the largest investors in the region, providing hundreds of billions of capital stock in U.S. dollars for businesses and industries in Northeast Asia.[899] In addition to capital investment, U.S. economic influence stems from its power to set regulatory terms for trade and investment. For example, the 1985 Plaza accord initiated by the United States caused the appreciation of the Japanese yen and reduced Japanese exports (which were perceived as a threat to U.S. economic interests).[900] The United States—Korea FTA—which the United States negotiated to change South Korea's regulatory systems and practices to create "an optimal business environment" for U.S. export industries—has increased U.S. exports to South Korea.[901] As discussed in the following subsection, the United States has significant economic and trade interests in Northeast Asia, and its regional economic influence is expected to continue.

6.2.2 U.S. economic and trade interests in Northeast Asia

Economic indicators demonstrate the strong economic and trade interests that the United States has in Northeast Asia. Half of the top six traders with the United States—China, Japan, and South Korea—are in Northeast Asia, collectively representing 21 percent of U.S. trade in goods.[902] Only two countries in North America (Canada and Mexico) and one in Europe (Germany) are in this group.[903] As of September 2022, the United States imported more goods from China (US$ 418 billion) than any other country despite its recent trade disputes with China.[904] China, Japan, and South Korea are also among the top seven export markets for the United States. Once a major destination of U.S. aid, Northeast Asia has become one of the most important regions for the United States' economic and trade interests. The Obama administration's "Pivot to East Asia" regional strategy in 2011[905] and its signing of the Trans-Pacific Partnership Agreement in 2016[906] signified the region's importance for U.S. interests.

Economic engagement with China, including trade expansion, has been at the core of the U.S. economic and trade interests in the region. The United States approved China's entry into the WTO in 2001. Since then, China has rapidly increased its trade and grown its economy. As Assistant Secretary of State for East Asian and Pacific Affairs David R. Stilwell recalled, the United States wanted an economically stronger China (to keep Russia in check) and was supportive of China's economic growth beginning in the 1980s.[907] Although increasing industrial competition from China has created some friction, causing trade disputes at times, the United States maintained a collaborative attitude toward China for decades.[908] However, this stance changed with the Trump administration in 2017. Donald Trump believed U.S. interests were not best secured by collaborative engagement with trade partners, including China. Instead, Trump thought it best for the United States to assert its own interests exclusive of the interests of its trade partners and extract concessions.[909] Accordingly, Trump adopted unilateral measures, such as the large tariffs imposed on a broad range of imports from China, at the risk of confrontation and disputes.[910]

Distrustful of cooperative trade engagement, the Trump administration withdrew from the TPP, which previous U.S. administrations had worked for years to conclude.[911] The Trump administration also targeted China by imposing unprecedented tariffs (as high as 25 percent) on hundreds of products imported from China.[912] The U.S. government cited China's unfair practices regarding IPRs as the grounds for the tariffs.[913] According to the United States, it voiced concerns on IPR issues repeatedly to China, but it was unwilling to offer meaningful modifications to its unfair practices.[914] Its industrial initiative, the Made in China 2025 Plan, announced China's aim for dominance in strategic industries, which the United States considered to be a challenge to its global position in industry and trade.[915] Unlike his predecessors, China's current leader Xi Jinping has adopted more aggressive, expansionary policies to achieve the "Chinese Dream," which he described as "the great rejuvenation of the Chinese nation."[916] For China, the era of "peaceful rise"[917] seems to have ended. In response, the United States has banned major Chinese IT companies, including Huawei, from operating in the United States, citing security reasons.[918] The ban signifies its strong reservations about China's economic ambitions, which are deemed adverse to the United States' economic and trade interests. The ban is perhaps symbolic of the end of the economic détente between the United States and China.

The United States seems to have reset the parameters of its economic and trade interests by excluding China, at least from strategic areas such as information technology and semiconductors. The Biden administration vowed to reverse the course (unilateral policies) adopted by the Trump administration but has yet to repeal the tariffs on China, although the WTO dispute settlement panel found those tariffs to be inconsistent with the rules of international trade law.[919] The United States discounted the panel decision, pointing out that it was not a final decision from the WTO Appellate Body (which has been made unfunctional because the United States blocked all of its new appointments).[920] The United States has clarified its intention to exclude China in the IT sector; after banning Huawei and China Telecom from operating in the United States, President Biden signed the Security Equipment Act in November 2021, which prohibited Huawei, ZTE, and other companies considered to be a national security threat to the United States from obtaining licenses for network equipment.[921]

The U.S. exclusion of China also applies to semiconductor supplies. Through the proposed Chip 4 Alliance, the Biden administration, in cooperation with the other major semiconductor supplying countries (South Korea, Japan, and Taiwan), seeks to secure semiconductors essential for U.S. industries to the exclusion of China.[922] The U.S. policy moves beyond securing non-Chinese semiconductor supplies. The policy also aims to deter China's development of advanced semiconductors—to meet this policy objective, the United States has placed export controls on semiconductor technology to China.[923] The United States also endeavors to limit the global availability of semiconductor producing equipment to China and pressured Japan and the Netherlands, major suppliers of advanced semiconductor producing equipment, to limit their equipment exports to China.[924] The U.S. policy also aims to influence investment for semiconductor production in China—semiconductor producers in the United States receiving subsidies from the U.S. government may not increase their investment for semiconductor production in China.[925]

Observers have expressed doubts that the United States can successfully safeguard its economic and trade interests by suppressing China's industrial expansion. For example, the Chip 4 Alliance, which is intended to exclude China from the semiconductor supply chain, may cover all of the major areas of the value chain, but China remains the biggest market for the alliance's participants, including South Korea, which may deter their full participation in the alliance.[926] An attempt to exclude China from the industry may also hurt U.S. firms. China imports US$ 350 billion worth of semiconductors annually, and U.S. semiconductor producers are a major supplier. This means that China may retaliate against U.S. firms for its exclusion.[927] Concerns have also arisen about the exclusion of Chinese IT companies. As a result of their exclusion, consumers will have to use more costly, inferior equipment and services, incurring losses.[928] Despite these concerns, the United States perceives China's dominance in strategic industrial areas as a long-term threat to its economic and military position; thus, the United States is unlikely to withdraw its containment policies against China, notwithstanding the risk of losses cited above.

6.2.3 *Russia's presence in Northeast Asia*

The dissolution of the Soviet Union and the communist bloc in the 1990s weakened Russia's global and regional position in Northeast Asia. The Russian economy experienced a downturn resulting from the economic turmoil associated with the dissolution of the Soviet Union.[929] Its military was also reduced.[930] However, despite its weakened position, Russia has remained a relevant player in the region as China and others have sought to build partnerships with Russia to maintain stability in Russia and (in the case of China) use Russia to counter the United States.[931] Russia and China found mutual interests in cooperation when the United States became the only superpower in the post-Soviet world. Throughout the 1990s, Sino-Russian cooperation continued to develop, with Jiang Zemin and Boris Yeltsin signing a strategic partnership in 1996 to balance against the hegemonic influence of the United States.[932] Russia also assisted China with its military buildup, resulting in a substantial increase in Russian arms sales to China in the 1990s.[933]

However, the weakening of post-Soviet Russia and China's economic and military rise meant that the power dynamic between the two countries changed in the 1990s. In the Soviet era, Russia maintained economic superiority over China. In 1988, China's GDP (US$ 312.3 billion) was only 56 percent of that of the Russian Federation (US$ 554.7 billion); however, their relative positions had reversed: by 1999, China's GDP (US$ 1.09 trillion) was over five times that of Russia's (US$ 195.9 billion).[934] As of 2021, the gap between the two countries' economies had further grown tenfold (US$ 17.73 trillion for China and US$ 1.78 trillion for Russia).[935] Due to the widening gap, Russia has become wary of its dependence on China as a regional partner and has sought to deepen its relationships with other countries in the region. For example, while cooperating with China, Russia also accepted assistance from the United States, which allocated approximately US$ 1.63 billion to Russia for the fiscal year 1994.[936] Russia has also sought to develop its diplomatic relationship with Japan, but those efforts have been largely stymied by long-standing territorial disputes over the Kuril Islands, a remnant of the Russo-Japanese imperial competition nearly a century earlier.[937]

Russia has also renewed its engagement with the Korean peninsula. Russia revised its diplomatic relationship with North Korea and eliminated its prior mutual defense obligations during the Soviet era.[938] Russia has tried to bolster its relationship with South Korea. South Korea provided Russia with loans to assist with its economic issues, and Russia repaid part of the loans by offering advanced Russian military equipment and technology to South Korea.[939] Russia's continued presence in Northeast Asia was highlighted by its participation in the Six Party Talks to resolve the North Korean nuclear issue. Russia was initially excluded from the multilateral negotiations regarding North Korea's nuclear weapons program, but it successfully inserted itself into the negotiations.[940] Russia (and China) has taken a different tone from that of the United States, South Korea, and Japan on the North Korean nuclear issue. While the latter group of countries demands the complete denuclearization of North Korea, Russia has pursued a resolution that will not only denuclearize North Korea but also strengthen regional security that will ensure the preservation of the North Korean regime.[941]

Russian presence in Northeast Asia entered a new era as Russia gradually recovered economically under President Vladimir Putin.[942] With its economic recovery, Russia regained geopolitical confidence, and Putin repeatedly emphasized the importance of retaining Russia's strategic position in Northeast Asia, including Moscow's ability to influence the terms of regional security.[943] The West has not welcomed Putin's expansionary ambition, as vividly demonstrated by Russia's annexation of the Crimean peninsula in 2014. The West responded to Russia's aggression by imposing economic sanctions on Russia (although their effectiveness has been questioned).[944] In response, Russia expanded its military cooperation with China, which had also been under increasing pressure from the West.[945] Russia has also renewed its economic interests in Northeast Asia. Russian territory in Northeast Asia has large deposits of oil, gas, and other minerals—all resources that Northeast Asian countries, such as South Korea and Japan, can utilize. Putin called for "a new generation of pioneers to revive the country's eastern frontier," emphasizing the importance of the development of Russia's Far East region.[946] However, the prospect of success is unclear. Economic cooperation with South Korea and Japan in the region is limited, particularly after these two countries joined the West-led economic sanctions against Russia for its invasion of Ukraine in February 2022.[947]

Russia's continued presence in Northeast Asia in the post-Soviet era has several geopolitical implications. First, Russia, with reduced economic and military power, is unlikely to retain the level of political, military, and economic influence in the region once held by the Soviet Union. Its regional influence may not be comparable to that of the United States and rising China. Russia has maintained a substantial military presence in the region, which has made Russia still relevant to regional security, but it remains to be seen whether Russia can maintain the level of its military presence after the Ukraine War. Second, Russia's continued diplomatic engagement has shown that it is still a viable player in the region's political sphere; for example, its participation in the Six Party Talks has supported North Korea's position that the purpose of its nuclear program is the protection of its own security.[948] This support, in turn, has solidified a standoff between the United States, South Korea, and Japan that push for the complete denuclearization of North Korea, and China, North Korea, and Russia that advocate for a gradual, quid-pro-quo type approach.[949] Third, Russia's interests in the economic development of its Far East territory, which requires assistance and cooperation from adjacent countries such as South Korea and Japan, might help to resolve the standoff between the two groups of countries, at least in the long term, although the present sanctions against Russia do not render such cooperation feasible in the near future.

6.3 Roles for the Future

6.3.1 United States: Restoring confidence in the region

The United States has traditionally promoted its economic and security interests in Northeast Asia in collaboration with its regional allies—South Korea and Japan.[950] The United States has also maintained a cooperative relationship with China and post-Soviet Russia, despite trade disputes and political tensions in recent decades.[951] However, this traditional approach changed with the Trump administration (2017–2021), which distrusted the traditional multilateral approach of prior administrations; it instead declared and pushed U.S. interests unilaterally over its allies' positions and interests without consultation and collaboration.[952] The Trump administration did not take a particularly confrontational stance toward Russia, but the administration targeted China through restrictive trade measures, including its most extensive tariffs in recent history.[953] The Trump administration continued these unilateralist policies, including withdrawal from the TPP, which previous U.S. administration negotiated with 11 other countries (Australia, Brunei, Canada, Chile, Japan, Malaysia, Mexico, New Zealand, Peru, Singapore, and Vietnam) and concluded after decades of work.[954] Although the Trump administration came to an end when Trump was defeated in the 2020 presidential election, its unilateralist policies substantially undermined U.S. global and regional leadership, and some of the policies are still in place today.[955]

For regional stability, it will be important for the United States to adjust its unilateralist policies still lingering from the Trump administration. As cited above, U.S. withdrawal from the TPP has raised questions about its credibility and leadership. The negotiated TPP provisions, such as strengthened IPR provisions, were highly favorable to the United States in terms of regulatory preferences.[956] With U.S. participation, the TPP also would have been the world's largest trade agreement, covering nearly 40 percent of the global economy.[957] The Biden administration, which vowed to reverse Trump's unilateralist policies, has not rejoined the TPP—evidencing a failure to overcome the trade protectionism reinforced during the Trump era. In the meantime, another group of Asian-Pacific countries, including China, South Korea, Japan, Australia, New Zealand, Brunei, Cambodia, Laos, Singapore, Thailand, and Vietnam, formed the Regional Comprehensive Economic Partnership (RCEP) Agreement in 2020.[958] China, a major RCEP participant, has formally submitted a request to accede to the Comprehensive and Progressive Agreement for Trans-Pacific Partnership Agreement (CPTPP),[959] which succeeded the TPP after U.S. withdrawal. The United States does not participate in either of these two most important trade agreements, weakening the U.S. trade and economic position in the region.

The U.S. position in international trade is essential for Northeast Asia because the U.S. allies in the region, South Korea and Japan, are major trading nations whose economies are substantially affected by trade. International trade is also vital to China, Mongolia (for mineral exports), and Russia (for oil and gas exports); thus, the stability of international trade in the region will influence the region's overall economic stability. However, the recent U.S. position in international trade has not gained regional confidence. For example, the United States has been blocking appointments to the WTO Appellate Body since 2016, rendering it inoperable due to a lack of quorum.[960] The United States may have decided to block the Appellate Body due to its continuing losses in trade disputes and other systemic concerns.[961] Regardless, such an intrusion of an international dispute settlement mechanism is contrary to the values which the United States advocates—the rule of law and an independent judiciary.

Moreover, such U.S. conduct is not conducive to regional economic stability. The Biden administration has yet to remove the controversial tariffs the Trump administration placed on China, despite the WTO dispute settlement panel decision that the tariffs are inconsistent with international trade law.[962] The Biden administration has also left in place the extensive tariffs that the Trump administration imposed on a broad range of steel and aluminum products (in addition to the tariffs imposed on China), whose compliance with international trade law is also questionable.[963] The Trump and Biden administrations replaced the steel and aluminum tariffs with export quotas for certain countries, but this also violates the rules of international trade law, which prohibit "gray-area measures" limiting the amount of exports by agreement.[964] As former United States Trade Representative Katherine Tai stated, the tariffs on Chinese goods might be "a significant piece of leverage" in the United States–China trade relationship.[965] But the administration's failure to remove the rule-breaching tariffs will have a longer-term adverse effect on global and regional confidence in the United States.

The United States also engaged in acts perceived as weakening its commitment to the security of its allies, including those in Northeast Asia. Former President Trump considered the U.S. security arrangements with its allies, including South Korea and Japan, to be costly endeavors that did not benefit the United States to a corresponding degree. This perception led Trump to make inappropriate financial demands on the U.S.' allies. For example, Trump reportedly demanded a *fivefold increase* in the amount South Korea contributes toward the cost of stationing U.S. forces in Korea.[966] Trump's lack of appreciation for the collective defense strategy utilized by the United States for several decades weakened the U.S. allies' confidence in its security commitments.[967] This weakened confidence may lead to regional instability—South Korea and Japan possess substantial nuclear capabilities, evidenced by extensive nuclear power plants in both countries and large quantities of plutonium that these countries already have or can extract.[968] They can develop their own nuclear weapons should the United States withdraw or substantially weaken its security commitments to them, which would be against the U.S. interests (and the region's) in the nonproliferation of nuclear weapons.[969]

The Biden administration has taken steps to restore its allies' confidence in U.S. security commitments, for instance, by resuming extensive military exercises with its allies,[970] which the Trump administration had avoided due to cost concerns. The National Security Strategy, released by the Biden administration, reaffirms the U.S. commitment to its military alliances in the region—notably to South Korea and Japan.[971] Arising under another U.S. initiative is the promotion of economic security, which means securing supplies of essential items for the economy, such as semiconductors. The Chip 4 Alliance is an important part of the U.S. endeavor although it is not clear, as discussed above, whether the exclusion of China from the semiconductor supply chain will be feasible or serve the interests of the U.S. trade partners in the region such as South Korea.[972] In May 2022, the Biden administration also launched a broader economic initiative: the "Indo-Pacific Economic Framework for Prosperity" (IPEF) with several other Asian-Pacific countries.[973] IPEF negotiations are focused on four "pillars": (1) trade; (2) supply chains; (3) clean energy, decarbonization, and infrastructure; and (4) tax and anti-corruption, but it is not clear whether the IPEF, which covers an extensive agenda, will generate any tangible benefits to its participants and restore the U.S. credibility in regional trade.[974]

6.3.2 *A moderating force*

In the postwar era, the United States successfully facilitated stability in Europe and Northeast Asia by supporting both its wartime allies and former enemies (Germany, Japan, and Italy) with their efforts to rebuild their destroyed countries and economies. This approach has set the United States apart from other hegemons in history. Instead of exploiting war-defeated countries or demanding large amounts of war reparations, as Britain and France did to a defeated Germany after World War I, the United States provided massive amounts of aid to war-destroyed European and Asian countries, including its former enemies. For example, under the Marshall Plan, U.S. Congress appropriated US$ 13.3 billion for the European recovery.[975] The United States was economically able to provide such support, unlike Britain and France after World War I, and the Marshall Plan was also motivated, at least in part, to secure markets for U.S. products.[976] However, regardless of self-interests, its reconciliatory postwar policies contributed to the recovery and postwar stabilization of Europe and Asia. Such a policy stance has continued—the United States also supported socialist China with its efforts for economic development by opening its market to Chinese exports.[977] The United States also provided aid to post-Soviet Russia. The United States is a superpower that competed and eventually defeated the communist bloc. Yet, it has also been a moderating force that supported its former enemies as well as its allies, promoting paths toward reconciliation.

The United States, as a moderating power, could continue to contribute to stability and peace in Northeast Asia. Unfortunately, the change in economic and military dynamics in the region, primarily associated with the rise of China, has led to a shift in U.S. policies. Donald Trump, who had been skeptical about the traditional U.S. role in international economy and politics, accelerated this shift and asserted U.S. interests over the interests of others, essentially ignoring the U.S. role as a moderating power.[978] Setting aside Trump's unilateralist preferences, China's rise does create considerable challenges to the United States in maintaining its moderating role in Northeast Asia and elsewhere. China's actions in Xinjiang and Hong Kong have vividly demonstrated that it does not respect civil freedom, which is a core value for Americans. China's repressive conduct creates considerable political difficulty for U.S. administrations to maintain a cooperative relationship with China over popular disapproval—according to a report, 82 percent of Americans expressed an unfavorable opinion of China.[979] China's state-supported industrial drive (*e.g.,* the Made in China 2025 Plan) and its confrontational military expansion are also perceived to be a threat to the United States' economic and security interests. The U.S. response to counter these Chinese ambitions could adversely affect the region's political and economic stability, even if such a response may seem to be in the legitimate interests of the United States.

Careful balancing and moderation will be required to ensure that the U.S. response will not undermine the region's political and economic stability. The Biden administration's Indo-Pacific Strategy, issued in February 2022, outlines the U.S. approach to the region, including its approach to China.[980] The strategy includes five major goals of U.S. policy toward the region, which are broadly concerned with good governance, alliances and multilateral cooperation, economic development and trade, military security and assistance, and addressing the ongoing impacts of COVID-19 and climate change.[981] The strategy also includes an action plan, which provides a series of promises to increase U.S. investment, military deployment, and diplomatic engagement.[982] The strategy identifies China as a potent force in the region that seeks to shape the region toward its own interests, while also emphasizing that the United States will seek to "manage competition" with China "responsibly."[983] It is difficult to determine from the outline of the strategy how the United States will respond to specific Chinese actions such as its maritime incursions in disputed ocean territories, but the emphasis on competition *management* and *responsibility* arguably suggests that the United States is aware of the need for balancing and moderation in its approach to China to maintain regional stability and peace.

The United States' regional moderating role may extend to the South Korea–Japan relationship, which has undergone considerable challenges in recent years. As discussed in Chapter 5, South Korea and Japan have not resolved their disagreements on Japan's war crime issues during World War II, such as the comfort women and the forced labor issues.[984] South Korea–Japan relations faced turbulence when Japan retaliated against the Korean Supreme Court's decision (ordering the responsible Japanese corporations to pay reparations for forced labor) by increasing regulatory control over essential items for the production of semiconductors, which are South Korea's key export product.[985] The United States reportedly attempted to mediate between the two countries and asked the Japanese government to suspend its measure (pending negotiations), although Japan was known to decline the mediation attempted by the United States.[986] On the comfort women issue, the United States supported the 2015 agreement between the two countries that aimed to resolve the issue "finally and irreversibly" in return for Japan's apology and a funding provision (although Korean civil societies criticized this agreement for being made without any consultation with the victims).[987] The South Korean–Japan relationship influences the region's stability as they form a vital security apparatus as two of the United States' most important allies.[988] The U.S. role as a mediator will be essential to suppress the outbreak of disputes and reduce tensions between them.

Lastly, to sustain peace and stability in the region, it will also be important for the United States to moderate its projection of self-interests. Alarmed by overseas supply constraints during the COVID-19 pandemic, the U.S. government has adopted industrial policies to increase domestic production of economically strategic items, including semiconductors and EV batteries, through legislation such as the Chips and Science Act and the Inflation Reduction Act (authorizing tax credits for the purchase of electric vehicles produced in the United States including the batteries installed therein).[989] The Chips and Science Act authorizes $280 billion in subsidies for the domestic production of semiconductors, but the subsidies are not available to producers expanding production capacity in China.[990] Thus, the U.S. policies attempt to increase domestic semiconductor production and curtail investment in China. The EV tax credit will also disadvantage overseas

EV producers, including U.S. allies, who use parts produced outside the United States, Canada, or Mexico.[991] This exclusion undermines the global value chain that has been working to the advantage of both producers and consumers, and it compromises the economic and trade interests of the U.S. allies, including South Korea and Japan.[992] Although there may have been a security dimension to this policy (*i.e.,* reducing reliance on the supply of semiconductors from China),[993] it would have been possible to devise a more moderate, inclusive industrial policy that reduces harm to its allies resulting from such exclusion and, accordingly, would be more supportive of the region's economic and trade stability.[994]

6.3.3 An unclear role for Russia

Russia's invasion of Ukraine in February 2022 is a critical development that has substantially diminished Russia's political credibility and economic future in the region. When Russia signed the 1994 Budapest Memorandum alongside Ukraine, the United States, and the United Kingdom, it agreed to respect the independence and sovereignty and the existing borders of Ukraine and to refrain from using force against Ukraine.[995] Ukraine, in turn, relinquished some 1,900 nuclear warheads, then the third largest nuclear arsenal in the world, in exchange for this assurance.[996] Russia's invasion of Ukraine is a clear breach of its commitment to Ukraine's security, and its justification for invasion—demilitarization and de-Nazification of Ukraine—lacks factual support and has been rejected by the international community.[997] The United Nations condemned Russia's invasion through a resolution by the General Assembly,[998] and Russia has not received support for its invasion from any country in the region except North Korea. Even Russia's long-standing ally, China, has reportedly expressed concerns over Russia's invasion and rejected Russia's request for war supplies.[999] South Korea, Japan, and the United States have objected to Russia's invasion and have implemented economic sanctions against Russia.[1000] Russia's invasion of Ukraine has resulted in its political isolation in the region.

The mounting war damage has raised a serious concern for the loss of life: for the first nine months of the war, military casualties and civilian deaths amounted to an estimated 200,000 and 40,000, respectively.[1001] Russia has attacked civilian targets in contravention of the rules of international law, causing civilian casualties and the destruction of civilian infrastructure.[1002] Particularly concerning is a large number of war crime reports—some 30,000 cases as of September 2022, committed mostly by the Russian side.[1003] Such an atrocity has raised a serious question as to whether Russia, as a permanent member of the U.N. Security Council, acts responsibly and upholds the norms of basic humanity. This concern has led to discussions about whether Russia should be expelled from the U.N. Security Council.[1004] Despite the controversy, Russia remains in the Security Council, but the U.N. General Assembly suspended Russia from the Human Rights Council.[1005] These developments have severely undermined Russia's political capital and caused its political isolation. However, China and North Korea were among the minority states that opposed Russia's suspension from the Human Rights Council. International relations scholars Yong-Chool Ha and Beom-Shik Shin have observed that these dynamics may drive Russia toward a closer relationship with China and North Korea in the region (although China has refused to support Russia in its war efforts).[1006]

Russia's military role in Northeast Asia is also expected to diminish. The war in Ukraine has substantially depleted Russia's military manpower and equipment—a report has indicated that Russia had lost 2,879 tanks, 5,808 armored vehicles, 1,865 artillery pieces, 278 aircraft, 261 helicopters, 480 cruise missiles, and 16 warships/boats by November 18, 2022.[1007] This is an unprecedented loss for the Russian military since the end of World War II. Russia has lost many modern combat tanks, advanced missiles, and other equipment to the extent that it had to mobilize older, outdated weapons and equipment on reserve.[1008] Russia has also begun to lose and retreat from the territory in Ukraine that it acquired at the beginning of the war.[1009] In September 2020, Russia announced a military buildup in the Far East,[1010] but Russia subsequently withdrew substantial military resources from the Far East due to its war in Ukraine.[1011] Additionally, Russia's poor battle performance in Ukraine may lead other countries to reassess Russia's military capability. The Russian military has demonstrated a substantial inability to move required supplies to battlefronts on time. Its reliance on foreign materials and parts, such as semiconductors, for the production of advanced weapons has rendered reproduction of the lost units impossible while economic sanctions are in place, which prohibits other countries from exporting such parts to Russia.[1012]

On the economic front, Russia's position in the region is also likely diminished. Russia's primary source of income and largest export has been oil and gas (accounting for 45 percent of Russia's federal budget revenue in 2021).[1013] However, economic sanctions have substantially curtailed Russia's oil and gas supply. The United States has banned the import of Russian oil, liquefied natural gas, and coal into the United States.[1014] South Korea and Japan have also substantially reduced their importation of Russian oil and gas.[1015] It seems unlikely that these countries will restore their oil and gas purchases from Russia to pre-invasion levels in the near future—Russia has threatened to reduce its gas supply to Europe over Europe's support for Ukraine,[1016] which demonstrates that future reliance on Russia's energy supply will carry a significant risk of interruption over political disputes.

The substantial withdrawal by South Korea and Japan from Russian energy creates significant implications for future economic cooperation between Russia and these countries, as any long-term economic project with Russia in the region will have to focus on energy development. The deterioration of Russian exports to these countries has also deepened Russia's dependence on China for exports of its energy resources. In 2022, China has emerged as the most dominant consumer of Russian energy exports, buying nearly US\$ 44 billion worth of coal, oil, and natural gas from Russia.[1017] China may also become the main financier for infrastructure building in Russia's Far East territory. China has financed the construction of a series of pipelines and assured Russia that it would take the lead in financing infrastructure projects along the Northern Sea Route.[1018] China's investment in Russia is aligned with its interest in securing energy sources to meet its significant industrial and consumer needs. Signifying its growing reliance on China, Russia has also recently granted China the use of Vladivostok, the strategic Russian Far East port, for domestic trade.

The future of Russia's role in Northeast Asia is uncertain and will be influenced significantly by the war in Ukraine.[1019] Regardless of the war's outcome, Russia has already lost much of its political credibility in the region, undermining its future prospect for economic cooperation with South Korea and Japan. Russia continues its oil and gas trade with China, but its engagement with Russia is also limited in that it is not supporting Russia's war effort, at least not directly, leaving North Korea as the sole regional supporter for Russia's war effort.[1020] Another factor influencing Russia's role in the region will be the increasing regional discontent toward Moscow. In Khabarovsk Krai (Russia's Far East province), thousands of protesters have rallied against Putin's continued rule in Russia since 2020,[1021] and the discontent increased following Russia's invasion of Ukraine.[1022] Rising regional discontent may weaken Russia's political position in Northeast Asia. In addition, Russia's significant difficulties in the Ukraine war have made Putin's continuing rule insecure. The loss of political stability in Russia, whether or not Putin remains in power, will also adversely affect Russia's role and position in the region, as was the case during Russia's political and economic instability following the end of the Soviet era.

Chapter 7

A HIDDEN PLAYER: MONGOLIA AND ITS ROLE IN THE POWER DYNAMICS OF NORTHEAST ASIA

7.1 An Independent Mongolia: Historical Context—From World Domination to the Fight for Independence

7.1.1 Pax Mongolica

Mongolia, the country that once dominated the world in the thirteenth and fourteenth centuries, is now the smallest power in Northeast Asia in terms of population (3.29 million) and economy (US\$ 15.1 billion GDP as of 2021).[1023] However, despite their modest presence in the present day, the Mongols, through their conquest and expansion throughout the thirteenth century, left a profound political, economic, and cultural impact on the Asian and European continents and changed the course of all nations therein.[1024] At its height, the Mongol Empire formed the largest land empire in history, spanning from the Pacific Ocean in the east to the Danube River in the west, as illustrated in Figure 7.1.

The Mongols' military success was unprecedented. The Mongols possessed an impressive cavalry, which could travel up to 100 miles (160 kilometers) a day and move without heavy supplies—unlike other armies at the time.[1025] The military genius of Mongolian leaders and generals (such as Chinggis Khan and General Subutai), supported by such powerful cavalry forces, led to unparalleled conquest within a few decades.[1026] The Mongol conquest was brutal and destructive, destroying the world's then greatest cities such as Herat, Kyiv, and Baghdad and claiming many lives therein. However, once the Mongol Empire had substantially completed its conquests by the mid-thirteenth century, it brought political unity and stability to the world, including Northeast Asia, often described as the "Pax Mongolica."[1027] The Mongols set up an extensive postal relay system ("jam" system) throughout their empire, which was comprised of fixed relay stations that provided official travelers with horses, lodging, and other necessities for their journeys.[1028]

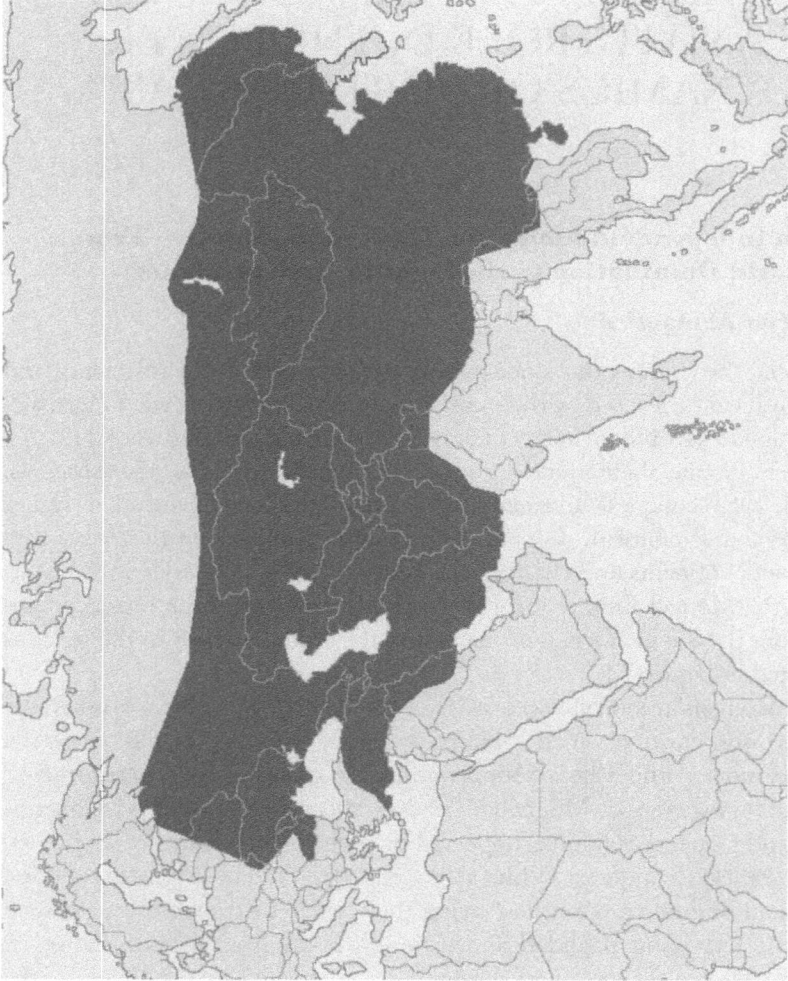

Figure 7.1 Territory of the Mongol Empire (thirteenth century). (*Source*: Mongol Empire Map, modified from https://commons.wikimedia. org/wiki/File:Mongol_Empire_map.gif)

The jam system expanded and became the most extensive network of communication and transportation in the pre-modern era, which facilitated the exchange of people, goods, information, and cultures between the East and the West.[1029]

The Mongol domination continued for over a century but ended with the dissolution of the Mongol Empire in 1368.[1030] The empire had been split into four Khanates (territories ruled by Mongolian leaders, "Khans"): the Golden Hordes in the Northwest (present-day Russia), the Yuan Dynasty in China, the Ilkhanate in the Southwest and Persia, and the Chagatai Khanate in Central Asia. These Khanates retained a strong sense of shared identity and ruled under the laws and traditions of Chinggis Khan, but they operated as autonomous states.[1031] The Mongols lost control of China with the fall of the Yuan Dynasty in 1368 and were pushed back to the north by the Han Chinese (the Ming Dynasty). The Pax Mongolica eventually dissipated, but its legacy remained. During Mongol rule, international trade and commerce proliferated, as safe trade routes and travel passages were guaranteed under the Pax Mongolica. The Mongols, through their empire, initiated the first global age by linking the East and West through trade and exchanges of culture, technology, and information.[1032]

7.1.2 A quest for independence

After the fall of the Yuan Dynasty and its successor in the north, the Northern Yuan Dynasty, some Mongol tribes in the east sought alliances with the rising Manchus. However, these alliances led to submission to the Manchus, and the tribes of Inner Mongolia lost their independence by the end of the seventeenth century.[1033] By the mid-eighteenth century, the Qing Dynasty had also conquered Outer Mongolia, completing its Mongol expeditions.[1034] Despite the conquest, large-scale revolts and rebellions erupted, causing Qing rulers to seek ways to weaken the Mongols' strength. The Qing replaced the Mongols' traditional clan system with the Manchu banner system under which Qing authorities chose the leader of each Mongol banner.[1035] This policy weakened relations among Mongol clans and instead increased their ties with the Qing court.[1036] The Qing also tried to keep the Mongol clans isolated and disconnected by restricting their movement beyond their banner's borders.[1037] Furthermore, the Qing promoted the settlement of the Han Chinese into Mongolia. The Han Chinese farmed hundreds of square kilometers in Inner Mongolia by the 1780s, and the Qing promoted the Han settlement in Mongol lands again in the early twentieth century.[1038] Despite these measures, the Mongols retained their national identity and desire for independence unlike other ethnic groups in China, including the Manchus, who lost their national identity and were absorbed into China.

The Qing Dynasty fell as a result of the 1911 Xinhai Revolution, and the Mongols found a window of opportunity for independence. Following the Mongolian Revolution in the same year, the Mongols installed the Jebtsundamba Khutuktu, the leader (primate) of Mongolian Lamaism, as the "holy king" (Bogd Khan) of the new Mongolian state in Outer Mongolia in December 1911.[1039] In 1913, Bogd Khan sent forces to Inner Mongolia and defeated Chinese forces therein, but Russia and China approved Mongolia's autonomous status within China instead of granting full independence.[1040] The Mongols initially contested but eventually accepted their autonomous status within China in the Treaty of Kyakhta in 1915.[1041] A movement to create a Mongol state continued. In February and March 1919, a pan-Mongolia conference was held in Chita, Siberia.[1042] The conference participants agreed to establish a Mongol state, including Outer Mongolia, Inner Mongolia, and Buryatia (present-day the Republic of Buryatia within Russia) and set up a provisional government.[1043]

However, the Chinese were not willing to allow Mongolia to stay autonomous or become independent. In 1919, a Chinese warlord army occupied the Mongol capital (Niislel Khüree) and deposed Bogd Khan, ending Mongol autonomy.[1044] In February 1921, Russian White Guard troops under the command of Baron Roman Nicolaus von Ungern-Sternberg drove the Chinese out of the capital city. However, his reign of terror provoked popular resistance,[1045] and Mongolian nationalist groups and revolutionists organized resistance. In July 1921, Mongolian revolutionist forces advanced on the capital and set up a "people's government," reinstating Bogd Khan as a constitutional monarch with limited powers.[1046] The Soviet Union assisted the Mongolian revolutionist forces and stationed its troops in Mongolia. In 1945, China approved the independence of Mongolia after a referendum, but Inner Mongolia remained a part of China. Under the influence of the Soviet Union, the Mongolian People's Revolutionary Party ruled Mongolia as a communist country until the overthrow of Mongolia's communist government in 1990. Its 1992 Constitution adopted an elective democracy, for the first time among all the communist countries in Asia, constituting a turning point for Mongolia.[1047]

7.2 Strategic Vulnerability and Economic Potential

7.2.1 Mongolia's strategic vulnerability

The Mongolian state has a substantial strategic vulnerability, which raises issues for its long-term security and independence. Mongolia's strategic vulnerability lies in its geographical location: the country is landlocked and wedged between Russia and China. A country's landlocked location does not necessarily raise security concerns. For example, Switzerland is a landlocked country, but it is surrounded by countries that maintain friendly relationships with it (Italy, France, and Germany), such that Switzerland's landlocked location does not threaten its security and independence. A landlocked country may also resolve security concerns by building superior political and military power with respect to contiguous neighbors. Throughout history, the land-locked locations of some Northern Asian tribes, including the Mongols, did not necessarily undermine their security and autonomy. On the contrary, with superior cavalry forces, they threatened the security and independence of neighboring powers, such as China, through invasions and conquests.[1048] The relative military, political, and economic strengths of landlocked countries vis-à-vis contiguous neighbors determine the existence or the degree of a security threat.

From this view—in terms of Mongolia's relative strength—the landlocked geographical location of contemporary Mongolia raises long-term security concerns. The population, military strength, and economic capacity of Mongolia are minute in comparison to those of its two giant neighboring countries, China and Russia. Mongolia is also among the most sparsely populated countries, with half of its population (around 1.6 million) living in its capital city, Ulaanbaatar. This concentration represents a vulnerability in a vital aspect of security—should Ulaanbaatar be occupied or destroyed, Mongolia would be deprived of key resources to continue any major military resistance (except, probably, sporadic guerrilla warfare in countryside). Mongolia, with its small military, would not be expected to withstand a full-scale military invasion by either China or Russia—although the likelihood of such an occurrence seems low in the foreseeable future.[1049] Despite deep-rooted anti-Chinese sentiment among the populace and occasional political tensions,[1050] Mongolia has not had a serious political dispute with either of these countries, which would warrant concern for a military response.

Mongolia has endeavored to overcome this security vulnerability by forming military partnerships with non-contiguous powers, such as the United States, and international organizations such as the North Atlantic Treaty Organization (NATO). The United States recently sent military personnel to assist with the training of Mongolian forces. In 2021, the U.S. Army's 5th Security Force Assistance Brigade initiated its first training activities in Mongolia with expectations to expand such cooperation in the future.[1051] The U.S. military has also participated in multinational Khaan Quest peace-keeping exercises hosted by Mongolia and has prioritized strengthening Mongolia's peacekeeping capacity and assisting Mongolian forces to enhance military reform, education, and professionalism.[1052] Mongolia has also been active with global peacekeeping operations. It sent troops to Iraq from 2003 to 2008 to assist the U.S.-led occupation of Iraq (and to secure U.S. assistance to modernize its old, outdated military), to Afghanistan to assist the NATO mission for 18 years, and to South Sudan on peacekeeping missions. Mongolia's bilateral and multilateral military cooperation will help to prevent China and Russia from dominating Mongolia with their militaries and to solicit international support in a time of need.

In addition to the abovementioned security concerns, Mongolia has a strategic vulnerability in the economic sphere due to its heavy dependence on China. Before the 1990s, Russia was a primary provider for Mongolia. Russia built Mongolia's railroad infrastructure in the 1960s, which is still used for commercial transport, and offered other subsidies (equating to 37 percent of Mongolia's GDP) in the communist era.[1053] Following the 1990 Mongolian Revolution, China replaced Russia as Mongolia's main developer. China has become Mongolia's largest source of investment, contributing 21 percent of Mongolia's FDI and more than 50 percent of the foreign equity comprising Mongolian enterprises.[1054] China needs Mongolia's rich mineral resources to meet its growing demand for commodities such as coal and copper, and the Mongolian economy relies on commodity exports to China. Commodity exports account for more than half of Mongolia's GDP, and over 80 percent of Mongolia's exports go to China.[1055] This means that Mongolia's economy is heavily influenced by China's demand for commodities, which is, in turn, affected by China's economic cycle and China's border measures, such as its recent border closure due to COVID-19.[1056] This heavy economic dependence weakens Mongolia's position concerning China given that China has a track record of weaponizing trade to extract political concessions from other countries.[1057]

Mongolia attempts to reduce its dependence on China by diversifying trade and investment with other countries through a policy it refers to as the "third neighbor" policy.[1058] For example, while China remains a destination for the vast majority of Mongolian exports (82.6 percent of its exports as of 2021), Mongolia has also exported to other countries, including Switzerland, Singapore, South Korea, and Russia. However, diversity is limited, and Switzerland is the only other country that makes up more than 5 percent of Mongolia's exports (by absorbing most of Mongolia's gold and silver exports).[1059] Mongolia has a weak manufacturing base, with manufacturing accounting for only 7.1 percent of its GDP as of 2021.[1060] Commodity exports, which make up over half of Mongolia's GDP are the main pillar of the Mongolian economy. The United States has shown interest in assisting Mongolia with diversifying its economic relations and building sustainable, inclusive, and private-sector-led economic growth.[1061] For employment abroad, South Korea has become a popular destination for Mongolians. In 2021, over 37,000 Mongolians lived and worked in South Korea, and over 300,000 Mongolians (some 10 percent of the total population) reportedly had living experience in South Korea.[1062] Considering China's tremendous impact on the Mongolian economy, it remains to be seen whether Mongolia will be able to reduce its economic dependency on China and thus reduce its strategic vulnerability.

7.2.2 Economic potential

Mongolia's capitalist economic reforms have resulted in rapid economic growth. Mongolia has been one of the fastest growing economies in the world; in 2011, the Mongolian economy peaked at a growth rate of 17.3 percent, which was the highest in the world that year.[1063] Mongolia's economic potential derives from its rich mineral endowments, which are valued between US$ 1 trillion and US$ 3 trillion.[1064] Mongolia has about 3,000 mineral deposits and 50 mineral commodities, including coal, copper, fluorspar, molybdenum, gold, iron, petroleum, tungsten, uranium, and zinc.[1065] Aided by the increase in exports (mostly commodity exports), from US$ 381 million in 1993 to US$ 9.03 billion in 2021,[1066] Mongolia's GDP increased rapidly from US$ 768 million to US$ 15.1 billion during the same period.[1067] Mongolia's per capita income also rose from US$ 510 in 1993 to US$ 3,760 in 2021.[1068] Figure 7.2 illustrates the trajectory of Mongolia's economy since 1993.

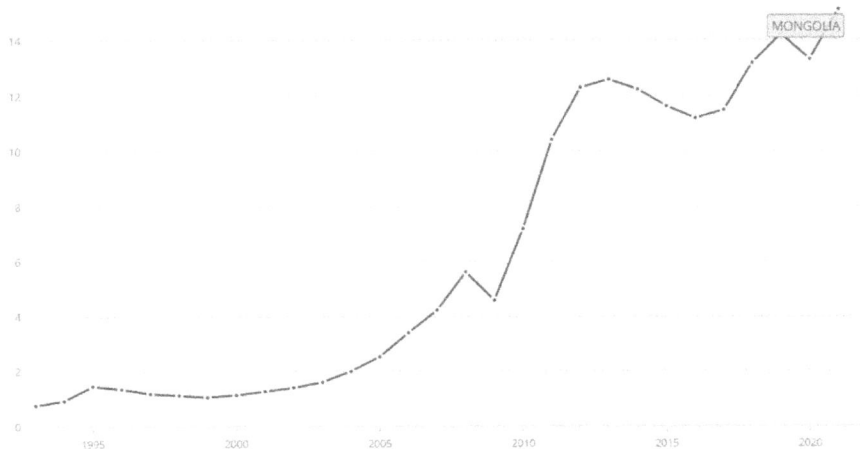

Figure 7.2 Gross domestic product of Mongolia (1993–2021) (unit US$ billion). (*Source*: World Bank, GDP (current US$)—Mongolia)

The World Bank, which has provided Mongolia with over US$ 1.6 billion in development financing for the last three decades, offers the following assessment of Mongolia's economic potential:

> With vast agricultural, livestock and mineral resources, and an educated population, Mongolia's development prospects look promising in the long-term assuming the continuation of structural reforms . . . . Rising private and public investments and household consumption are expected to support domestic demand.[1069]

A politically democratic and economically affluent Mongolia is a positive influence in Northeast Asia and could prove a helpful reference point for a country like North Korea, which has a keen interest in economic development. Private corporations such as the Mongolian Mining Corporation are an embodiment of Mongolia's capitalist economic reform. Mongolia's young population will also support its economic dynamism: about 59 percent of its citizens are under the age of 30 (with the average age being 27.5 years), which is also a positive factor for continuing economic development in the future.[1070]

Despite this positive assessment, several problems could prove to be obstacles to materializing Mongolia's full economic potential. First, there is substantial economic disparity. The country's poverty rate is high, comprising 27.8 percent of the population as of 2020.[1071] The World Bank has observed a downward trend in the poverty rate and opined that it would have been reduced further absent the outbreak of COVID-19.[1072] Nevertheless, the government will have to support inclusive growth to reduce poverty without overspending, and this balancing act could prove a challenging task. For example, proposed child cash subsidies and free water and electricity for households, in response to the economic difficulties associated with COVID-19, might prove unsustainable considering the lack of sufficient government funding.[1073] For inclusive growth, employment opportunities and wages will have to increase through the diversification of the economy and economic growth. Economic diversification is also necessary to reduce economic volatility caused by overdependency on commodity exports. Mongolia's economic growth has been heavily influenced by China's demand for commodities—when China's demand started to decline in 2014 and commodity prices fell, the Mongolian economy also slowed down, evidenced by the fall of its per capita income.[1074] Diversification will require reinforcement of Mongolia's manufacturing sector, improvement of its agricultural base, and strengthening of its banking and financial sector.

Lack of infrastructure is another problem for the Mongolian economy. Mongolia's infrastructure, such as roads and railroads, is insufficient to support industries (including the mining industry) and facilitate exports.[1075] This problem undermines Mongolia's economic potential and hampers its economic performance in both the short and long term by driving up logistics costs, including the cost of shipping and storage, which has led potential importers and investors to find import sources and investment destinations elsewhere.[1076] Investment in key areas, such as mining, is insufficient, despite substantial FDI flowing into the country (US$ 27.1 billion as of the second quarter of 2022),[1077] and some existing investment projects have been delayed. For example, Rio Tinto, a major multinational mining corporation, has been developing one of the world's largest copper mines at the Oyu Tolgoi site in southern Mongolia.[1078] Its projected US$ 5 billion mining expansion was, however, halted due to disagreements with the government over ownership shares and royalties, environmental concerns, and corruption problems.[1079] Rio Tinto initially projected that copper production at Oyu Tolgoi would begin in 2021—more than two decades after the initial discovery of deposits there—but production has since been delayed.[1080]

Economic governance is another issue. In addition to the government's questionable handling of the mining investment cited above, its overall fiscal management has raised concerns. The Mongolian government took out substantial loans during the commodity boom by leveraging its mining assets but later could not service its debt when commodity export revenues were down. As a result, the government went into a financial crisis and was compelled to request a bailout package from the IMF in 2017.[1081] Better financial management and economic governance would be necessary to materialize Mongolia's economic potential. For example, frequent changes in laws and policies concerning investment have lowered the confidence of potential investors and discouraged investments.[1082] The lack of transparency with the government's administrative process, as well as substantial corruption within the public sector (*e.g.*, the bribing of public officials), has also deterred investments.[1083] The World Bank has pointed out that to ensure growth and reduce poverty, Mongolia will need to "strengthen governance; build institutional capacity to manage public revenues efficiently; allocate its resources effectively among spending, investing, and saving; and ensure equal opportunities to all its citizens in urban and rural areas."[1084]

Rampant environmental problems in Mongolia are yet another issue that adversely affects Mongolia's economic performance. Mongolia has a vast, sparsely populated territory (1,564,116 square kilometers making it the 18th largest country), but it has significant water and air pollution issues. With regard to the water issue, mining operations have caused water pollution and water shortages in adjacent areas, and lack of access to clean water has threatened the livelihoods of a substantial number of Mongolians who live on herding and other agricultural activities.[1085] Climate change has also caused water shortages and desertification in Mongolia.[1086] In urban areas, particularly the capital city of Ulaanbaatar, air pollution has become a serious issue, due in part to the extensive use of coal for heating in informal settlements ("ger" districts).[1087] Improvement of Mongolia's heating systems or use of alternative fuel would be important to solve the problem. The government has subsidized refined coal briquettes to reduce air pollution and has also sought to cooperate with other countries such as South Korea to find alternative, affordable heating sources.[1088] However, the impact of the government's efforts is unclear, and as of December 2022, Ulaanbaatar remains one of the world's most polluted cities.[1089] A clean and healthy environment is important to sustaining a productive labor force for the economy, which comprises a core element of Mongolia's economic potential.

Mongolia's rich mineral endowment, its young and educated population, and its new generation of leaders with economic vision (such as Mongolia's vision 2050) demonstrate substantial economic potential for the country. However, there is a risk that Mongolia's current dependency on commodity exports may push it into a "resource curse," thereby leading to a state of perpetual economic degradation, instead of economic prosperity.[1090] A combination of corruption, inconsistent economic policies, and environmental damage existing in Mongolia today deepens this concern. This concern is further reflected by recent civil protests against the government's corruption regarding a US$ 120 million unauthorized coal delivery to China.[1091] Corruptive, untransparent, and ineffective economic governance is not unique to Mongolia, but successful countries manage to reduce these issues. To realize its full economic potential, Mongolia will have to build the needed infrastructure to support its industries and exports, attract foreign investments, pull domestic resources to diversify its economy, suppress corruption, support private entrepreneurship, and reinforce its banking and financial industry.

7.3 The Role of Mongolia in Northeast Asia

7.3.1 Mongolia's desired role in the region

The Mongols have historically been both conquerors and diplomats. In the process of its global conquest, the Mongol Empire used diplomacy as extensively as military operations. Dr. Francesca Fiaschetti described this dual Mongol strategy as follows:

> In building his empire, Chinggis Khan (r. 1206–27) alternatingly combined military and diplomatic efforts to integrate his subjects and

neighbors into his project of conquest. He brought forth traditions of the Inner Asian cultural complex, and expanded them even further to set up a network of more or less formalized dependencies. Such a network was meant to determine with whom one could trade, with whom one could intermarry and against whom one would fight—something which did not necessarily prevent the trade exchanges but rather complemented them (*e.g.*, forced trade) (footnote omitted).[1092]

Mongolia's diplomatic tradition continues today. With its small population (3.29 million), modest economy (US$ 15.1 billion GDP), and limited military power (ranked 102 out of 142 by the 2022 Global Fire Power Review),[1093] contemporary Mongolia would be unable to impose its position on any other Northeast Asian country with a larger economy and stronger military force. Instead, Mongolia has actively sought a mediatory or conciliatory role in the region to safeguard its interests. For example, shortly after the announcement of the 2018 United States–North Korea summit, Mongolia proposed to provide a forum for the summit.[1094] Former Mongolian President Tsakhiagiin Elbegdorj was also the first foreign leader to visit North Korea in 2013 after Kim Jong-Un became North Korea's leader following the death of his father Kim Jong-Il.[1095] During his visit to North Korea, Elbegdorj offered Mongolia as a mediator in the nuclear crisis.[1096] In an impressive speech at Kim Il Sung University (Pyongyang, North Korea), Elbegdorj advocated for democracy and freedom in one of the most authoritarian countries in the world. His speech aptly reflected Mongolia's status as a democracy with an aspiration to contribute to regional peace and stability. Mongolia maintains close ties with North Korea, as demonstrated by Japanese Foreign Minister Taro Kono's 2019 visit to Mongolia to request assistance in resolving an issue of Japanese citizens abducted in North Korea.[1097]

Mongolia's proposed mediatory role over North Korea's nuclear issue, although not yet materialized, would be well supported by its good relationship with both South and North Korea and its balanced policy interests in the region that appear to have won the goodwill and trust of its neighbors.[1098] This trust has indeed allowed for the facilitation of Mongolia's initiative of the "Ulaanbaatar (UB) Dialogue on Northeast Asia Security."[1099] The UB Dialogue, whose objective is to reduce distrust among nations and improve cooperation and peace, held its first meeting in June 2014 with representatives from South and North Korea, the United States, China, Russia, and Japan, as well as some European countries. The Dialogue has convened annually since then, marking its seventh meeting in 2022.[1100] The Dialogue uniquely combines official governmental participants and non-governmental (academic, think tank, and NGO) participants in two separate tracks, each addressing a broad range of regional issues including economic cooperation, military transparency, environmental protection, non-traditional security threats, regional stability, and cultural and educational exchanges.[1101] The Dialogue is a consultative program that has the potential to bring together international policy makers, civil societies, and regional entrepreneurs.[1102]

"Neutrality" is a key word that characterizes Mongolia's approach to its regional role. Mongolia endeavors to remain a neutral force in the region; in 2015, then president Elbegdorj publicly announced that Mongolia was effectively a neutral state, although it did not officially declare itself as such.[1103] The latter non-declaration will accord Mongolia some political space when it requires military cooperation with other countries, such as the United States.[1104] Despite pursuing neutrality, Mongolia has invited the U.S. military to participate in its multilateral peacekeeping exercises (Khaan Quest), and Mongolia has also actively participated in global peacekeeping operations under the U.S. lead, such as peacekeeping missions in Iran and Afghanistan.[1105] Mongolia is also engaged in cooperation with the Chinese and Russian militaries. In 2020, China's Ministry of National Defense delivered 100,000 COVID-19 vaccine doses to Mongolian military personnel, indicating a "high level of collaboration" between the two militaries.[1106] That same year, Russia and Mongolia held Selenga 2020, a military exercise, the purpose of which was to test new methods of combating "illegal armed groups."[1107]

Mongolia's bilateral and multilateral engagements in military cooperation, ironically, demonstrate Mongolia's inherent limits as the "Geneva" of Northeast Asia.[1108] As mature and creative as Mongolia's foreign policy has become, as demonstrated by its regional initiatives discussed earlier, its geographical vulnerability—sandwiched between the two giants, China and Russia—has forced Mongolia to tread carefully when engaging with those global powers to maintain its independence. While Mongolia cooperates with the Chinese and Russian militaries as discussed above, it also finds it necessary to invite U.S. military personnel to participate in its Khaan Quest. In contrast, other neutral states such as Switzerland have never been compelled to engage other powers to counter the influence of other neighboring countries. Unlike Switzerland, Mongolia is a developing country with lower-middle per capita income (US\$ 3,760 as of 2021) and modest financial and industrial capacity, which means that the influence of its otherwise creative diplomatic efforts is likely limited. For example, Mongolia, despite its stated willingness, has not been able to "mediate" North Korea's nuclear issues. The UB Dialogue, as constructive as it may be, has yet to create any breakthroughs on major security issues in Northeast Asia.

Mongolia's limited political, military, and economic capacity renders its desired role as the region's mediator somewhat aspirational. As discussed in Chapter 4, South Korea contemplated a similar role for itself in the region, but its political, military, and economic influence is insufficient to undertake such a role, despite commanding much larger resources than Mongolia.[1109] However, that does not mean that Mongolia cannot play a meaningful role in Northeast Asia. Mongolia may not be able to coordinate conflicting interests among its larger neighbors in the region, such as those involving North Korea's nuclear issues, but its initiatives for dialogues and consultations, such as the UB Dialogue, can create a regional platform for interested parties to address these issues and explore possible solutions for the future. For example, North Korea's participation in the Dialogue has been important, especially for Japan, who wants to discuss its bilateral concerns with North Korea during the Dialogue.[1110] The facilitation of multilateral and bilateral dialogues, security conferences, and multilateral peacekeeping exercises such as the Khaan Quest gives Mongolia an important role in the region, and Mongolia will be able to serve in this role as long as it is perceived to be a functional and neutral party with political credibility.[1111]

7.3.2 *Current political landscape*

Mongolia's role in the region is also influenced by its domestic politics, which could affect its credibility. Political development and democratization in the 1990s earned Mongolia some political credibility. Mongolia has since implemented an elective democracy, successfully holding 8 presidential and 8 legislative elections and producing 6 elected presidents and 14 prime ministers (excluding acting or interim prime ministers).[1112] Under Mongolia's 1992 Constitution (amended in 2001), Mongolia is categorized as a semi-presidential system under which executive power is vested with the prime minister, who is the head of the government.[1113] The president is the head of state and possesses veto power over legislation and full authority over foreign affairs but has limited authority over the executive branch of the government.[1114] Elected members of parliament (The State Great Khural) exercise legislative power, and the judiciary is independent of the executive and legislative branches.[1115] The constitution establishes a representative democracy, guaranteeing freedom of religion, property rights, travel, expression, unalienable rights, and fair elections.[1116] Free elections have shifted power to different political parties over the years, such as the Democratic Party and the Mongolian People's Party (MPP, which succeeded the Mongolian People's Revolutionary Party that ruled Mongolia during the communist era), making Mongolia the only post-communist democracy in Asia.[1117]

As of December 2022, the MPP controls both the presidency and the cabi-net. President Ukhnaagiin Khürelsükh and Prime Minister Luvsannamsrain Oyun-Erdene were both elected into office in 2021. They represent young Mongolian leadership—President Khürelsükh was born in 1968 and Prime Minister Oyun-Erdene in 1980—but each possesses years of political experience. Khürelsükh became a member of the parliament in 2000 and Oyun-Erdene started his political career in 2008.[1118] Khürelsükh became Mongolia's prime minister in 2017, leading the MPP's landslide victory in the 2020 parliamentary election, but resigned in January 2021 on account of pro-tests over an incident involving the government's handling of the COVID-19 pandemic.[1119] (The incident involved the forced relocation of a mother and a newborn to a specialized quarantine facility.) Khürelsükh's resignation came as a surprise because his handling of COVID-19 had been praised by the World Health Organization.[1120] The new prime minister, Oyun-Erdene, a Harvard graduate, had worked under the Khürelsükh administration and designed Mongolia's vision 2050 initiative, aiming to boost Mongolia's devel-opment in several areas including education, digital technology, science, and green development.[1121]

Despite the prospects of young, promising leadership in Mongolia, cau-tion has been raised about the MPP's consolidation of powers.[1122] According to a report, Prime Minister Khürelsükh's sudden resignation in 2021, over the above cited COVID-19 related incident, was allegedly a ploy to protect himself from the effect of the pandemic and to secure the presidency.[1123] This claim has been supported by a series of questionable events that led to the removal of other presidential candidates (such as Khaltmaagiin Battulga and Sainkhüügiin Ganbaatar) from the presidential race.[1124] As a result, Khürelsükh, who gained support from Mongolia's economic and political elite, ran against weaker candidates and won the race by a massive margin (68 percent of the vote).[1125] The process of this presidential election has been criticized. According to the Office for Democratic Institutions and Human Rights of the Organization for Security and Cooperation in Europe, "a highly prescriptive campaign framework, apparent inequality of resources, excessive limitations on candidacy, overly restrictive media regulations, lack of inde-pendent information on candidates and the absence of debate had affected voters' ability to make an informed choice."[1126]

Concerning also is the possibility of foreign influence over Mongolia's electoral process. China stopped COVID-19 vaccine deliveries to Mongolia until Mongolia's Constitutional Court rendered a decision as to whether then-sitting president Khaltmaagiin Battulga, who was known to be a "Sinophobe," should be allowed to run again for the presidency. Vaccine deliveries later resumed when parliament accepted the court's ruling against his run.[1127] Xi

Jinping has called for close cooperation between China's CCP and Mongolia's MPP "at all levels and in all fields to lead the China-Mongolia comprehensive strategic partnership to greater development."[1128] The MPP has frequently participated in "CCP in Dialogue with World Political Parties" conferences, through which the CCP aims to gain international support for its proposition that a country does not have to be democratic to develop.[1129] Mongolian economic and political elite groups who support the MPP are reportedly concerned about the impact that frequent regime changes have on economic development.[1130] Considering Mongolia's economic dependence on China, the CCP's argument—political stability over democracy—has some bearing on Mongolian politics.[1131] Political analyst Munkhnaran Bayarlkhagva concludes that the MPP has taken Mongolia down a path toward authoritarianism by unduly preventing otherwise competitive opposition candidates from running for office and suppressing strong dissents to ensure election victories.[1132]

Notwithstanding the CCP's argument, authoritarianism alone does not facilitate economic development. It is true that several East Asian countries that have successfully developed their economies since the end of World War II (such as South Korea, Taiwan, Singapore, and later China) had periods of authoritarian regimes or still undergo periods of such regimes (in the cases of Singapore and China). However, in all these countries, authoritarian leadership has adopted effective economic development policies centering on the promotion of manufacturing and exports with strong public support.[1133] Democracy may not have been an absolute condition for economic development, as the CCP argues, but its removal does not guarantee economic success either. Unlike the other abovementioned successful countries, Mongolia has not implemented effective manufacturing-based, export-led development policies that would arguably benefit from efficient authoritarian organization or leadership. Rather, Mongolia has relied on commodity exports, and many other authoritarian countries relying heavily on commodity exports for their economies are among the poorest countries in the world.[1134]

Additionally, the weakening of Mongolia's democracy is likely to spur dissent among the public, rather than draw support for the government. Mongolians have enjoyed a working democracy since the 1990s, and its undermining would weaken support for the government, which will be essential to effectively implement economic development policies. Further, it should be noted that those countries that have successfully developed under authoritarian rule have paid high prices in the process of democratization. For example, South Korean dissidents fought the authoritarian government for decades to win freedom and democratic governance for the people, which provoked violent government responses causing social and political divisions and considerable human costs. This is perhaps another important lesson for Mongolian elites who support the CCP's argument. As Mongolia's former president Tsakhiagiin Elbegdorj aptly pointed out in his 2013 speech in North Korea, "the desire of the people to live free" is "the eternal power."[1135] Mongolian leadership could alternatively seek ways to implement effective economic development policies within the parameters of democratic governance, perhaps in collaboration with another democracy in the region such as South Korea.

7.3.3 The Korea-Mongolia union: Possibilities

A closer affiliation between the two countries could create new political and economic dynamics in Northeast Asia, contributing to regional stability and economic prosperity and providing strong traction for Mongolia's "third neighbor" policy. In 2007, in a publicized seminar in Seoul, senior scholars and high-level diplomats, including then the Mongolian Ambassador to South Korea, discussed the necessity and feasibility of forming a national union between Korea and Mongolia.[1136] Korea's presidential candidates had also discussed this idea, raising substantial interest from both the academic and political circles of both countries.[1137] The discussion has since subsided, and neither the South Korean or Mongolian government has formally proposed such a national union between the two countries. Regardless, this chapter introduces the proposed union for its potential political and economic ramifications. Preliminary observations indicate that Mongolians and South Koreans might be receptive to this idea—the author has conducted interviews with young Mongolian citizens, and they found the proposed union potentially mutually beneficial, provided that the peoples of both countries enjoy equal rights under the union without discrimination.[1138]

This optimism stems from the belief that South Korea and Mongolia can complement each other economically and politically, fulfilling each other's needs through a closer union. As discussed earlier, Mongolia's economic dependency on China creates a substantial strategic vulnerability for Mongolia. To preserve its autonomy and independence, Mongolia seeks to diversify its political and economic relations beyond China and Russia. South Korea has become a promising partner for Mongolia. Although Mongolia's trade with South Korea (US$ 531 million) is small in comparison to its trade with China (US$ 10 billion), Korea is a major potential market for Mongolia due to its strong demand for commodities (over US$ 30 billion per month). South Korea requires large quantities of commodities to support its extensive manufacturing industry.[1139] For Mongolia, South Korea's capital and technology could make an essential contribution to Mongolia's economic development, which will be necessary to improve the standard of living for Mongolians.

Beyond their mutual economic needs, Korea and Mongolia also share historical roots, cultural proximity, and popular affinity—more Mongolians have visited, worked, and lived in South Korea than any other country since the 1990s (some 300,000 Mongolians equivalent to 10 percent of Mongolia's population).[1140] While many Mongolians reportedly perceive China as an aggressive and exploitive power because of history (*i.e.,* China's occupation of Mongolia) and some of its present policies (such as the suppression of the Mongolian language and culture in Inner Mongolia),[1141] Mongolians' perception of Korea tends to be more positive, as demonstrated by the large number of Mongolians living and working in South Korea.[1142] As for the Koreans, some may harbor an uncomfortable historical memory—the Mongol Empire invaded Korea nine times over the course of its global conquest in the thirteenth century, and much of Korea was devastated and destroyed in the process. Yet, others allege that the Mongols treated Koreans with preference in the aftermath of the invasions; when the Koreans eventually capitulated, the Mongols preserved the Korean dynasty (Goryeo) that had fought the Mongols for decades in return for subordination to the Mongolian court. They further argue that such preferential treatment was not granted to most other nations that the Mongols conquered.[1143] Despite that historical memory, many contemporary Koreans, who are constrained by their relatively small territorial space and lack of natural resources, are mindful of the cultural and ethnic proximities between the two nations and appear to be open to the idea of such a union.[1144]

Despite the prior discussion of the proposed union, advocates never reached a consensus as to a specific form of the union. Discussions have included forming a loose union under which Mongolia and Korea would each maintain their national autonomy and sovereignty with some shared policies (such as the free movement of goods and people) and institutions to implement them.[1145] Other possibilities, which might be less feasible for initial implementation, include a federal state, where the national sovereignty of Mongolia and Korea would become subordinate to a newly formed federal government, as well as a unitary state in which Mongolia and Korea would have more limited regional autonomy and cede stronger control to a central government.[1146] As mentioned, neither government has made any official proposal, and forming such a national union would likely conflict with Mongolia's announced pursuit of neutrality in the region because South Korea is a close U.S. ally. The proposed union could also alarm Mongolia's most important economic partner, China, which seeks to increase its influence over Mongolia through its leverage over the Mongolian economy.[1147] Conversely, Russia might not oppose the union if it believes that it would help to counter China's growing influence in Siberia and Primorsky Krai, provided that the union maintains collaborative relations with Russia and accommodates Russia's economic interests in the region.[1148]

Mongolia stands to benefit from the proposed union. It would create an institutional framework from which Mongolians could reference and apply South Korea's experience in its successful development, which converted Korea from one of the poorest countries in the world to an advanced, high-income economy, and from an authoritarian regime to an elective democracy based on the rule of law—all within three decades.[1149] The union could also expedite investments from South Korea in areas of need, such as roads, railroads, mines, power plants (including nuclear power plants), mineral processing plants, manufacturing plants, banking and financing, communications, and information technology (provided that local economic governance would not hamper Korean investment interests). Politically, a union with a democratic country like South Korea would encourage and enhance Mongolia's democracy, while a closer association with China, which justifies and advocates for authoritarian rule,[1150] bears a risk of weakening it. For South Korea, the union would help to secure an important source of commodities that are essential to its economy and a much larger territorial space for its population to settle and explore (since Mongolia is nearly 16 times the size of South Korea). Mongolia's young and rising population would also complement South Korea's aging and declining population, which has been a rising concern for the Korean government.[1151]

The union could also bring positive political dynamics conducive to sustainable peace and stability in the region. As discussed in Chapter 4, unification between South and North Korea, which had been a united state for over 1,300 years, would be an important long-term solution to resolve current regional risks such as North Korea's nuclear pursuit.[1152] Despite the importance of unification, there remain drastic differences in political governance, economies, ideologies and cultures between the South and North—all of which would create substantial obstacles to unification.[1153] The proposed union between South Korea and Mongolia, if it also extended to include North Korea, could be used as a structural bridge to address these problems. Mongolia, with decades of experience in both communism and capitalism, could function as an intermediary between the South and North, alleviating clashes between them as a third party and moderator in the union. The existence of such a union would also require approval and cooperation from the neighboring countries—particularly China—because the territories of Korea and Mongolia are not adjacent but separated by China's northeastern territory. This means that such a union, which can only exist in cooperation with China, would bring cooperative dynamics to the region that would thereby enhance regional stability.

There is an argument that the proposed union is unfeasible due to the likelihood of an objection from China.[1154] China may oppose because the union would reduce Mongolia's economic dependency on China and counter China's influence in the area.[1155] Although there is some truth to this observation, the proposed union would not necessarily be against China's long-term interests. Mongolia has declared neutrality and attempts to diversify its political and economic relations, as discussed earlier.[1156] The United States has shown interest in supporting Mongolia's efforts. The United States military has participated in Mongolia's peacekeeping exercises on Mongolian territory, which reinforces the U.S. presence in Mongolia and is out of China's control. Such relations with the U.S. military are likely not preferable to China when compared to the prospect of a peaceful union between Korea and Mongolia, over which China could exert some control because the union would not exist without China's cooperation. If the union also included North Korea, it could permanently resolve North Korea's nuclear issue, which would also be in China's long-term security interests. Additionally, Mongolia's successful economic development, which would be supported by South Korea once the union was formed, would present economic opportunities for China. The trilateral union (South and North Korea and Mongolia) could also be the beginning of a larger community in Northeast Asia should it be open to accepting additional participants beyond South and North Korea and Mongolia. However, this expansion would require a high degree of common political, economic, and cultural interests and affinities, as observed in contemporary Europe—which currently may not exist among Northeast Asian countries but could emerge in the future.

Chapter 8

PATHWAY TO PEACE AND STABILITY IN NORTHEAST ASIA

8.1 Deciphering the Historical, Cultural, Political, and Economic Codes of Northeast Asia

8.1.1 Contextual inquiry

Northeast Asia exhibits complex political, military, and economic dynamism that generates conflicts—often in a manner not easily comprehensible to those unaware of the region's historical, cultural, political, and economic contexts. For example, both South Korea and Japan are close U.S. allies, sharing common values, such as democracy, the rule of law, civil freedoms, and basic human rights.[1157] Both countries also form a cooperative security platform with the United States against North Korea (and potentially China and Russia), although South Korea and Japan are not officially "allies." Yet, intense political and economic tensions have existed between South Korea and Japan over several issues including the comfort women issue, trade conflict (e.g., Japan's restrictive export measure imposed in response to the South Korean court order requiring compensation for forced labor during World War II), and the territorial dispute over the Dokdo Islands.[1158] Those who are not aware of the relevant contexts might wonder why two advanced Northeast Asian democracies and close U.S. allies—South Korea and Japan—have been unable to resolve these issues for several decades, creating intense tensions not only for themselves but also for the region.

Another example is the statement made by China's Foreign Minister, Wang Yi, in his recent meeting with the South Korean foreign minister, reportedly calling the United States a rule breaker and suggesting that each country must stand up to the United States, when he must have known that South Korea, one of the closest U.S. allies, would be unlikely to join China in such an action.[1159] Again, for outsiders, Wang Yi's comment raises a contextual inquiry as to what relationship he presumed exists between South Korea and China that could take precedence over the strong alliance between South

Korea and the United States. To understand these seemingly incomprehensible calls to action and long-standing tensions, it is necessary to identify and decipher the historical, political, cultural, and economic "codes" of Northeast Asia that cause, at times, unexpected moves affecting peace and stability in the region.

8.1.2 Nationalism and economic development

The first such code to decipher is "nationalism," which promotes the interests of a nation (however it is defined) and its political independence.[1160] Historically, Korea, Mongolia, China, and Japan all strived for their national preservation and independence, often against each other. Korea, for example, withstood repeated Mongol invasions for several decades, perhaps longer than any other nation invaded by the mighty Mongols in the thirteenth century, to preserve its independence.[1161] Mongolia, after passing its prime, also fought for its independence—it was conquered by the Manchus in the eighteenth century but eventually secured national independence for Outer Mongolia.[1162] The Chinese (or the Han Chinese) were also conquered by the Mongols in the thirteenth century and the Manchus in the seventeenth century, but they endured foreign occupations and drove the Mongols to the north, eventually restoring their dynasty (the Ming Dynasty). They also overthrew the Qing Dynasty through a revolution, which marked the beginning of the first Chinese republic in 1912.[1163] China also faced invasions from the West and Japan in the nineteenth and twentieth centuries, respectively, but preserved its national independence through enormous sacrifices. Finally, Japan underwent treacherous national reforms in the nineteenth century, underwent internal conflicts and civil wars, and embarked on colonial expansion into the Korean peninsula and beyond—all to promote what it considered to be in its own national interests.[1164]

In the modern context, nationalism is key to understanding the political and economic dynamics generated by the actions of Northeast Asian countries. For Korea, just resolution of Japan's past war crime issues (*e.g.*, the comfort women issue) is not just a question of compensation or reparation for the harm inflicted on its people but is a matter of restoring its national honor, which was undermined by Japan's invasion and colonial rule. For Japan, accepting Korea's demands on these issues (such as recognition of its responsibilities for war crimes) could be perceived as undermining its national pride and prestige.[1165] Thus, the comfort women issue, considered independently of the two nations' common security concerns calling for cooperation, is a source of intense tension and conflict between the two countries. An additional example is Mongolia's quest for the preservation of its national independence and autonomy, which explains why it has taken a keen interest in strengthening its relations with South Korea, to the point that its Ambassador to South Korea discussed the feasibility of a national union in an open seminar.[1166] While an association with South Korea, such as the proposed union, might alarm China, on whom Mongolia substantially relies for its economy,[1167] it would also enable Mongolia to reduce its reliance on China and improve its national autonomy. Nationalism also explains China's recent actions. Xi Jinping's "Chinese Dream," which is understood as the "great rejuvenation of the Chinese nation,"[1168] demonstrates China's pursuit of national prominence and superiority, even at the risk of economic loss and political confrontations with the West, particularly the United States.[1169]

The second code to explain political and economic dynamics in Northeast Asia is economic development. Northeast Asian countries, including Korea, China, and Japan, were all in poverty after the end of World War II. The war destroyed much of China and Japan, leaving their populations in serious economic deprivation. The Korean War also devastated both South and North Korea, leaving behind millions of refugees and the destruction of infrastructure. All of these countries focused on economic development, mobilizing available resources for decades in this pursuit.[1170] South Korea and Japan successfully improved their economies, achieving high-income status, but due to a lack of natural resources and the constraints of their domestic markets, they focused on export-led industrialization to overcome these obstacles.[1171] China, following its economic reform in the late 1970s, pursued market-based economic development, again, focusing on export promotion to overcome its insufficient domestic purchase power at the time.[1172] China has become a middle-income economy as a result of successful economic development, but a substantial portion of its population remains in poverty.[1173] This means that China needs to continue pursuing economic development based on export promotion and acquisition of superior technologies, which, in turn, poses a threat to competing industries in other countries, such as the United States. These concerns have led to the invocation of restrictive trade measures such as tariff hikes and technology export controls against China.[1174]

8.1.3 Confucianism and liberalism

The third code explaining the region's political and cultural dynamism is Confucianism, the ideology that historically supported the political order in Northeast Asia under Chinese supremacy, where the dominant power leads all other states with virtue rather than force in exchange for the latter's voluntary subordination.[1175] Chapter 3 has explained why such a Confucian-based rule (Sinocentrism) would not work in today's context.[1176] Despite its unfeasibility, China has tried, albeit implicitly, to revive the Confucian order in a modern context. These efforts can be seen through China's establishment of Confucius Institutes throughout the world (to introduce Confucian values and ideals) and through its China-centric conduct, such as Wang Yi's recent comment encouraging South Korea to oppose the United States on its economic policies under China's (virtuous) lead, notwithstanding Korea's alliance with the United States.[1177] Thus, what Wang Yi presumed exists between the two countries is China's right to lead on the strength of its Confucian virtue—its righteous claim against the United States in this case—which from a Sinocentric perspective takes precedence over any alliance South Korea may have.

As discussed in Chapter 2, Confucianism has also influenced North Korea's political governance, justifying the absolute rule by the Kim regime.[1178] Confucianism also explains, at least in part, the conduct of the South Korean political establishment that expelled the elected head of South Korea's ruling party.[1179] Confucianism has also profoundly influenced Japanese society, prescribing what proper conduct is in the political arena.[1180] Confucianism, as a political ideology, has been formally displaced by other modern ideologies such as democracy. Therefore, Confucian order is implicit rather than explicit—none of the Northeast Asian countries' constitutions refer to Confucianism, and no government in Northeast Asia has formally announced or suggested that it has revived Confucianism as a guiding principle. In China, Confucianism was condemned during the Cultural Revolution, and political reforms after Mao's death did not include the revival of Confucianism as a political ideology. Nevertheless, implicit as it may have been, its influence over domestic and regional politics in Northeast Asia remains.

The fourth code that influences political dynamics in Northeast Asia is liberalism. The pursuit of liberalism might at first appear to contradict the continuance of Confucianism, which justifies a hierarchical political order. Yet, liberalism and Confucianism might not necessarily be mutually exclusive, as shown by South Korea, where Koreans have developed liberal political governance (an elective democracy) but also preserved Confucian values in society.[1181] Political scientist Professor Brooke Ackerly also argued that Confucianism in many ways is compatible with liberalism.[1182] However, the pursuit of political equality and freedom, which is a core tenet of liberalism, does not squarely fit within the confines of Confucianism, which prioritizes social stability with a hierarchical order. Such creates a unique, but not always comfortable, cohabitation between liberalism (as a norm for political governance) and Confucianism (as a social and cultural norm).

The United States advocated for political liberalism in its occupied territories after the end of World War II, and both South Korea and Japan, under U.S. influence, formed liberal political democracies (although South Korea underwent periods of authoritarian rule until 1987).[1183] Liberalism has also heavily influenced Mongolia, as demonstrated by its 1990 Revolution that overthrew the communist regime and the subsequent political reforms that developed its liberal democracy.[1184] In China, authoritarian communist rule continues, but liberalist demands have been emerging among the populace. In the recent protests against the government's stringent COVID-19 policies, demonstrators have demanded that Xi step down and honor their freedom of speech.[1185] Liberal protests have also occurred in Russia's Far East territory, opposing the constitutional amendment extending Putin's rule. Liberalism and the pursuit of freedom have also driven a large number of North Korean refugees to seek asylum in South Korea, risking their lives in the process. It is not clear whether liberalism will eventually alter the current practices of authoritarian rule in China, Russia, and North Korea, but regardless, liberalism is a code that explains these political developments in Northeast Asia.[1186]

8.1.4 The balance of power

Lastly, the pursuit of the balance of power is another code that explains the political, military, and economic dynamics in the region. As Kenneth Waltz explained, the balance of power is an innate pursuit of states that endeavor to preserve themselves,[1187] and Northeast Asian countries have not been an exception. In addition to Kenneth Waltz, leading scholars such as Hans Morgenthau, Hedley Bull, Robert Gilpin, Stephen Walt, Robert Little, Robert Jervis, and John Mearsheimer endeavored to explain complex power dynamics among states, including the feasibility and nature of the balance of power and its relation to the international order.[1188] Professor Stephen Haggard opined that there are limits to applying major international relations theories in the Northeast Asian context.[1189] In his view, democratic peace theory (which posits that democracies are less likely to engage in armed conflict with other identified democracies)[1190] would be less useful in understanding some of the core dynamics in Northeast Asia in the presence of long-lasting authoritarian regimes such as China and North Korea.[1191]

The political dynamics in Northeast Asia may be outside the parameters of some of these theories, but democratic peace theory might be relevant to the discussion of the potential impact of China's internal governance reform on the regional political dynamics as discussed in Chapter 3.[1192] Historical references will be useful to address the pursuit of the balance of power in Northeast Asia. Northeast Asian countries have accepted China's supremacy in return for the preservation of their national autonomies, which had formed an inherent balance of power in the region.[1193] For example, China offered military support to Korea (Joseon) when Korea was invaded by Japan in the sixteenth century, and Korea sent troops to China in the following century when it faced challenges from the Manchus.[1194] Once the Manchus conquered China and replaced the Han Chinese as the dominant power in the region, the combined forces of the Qing and Joseon stopped the advance of Russian forces from the north in 1654 and 1658, again, to preserve the balance of power in the region[1195]

In the modern context, the balance of power in Northeast Asia is one between a group of democracies including South Korea, Japan, and the United States and another group including China, Russia, and North Korea.[1196] The United States has adopted political, military, and economic policies to suppress China's expansion beyond what it considers to be an appropriate balance of power in the region (although the rivalry between the United States and China is not contained in Northeast Asia) and encourages its allies to follow its lead (with the Chip 4 Alliance, for example).[1197] China, believing the United States is unduly attempting to contain it, pressures other countries in the region (with its substantial leverage over their economies) not to cooperate with the United States on its containment policies against China.[1198] The conflict between the United States and China is a significant destabilizing factor in Northeast Asia, which is further discussed in the following section.

8.2 Necessity for a New Power Balance in the Region

8.2.1 Political instability

Substantial political and economic instability in the region, as discussed in previous chapters, undermines sustainable peace and raises the risk of military conflict in the region. North Korea's nuclear issue has not been resolved and is an ongoing concern. The 2019 Hanoi Summit between the United States and North Korea was unsuccessful in reaching an agreement on North Korea's nuclear issue.[1199] North Korea subsequently resumed missile tests (over 90 cruise and ballistic missile launches in 2022), demonstrating its capability to deliver nuclear warheads at both short and long ranges.[1200] Kim Jong-Un has declared that North Korea will never give up its nuclear weapons, reversing his previous commitment to South Korea and the United States to denuclearize the Korean peninsula.[1201] North Korea has also adopted a law that authorizes preemptive nuclear strikes when it deems a military attack on its leadership—either nuclear or non-nuclear—to be imminent or if it believes such is necessary to prevent "the expansion and protraction of a war."[1202] Kim has vowed to expand North Korea's nuclear arsenal and use it not only as a deterrent but also as a means of protecting North Korea's "fundamental interests."[1203] Kim's position that North Korea will not "negotiate" or use nuclear weapons as a "bargaining chip" diminishes the prospect for the denuclearization of North Korea through negotiation.[1204]

Tensions are mounting over North Korea's nuclear issue. The United States has warned North Korea that "any nuclear attack by North Korea against the United States or its allies and partners is unacceptable and will result in the end of that regime" and that "there is no scenario in which the Kim regime could employ nuclear weapons and survive."[1205] The United States has not precluded the use of its own nuclear weapons against any conventional "rapid strategic attacks" by North Korea.[1206] South Korea has also expressed concerns, noting that North Korea is ready to conduct a nuclear test whenever Kim Jong-Un wishes, and South Korea's defense minister has called for a shift in its defense strategy regarding North Korea to deter its use of nuclear weapons.[1207] In response to the increasing threat from the North, South Korea has increased its joint military exercises with the United States.[1208] Japan also has serious security concerns about North Korea's repeated missile launches over Japan and has warned residents to seek shelter after recent launches.[1209] China and Russia, whose relationships with the United States have recently been deteriorating, blame the United States for the worsening situation, citing its political and economic pressure on North Korea as the reason for escalation.[1210] With such a division of positions, North Korea's nuclear issue is not likely to be resolved and remains a significant factor creating instability in the region.

The intensifying rivalry between the United States and China is another destabilizing factor in Northeast Asia. The United States has described China as "the only competitor capable of combining its economic, diplomatic, military, and technological power to mount a sustained challenge to a stable and open international system" (*i.e.*, the international order set by the United States and its allies).[1211] The United States also views China's goal by 2049, the centenary year of the establishment of the People's Republic of China, as displacing U.S. alliances and security partnerships in the Indo-Pacific and revising the international order to one that is controlled by China.[1212] The United States has responded to these perceived challenges from China by increasing its military presence, particularly in South Korea and Japan, where 80,000 U.S. troops are currently stationed.[1213] China has objected to this increased U.S. military presence in Northeast Asia, as demonstrated by its protests over the U.S. deployment of the THAAD missile defense system in South Korea. China argued that its radar coverage would include the eastern part of China (despite U.S. assurance that it was not set to monitor China) and that its deployment would politically and militarily destabilize the region as a result of intensified scrutiny over China's military operations. In response, China adopted retaliatory trade measures against South Korea for authorizing its deployment.[1214]

Xi Jinping has consolidated his powers and strengthened authoritarian rule in China, as vividly demonstrated through several events: the violent suppression of civil protests in Hong Kong, the continuing oppression in Xinjiang and Tibet, and the coercive COVID-19 shutdowns, which have provoked nationwide protests. Additionally, China's aggressive approaches to territorial disputes in the South China Sea and the Taiwan issue have also increased anti-Chinese sentiment around the world and made it increasingly difficult for the United States and its allies to find solutions to reduce political tension in the region and improve relations with China.[1215] Reflective of the growing concerns about China is that its international initiatives have been met with suspicion. For example, in the case of China's Belt and Road Initiative, which is a large-scale international project to promote development throughout Asia, China is suspected to be attempting to take for itself most of the benefit without consideration for the interests of other stakeholders, particularly private stakeholders including businesses, civil society organizations, and local communities.[1216] This project has caused financial distress for over a third of participating countries due to problematic debt management.[1217] The United States has been called upon to address the shared concerns of a growing number of countries over China's lack of economic reciprocity, dominant technological policies, coercive foreign policy practices, and regional military ambitions.[1218] The U.S. response to this call could increase, rather than reduce, political tension with China.

8.2.2 Current economic instability

Political tensions between the United States and China have also transformed into economic tensions. The United States has adopted extensive tariff measures against a wide range of imports from China for its objectionable IPR practices.[1219] China relies on exports to the United States and other countries for its economic growth;[1220] thus, the increased tariffs have had a negative impact on the Chinese economy. China has responded with its own retaliatory tariffs against exports from the United States,[1221] and the exchange of these trade restrictive measures between the two countries has caused disruptions to international trade.[1222] As discussed earlier, China announced its plans to dominate in key technologies (e.g., the Made in China 2025 Plan), and the United States has perceived China's plans as a direct challenge to its economic and industrial supremacy.[1223] In response, the United States has also imposed technology export controls against China in strategic areas such as semiconductors.[1224] This confrontational standoff between the United

States and China signifies the end of cooperative economic relations between the two countries, raising economic instability for the region.

The recent U.S. policy to locate the production of "strategic items" such as semiconductors and EV batteries in the United States (which is supported by massive subsidies to incentivize domestic production) has also caused economic disruption.[1225] The United States has cited its national security as a justification for this policy but did not identify any specific security grounds that require domestic production (other than generalized statements that they are important to national defense).[1226] The policy disrupts international trade by pressuring producers, including overseas producers, to move production to the United States to secure access to the U.S. market. Such a policy also has the potential to cause economic losses (loss of employment and investment opportunities) in other countries, including U.S. allies in Northeast Asia, where producers seek to relocate its production to the United States due to the new U.S. policy.[1227] This type of policy hardly enhances economic stability in the region. Adding further instability to the regional economy is that China and Japan have also "weaponized" international trade to press their political demands on their trade partners. China has imposed trade restraint measures against South Korea over the THAAD issue, including bans on tours and cultural events, and against Japan for a conflict over the Senkaku Islands.[1228] Japan has imposed export control measures against South Korea over the Korean court order requiring compensation for forced labor during World War II.[1229]

There are also structural issues with the Northeast Asian economy adding to regional economic instability. China is the largest export market to Northeast Asian countries, creating economic dependency on China, albeit, to various degrees: as of 2021, Mongolia, South and North Korea, and Japan sent anywhere from 23 to 82 percent of their exports to China.[1230] Their reliance on China raises two important issues. First, when the Chinese economy slows down, their economies are directly impacted by its reduced demand for their exports. For example, China's stringent COVID-19 shutdown policies have slowed down the Chinese economy, which, in turn, has substantially reduced China's demand for their exports.[1231] Lack of transparency also creates uncertainty for the economic policies that China may adopt, which increases vulnerability for Northeast Asian countries that rely on exports to China, while adding to regional economic instability. Additionally, the United States, in its effort to contain China, has been formulating a systemic approach to control supply chains. The United States seeks to suppress China's technological expansion by excluding China from the semiconductor supply chain with its allies and reducing foreign investment in China in strategic areas.[1232] China could also respond to such joint efforts with its own retaliatory measures, which would also increase economic instability in the region.

Finally, long-term economic stagnation in some major economies in the region could breed regional instability. For example, the Japanese economy has been stagnant since the 1990s, chronically suffering from a lag in domestic demand.[1233] Former Japanese prime minister Abe Shinzo attempted to revive the Japanese economy by infusing cash into it ("Abenomics"), but his policy failed to facilitate long-term economic growth.[1234] Economic stagnation in Japan has also empowered its conservative right-wing faction, which advocates a confrontational stance against Korea and China over the Japanese war crime issues from World War II, and such a political shift has also increased tension in the region.[1235] A similar political shift is also occurring in Mongolia, where its recent economic problems have induced the consolidation of powers in Mongolia's conservative party (MPP), and concerns have arisen that such a development could weaken democracy and increase reliance on China.[1236] A possible economic downturn in China also raises concerns. Economic stagnation is expected in the coming years, which could increase public discontent.[1237] Depending on the extent of public discontent and the political instability it generates, China's leadership could attempt to adopt diversionary measures, including military action against Taiwan. While such an effort would be aimed at shifting public attention from economic issues, it could undoubtedly create substantial instability in Northeast Asia.[1238]

8.2.3 The confrontational nature of the current power arrangements

The current power arrangements in Northeast Asia, as discussed in Chapter 3, create a "confrontational balance" between the United States, South Korea, and Japan on the one hand and China, North Korea, and Russia on the other, generating political and economic tensions in the region. The United States, China, and Russia, being global powers, infuse their own global interests into their Northeast Asian policies, which complicates regional political dynamics. Considering these complex regional dynamics, achieving sustainable peace through creating a balance of power would be a challenging, and perhaps unfeasible task, as such a balance is inherently "uncertain, unreal, and inadequate," as Morgenthau explained.[1239] It is unclear whether the United States and China can accurately assess each other's power, which is not always measurable, to assess the balance of power between them.[1240] Even if it is measurable, it would still be difficult for the United States and China to agree on what is an acceptable point of balance between them when China seeks to play a larger role in the region (and globally) and the United States wants to suppress China's expansion to maintain its own political and economic influence. Considering the rivalry and competition between the two countries, a more effective form of the balance of power that can improve regional stability might not be bilaterally achieved but needs to be multilaterally approached and institutionalized in a regional framework (such as the EU).

The current regional security and economic arrangements generate continuous political tension and confrontational dynamics. The current security arrangement among the United States, South Korea, and Japan aims to protect not only their common security interests but is also based on core political values, such as democracy, the rule of law, civil freedoms, and fundamental human rights. On this point, the 2022 Phnom Penh Statement on US–Japan–Republic of Korea Trilateral Partnership for the Indo-Pacific has affirmed that their "trilateral partnership" is "guided by *shared values*, driven by innovation, and committed to shared prosperity and security" (emphasis added).[1241] This suggests that the divide between the two groups of Northeast Asian countries not only represents differences in shared military and security interests but also forms an ideological front, which is bound to generate tension and debate over political values that are not amenable to an agreement. For instance, China has raised the ideological argument in forums such as the CCP in Dialogue with World Political Parties conference that a liberal democracy is unnecessary for a country's development.[1242] Political confrontations over ideologies could worsen as public discontent increases in China, where demonstrators have openly demanded an election and for Xi to step down. Such public unrest may well drive the Chinese government to strengthen its ideological platform.[1243]

Regional tensions and confrontations also result from current military arrangements in the region. Under its defense treaties with South Korea and Japan,[1244] the United States stations massive naval and ground forces in South Korea and Japan, closely monitoring the movement of the North Korean, Chinese, and Russian militaries. The combined forces of the United States, South Korea, and Japan would be formidable to any power in the region, including China, and the military presence of the United States is a significant security concern for China, as demonstrated by its vehement objection to the U.S. deployment of the THAAD system in South Korea.[1245] The presence of the U.S. Navy in Northeast Asia is also a physical deterrent to China's attempts to control the South and East China Seas, creating substantial tensions between the two countries. The primary purpose of the military alliance between the United States and South Korea is the defense of South Korea from invasions from the North. The South Korean military has become a world-class force with substantial capabilities over the past several decades, and the allied forces of the United States and South Korea present an insurmountable military obstacle to North Korea. In response, North Korea has developed nuclear weapons and ballistic missiles to bridge the gap, and its nuclear arsenal now represents the most acute security threat in Northeast Asia, raising the risk of intense political confrontation.

On the economic front, the current trade and economic frameworks in Northeast Asia have proven to be insufficient to meet the trade and economic interests of Northeast Asian countries. Northeast Asia is a part of the world's most extensive free trade area due to the creation of RCEP (the Regional Comprehensive Economic Partnership), in which China, South Korea, and Japan are all members. These three countries have also formed a trilateral free trade agreement,[1246] while China and South Korea have signed a bilateral free trade agreement. All of these FTAs or regional trade agreements ("RTAs") aim to eliminate tariff and certain nontariff barriers to trade, but these frameworks have not deterred restrictive trade measures adopted to extract political concessions, such as China's trade measures against South Korea over the THAAD dispute and Japan's export restraint measures against South Korea cited earlier.[1247] China has become the most important economic player in Northeast Asia, as it provides the largest export market to Northeast Asian countries. Although China is in a position to foster economic growth for the region, it has instead leveraged its economic position to extract political concessions, which has generated political tensions that the current regional trade and economic frameworks have been unable to resolve.[1248]

The absence of the United States from the cited regional trade and economic frameworks is also problematic. Although the United States has an FTA bilaterally with South Korea,[1249] the Trump administration withdrew from the TPP Agreement, which would have created the largest free trade agreement in the Asia-Pacific region.[1250] Thus, U.S. efforts to exclude China from strategic supply chains (*e.g.*, semiconductors) are outside the purview of any of the regional trade and economic frameworks currently in place. The United States instead promotes the IPEF (Indo-Pacific Economic Framework for Prosperity), whose participants include major Asian-Pacific economies (including Australia, Brunei, Fiji, Indonesia, Japan, South Korea, Malaysia, New Zealand, Philippines, Singapore, Thailand, and Vietnam).[1251] Just as the United States is not a member of any RTA that includes China as a member, China is not a participant in this initiative. The absence of a regional trade and economic framework that includes both the United States and China reflects the inherent economic tension between the two powers. Creating a more inclusive regional framework that secures the participation of both the United States and China may not necessarily resolve economic tension and conflict between the two countries, but it could function as a venue where participants could attempt to moderate between the two powers in the common interests of all.

8.3 Toward Sustainable Peace in Northeast Asia

8.3.1 The role of China in sustaining peace in the region

China is the most important and influential factor influencing sustainable peace in Northeast Asia. Its sheer size (in terms of its territory, population, military, and economy) is unmatchable by any other country in the region. Its governmental revenues alone (US$ 3.20 trillion) are 1.7 times larger than the entire GDP of South Korea (the third largest economy in the region) and nearly two-thirds the size of the GDP of Japan (the third largest economy in the world).[1252] China's population (over 1.4 billion in 2021) is several times larger than all other Northeast Asian countries combined, and its military is also the largest among all Northeast Asian countries. The state capacity of the United States is comparable or superior to China's, as discussed in Chapter 6, but the United States is essentially an outsider to the region (due to its territory being located on another continent), although its tremendous political and economic influence and historical connections with other Northeast Asian countries have earned it a significant insider role.[1253] Russia, another outsider, has territory in Northeast Asia but has seen its influence diminished, particularly after its invasion of Ukraine, and it cannot compete with China's political and economic influence in the region. As discussed earlier,[1254] China alone may not control the outcome of peace and war in the region, but it nevertheless has the capacity to have a crucial effect on it.

China does not seem to be politically content with the status quo. It has felt the threat of encirclement by the United States and its allies,[1255] and the United States has tried to "shape the strategic environment around Beijing" to advance its interests.[1256] Since Xi Jinping took power in 2012, China has reinforced its expansionary policies and amplified its territorial claims over the East and South China Seas against the Philippines, Vietnam, Malaysia, Brunei, Indonesia, Taiwan, and Japan.[1257] China also sought to strengthen its partnership with Russia only a few weeks before Russia's invasion of Ukraine—offering support to Putin's criticism of NATO.[1258] Domestically, China's authoritarian rule has escalated, as demonstrated by its violent suppression of civil protests in Hong Kong, as well as its oppression of minorities and repression of free speech and assembly in Xinjiang and Tibet. The Chinese government has also attempted to undermine the cultural autonomy of ethnic minorities, evidenced by its curtailment of classes teaching the Mongolian language in Inner Mongolia.[1259] The United States views China's conduct as moving away "from the universal values that have sustained so much of the world's progress"[1260] and justifying its containment policy against China.

China's aggressive and coercive domestic and foreign policies, which have become more intense under the Xi regime, weaken its political credibility in the region and diminish its political and economic roles in Northeast Asia. The coercive nature of China's foreign policy stems from its authoritarian domestic ruling style, which has been reinforced under Xi's rule and can be seen through its oppressive and highly protested zero-COVID policy that continued for three years.[1261] As discussed in Chapter 3, Xi dismantled a collective governance system implemented by China's earlier leader, Deng Xiaoping, who was cognizant of the danger of one-person rule—a lesson learned through the turmoil of the Cultural Revolution. Xi has abolished the presidential term limit, weakened the CCP's standing committee, and consolidated powers under his control.[1262] Rebalancing power within China through a return to the more deliberative governance that it used to have and the implementation of some separation of power would be necessary before more balanced, reconciliatory, and regionally agreeable foreign policies can emerge from Beijing.[1263]

On the political-economic front, the United States has warned of China's ambitions. According to U.S. Secretary of State Antony Blinken, "Beijing wants to put itself at the center of global innovation and manufacturing, increase other countries' technological dependence, and then use that dependence to impose its foreign policy preferences."[1264] Blinken also stated that China has benefited from the rule-based international trading system more than any other country, but instead of "using its power to reinforce and revitalize the laws, agreements, principles and institutions that enabled its success, so other countries can benefit from them too, Beijing is undermining it."[1265] In this area, the United States itself has not been setting a good example either; the United States has been unduly blocking the appointments of WTO Appellate Body members since 2016, which renders the Appellate Body non-functional, and has adopted and maintained rule-breaching tariffs on a broad range of products from China despite their inconsistency with international trade law (as found by the WTO dispute settlement panel).[1266] Regardless of U.S. action, China's extensive use of restrictive trade measures as a means to extract political concessions from its trade partners is concerning.[1267] Such measures diminish China's credibility in economic governance and also lead to long-term losses. South Korean companies divested from China after it adopted retaliatory trade measures against South Korea over the THAAD issue, and Australian exporters found alternative markets after China implemented politically-motivated trade measures.[1268]

Attempts to achieve victory over the United States and its allies through coercive and confrontational policies may not fulfill Xi Jinping's Chinese Dream. Such an approach will instead raise widespread concerns and might prove to be counterproductive. Deliberative and accountable political governance processes that produce more balanced, inclusive, and reconciliatory domestic and foreign policies may indeed bring China closer to the ideals of Xi's Dream—the great rejuvenation of the Chinese nation.[1269] China has shown that it possesses such a capacity—what dissolved the occupying Manchus' power after its invasion in the seventeenth century was not China's military, but rather its culture, economy, and the great society into which the Manchus were absorbed, without any coercion, compulsion, or conflict. A peaceful and reconciliatory China with an internal balance of power and deliberative governance could have an enormous political and economic capacity to influence the region and beyond. China's vast open market would provide unparalleled economic opportunities to adjacent countries and more. Its scientific and technological innovations (supported by perhaps the largest number of scientists and engineers in the world) would chart new paths to discovery and industrial prosperity. Its reconciliatory political stance would draw regional and global support; its confrontations with the United States and its allies would be dissolved and a higher level of cooperation and collaboration would become feasible. Therefore, it would arguably be in the long-term interests of China to reassess the wisdom of its current policy stance and reform its authoritarian governance into collaborative governance that is deliberative, inclusive, and accountable. China was once more aligned with the latter form of governance when it was growing rapidly following Deng Xiaoping's economic reforms, which attracted broader international support.

8.3.2 Call for a regional framework for peace in Northeast Asia

The preceding section discussed how current regional arrangements for security and economic governance do not effectively promote political and economic stability in Northeast Asia.[1270] Northeast Asia lacks a multilateral security apparatus, such as NATO in Europe or the Association of Southeast Asian Countries (ASEAN) in Southeast Asia.[1271] Northeast Asian countries have developed a multilateral forum for security cooperation, namely the Six Party Talks, to negotiate the denuclearization of North Korea; however, this framework has not expanded to cover broader regional security issues or even to resolve the North Korean nuclear issue itself.[1272] Any functional multilateral security framework in Northeast Asia must include both China and the United States, but the power struggle between the two countries casts a long shadow over prospects for success with such a framework. Considering the decades of acute political and economic tensions, it is difficult to imagine the United States and Chinese militaries serving under a common command, as is the case for North American and European countries under NATO, or South and North Korean forces operating under a common security framework. Even between South Korea and Japan, both of which are U.S. allies, cooperation under a formal, multilateral security framework might be politically challenging—as evidenced by former South Korean President Moon Jae-In's statement that Japan is not South Korea's ally.[1273]

The development of a regional security framework would clearly be conducive to sustainable regional peace, but its precondition is the substantial improvement of bilateral relationships among Northeast Asian countries. With the United States and China, since the Obama administration's "Pivot to Asia," China has viewed U.S. engagement in the region as a containment policy designed to weaken and impede China's regional influence, which, in turn, has made China distrustful of U.S. intentions during security negotiations.[1274] From the U.S. perspective, China has been implementing its expansionary policies with the intent to replace U.S. political and economic influence with its own; this perception is the basis on which the United States justifies its containment policies against China.[1275] A functional multilateral security framework in Northeast Asia will not be feasible until the United States and China develop a degree of common understanding about each other's objectives. Insufficient trust is an issue. A representative of the Chinese government has denied that China's objective is to challenge the U.S. position in the world,[1276] but the United States does not seem to trust China. As discussed earlier, the development of more deliberative and transparent internal governance would improve China's political credibility with its announced positions.[1277]

A functional regional security framework must also include North Korea if it were to effectively address the North Korean nuclear issue. Such inclusion will require a politically challenging process to improve the current distrust and hostility between North Korea on the one hand and the United States and its allies on the other. With the nuclear issue, both sides will have to agree to a set of parameters, procedures, and steps for resolution of the problem, even if that does not immediately result in the complete denuclearization of North Korea. Participants will also have to address concerns about the serious human rights violations in North Korea for it would be challenging for participating democracies to develop a common security framework with a country that operates concentration camps for political prisoners.[1278] Participants will have to agree on steps to address these issues. To initiate such efforts with North Korea, the role of a neutral party such as Mongolia (who maintains good relations with both North Korea and the other participating countries) could be important. The relationship between South Korea and Japan must also improve before a functional regional security framework would be plausible. Many South Koreans share the aforementioned sentiment expressed by former South Korean President Moon about Japan—they do not have enough confidence in Japan to form a security alliance with it. To build such trust, both countries will have to come to an understanding, as Germany has done with its neighbors, on points of concern, such as the atrocities of Japanese colonial rule and its war crimes in World War II (*e.g.,* the comfort women and forced labor issues).[1279]

The cited preconditions are politically challenging and may be impossible to meet in the near term. A possible step that could be taken beforehand is the development of a low-level security initiative, such as the Northeast Asia Peace and Cooperation Initiative (NAPCI) proposed by South Korea in 2013.[1280] Instead of tackling difficult negotiations on hard security issues like arms control, the NAPCI sought to initiate dialogues on softer issues, such as nuclear safety and cyberspace. With this foundation, former South Korean President Park Geun-Hye sought to lay the groundwork for future conversations on more difficult issues.[1281] Park also emphasized the importance of dialogue and cooperation over specific rules and agreements, to avoid years of stagnating negotiations.[1282] The NAPCI seemed promising, and the subsequent South Korean government tried to expand the initiative, but it eventually dissipated due to its failure to deliver regional political changes.[1283] The UB (Ulaanbaatar) Dialogue on Northeast Asia Security, which has annually convened since 2014 in Mongolia, adopts a similar approach, offering an opportunity for dialogues on a broad range of regional issues in two tracks: one for official governmental participants and another for non-governmental participants.[1284] The question is whether this type of soft approach can be transitioned into a more solid framework that produces binding policies, shared commitments, and hard agreements among participants.

On the economic front, Northeast Asia does not have a regional trade and economic framework that includes both of its two most important players: the United States and China. As discussed, the United States does not participate in RCEP (of which China is a member), and China did not participate in the TPP (although it subsequently applied for membership after U.S. withdrawal). The United States promotes the IPEF (Indo-Pacific Economic Framework for Prosperity) with other Asian-Pacific countries, which is a broader economic cooperative framework, but it is not clear whether the IPEF will provide its participants with tangible benefits such as tariff reductions and specific market access as granted by other RTAs.[1285] The development of a Northeast

Asian FTA—which admits all of the constituent countries (the United States, China, South and North Korea, Japan, and Mongolia) and grants appropriate concessions to developing country members—would mark the beginning of economic integration in Northeast Asia. Regional economic integration would contribute to stabilizing trade and economic relations in Northeast Asia, although it is not an absolute deterrent to abusive trade practices. Such an economic integration could also lead to regional political and security cooperation as seen by the development of the European Economic Community into the EU.[1286] This might be a possible path for Northeast Asia in the future.

8.3.3 Concluding remarks

Sustainable peace in Northeast Asia is one of the most pressing issues today. The region is economically one of the most vibrant places in the world but simultaneously is one of the most volatile places from a military and political standpoint. The region is home to North Korea, a country that has threatened to use nuclear weapons to protect its "fundamental interests," which could justify nearly any use that its authoritarian regime deems fit.[1287] Besides North Korea, Northeast Asia includes three of the largest military forces in the world (the United States, China, and Russia) and other leading militaries (South Korea and Japan), which are ranked within the world's top 10.[1288] Substantial political and economic tensions among these countries create a substantial risk of conflict. As seen by the outbreak of war in Ukraine, war is not always predictable. A war in the region would have a devastating impact on the global economy and could result in millions of casualties. Conversely, a major conflict among the global powers outside the region, such as a conflict between the United States and China in the South China Sea, would have an immediate impact in Northeast Asia. The political, military, and economic dynamics in Northeast Asia are globally linked—the question of sustainable peace in Northeast Asia is a question of global interest.

Achieving sustainable peace in Northeast Asia would be a challenging task. Northeast Asia was at the forefront of the Cold War, as demonstrated by the tragic Korean War (1950–1953) and the decades of political and military confrontations that followed. The end of the Cold War, however, did not bring sustainable peace to the region. Under the leadership of Deng Xiaoping, China adopted a (socialist) market economy and achieved unprecedented economic growth, lifting hundreds of millions of its population out of poverty. However, the reform did not include a change in China's authoritarian communist rule; China's regime suppressed the 1989 Tiananmen Square protest, which could have been an opportunity for democratic reform, and the current Chinese leader Xi Jinping has strengthened his authoritarian control. China's increased economic resources and its enhanced military capabilities, both secured as the result of successful economic development, renders Xi's authoritarian rule more powerful today. In the closing ceremony of a congress of the CCP, China's former president Hu Jintao was escorted out.[1289] It is not clear whether he was removed from the venue against his will or for another reason (such as health issues), but to many who have seen his removal, it was a symbolic end of an era of collective governance, which Hu's presidency represented, and the beginning of a new era, which Xi's one-person rule will control.

Post-Soviet Russia, a country that initially showed democratic aspirations, has also fallen to the once popular but increasingly autocratic Vladimir Putin, who has started a costly war in Ukraine that has resulted in the loss of hundreds of thousands of both Ukrainian and Russian lives. Along with this loss, Russia has substantially damaged its political credibility and global reputation by waging this war. It remains to be seen whether Russia can recover from this downfall and restore its influence in Northeast Asia, although its prospect does not appear strong. Equally concerning are the political and economic circumstances in North Korea. North Koreans are currently living under the world's most authoritarian rule and in serious economic deprivation. The Kim regime has a dismal track record of human rights violations and has also openly threatened to use nuclear weapons, adding a significant risk to the region.[1290] The South Korea–Japan relationship also raises concerns. These two major democracies in Northeast Asia have achieved economic prosperity and industrial advancement, but their relationship is tenuous due in large part to decades-long disagreements over war crimes and territorial disputes (over the Dokdo Islands), another unsettling factor for the region (despite the Yoon administration's recent reconciliatory policy toward Japan).

China is the largest political and economic power in Northeast Asia and has the ability to influence the trajectory of the region's future. A China with stable, inclusive, and deliberative internal governance as well as balanced and temperate foreign policies would enhance regional stability and promote sustainable peace. Xi Jinping has expressed his resolve to unify China and Taiwan.[1291] Having witnessed China's undermining of Hong Kong's political autonomy despite China's earlier commitment to guarantee it, Taiwan has rejected, not surprisingly, China's "one country, two systems" proposal.[1292] China has indicated that it is willing to use force to achieve unification if necessary,[1293] in which case China would likely face fierce resistance from Taiwan—as Russia experienced in Ukraine. As also happened to Russia, China's invasion of Taiwan would critically damage its global and regional political credibility. As imaginative as it may seem, the democratization of China could present a less costly avenue for unification, especially with a history of cooperation between the CCP and now Taiwan's Nationalist Party.

Both parties sought to cooperate and formed a "United Front" (1924–1927 and 1937–1945) to broaden their constituencies (the First United Front) and to resist Japan during World War II (the Second United Front).[1294] If China were to allow free, general elections, as demanded by recent protests,[1295] and then propose uniting mainland China and Taiwan to form a democratic government based on the rule of law and a multiparty system, Taiwan may be more receptive to the idea (although those who regard Taiwan as a separate nation and support an independent Taiwan may still oppose).

The North Korean nuclear issue is the most serious security problem in Northeast Asia, and negotiations for its denuclearization have so far proved unsuccessful. No power in Northeast Asia, including North Korea's traditional allies (China and Russia), has officially accepted a nuclear North Korean state, but no consensus has emerged on how to address the issue. Meanwhile, North Korea has affirmed its resolve not to denuclearize and has threatened to use its nuclear weapons proactively to protect its "fundamental interests."[1296] North Korea could use its nuclear arsenal as a bargaining chip, despite its insistence otherwise, in return for political and economic concessions. Nevertheless, it seems unlikely that the North Korean regime would entirely abandon its nuclear weapons and long-range missiles (which have the capability of delivering nuclear warheads). The unification of South and North Korea, which remains an objective of both countries, would provide a lasting solution to the nuclear problem. Like Taiwan, South Korea will not accept a unification if it does not institutionally guarantee freedom and elective democracy; thus, unification will have to be achieved in a manner that provides such a guarantee. The unification of South and North Korea would require a substantial improvement in their relationship, the building of mutual trust, and an improvement in the atrocious human rights situation in the North.

Achieving sustainable peace in Northeast Asia would require the implementation of supportive regional institutional frameworks such as NATO and the EU. Given the present power struggle between the United States and China, the two most important powers in the region, it could take decades before such institutional frameworks emerge. It remains to be seen whether a soft approach to security issues, such as the one taken by the UB Dialogue, could be developed into a more solid framework that is binding among participants. The support of the United States will be important in building such regional institutions. The United States has lost some of its political credibility due to the Trump administration's unilateralist policies that failed to consider the interests of U.S. allies and partners, including those in Northeast Asia.[1297] Some of these unilateral policies remain today, including rule-breaching tariffs against China (found by the WTO dispute settlement body to be inconsistent with the rules of international trade law)[1298] and economic policies favoring domestic production (potentially in breach of international trade law).[1299] As was the case for China, the United States has also benefited from the open, rule-based international system, and its selective compliance with the latter has set a negative example for other countries like China. The United States, by renouncing its unilateralist policies and reaffirming its support of multilateralism and the open international system, would function, once again, as a beacon of freedom, accountability, and shared prosperity. Such a return would help to facilitate sustainable peace in Northeast Asia.

The political and economic tensions between South Korea and Japan are not conducive to sustainable peace in the region and require a long-term solution. On December 16, 2022, the Japanese government announced that it would acquire the ability to "strike enemy bases" and double its defense spending.[1300] Under this new strategy, Japan may choose to strike an enemy base on foreign soil in the event of an attack on Japan or on a "friendly nation." This new strategy expands the parameters of self-defense under the Japanese Constitution (subverting the Constitution's prohibition on the use of force).[1301] Although the United States welcomed Japan's announcement,[1302] concerns have been raised in South Korea.[1303] Japan's increasingly unapologetic attitude about its past aggression, its continuing claims over Korean territory (the Dokdo Islands), and its uncooperative approach toward South Korea about its potential use of force against the Korean peninsula have raised concerns among Koreans about Japan's increased military capabilities.[1304]

Japan is in a position to relieve Korea's concerns and improve its relationship with South Korea by adjusting its approaches. Japan's right-wing faction has influenced its politics and induced the government to adopt nationalist policies, but it is doubtful that such an approach (disregarding the concerns and historical trauma of its neighbors caused by its past aggression) is in Japan's long-term interests. Japan needs to maintain supportive relationships with other Northeast Asian countries, not just the United States, to secure its long-term security interests. The example set by Germany would be an important reference. Germany has regained the trust of the rest of Europe despite its past atrocities by taking responsibility for its actions and reconciling with Nazi victims through unconditional reparations.[1305] The Japanese government, through the 1993 Kono Statement, expressed its resolve to face the historical facts instead of evading them and "never to repeat the same mistake" "through the study and teaching of history."[1306] The difficulty in the Korea-Japan relationship could likely be resolved if Japan were to return to the positions reiterated in the Kono Statement.

As cliché as it may sound, trust is key to sustainable peace in Northeast Asia. For example, increased trust between South Koreans and Mongolians, as well as their mutual economic needs, cultural affinities, and political aspirations, led scholars and politicians of both countries to discuss the possibility of a national union between the two countries.[1307] The proposed union could fulfill the needs of both countries (*i.e.*, capital, technology, and markets for Mongolians and mineral resources and territorial space for South Koreans). In addition, such a political framework could facilitate unification between South and North Korea if it could be expanded to include North Korea (which might otherwise be unwilling to negotiate unification bilaterally with South Korea due to fears of being absorbed into South Korea with a much larger capacity compared to North Korea's smaller population and economy). Mongolia, which has good relations with both South and North Korea, could function as a moderator between them.[1308] The proposed union could also function as an open institutional platform to include other Northeast Asian countries with the prospect of growing into an even larger union—similar to the European Union. Once Northeast Asian countries share some common values, such as basic human rights and civil freedoms, they can use these values as a basis upon which to build trust. When they have built sufficient trust to pursue an economic and political integration of the region, sustainable peace in Northeast Asia will finally be in sight.[1309]

NOTES

Chapter 1. Introduction

1 See World Bank, *GDP (current US$)*, https://data.worldbank.org/indicator/NY.GDP
.MKTP.CD [https://perma.cc/UJ53-S2T9]. The content of this book is generally
updated as of December 2022.

2 World Trade Organization, *World Trade Statistical Review 2022*, Table A6, https://
www.wto.org/english/res_e/booksp_e/wtsr_2022_e.pdf [https://perma.cc/UYJ7
-DDAS]. The terms "region" or "regional" refers to Northeast Asia throughout this
book unless indicated otherwise. "Northeast Asian countries" refer to China, South
Korea, North Korea, Japan, and Mongolia. This book discusses two outside powers,
Russia and the United States, for their influence in the region.

3 Bank of Korea, *Gross Domestic Product Estimates for South and North Korea*, https://
knoema.com/KPKRGDPE2017/gross-domestic-product-estimates-for-north-and
-south-korea (accessed December 30, 2022). See also Soo-Bin Park, *The North Korean
Economy: Current Issues and Prospects, Association of Korean Studies* (2003), https://carle-
ton.ca/economics/wp-content/uploads/cep04-05.pdf?origin=publication_detail
[https://perma.cc/H5EB-FNUU].

4 Data compiled from the World Steel Association, *World Steel in Figures 2022* (2022),
https://worldsteel.org/steel-topics/statistics/world-steel-in-figures-2022/ [https://
perma.cc/S9WQ-A2LB].

5 Data compiled from the U.S. Department of Transportation's Bureau of
Transportation Statistics, *World Motor Vehicle Production, Selected Countries*, https://www
.bts.gov/content/world-motor-vehicle-production-selected-countries [https://perma
.cc/L653-ZVPC].

6 Data from the United Nations Conference on Trade and Development (UNCTAD),
https://unctadstat.unctad.org/wds/TableViewer/tableView.aspx?ReportId=89493
(accessed December 30, 2022).

7 Santosh Das, *Top 10 Consumer Electronics Companies in the World* (October 4, 2021),
http://www.electronicsandyou.com/blog/top-10-consumer-electronics-companies
-in-the-world.html [https://perma.cc/E53R-YFMW].

8 Thomas Alsop, *DRAM Manufacturers Revenue Share Worldwide from 2011 to 2021, by
Quarter* (May 12, 2021), https://www.statista.com/statistics/271726/global-market
-share-held-by-dram-chip-vendors-since-2010/ [https://perma.cc/8SYC-F64M].

9 CEIC, *China Exports: ICT Goods*, https://www.ceicdata.com/en/indicator/china/
exports-ict-goods [https://perma.cc/5837-6WAP].

10 See World Bank, *The Global Economic Outlook During the COVID-19 Pandemic: A Changed World*,
https://www.worldbank.org/en/news/feature/2020/06/08/the-global-economic-

outlook-during-the-covid-19-pandemic-a-changed-world [https://perma.cc/MZ29
-JJ7J], See also The Centre for Economics and Business Research, *World Economic League Table* (December 2020), p. 71, https://cebr.com/wp-content/uploads/2020/12/WELT-2021-final-29.12.pdf [https://perma.cc/7UFK-WE89].

11 See Elena Holodny, "The Rise, Fall, and Comeback of the Chinese Economy Over the Past 800 Years," *Business Insider*, January 8, 2017, https://www.businessinsider.com/history-of-chinese-economy-1200-2017-2017-1 [https://perma.cc/S2VN-8CLV].

12 World Trade Organization, *supra* note 2.

13 "Russia" may refer to the Soviet Republic or the Soviet Union (1917–1991) as well as Imperial Russia or the Russian Federation (1991–). The terms "Soviets" and "Russians" may be used interchangeably without distinction.

14 For a discussion of the Korean War, see Max Hastings, *The Korean War* (Simon and Schuster, 1987); Steven Hugh Lee, *The Korean War* (Longman, 2001); and Bruce Cumings, *The Origins of the Korean War* (Princeton University Press, 1981).

15 For example, the Regional Comprehensive Economic Partnership (RCEP) Agreement, which aims to form a free trade area, includes all of the countries in Northeast Asia except Mongolia and North Korea. China is the largest export market for South Korea and Japan, and the United States and Japan are China's largest and fourth largest export markets, respectively, indicating close economic and trade relations among these countries.

16 For a relevant discussion, see Christopher Layne, "China's Challenge to US Hegemony" (2008) 107 *Current History* 13–18.

17 See *supra* note 15 (explaining that China is the largest export market for South Korea and Japan).

18 For example, China has economically retaliated against South Korea for allowing the deployment of the "THAAD"—Terminal High Altitude Area Defense system, stationed in South Korea by the United States—by adopting measures affecting trade and Korean businesses. For a discussion of these measures, see Yong-Shik Lee, "Should China be Granted Market Economy Status?: In View of Recent Development" (2017) 3(2) *China and WTO Review* 319–341.

19 "Biden says US will defend Taiwan if China attacks," *BBC News*, October 22, 2021, https://www.bbc.com/news/world-asia-59005300 (accessed December 30, 2022).

20 Allan R. Millett, "Korean War," *Encyclopaedia Britannica* (June 18, 2021), https://www.britannica.com/event/Korean-War [https://perma.cc/8TA8-SPRF].

21 See, *e.g.*, Daniel Calingaert, "Nuclear Weapons and the Korean War" (1988) 11(2) *Journal of Strategic Studies* 177–202.

22 These countries included the United States, Japan, Australia, Peru, Malaysia, Vietnam, New Zealand, Chile, Singapore, Canada, Mexico, and Brunei.

23 The Comprehensive and Progressive Agreement for Trans-Pacific Partnership (CPTPP), which replaced the TPP, was formed among 11 countries, including Australia, Brunei, Canada, Chile, Japan, Malaysia, Mexico, New Zealand, Peru, Singapore, and Vietnam.

24 For a discussion of the TPP and RCEP, see Yong-Shik Lee, "The Eagle Meets the Dragon – Two Superpowers, Two Mega RTAs, and So Many In Between: Reflections on TPP and RCEP" (2016) 50(3) *Journal of World Trade* 479–500.

25 World Bank, *GDP (current US$) – Mongolia*, https://data.worldbank.org/indicator/NY.GDP.MKTP.CD?locations=MN [https://perma.cc/QQ66-DHD4]. Dollar values denoting domestic income (*e.g.*, GDP) or per capita income (*e.g.*, GNI per capita) are current (current US$) throughout this book unless indicated otherwise.

26 North Korea's economy was superior to that of South Korea until the 1970s, but it has faced difficulties and declined since the 1980s. Both Mongolia and North Korea have rich mineral deposits, including copper, coal, gold, silver, iron ore, zinc, fluorspar, molybdenum, uranium, tin, tungsten, natural gas and petroleum (for Mongolia) and graphite, zinc, tungsten, gold, barite, apatite, molybdenite, limestone, magnesite, and copper (for North Korea).

27 For a discussion of Sinocentrism, see John King Fairbank (ed.), *The Chinese World Order* (Harvard University Press, 1968), at 1–4, 20–22. See also Sinan Chu, *Whither Chinese IR? The Sinocentric subject and the paradox of Tianxia-ism* (Cambridge University Press, 2020).

28 For further discussion of the Sino-Japanese War, see S. C. M. Paine, *The Sino-Japanese War of 1894–1895: Perceptions, Power, and Primacy* (Cambridge University Press, 2003).

29 Henry McAleavy, *The Modern History of China* (Praeger, 1967), at 201; Kenneth Scott Latourette, *A History of Modern China* (London and Baltimore: Penguin Books, 1954), at 120–121.

30 McAleavy (1967), *ibid.*, at 201; Latourette (1954), *ibid*, at 120–121.

31 Charles R. Bawden, *The Modern History of Mongolia* (Kegan Paul International, 1989), at 188.

32 Michael J. Seth, *A History of Korea: From Antiquity to the Present* (Rowman & Littlefield, 2011), at 250–252.

33 For a discussion of the Meiji Restoration, see W. G. Beasley, *The Meiji Restoration* (Stanford University Press, 1972).

34 *Ibid.*

35 Christopher Martin, *The Russo-Japanese War* (Abelard-Schuman, 1967), at 224–225.

36 Kirk W. Larsen and Joseph Seeley, "Simple Conversation or Secret Treaty? The Taft-Katsura Memorandum in Korean Historical Memory" (2014) 19(1) *Journal of Korean Studies* 59–92.

37 David H. James, *The Rise and Fall of the Japanese Empire* (Routledge, 2011), at 380.

38 *Ibid.*, at 381.

39 *Ibid.*, at 256–266.

40 See, *e.g.*, Yong-Shik Lee, Natsu Taylor Saito, and Jonathan Todres, "The Fallacy of Contract in Sexual Slavery" (2021) 42(2) *Michigan Journal of International Law* 291–319.

41 Jeffrey Record, *Japan's Decision for War in 1941: Some Enduring Lessons* (U.S. Army War College, Strategic Studies Institute, 2009).

42 See Brandon Palmer, "Imperial Japan's Preparations to Conscript Koreans as Soldiers, 1942—1945" (2007) 31 *Korean Studies* 63–78; Wook Shin and Daniel Sneider, *Divergent Memories* (Stanford University Press, 2016), at 195–213.

43 For an account of China's civil war, see Diana Lary, *China's Civil War: A Social History, 1945–1949* (Cambridge University Press, 2015).

44 *Ibid.*

45 *Ibid.*

46 Ernest R. May, "The United States, the Soviet Union, and the Far Eastern War, 1941–1945" (1955) 24(2) *Pacific Historical Review* 153–174.

47 *Ibid.*

48 Hastings (1987), *supra* note 14; Cumings (1981), *supra* note 14.

49 See Wei Li and Dennis Tao Yang, "The Great Leap Forward: Anatomy of a Central Planning Disaster" (2005) 113(4) *Journal of Political Economy* 840–877.

50 *Ibid.*

51 Roderick MacFarquhar and Michael Schoenhals, *Mao's Last Revolution* (Harvard University Press, 2006), at 4.

52 *Ibid.* See also Frank Dikötter, *The Cultural Revolution: A People's History, 1962–1976* (Bloomsbury Press, 2017).

53 MacFarquhar and Schoenhals (2006), *supra* note 51, at 3, 350–352.

54 For a discussion of the socialist market economy, see Xiaoqin Ding, "The Socialist Market Economy: China and the World" (2009) 73(2) *Science and Society* 235–241.

55 Yong-Shik Lee and Xiaojie Lu, "China's Trade and Development Policy under the WTO: An Evaluation of Law and Economics Aspect" (2016) 2(2) *China and WTO Review* 339–360.

56 Yong-Shik Lee, "Weaponizing International Trade in Political Disputes: Issues under International Economic Law and Systemic Risks" (2022) 56(3) *Journal of World Trade* 405–428.

57 Susan L. Shirk, "China in Xi's 'New Era': The Return to Personalistic Rule" (2018) 29(2) *Journal of Democracy* 22–36.

58 See, *e.g.*, Tomoyuki Tachikawa, "FOCUS: Chinese Citizens Support Xi's Hard-Line Policy Against Hong Kong," *Kyoto News*, March 6, 2021, https://english.kyodonews .net/news/2021/03/39fe8d7e5ccd-focus-chinese-citizens-support-xis-hard-line-pol-icy-against-hong-kong.html [https://perma.cc/GLP5-73QT].

59 For further discussion of Korea's economic development, see Yong-Shik Lee, "Law and Development: Lessons from South Korea" (2018) 11(2) *Law and Development Review* 433–465.

60 See Fairbank (ed.), *supra* note 27.

61 See, *e.g.*, Gi-Wook Shin, "The Rise of Anti-Chinese Sentiments in South Korea: Political and Security Implications," *FSI News* (Stanford Freeman Spogli Institute for International Studies), October 7, 2021.

62 Sino-North Korean Mutual Aid and Cooperation Friendship Treaty. Article 2 provides that both China and North Korea undertake all necessary measures to oppose any country or coalition of countries that might attack either nation.

63 Mar O'Neill, "Soviet Involvement in the Korean War: A New View from the Soviet-era Archives" (2000) 14(3) *OAH Magazine of History* 20–24.

64 "North Korean artillery hits South Korean island," *BBC News*, November 23, 2010, https://www.bbc.com/news/world-asia-pacific-11818005 (accessed December 30, 2022).

65 See Andrei Lankov, "'The big hunt': When North Korean Agents Almost Killed South Korea's President," *NK News*, January 21, 2021, https://www.nknews.org/2021 /01/the-big-hunt-when-north-korean-agents-almost-killed-south-koreas-president/ [https://perma.cc/D9SK-T7JS].

66 See, *e.g.*, Jonathan Cheng, "How Seoul Would Defend Itself Against a North Korean Attack," *Wall Street Journal*, August 11, 2017, https://www.wsj.com/articles/how-seoul -would-defend-itself-against-a-north-korean-attack-1502466710 [https://perma.cc/ G4WL-BZSS].

67 Elizabeth Wishnick, "The Sino-Russian Partnership and the North Korean Nuclear Crisis," *The National Bureau of Asian Research* (June 14, 2019), https://www.nbr.org /publication/the-sino-russian-partnership-and-the-north-korean-nuclear-crisis/ [https://perma.cc/8CDA-8M2V]. See also Sara Zheng, "Three reasons China will not accept a nuclear armed North Korea," *South China Morning Post*, September 19, 2017, https://www.scmp.com/news/china/diplomacy-defence/article/2111788/three -reasons-china-will-not-accept-nuclear-armed-north [https://perma.cc/X3Q8-86XD].

68 U.S. Energy Information Administration, *North Korea* (June 2018), https://www.eia
.gov/international/analysis/country/PRK [https://perma.cc/7JKX-JGHE].

69 See Suk Hi Kim and Mario Martin-Hermosillo, "The Effectiveness of Economic
Sanctions Against a Nuclear North Korea" (2013) 9(2) *North Korea Review* 99–110.

70 "North Korea says new missile puts all of US in striking range," *BBC News*, November
29, 2017, https://www.bbc.com/news/world-asia-42162462 (accessed December 30,
2022).

71 Gregory Hellman, "U.S. Prepared to Launch Preemptive Strike on North Korea,"
Politico, April 14, 2017, https://www.politico.com/tipsheets/morning-defense/2017
/04/officials-warn-us-could-launch-preemptive-strike-on-north-korea-219774
[https://perma.cc/3WV6-PU2Z].

72 For an assessment of the Singapore Summit, see Victor Cha, *Assessment of the Singapore
Summit* (June 12, 2018), https://www.csis.org/analysis/assessment-singapore-summit
[https://perma.cc/4GF4-LY8J].

73 Kelly A. Grieco "Assessing the Singapore Summit—Two Years Later" (2020) 14(3)
Strategic Studies Quarterly 12–21.

74 See Steve Chan, "Human Rights in China and the United States: Competing Visions
and Discrepant Performances" (2002) 24(4) *Human Rights Quarterly* 1035–1053.

75 See William Zheng, "China's Communist Party Backs Xi Jinping's Firm Hand on
Hong Kong and Taiwan," *South China Morning Post*, November 12, 2021, https://www
.scmp.com/news/china/politics/article/3155755/chinas-communist-party-backs-xi
-jinpings-firm-hand-hong-kong [https://perma.cc/3K88-NYP4].

76 James McBride and Andrew Chatzky, *Is 'Made in China 2025' a Threat to Global Trade?*
Council on Foreign Relations (May 13, 2019), https://www.cfr.org/backgrounder/
made-china-2025-threat-global-trade [https://perma.cc/J3RN-QKDU].

77 Lee (2022), *supra* note 56.

78 "Biden Says US Will Defend Taiwan If China Attacks," *BBC News*, October 22, 2021,
supra note 19.

79 See Lindsay Maizland, *China's Repression of Uyghurs in Xinjiang* (September 22, 2022),
https://www.cfr.org/backgrounder/china-xinjiang-uyghurs-muslims-repression-gen-
ocide-human-rights [https://perma.cc/A9LB-KZ6Z].

80 Humeyra Pamuk and David Brunnstrom, "U.S. Criticises China's Hong Kong Move,
Set to Raise Xinjiang Genocide Charge in Talks," *Reuters*, March 11, 2021, https://www
.reuters.com/article/us-usa-china-hongkong/u-s-criticises-chinas-hong-kong-move-set
-to-raise-xinjiang-genocide-charge-in-talks-idUSKBN2B32TC (accessed December
30, 2022); "US Calls on China, Hong Kong to Release Stand News Staff," *France 24*,
December 30, 2021, https://www.france24.com/en/asia-pacific/20211230-us-calls-on
-china-hong-kong-to-release-stand-news-staff [https://perma.cc/ZB8P-WEJR].

81 Pamuk and Brunnstrom (2021), *ibid.*

82 "Britain's Queen Elizabeth Aircraft Carrier to Visit Japan, S Korea on Maiden
Deployment," *Reuters*, April 26, 2021, https://www.reuters.com/world/uk/brit-
ain-says-queen-elizabeth-aircraft-carrier-visit-japan-s-korea-maiden-2021-04-26/
(accessed December 30, 2022).

83 South Korea and Japan signed the treaty normalizing their diplomatic relations.
Treaty on Basic Relations Between Japan and the Republic of Korea (1965), https://
treaties.un.org/doc/Publication/UNTS/Volume%20583/volume-583-I-8471
-English.pdf [https://perma.cc/K2JH-RLTD]. Japan, which had occupied Korea
from 1910 to 1945, left Korea in 1945 after its defeat in World War II.

84 Agreement on the settlement of problems concerning property and claims and on economic co-operation (1965), https://treaties.un.org/doc/Publication/UNTS/Volume%20583/volume-583-I-8473-English.pdf [https://perma.cc/F6Y3-QGNU].

85 For a discussion of the "comfort women," see George Hicks, *The Comfort Women: Japan's Brutal Regime of Enforced Prostitution in the Second World War* (W. W. Norton & Company, 1997) and Yoshiaki Yoshimi, *Comfort Women* (New York: Columbia University Press, 2002). See also "Forced laborers seeking justice 70 years on," *Korea Herald*, August 9, 2013, http://www.koreaherald.com/view.php?ud=20130809000689 [https://perma.cc/V3XM-2WQM].

86 Yong-Shik Lee, "Mimicking President Trump? – Trade and Politics in Japan's Recent Export Measure" (2020) 14(1) *Review of Institution and Economics* 1–5.

87 *Ibid.*

88 The ongoing conflict between South Korea and Japan has been described as one resulting from "identity clashes between a group of Japanese conservative elites and the South Korean public, manifested through the elite-led process of symbolic politics in Japan and the mass-led process in South Korea." Ji Young Kim, "Escaping the Vicious Cycle: Symbolic Politics and History Disputes Between South Korea and Japan" (2014) 38(1) *Asian Perspective* 31–60.

89 For a discussion of the dispute over the Dokdo Islands and its colonial origin, see Chinsoo Bae, "Territorial Issue in the Context of Colonial History and International Politics: The Dokdo Issue Between Korea and Japan" (2012) 26(1) *Journal of East Asian Affairs* 19–51.

90 *Ibid.*

91 Im Byung Do, "Japanese Patrol Boats Appear 440 Times Near Dokdo Islands for the Last Five Years" (in Korean), *IMPeter News*, October 5, 2021, http://www.impeter-news.com/news/articleView.html?idxno=60398 [https://perma.cc/JUZ6-PV2L].

92 Bae (2012), *supra* note 89.

93 See Hui-Yi Katherine Tseng, "China's Territorial Disputes with Japan: The Case of Senkaku/Diaoyu Islands" (2014) 1(2) *Journal of Territorial and Maritime Studies* 71–95; Yutaka Okuyama, "The Dispute Over the Kurile Islands between Russia and Japan in the 1990s" (2003) 76(1) *Pacific Affairs* 37–53.

94 See Jennifer Lind and Daryl G. Press, "Should South Korea Build Its Own Nuclear Bomb?" *Washington Post*, October 7, 2021, https://www.washingtonpost.com/outlook/should-south-korea-go-nuclear/2021/10/07/a40bb400-2628-11ec-8d53-67cfb452aa60_story.html [https://perma.cc/3KKR-EB23]. See also Kyle Mizokami, "Surprise: Japan Could Quickly Build Nuclear Weapons in a Crisis," *National Interest*, July 21, 2021, https://nationalinterest.org/blog/reboot/surprise-japan-could-quickly-build-nuclear-weapons-crisis-190089 [https://perma.cc/S665-LBET].

Chapter 2. The Heritage from the Cold War—North Korea and the Nuclear Crisis

95 David E. Sanger, "North Korea Say They Tested Nuclear Device," *New York Times*, October 9, 2006, https://www.nytimes.com/2006/10/09/world/asia/09korea.html [https://perma.cc/8ENQ-EG7U].

96 Justin McCurry, "North Korea Confirms Test of Its Largest Intercontinental Ballistic Missile Yet," *The Guardian*, March 25, 2022, https://www.theguardian.com/world/2022/mar/24/n-korea-confirms-missile-testing-ahead-of-long-confrontation-with-us [https://perma.cc/JY2J-YDAY].

97 See Paul D. Shinkman, "North Korea Threatens U.S.: Nuclear Attack 'The Only Option Left,'" *U.S. News and World Report*, June 26, 2020, https://www.usnews.com /news/world-report/articles/2020-06-26/north-korea-threatens-us-with-nuclear -attack (accessed December 30, 2022). See also "North Korea's Kim Jong Un Threatens to Use Nuclear Weapons Preemptively 'if necessary,'" *CBS News*, April 30, 2022, https://www.cbsnews.com/news/north-korea-nuclear-weapons-kim-jong -un-preemptively/ [https://perma.cc/UGM3-35YB].

98 "North Korea's Military Capabilities," *Council on Foreign Relations*, December 22, 2021, https://www.cfr.org/backgrounder/north-korea-nuclear-weapons-missile -tests-military-capabilities [https://perma.cc/WJ2H-ZEMH].

99 W. C. Clemens, "North Korea's Quest for Nuclear Weapons" (2010) 10(1) *Journal of East Asian Studies* 127–154.

100 *Ibid.*

101 *Ibid.*

102 *Ibid.*

103 *Ibid.*

104 *Ibid.*

105 *Ibid.*

106 Jacques E. C. Hymans, "Assessing North Korean Intentions And Capacities: A New Approach" (2008) 8 *Journal Of East Asian Studies*, 259–292.

107 Clemens (2010), *supra* note 99.

108 *Ibid.*

109 Mun Suk Ahn, "What Is the Root Cause of the North Korean Nuclear Program?" (2011) 38(4) *Asian Affairs* 175–187.

110 Daniel Wertz, Matthew McGrath, and Scott Lafoy, "North Korea's Nuclear Weapons Program," *Issue Brief*, The National Committee on North Korea (April 2018), https://www.ncnk.org/sites/default/files/issue-briefs/NCNK_IssueBrief _NorthKoreaNuclearWeapons_April2018.pdf [https://perma.cc/3RGU-2Z3R].

111 For further discussion on the Geneva Agreed Framework, see Eunyoung Ha and Christopher Hwang, "The U.S.-North Korea Geneva Agreed Framework: Strategic Choices and Credible Commitments" (2015) 11(1) *North Korea Review* 7–23.

112 For further discussion on the Six Party Talks, see Jayshree Bajoria and Beina Xu, *The Six Party Talks on North Korea's Nuclear Program* (September 30, 2013), https:// www.cfr.org/backgrounder/six-party-talks-north-koreas-nuclear-program [https:// perma.cc/8WPR-BKR7].

113 Wertz, McGrath, and Lafoy (2018), *supra* note 110.

114 *Ibid.*

115 *Ibid.*

116 *Ibid.*

117 Uri Friedman, "North Korea Says It Has 'Completed' Its Nuclear Program," *The Atlantic*, November 29, 2017, https://www.theatlantic.com/international/archive /2017/11/north-korea-nuclear/547019/ [https://perma.cc/MR82-DLDA].

118 For a discussion of economic sanctions against North Korea, see Rüdiger Frank, "Economic Sanctions against North Korea" (2018) 13(3) *Asia Policy* 5–12.

119 *Ibid.*

120 *Ibid.*

121 There has been controversy about the effectiveness of the economic sanctions. Rüdiger Frank summarizes his impression from his trips to North Korea as follows:

"I would say that no immediate impact of sanctions could be observed. The country remains far behind South Korea or China in its economic development, but progress is visible and the mood among those people who were willing to talk to me was optimistic. The sanctions were often problematized as a reason for the lack of even stronger progress." *Ibid.*, at 10.

122 Bennett Ramburg. *North Korea's Ongoing Nuclear Missile Tests Prove It's Time to Normalize Relations*, *NBC News*, October 21, 2021, https://www.nbcnews.com/think/opinion/north-korea-s-ongoing-nuclear-missile-tests-prove-it-s-ncna1282118 [https://perma.cc/8FT8-TE4V].

123 Evans J. R. Revere, *North Korea's Economic Crisis: Last Chance for Denuclearization?* Brookings Institute Report (February 26, 2021), at 7, https://www.brookings.edu/research/north-koreas-economic-crisis-last-chance-for-denuclearization/ [https://perma.cc/TV6M-6W7Z].

124 Choe Sang-Hun, "North Korea Adopts New Law Hardening Its Nuclear Doctrine," *New York Times*, September 9, 2022, https://www.nytimes.com/2022/09/09/world/asia/north-korea-kim-weapons-law.html [https://perma.cc/FX4K-KNBY].

125 Min-hyung Kim, "Why Nuclear? Explaining North Korea's Strategic Choice of Going Nuclear and Its Implications for East Asian Security" (2021) 56(7) *Journal of Asian and African Studies* 1488–1502.

126 See, *e.g.*, Eleanor Albert, *The China–North Korea Relationship* (June 25, 2019), https://www.cfr.org/backgrounder/china-north-korea-relationship [https://perma.cc/BBB5-4UXM].

127 See Anthony H. Cordesman, *The Korean Civil-Military Balance*, Center for Strategic and International Studies Report (May 24, 2018), https://www.csis.org/analysis/korean-civil-military-balance [https://perma.cc/969N-AJT8].

128 Kim (2021), *supra* note 125.

129 *Ibid.*

130 *Ibid.*

131 *Ibid.*

132 *Ibid.*

133 Hanah Fischer, *North Korean Provocative Actions, 1950–2007*, CRS Report for Congress (April 20, 2007), https://sgp.fas.org/crs/row/RL30004.pdf [https://perma.cc/WR8Z-PJTQ].

134 Mitch Shin, "North Korea Issues Warning Over South Korea-US Joint Military Exercises," *The Diplomat*, August 12, 2021, https://thediplomat.com/2021/08/north-korea-issues-warning-over-south-korea-us-joint-military-exercises/ [https://perma.cc/NM6V-2BKU].

135 Revere (2021), *supra* note 123.

136 Jai S. Mah, "Patterns of International Trade and the Industrial-Led Economic Development of North Korea" (2018) 30(6) *Post-Communist Economies* 830–832.

137 Kim (2021), *supra* note 125.

138 *Ibid.*

139 *Ibid.*

140 Sangsoo Lee. *North Korea's Economy Is Recentralised and China-Reliant*, East Asia Forum (April 10, 2021), https://www.eastasiaforum.org/2021/04/10/north-koreas-economy-is-recentralised-and-china-reliant/ [https://perma.cc/2HLM-7XTC].

141 Kim (2021), *supra* note 125.

142 Revere (2021), *supra* note 123, at 7.

143 Cui Lei, "Why It's Nearly Impossible to Denuclearize North Korea," *The Diplomat,* June 22, 2018, https://thediplomat.com/2018/06/why-its-nearly-impossible-to-denucl earize-north-korea/ [https://perma.cc/CM87-GM7G].

144 Kim (2021), *supra* note 125.

145 For a discussion of South Korea's economic development, see Lee (2018), *supra* note 59.

146 No Jae-Whan, "A Russian Report Says, 'South Korea Will Absorb North Korea into Reunification'" (in Korean), *Radio Free Asia*, November 4, 2011, https://www.rfa.org/korean/in_focus/russiareport-11042011114933.html [https://perma.cc/TW5A-PHPJ].

147 Shane Smith, *North Korea's Evolving Nuclear Strategy*, US-Korea Institute at SAIS (August 2015), https://www.38north.org/wp-content/uploads/2015/09/NKNF _Evolving-Nuclear-Strategy_Smith.pdf [https://perma.cc/4ALC-HA42].

148 Kim (2021), *supra* note 125.

149 Edward Howell, "The Juche H-bomb? North Korea, Nuclear Weapons and Regime-State Survival" (2020) 96(4) *International Affairs* 1051–1068, at 1057. The influence of *juche* is also a significant factor in explaining Pyongyang's discomfort regarding its dependence on China; see Kim (2021), *supra* note 125, at 1495.

150 Howell (2020), *ibid.*

151 *Ibid.*

152 *Ibid.*

153 *Ibid.*

154 *Ibid.*

155 *Ibid.*

156 *Ibid.*

157 Kim (2021), *supra* note 125.

158 *Ibid.*

159 *Ibid.*

160 Andrei Lankov, "North Korea's Perfectly Logical Strategy of Missile Launches and Dialogue," *NK News*, October 14, 2021, https://www.nknews.org/2021/10/north-koreas-perfectly-logical-strategy-of-missile-launches-and-dialogue/ [https://perma.cc/NR7E-DNDU].

161 Ahn Young-Joon, "North Korea's Kim Jong Un Threatens to Use Nuclear Weapons in Potential Conflicts with South Korea and United States," *CBS News*, July 28, 2022, https://www.cbsnews.com/news/kim-jong-un-threatens-to-use-nukes-amid -tensions-with-us-south-korea/ [https://perma.cc/7Q7B-PTVT].

162 Lankov (2021), *supra* note 160.

163 *Ibid.*

164 *Ibid.*

165 Ahn (2022), *supra* note 161.

166 Ohn Chang-Il, "The Causes of the Korean War 1950–1953" (2010) 14(2) *International Journal of Korean Studies* 19–44.

167 *Ibid.*

168 See, *e.g.,* Charles K. Armstrong, *The North Korean Revolution, 1945–1950* (Cornell University Press, 2003).

169 *Ibid.*

170 *Ibid.*

171 *Ibid.*

172 Jong-Ju Yoon, "People Who Left Home" (in Korean), *Encyclopedia of Korean Culture* (1995), http://encykorea.aks.ac.kr/Contents/Item/E0033696 [https://perma.cc /5HXN-PFVJ].

173 Armstrong (2003), *supra* note 168.
174 Joel R. Campbell, "The Wrong War: The Soviets and the Korean War, 1945–1953" (2014) 88(3) *International Social Science Review* 1–29.
175 Armstrong (2003), *supra* note 168. See also Avram Agov, "North Korea's Alliances and the Unfinished Korean War" 18(2) (1979) *Journal of Korean Studies* 225–262.
176 H.-K. Park, "American Involvement in the Korean War" (1983) 16(4) *The History Teacher* 249–263, at 250.
177 Carl Berger, *The Korea Knot: A Military-Political History* (University of Pennsylvania Press, 1965).
178 Jong Won Lee, "The Impact of the Korean War on the Korean Economy" (2001) 5(1) *International Journal of Korean Studies* 97–118.
179 *Ibid.*
180 Priscilla Roberts, "New Light on a "Forgotten War": The Diplomacy of the Korean Conflict" (2000) 14(3) *OAH Magazine of History* 10–14.
181 "Kim Il-Sung," *Encyclopaedia Britannica* (July 4, 2022), https://www.britannica.com/biography/Kim-Il-Sung [https://perma.cc/9E75-HRZJ].
182 Robert Jervis, "The Impact of the Korean War on the Cold War" (1980) 24(4) *Journal of Conflict Resolution* 563–592, at 579.
183 *Ibid.*
184 U.S. Senate Committee on Appropriations, *Hearings on Appropriations for 1951* (U.S. Government Printing Office, 1950).
185 For further discussion of the Cold War confrontations, see John Lewis Gaddis, *The Cold War: A New History* (Penguin Books, 2006) and Odd Arne Westad, *The Cold War: A World History* (Basic Books, 2019).
186 See, *e.g.,* Erik van Ree, "The Limits of Juche: North Korea's Dependence on Soviet Industrial Aid, 1953–76" (1989) 5(1) *Journal of Communist Studies* 50–73.
187 Y.S. Lee, Young-Ok Kim, and Hye Seong Mun, "Economic Development of North Korea: International Trade Based Development Policy and Legal Reform" (2010) 3(1) *Law and Development Review* 136–156.
188 Joan Robinson, "Korean Miracle" (1965) 16(9) *Monthly Review* 541–549.
189 Lee, Kim, and Mun (2010), *supra* note 187.
190 See also Yong-Shik Lee, "New General Theory of Economic Development" (2020) 24(2) *Review of Development Economics* 402–423.
191 *Ibid.* See also Lee, Kim, and Mun (2010), *supra* note 187.
192 Lee, Kim, and Mun (2010), *supra* note 187. See also Semoon Chang, "The Saga of U.S Economic Sanctions Against North Korea" (2006) 20(2) *Journal of East Asian Affairs* 109–139. For a broader discussion on the United States-North Korean relationship during the Cold War, see Edward A. Olsen, "U.S.–North Korean Relations: Foreign Policy Dilemmas" (2005) 1 *North Korean Review* 63–75.
193 See, *e.g.,* Lee (2018), *supra* note 59.
194 Lee, Kim, and Mun (2010), *supra* note 187.
195 World Bank, *GDP (current US$) – Korea, Rep.*, https://data.worldbank.org/indicator/NY.GDP.MKTP.CD?locations=KR [https://perma.cc/254J-FEYA].
196 Bank of Korea, *North Korea's GDP Estimation Result in 1996* (in Korean) (December 2, 1997), https://www.bok.or.kr/portal/bbs/P0000559/view.do?nttId=1023&menuNo=2&pageIndex=1131 (accessed December 30, 2022).
197 "Kim Il-Sung," *Encyclopaedia Britannica* (2022), *supra* note 181.
198 *Ibid.*

199 Andrei Lankov, "Kim Takes Control: The 'Great Purge' in North Korea, 1956–1960" (2002) 26(1) *Korean Studies* 87–119.

200 See, *e.g.,* Brian Bridges, "North Korea after Kim Il-Sung" (1995) 51(6) *The World Today* 103–107.

201 Lee, Kim, and Mun (2010), *supra* note 187.

202 Dae-Sook Suh, "Military-First Politics of Kim Jong Il" (2002) 26(3) *Asian Perspective* 145–167.

203 "Current Status of Support for North Korea" (in Korean), *National Index* (July 11, 2022), https://web.archive.org/web/20221008235217/https://www.index.go.kr/potal/main/EachDtlPageDetail.do?idx_cd=2784 (accessed December 30, 2022).

204 Choe Sang-Hun and David E. Sanger, "Kim Jong-il, North Korean Dictator, Dies," *New York Times*, December 19, 2011, https://www.nytimes.com/2011/12/19/world/asia/kim-jong-il-is-dead.html [https://perma.cc/2RCH-PWJG].

205 Ben Westcott, "Kim Jong Un 'ordered' Half Brother's Killing, South Korean Intelligence Says," *CNN*, February 28, 2017, https://www.cnn.com/2017/02/27/asia/kim-jong-nam-north-korea-killed [https://perma.cc/WS5J-K57B].

206 Evans J. R. Revere, *Kim Jong-Un Will Not Give Up North Korea's Nuclear Weapons* (April 9, 2018), https://www.brookings.edu/blog/order-from-chaos/2018/04/09/kim-jong-un-will-not-give-up-north-koreas-nuclear-weapons/ [https://perma.cc/3BPF-FCGA].

207 *Ibid.*

208 See Lee, Kim, and Mun (2010), *supra* note 187.

209 *Ibid.*

210 See United Nations Human Rights Council, *Report of the Commission of Inquiry on Human Rights in the Democratic People's Republic of Korea*, A/HRC/25/63 (February 7, 2014).

211 Lee (2020), *supra* note 190.

212 Lee, Kim, and Mun (2010), *supra* note 187.

213 Ministry of Unification (South Korea), *Current Status* (in Korean), https://www.unikorea.go.kr/unikorea/business/NKDefectorsPolicy/status/lately/ [https://perma.cc/FXJ4-K4TS].

214 Julie Makinen, "North Korean Leader Unveils 5-Year Plan for Economy, But No Radical Reforms," *Los Angeles Times*, May 8, 2016, https://www.latimes.com/world/asia/la-fg-north-korea-economy-20160508-story.html [https://perma.cc/UVY4-TRQX]. See also Victor Cha, "The North Korean Question" (2016) 56(2) *Asian Survey* 243–269 for a broad discussion of the state of North Korea under young leadership.

215 *Ibid.*

216 Korea Institute for National Unification, *Analysis on North Korea's 4th Plenary Meeting of the 8th Central Committee of the Workers' Party of Korea* (January 4, 2022), https://www.kinu.or.kr/pyxis-api/1/digital-files/b4062b0f-180d-4647-9c8b-96ba26380fdc [https://perma.cc/Y5BL-HKPN].

217 *Ibid.*

218 W-J Min and S. Han, "Economic Sanctions Against North Korea: The Pivotal Role of US–China Cooperation" (2020) 23(2) *International Area Studies Review* 177–193.

219 Rick Gladstone, "U.N. Security Council Imposes Punishing New Sanctions on North Korea," *New York Times*, August 5, 2017, https://www.nytimes.com/2017/08/05/world/asia/north-korea-sanctions-united-nations.html [https://perma.cc/4EBQ-F98E].

220 Makinen (2016), *supra* note 214.

221 Lee (2020), *supra* note 190.

222 See Cha (2018), *supra* note 72.

223 Patrick Köllner, "The Denuclearisation of North Korea: From Maximum Demands to Arms Control," *GIGA Focus*, no. 2 (February 2019), 1–10. See also Rohan Mishra, "Toward A Nuclear Recognition Threshold" (2020) 120(4) *Columbia Law Review* 1035–1076 (discussing the definition of de facto nuclear war states and whether North Korea meets the standard for nuclear recognition).

224 *Ibid.*

225 Grieco (2020), *supra* note 73.

226 Mary Beth D. Nikitin and Samuel D. Ryder, "North Korea's Nuclear Weapons and Missile Programs," *CRS Report*, IF10472 (January 5, 2021), at 1, https://crsreports.congress.gov/product/pdf/IF/IF10472/19 (accessed December 30, 2022).

227 Alexander Ward and Quint Forgey, "North Korea Tested Its First ICBM Since 2017," *Politico*, March 10, 2022, https://www.politico.com/newsletters/national-security-daily/2022/03/10/north-korea-tested-its-first-icbm-since-2017-00016206 [https://perma.cc/WAD3-FGGY].

228 *Ibid.*

229 Choe (2022), *supra* note 124.

230 Gawon Bae and Jessie Yeung, "North Korea Rejects South's Aid Offer, Calls President Yoon 'really simple,'" *CNN*, August 19, 2022, https://www.cnn.com/2022/08/19/asia/north-korea-south-korea-aid-denuclearization-intl-hnk/index.html [https://perma.cc/ZXP9-CYFV].

231 See Ward and Forgey (2022), *supra* note 227.

232 U.S. Department of Defense, *2022 National Defense Strategy of the United States* (October 2022), at 12, https://media.defense.gov/2022/Oct/27/2003103845/-1/-1/1/2022-NATIONAL-DEFENSE-STRATEGY-NPR-MDR.PDF [https://perma.cc/57D6-HE2D].

233 Hyung-Jin Kim, "Kim Threatens to Use Nukes Amid Tensions with US, S. Korea," *AP News*, July 28, 2022, https://apnews.com/article/covid-health-seoul-south-korea-nuclear-weapons-e285be60ef404092fe3324748fa60707 [https://perma.cc/9XJ5-GHF6].

234 Ahn (2011), *supra* note 109.

235 For further discussion of North Korea's hereditary succession, see Jae-Cheon Lim, "North Korea's Hereditary Succession, Comparing Two Key Transitions in DPRK" (2012) 52(3) *Asian Survey* 550–570.

236 For further discussion of the Confucian influence in North Korea, see Jin Woong Kang, "Political Use of Confucianism in North Korea" (2011) 16(1) *Journal of Korean Studies* 63–87.

237 *Ibid.*

238 *Ibid.*

239 For further discussion of the *Juche* ideology, see Geir Helgesen, "Political Revolution in a Cultural Continuum: Preliminary Observations on the North Korean 'Juche' Ideology with Its Intrinsic Cult of Personality" (1991) 15(1) *Asian Perspective* 187–213. See also David W. Shin, "North Korea's Post-Totalitarian State: The Rise of the Suryong (Supreme Leader) and the Transfer of Charismatic Leadership" (2016) 33(1) *American Intelligence Journal* 31–48.

240 For further discussion of North Korea's purges, see James Person, "North Korea's Purges Past," *National Interest*, December 30, 2013, https://nationalinterest.org/commentary/north-koreas-purges-past-9628 [https://perma.cc/U5ZM-YCKM].
241 United Nations Human Rights Council (2014), *supra* note 210.
242 *Ibid.*
243 *Ibid.*
244 See also Kenneth Roth, *World Report 2022: North Korea (2022)*, https://www.hrw.org/world-report/2022/country-chapters/north-korea [https://perma.cc/4FYE-6XZP].
245 See, *e.g.*, PSCORE, *Forced to Hate*, http://pscore.org/life-north-korea/forced-to-hate/ [https://perma.cc/ABV3-TM6S].
246 Choe Sang-Hun, "Kim Jong-un Calls K-Pop a 'Vicious Cancer' in the New Culture War," *New York Times*, June 10, 2021, https://www.nytimes.com/2021/06/11/world/asia/kim-jong-un-k-pop.html [https://perma.cc/44GY-YDGX].
247 Jeong Yong-Hwan and Park Eun-Jee, "18 Percent of North Koreans Now Thought to Own Mobile Phones," *JoongAng Daily*, August 11, 2020, https://koreajoongangdaily.joins.com/2020/08/11/business/tech/North-Korea-smartphone/20200811180400430.html [https://perma.cc/6H7N-9P8U].

Chapter 3. The New Asian Paradigm or Return to the Old Asia—Rise of China and Its Role in the Region

248 World Population Review, *Largest Countries in the World 2022* (2022), https://worldpopulationreview.com/country-rankings/largest-countries-in-the-world [https://perma.cc/MT79-LNZC].
249 For further discussion of the American Civil War, see Gerald Gunderson, "The Origin of the American Civil War" (1974) 34(4) *Journal of Economic History* 915–950.
250 For more information on the Zhou Dynasty's feudal system, see Li Feng, "'Feudalism' and Western Zhou China: A Criticism" (2003) 63(1) *Harvard Journal of Asiatic Studies* 115–144.
251 Sophia-Karin Psarras, "Han and Xiongnu: A Reexamination of Cultural and Political Relations (II)" (2004) 52 *Monumenta Serica* 37–93.
252 John W. Dardess, "From Mongol Empire to Yuan Dynasty: Changing Forms of Imperial Rule in Mongolia and Central Asia" 30 *Monumenta Serica* 117–165 and Piero Corradini, "The Legitimization of the Qing Dynasty" (2002) 46(1) *Central Asiatic Journal* 112–127.
253 *Ibid.*
254 Walter J. Meserve and Ruth I. Meserve, "Theatre for Assimilation: China's National Minorities" (1979) 13(2) *Journal of Asian History* 95–120, at 95.
255 See Seth (2011), *supra* note 32.
256 *Ibid.*
257 *Ibid.*
258 "GDP, 1000 to 2018," *Our World in Data* (2020), https://ourworldindata.org/grapher/gdp-world-regions-stacked-area?country=CHN~OWID_WRL [https://perma.cc/T2X3-3H2J].

259 Peter C. Perdue, "Boundaries and Trade in the Early Modern World: Negotiations at Nerchinsk and Beijing" (2010) 43(3) *Eighteen-Century Studies* 341–346.
260 See William T. Rowe, *China's Last Empire: The Great Qing* (Belknap Press, 2012).
261 See Jonathan Fenby, *Modern China: The Fall and Rise of a Great Power, 1850 to the Present* (HarperCollins, 2008).
262 *Ibid.*
263 *Ibid.*
264 *Ibid.*
265 Contemporary China includes 55 ethnic groups, but the dominant group has always been Han Chinese (漢族), which occupies 92 percent of China's population of 1.4 billion people. "Han Chinese," *New World Encyclopedia* (2022), https://www.newworl dencyclopedia.org/entry/Han_Chinese [https://perma.cc/RD7V-93SB].
266 Fenby (2008), *supra* note 261.
267 *Ibid.*
268 *Ibid.*
269 Paine (2003), *supra* note 28.
270 For further discussion of the Xinhai Revolution, see Rana Mitter, "1911: The Unanchored Chinese Revolution" (2011) 208 *China Quarterly* 1009–1020.
271 See also Harold M. Tanner, *China: A History: From the Great Qing Empire through The People's Republic of China (1644 - 2009)*, vol. 2 (Hackett Publishing Company, 2010).
272 *Ibid.*
273 Lary (2015), *supra* note 43.
274 *Ibid.*
275 For further discussion of the history of the CCP, see Tony Saich, *From Rebel to Ruler: One Hundred Years of the Chinese Communist Party* (Harvard University Press, 2021).
276 Lary (2015), *supra* note 43.
277 Li and Yang (2005), *supra* note 49.
278 Ilya Somin, "Remembering the Biggest Mass Murder in the History of the World," *Washington Post*, August 3, 2016, https://www.washingtonpost.com/news/volokh -conspiracy/wp/2016/08/03/giving-historys-greatest-mass-murderer-his-due/ [https://perma.cc/8NMN-ARKU].
279 For further discussion of the Cultural Revolution, see MacFarquhar and Schoenhals (2006), *supra* note 51. See also Julian Gewirtz, *Chinese Reformers, Western Economists, and the Making of Global China* (Harvard University Press, 2017) (discussing how Chinese intellectuals and leaders, facing a ruined economy at the end of the Cultural Revolution, sought the help of foreign economists to rebuild).
280 Fenby (2008), *supra* note 261.
281 Wayne M. Morrison, *China's Economic Rise: History, Trends, Challenges, and Implications for the United States*, Congressional Research Service, RL33534 (2019).
282 Fenby (2008), *supra* note 261.
283 For further discussion of the socialist market economy, see Barry Naughton, "Is China Socialist?" (2017) 31(1) *Journal of Economic Perspectives* 3–24 and Ding (2009), *supra* note 54.
284 See Yong-Shik Lee, *Law and Development: Theory and Practice* (2d ed., Routledge, 2022).
285 Lee, "New General Theory of Economic Development" (2020), *supra* note 190.
286 Lee and Lu (2016), *supra* note 55.
287 *Ibid.* See also Isabella M. Weber, *How China Escaped Shock Therapy: The Market Reform Debate* (Routledge, 2021).

288 Lee and Lu (2016), *supra* note 55.

289 *Ibid.*

290 Yong-Shik Lee, *Reclaiming Development in the World Trading System* (2d ed., Cambridge University Press, 2016).

291 Lee and Lu (2016), *supra* note 55.

292 *Ibid.*

293 *Ibid.*

294 *Ibid.*

295 "China Is the World's Factory, More Than Ever," *The Economist*, September 8, 2021, https://www.economist.com/finance-and-economics/2021/09/08/china-is-the-worlds-factory-more-than-ever [https://perma.cc/9PB2-YFTT].

296 See Yong-Shik Lee, "International Trade Law Post Neoliberalism" (2020) 68(2) *Buffalo Law Review* 413–478.

297 For a related discussion, see Yong-Shik Lee, "National Security as a Means to a Commercial End—Call for a New Approach," *SSRN* (May 27, 2022), https://papers.ssrn.com/sol3/papers.cfm?abstract_id=4117777.

298 Statista, *China is the World's Manufacturing Superpower* (May 4, 2021), https://www.statista.com/chart/20858/top-10-countries-by-share-of-global-manufacturing-output/ [https://perma.cc/98Z5-FMBB].

299 Li and Yang (2005), *supra* note 49.

300 World Bank, *Manufacturing, Value-Added (Current US$) – China*, https://data.worldbank.org/indicator/NV.IND.MANF.CD?locations=CN [https://perma.cc/4N25-9AEK].

301 Estimated from U.S. government statistics. United States Statistics Division, *Value Added by Economic Activity, at Current Prices – US Dollars* (Mining Manufacturing, and Utilities), https://unstats.un.org/unsd/snaama/Basic (accessed December 30, 2022).

302 In 2021, 48,000 foreign-invested enterprises were set up in China. Orange Wang, "How Much Is China's Foreign Direct Investment and Is It Still a Good Destination for Overseas Investors?" *South China Morning Post*, June 10, 2022, https://www.scmp.com/economy/economic-indicators/article/3181037/how-much-chinas-foreign-direct-investment-and-it-still [https://perma.cc/8B9C-W4FA]. By the end of 2020, a total of 1,040,480 foreign companies were registered in China. "How Many Foreign Companies in China?" *RegistrationChina* (November 2, 2021), https://www.registrationchina.com/articles/how-many-foreign-companies-in-china/ [https://perma.cc/R683-EKK6].

303 For a more detailed account of the development of China's manufacturing sector, see Lianshui Li and Zhanyuan Du (eds.), *A Research Report on the Development of China's Manufacturing Sector (2016)* (Springer, 2017).

304 Wang (2022), *supra* note 302.

305 "How many Foreign Companies in China?" *RegistrationChina* (2021), *supra* note 302.

306 Lee (2022), *supra* note 284.

307 See Peter Brennan, *Push to Reshore US Manufacturing Challenged by Reliance on Global Supply Chain* (April 14, 2022), https://www.spglobal.com/marketintelligence/en/news-insights/latest-news-headlines/push-to-reshore-us-manufacturing-challenged-by-reliance-on-global-supply-chain-69752018 [https://perma.cc/L39K-BD3W].

308 World Bank, *GDP Per Capita (Current US$) – China*, https://data.worldbank.org/indicator/NY.GDP.PCAP.CD?locations=CN [https://perma.cc/AH9M-BMC5].

309 Statista, *Share of the Leading Merchandise Importers Worldwide in 2020, by Importing Nation* (October 11, 2021), https://www.statista.com/statistics/252140/share-of-the-lead-ing-merchandise-importers-worldwide-by-importing-nation/ [https://perma.cc/U93A-D6TT].

310 See, *e.g.*, International Trade Administration, *U.S. Trade in 2021: U.S. Exporters on Road to Recovery* (February 11, 2022), https://blog.trade.gov/2022/02/11/u-s-trade-in-2021-u-s-exporters-on-road-to-recovery/#:~:text=The%20top%20four%20U.S.%20goods,followed%20by%20China%20and%20Japan [https://perma.cc/3F52-735G].

311 Ding (2009), *supra* note 54.

312 For a discussion of the changes within China's Communist Party, See Chun Han Wong, "Is China's Communist Party Still Communist?" *Wall Street Journal*, June 30, 2021, https://www.wsj.com/articles/is-chinas-communist-party-still-communist-11625090401 [https://perma.cc/D2HB-84CC].

313 Lee (2017), *supra* note 18.

314 *Ibid.*

315 *Ibid.*

316 *Ibid.*

317 For further discussion of China's perception of national security, see Yi Wang, "The Backward Will Be Beaten: Historical Lesson, Security, and Nationalism in China" (2020) 29(126) *Journal of Contemporary China* 887–900.

318 Edward White, Song Jung-a, and Kang Buseong, "Lotte's China Woes a Harbinger of South Korean Exodus," *Financial Times*, June 20, 2019, https://www.ft.com/content/3a2eaeb2-9330-11e9-aea1-2b1d33ac3271 [https://perma.cc/7U22-J4ZM].

319 Amir Guluzade, "How Reform Has Made China's State-Owned Enterprises Stronger," *World Economic Forum* (May 21, 2020), https://www.weforum.org/agenda/2020/05/how-reform-has-made-chinas-state-owned-enterprises-stronger/ [https://perma.cc/KGK8-YDW3].

320 For further discussion of China's SOEs, see Karen Jingrong Lin, Xiaoyan Lu, Junsheng Zhang, and Ying Zheng, "State-Owned Enterprises in China: A Review of 40 Years of Research and Practice" (2020) 13(1) *China Journal of Accounting Research* 31–55.

321 *Ibid.*

322 For further discussion of the role of China's SOEs, see Fan Gang and Nicholas Hope, *The Role of State-Owned Enterprises in the Chinese Economy*, https://www.chinausfocus.com/2022/wp-content/uploads/Part+02-Chapter+16.pdf (accessed December 30, 2022).

323 Lee (2017), *supra* note 18.

324 S. Donnan, L. Hornby, and A. Beesley, "China Challenges EU and US Over Market Economy Status," *Financial Times*, December 13, 2016, https://www.ft.com/content/6af8da62-bf5d-11e6-9bca-2b93a6856354?mhq5j=e2 (accessed December 30, 2022).

325 S. Donnan, "Trump Trade Tsar Warns Against China 'market economy' Status," *Financial Times*. June 22, 2017, https://www.ft.com/content/4d6ba03e-56b0-11e7-9fed-c19e2700005f (accessed December 30, 2022).

326 Donnan, Hornby, and Beesley (2016), *supra* note 324.

327 For further discussion of China's challenge, see David Dollar and Ryan Hass, *Getting the China challenge right* (January 25, 2021), https://www.brookings.edu/research/getting-the-china-challenge-right/ [https://perma.cc/JGL2-NYTF].

328 For example, China has agreed with Russia to use their own currencies, instead of US dollars, to pay for petroleum from Russia. This is intended to weaken the economic sanctions against Russia, which are led by the United States and imposed for Russia's military invasion of Ukraine. "Russia Says China Will Start Paying for Gas in Rubles and Yuan," *CNN Business*, September 6, 2022, https://www.cnn.com /2022/09/06/energy/china-russian-gas-payments-ruble-yuan/index.html [https:// perma.cc/L3U2-S6C7].

329 Lee (2020), *supra* note 296.

330 *Ibid.*

331 See Sean Keane, "Huawei Ban Timeline: Detained CFO Makes Deal with US Justice Department," *CNET* (September 30, 2021), https://www.cnet.com/news /privacy/huawei-ban-timeline-detained-cfo-makes-deal-with-us-justice-depart- ment/ [https://perma.cc/82C5-CNTV]; Simon Denyer, "Japan Effectively Bans China's Huawei and ZTE from Government Contracts, Joining U.S.," *Washington Post*, December 10, 2018, https://www.washingtonpost.com/world/asia_pacific/ japan-effectively-bans-chinas-huawei-zte-from-government-contracts-joining-us /2018/12/10/748fe98a-fc69-11e8-ba87-8c7facdf6739_story.html [https://perma.cc /WLF3-HDS2].

332 Lee (2020), *supra* note 296.

333 Joe McDonald, "China Criticizes US Action Against Huawei," *AP News*, May 16, 2019, https://apnews.com/article/china-technology-united-states-ap-top-news-bei- jing-6dffae234a3e45a8b1e7ede17480839d [https://perma.cc/WLF3-HDS2].

334 Congressional Research Service, *China Naval Modernization: Implications for U.S. Navy Capabilities—Background and Issues for Congress*, RL33153 (March 8, 2022), https://sgp .fas.org/crs/row/RL33153.pdf [https://perma.cc/X3PL-74ZA].

335 *Ibid.*

336 Lee (2017), *supra* note 18.

337 Son Ji-hyoung, "Chinese Envoy Warns Korea Against 'interference' in Chip Supply Chain," *Korea Herald* (July 26, 2022), https://www.koreaherald.com/view.php?ud =20220726000627 [https://perma.cc/MV22-T83M].

338 See In-Chan Hwang, "Xi Jinping Says Korea Was a Part of China," *Dong-A Ilbo*, April 20, 2017, https://www.donga.com/en/article/all/20170420/902176/1 [https://perma.cc/R38F-DZFG].

339 For further discussion of the Northeast Project, see Yeo Hokyu, "China's Northeast Project and Trends in the Study of Koguryŏ History" (2006) 10 *International Journal of Korean History* 121–155.

340 Northeast Asian History Network, *Korea-China History Awareness*, http://contents .nahf.or.kr/english/item/level.do?itemId=iscd [https://perma.cc/G2B5-Y5ST].

341 See also Jae Ho Chung, "Korean Views of Korea-China Relations: Evolving Perceptions and Upcoming Challenges" (2012) 36(2) *Asian Perspective* 219–236.

342 Bruce Stokes, *Hostile Neighbors: China vs. Japan* (September 13, 2016), https://www .pewresearch.org/global/2016/09/13/hostile-neighbors-china-vs-japan/ [https:// perma.cc/A5CN-CKR8].

343 See Tseng (2014), *supra* note 93.

344 Antoine Roth and Andrea A. Fischetti, "Japan's Growing Reliance on the Chinese Market," *Tokyo Review* (2021), https://www.tokyoreview.net/2021/02/japans-grow- ing-reliance-on-the-chinese-market/ [https://perma.cc/CF33-Z2HQ].

345 Isabel Reynolds and Emi Nobuhiro, "China Says Unfair Treatment of Huawei Could Damage Japan Ties," *Bloomberg*, March 29, 2019, https://www.bloomberg.

com/news/articles/2019-03-29/china-says-unfair-treatment-of-huawei-could-dam-age-japan-ties [https://perma.cc/S3HZ-ZF46].

346 For further discussion of this conflict, see Michael S. Gerson, *The Sino-Soviet Border Conflict* (November 2010), https://www.cna.org/archive/CNA_Files/pdf/d0022974 .a2.pdf [https://perma.cc/3GQ2-X6RZ].

347 Richard Lowenthal, "Russia and China: Controlled Conflict" (1971) 49(3) *Foreign Affairs* 507–518.

348 Paul D. Shinkman, "China Indicates to Biden It Won't Send Weapons to Russia," *The U.S. News and World Report*, March 18, 2022, https://www.usnews.com/news/ world-report/articles/2022-03-18/china-indicates-to-biden-it-wont-send-weapons -to-russia-as-bloody-war-in-ukraine-grinds-on (accessed December 30, 2022).

349 "China to Enforce UN Sanctions Against North Korea," *The Guardian*, September 23, 2017, https://www.theguardian.com/world/2017/sep/23/china-to-enforce-un -sanctions-against-north-korea [https://perma.cc/6XX3-FQPQ].

350 Ben Frohman, Emma Rafaelof, and Alexis Dale-Huang, *The China-North Korea Strategic Rift: Background and Implications for the United States* (January 24, 2022), https:// www.uscc.gov/sites/default/files/2022-01/China-North_Korea_Strategic_Rift.pdf [https://perma.cc/45FZ-EYCM].

351 "Mongolia Under Pressure to Align with Russia and China," *The Guardian*, May 31, 2022, https://www.theguardian.com/world/2022/may/31/mongolia-under-pres-sure-to-align-with-russia-and-china [https://perma.cc/FV7H-V9XR].

352 See, *e.g.*, Bard Nikolas Vik Steen, "Is Pacific Asia Returning to Sinocentrism?" *E-International Relations* (September 14, 2014), https://www.e-ir.info/2014/09/14/is -pacific-asia-returning-to-sinocentrism/ [https://perma.cc/FLV4-V9HC]. See also Suisheng Zhao, "Rethinking the Chinese World Order: The Imperial Cycle and the Rise of China" (2015) 24(96) *Journal of Contemporary China* 961–982. For a proponent of Sinocentrism, see Feng Zhang, "Chinas Rise Will Be Peaceful," *in* Robert S. Ross and Zhu Feng (eds.), *China's Ascent-Power, Security, and the Future of International Politics* (Cornell University Press, 2008), at 34–54. Sinocentrism, some scholars argue, pre-sents a shift in the paradigm in global history. See Manuel Perez Garcia, "From Eurocentrism to Sinocentrism: The New Challenges in Global History" (2014) 119(3) *European Journal of Scientific Research* 337–352.

353 See Fairbank (ed.) (1968), *supra* note 27.

354 For further discussion of the political development of China, see David M. Lampton, *Following the Leader: Ruling China, From Deng Xiaoping to Xi Xingping* (University of California Press, 2014).

355 Ministry of Foreign Affairs of the People's Republic of China, *Wang Yi: Promote Sound and Steady Growth of China-ROK Strategic Cooperative Partnership with a Five-Point Commitment* (August 9, 2022), https://www.fmprc.gov.cn/mfa_eng/wjdt_665385 /wshd_665389/202208/t20220810_10740381.html [https://perma.cc/PYZ7 -GPGM].

356 See, *e.g.*, "No to Three No's," *Korea Herald* (August 12, 2022), https://www.koreaher-ald.com/view.php?ud=20220811000838 [https://perma.cc/B4JF-DL3J].

357 Young-Hwan Kim, "Confucianism as Sinocentrism" (in Korean) (2011) 40 *Journal of Philosophical Ideas* 3–33.

358 See A. James Gregor and Maria Hsia Chang, "Anti-Confucianism: Mao's Last Campaign" (1979) 19(11) *Asian Survey* 1073–1092.

359 According to the WTO, a total of 353 FTAs (also called "regional trade agreements" or "RTAs") were in force as of September 2022. World Trade Organization, *Regional*

Trade Agreements Database (September 16, 2022), http://rtais.wto.org/UI/PublicM aintainRTAHome.aspx [https://perma.cc/D22X-6LVR]. South Korea and Japan each have signed eighteen FTAs.

360 According to a national power ranking, China is ranked at number 2, behind the United States; other countries in the region, such as Japan, South Korea, and Russia, are ranked at 6, 8, and 3, respectively, showing that China's economic and political dominance in the region is not established. "Power," *The U.S. News and World Report*, https://www.usnews.com/news/best-countries/rankings/power (accessed December 30, 2022).

361 Gordon Chang, *China's Conception of the World and Model of Global Governance*, https:// www.hoover.org/sites/default/files/gordon_chang_paper.pdf (accessed December 30, 2022).

362 *Ibid.*

363 Joshua P. Meltzer and Neena Shenai, *The US-China Economic Relationship: A Comprehensive Approach* (February 28, 2019), https://www.brookings.edu/research/ the-us-china-economic-relationship-a-comprehensive-approach/ [https://perma.cc /FR8S-VAZS].

364 See James Stavridis, "A US-China War Over Taiwan Isn't Happening Anytime Soon," *Bloomberg*, August 9, 2022, https://www.bloomberg.com/opinion/articles /2022-08-09/a-us-china-war-over-taiwan-isn-t-happening-anytime-soon?lead-Source=uverify%20wall [https://perma.cc/7WCY-5W7T].

365 See discussion *supra* Sections 3.1 and 3.2.

366 Sangchul Yoo, "Xi's Power Is at Climax...Why Voices Missing Hu Jintao?" (in Korean), *JoongAng*, October 27, 2019, https://www.joongang.co.kr/article/23616322 #home [https://perma.cc/AU59-EL2R].

367 *Ibid.*

368 *Ibid.*

369 "What Does Xi Jinping's China Dream Mean?" *BBC News*, June 6, 2013, https:// www.bbc.com/news/world-asia-china-22726375 (accessed December 30, 2022).

370 *Ibid.*

371 U.S. Chamber of Commerce, *Made in China 2025: Global Ambitions Built on Local Protections* (2017), https://www.uschamber.com/assets/archived/images/final_made _in_china_2025_report_full.pdf [https://perma.cc/YU48-CXW9].

372 See "America's Top Brass Responds to the Threat of China in the Pacific," *The Economist*, March 11, 2021, https://www.economist.com/asia/2021/03/11/americas -top-brass-responds-to-the-threat-of-china-in-the-pacific [https://perma.cc/2G52 -QEFT].

373 See Lindsay Maizland, *Hong Kong's Freedoms: What China Promised and How It's Cracking Down* (May 19, 2022), https://www.cfr.org/backgrounder/hong-kong-freedoms -democracy-protests-china-crackdown [https://perma.cc/9HTZ-CBH4]. See also Joint Declaration on the question of Hong Kong (December 19, 1984), https://trea-ties.un.org/doc/Publication/UNTS/Volume%201399/v1399.pdf [https://perma .cc/T8WC-UZ5A].

374 "China Reaffirms Threat of Military Force to Annex Taiwan," *Voice of America*, August 10, 2022, https://www.voanews.com/a/china-reaffirms-threat-of-military -force-to-annex-taiwan-/6695555.html [https://perma.cc/LY7A-4H6N].

375 See, *e.g.*, United Nations Human Rights Office of the High Commissioner, *OHCHR Assessment of Human Rights Concerns in the Xinjiang Uyghur Autonomous Region, People's Republic of China* (August 31, 2022), https://www.ohchr.org/sites/default/files/

documents/countries/2022-08-31/22-08-31-final-assesment.pdf [https://perma.cc/M8VT-5PUL]. See also Maizland (2022), *supra* note 79.

376 Lee (2020), *supra* note 296.

377 See Cheng Hung-ta and Evelyn Kao, "U.S.-Led Chip Alliance Aimed at Curbing China Influence: Analyst," *Focus Taiwan*, August 21, 2022, https://focustaiwan.tw/business/202208210007 [https://perma.cc/JTS8-4U46].

378 Zolan Kanno-Youngs and Peter Baker, "Biden Pledges to Defend Taiwan if It Faces a Chinese Attack," *New York Times*, May 23, 2022, https://www.nytimes.com/2022/05/23/world/asia/biden-taiwan-china.html [https://perma.cc/FM2H-2STW].

379 See, *e.g.*, U.S. Department of State, *2021 Country Reports on Human Rights Practices: China (Includes Hong Kong, Macau, and Tibet)*, https://www.state.gov/reports/2021-country-reports-on-human-rights-practices/china/ [https://perma.cc/GP97-597E].

380 See Nectar Gan, "'Stop asking why': Shanghai Intensifies Covid Lockdown Despite Falling Cases," *CNN*, May 9, 2022, https://www.cnn.com/2022/05/09/china/china-covid-shanghai-restrictions-escalate-intl-hnk/index.html [https://perma.cc/AQJ6-QXAS].

381 Grady McGregor, "China's Lockdowns to Contain Omicron Snarled the Global Economy. Lockdowns to Contain Subvariant BA.5 Could Be Even Worse," *Fortune*, July 11, 2022, https://fortune.com/2022/07/11/china-covid-lockdowns-omicron-ba-5-subvariant-economy-shanghai/ [https://perma.cc/EJN9-YTRY].

382 China subsequently announced the discontinuation of its zero-COVID policy due to widespread protests, and the number of COVID infections and related deaths have rapidly increased as authorities have given up on response measures such as mass testing requirements. See "China will stop reporting asymptomatic COVID cases after dropping mass testing requirements," *PBS*, December 14, https://www.pbs.org/newshour/world/china-will-stop-reporting-asymptomatic-covid-cases-after-dropping-mass-testing-requirements [https://perma.cc/8CRF-YTBT]. The rapid increase in COVID infections in China does not indicate that its coercive zero-COVID policy was justified. Rather, it shows that China lacked plans and preparations for an exit plan. See Farah Master and David Stanway, "China Lacked a 'zero COVID' Exit Plan. Its People Are Paying the Price," *Reuters*, December 22, 2022, https://www.reuters.com/world/china/china-lacked-zero-covid-exit-plan-its-people-are-paying-price-2022-12-23/ [https://perma.cc/2PMT-XA7R].

383 For further discussion of the Trans-Pacific Partnership Agreement, see Yong-Shik Lee, "Future of Trans-Pacific Partnership Agreement: Just a Dead Trade Initiative or a Meaningful Model for the North-South Economic and Trade Integration?" (2017) 51(5) *Journal of World Trade* 1–26.

384 Steve Herman, "White House Ordered to Return Press Pass to CNN Reporter," *Voice of America*, November 17, 2018, https://www.voanews.com/a/white-house-ordered-to-return-press-pass-to-cnn-reporter/4661693.html [https://perma.cc/6GGJ-ETY9].

385 Daniella Diaz, "Top General Says He'd Push Back Against 'illegal' Nuclear Strike Order," *CNN*, November 20, 2017, https://www.cnn.com/2017/11/18/politics/air-force-general-john-hyten-nuclear-strike-donald-trump [https://perma.cc/MS3F-S548].

386 Lee (2022), *supra* note 284.

387 *Ibid.* See also Yong-Shik Lee, "General Theory of Law and Development" (2017) 50(3) *Cornell International Law Journal* 415–471.

388 Lee (2017), *supra* note 387.

389 According to the World Bank, China's per capita income in 2021 was US$ 12,556. World Bank, *GDP Per Capita (Current US$) – China*, https://data.worldbank.org/indicator/NY.GDP.PCAP.CD?locations=CN [https://perma.cc/LR4S-QNSU].

390 Lee (2017), *supra* note 387.

391 Lee (2022), *supra* note 56.

392 "Alibaba And Tencent Fined in China Tech Crackdown," *Forbes*, July 13, 2022, https://www.forbes.com/sites/qai/2022/07/13/alibaba-and-tencent-fined-in-china-tech-crackdown/?sh=71737b083dac (accessed December 30, 2022).

393 Kenneth N. Waltz, *Theory of International Politics* (Addison-Wesley, 1979), at 118.

394 Researchers have demonstrated that democracy has a negative effect on the likelihood of conflict or escalation. See Zeev Maoz and Bruce Russett, "Normative and Structural Causes of Democratic Peace, 1946-1986" (1993) 87(3) *American Political Science Review* 624–638. See also Michael R. Tomz and Jessica L. P. Weeks, "Public Opinion and the Democratic Peace" (2013) 107(4) *American Political Science Review* 849–865. For an opposing view, see Sebastian Rosato, "The Flawed Logic of Democratic Peace Theory" (2003) 97(4) *American Political Science Review* 585–602.

395 Yoo (2019), *supra* note 366.

396 "China Says 2021 Fiscal Revenues Rise 10.7% y/y, Boosted by Economic Recovery," *Reuters*, January 25, 2022, https://www.reuters.com/markets/rates-bonds/china-says-2021-fiscal-revenues-rise-107-yryr-2022-01-25/ (accessed December 30, 2022).

397 For further discussion of China's military, see Congressional Research Service, *China's Military: The People's Liberation Army (PLA)* (June 4, 2021), https://crsreports.congress.gov/product/pdf/R/R46808 (assessed December 20, 2022).

398 McGregor (2022), *supra* note 381.

399 Scott McDonald, "NY Governor Cuomo Says a Federal Quarantine by Trump Would be a 'Declaration of War,' Trump Renegotiates," *Newsweek*, March 28, 2020, https://www.newsweek.com/ny-governor-cuomo-says-federal-quarantine-ordered-trump-would-declaration-war-states-1494857 [https://perma.cc/7DLL-4BPC].

400 *Ibid.*

401 For further discussion on the relationship between judicial independence and democratic governance, see Christopher M. Larkins, "Judicial Independence and Democratization: A Theoretical and Conceptual Analysis" (1996) 44 *American Journal of Comparative Law* 605–626 and Roderick A. Macdonald and Hoi Kong, "Judicial Independence as a Constitutional Virtue," *in* Carles Boix and Susan C. Stokers (eds.), *Oxford Handbook of Comparative Politics* (New York, 2012), at 831–858.

402 Article 126, Constitution of the People's Republic of China.

403 Congressional-Executive Commission on China, *Judicial Independence in the RPC*, https://www.cecc.gov/judicial-independence-in-the-prc (assessed September 19, 2022).

404 *Ibid.*

405 *Ibid.*

Chapter 4. A New Balancer in the Region? South Korea at the Crossroads

406 Seth (2011), *supra* note 32.

407 *Ibid.*

408 *Ibid.*, See also Mark Cartwright, "The Japanese Invasion of Korea, 1592-8 CE," *World History Encyclopedia* (June 11, 2019), https://www.worldhistory.org/article/1398 /the-japanese-invasion-of-korea-1592-8-ce/ [https://perma.cc/2F3E-L8TM].

409 Seth (2011), *supra* note 32 and Cartwright (2019), *ibid.*

410 The details of the Qing's invasion were chronicled in George Kallander (trans.), *The Diary of 1636: The Second Manchu Invasion of Korea* (Columbia University Press, 2020).

411 James (2011), *supra* note 37.

412 Seth (2011), *supra* note 32.

413 Fischer (2007), *supra* note 133.

414 See, *e.g.*, Kim Bo Kwang, "Diplomatic Issue between Goryeo-Song relation in the Early 12th Century" (in Korean) (2016) 60 *Dongguk Journal of History* 43–84.

415 Seung-Chul Son, "Sa-Dae-Gyo-Rin" (in Korean), *Encyclopedia of Korean Culture* (1998), http://encykorea.aks.ac.kr/Contents/Index?contents_id=E0025448 [https:// perma.cc/7H76-QLY6].

416 Seth (2011), *supra* note 32.

417 *Ibid.* See also Kevin N. Cawley, "Korean Confucianism," *Stanford Encyclopedia of Philosophy* (November 24, 2021), https://plato.stanford.edu/entries/korean-confu-cianism/ [https://perma.cc/K8VX-JL9C].

418 Cawley (2021), *ibid.*

419 See, *e.g.*, Yi Myonggu and William A. Douglas, "Korean Confucianism Today" (1967) 40 *Pacific Affairs* 43–59.

420 Brianna Jackson, "Confucianism and Korean Dramas: How Cultural and Social Proximity, Hybridization of Modernity and Tradition, and Dissimilar Confucian Trajectories Affect Importation Rates of Korean Broadcasting Programs between Japan and China," *Virginia Commonwealth University Scholars Compass* (2017), https:// scholarscompass.vcu.edu/cgi/viewcontent.cgi?article=1041&context=auctus (accessed December 30, 2022).

421 Tae-Ho Choi, "Trade," *Encyclopedia of Korean Culture* (1995), http://encykorea.aks.ac .kr/Contents/Item/E0019151 [https://perma.cc/9YZE-JBLV].

422 See Seth (2011), *supra* note 32.

423 Choi (1995), *supra* note 421.

424 *Ibid.*

425 World Bank, *Gross Domestic Product 2021*, https://databankfiles.worldbank.org/data/ download/GDP.pdf [https://perma.cc/ZH97-G9JB].

426 United Nations Statistics Division, *supra* note 301 (Manufacturing, value added).

427 Ministry of Trade, Industry and Energy (South Korea), *Exports and Trade in 2011: The Largest in History* (in Korean) (January 4, 2022), https://www.korea.kr/news/ visualNewsView.do?newsId=148897615 [https://perma.cc/3P55-EXGK].

428 Global Firepower, *2022 Military Strength Ranking*, https://www.globalfirepower.com/ countries-listing.php [https://perma.cc/B78N-DN23].

429 "Power," *US News and World Report*, https://www.usnews.com/news/best-countries/ rankings/power (accessed December 30, 2022).

430 Bank of Korea, *Korea's Major Industrial Production Map* (in Korean) (June 2021), https://www.bok.or.kr/viewer/skin/doc.html?fn=202106080424430000.pdf&rs=/ webview/result/P0002125/202106 [https://perma.cc/4DZ3-LHS4].

431 Global Edge, *South Korea: Trade Statistics*, https://globaledge.msu.edu/countries/ south-korea/tradestats [https://perma.cc/Z9U5-7ZNW].

432 For further discussion of economic cooperation, see Semoon Chang, "Economic Cooperation Between the Two Koreas" (2012) 8(2) *North Korean Review* 6–16.

433 Lee, Kim, and Mun (2010), *supra* note 187.

434 Camp Humphreys, located along the western coast of South Korea within the seaport city of Pyeongtaek, and approximately 40 miles (64 kilometers) south of Seoul, is the largest overseas U.S. Military installation in the world. *U.S. Army Garrison Humphreys*, https://home.army.mil/humphreys/index.php [https://perma.cc/EMV2-RB4Q].

435 For further discussion of the United States-South Korea alliance, see Hyun-Wook Kim and Won K. Paik, "Alliance Cohesion in the Post-Cold War US-South Korea Security Relations" (2009) 23(2) *Journal of Asian Affairs* 1–40.

436 See, *e.g.*, "South Korea and U.S. Begin Their Largest Military Drills," *CNBC*, August 22, 2022, https://www.cnbc.com/2022/08/22/s-korea-and-us-begin-largest-military-drills-amid-n-korea-backlash.html [https://perma.cc/V8HL-77DJ].

437 According to a report, South Korea's military defense budget was a mere US$ 280 million in 1960, thereby necessitating U.S. aid for its security. The budget has increased to US$ 45.74 billion in 2022, which is the seventh largest in the world. Microtrends, *South Korea Military Spending/Defense Budget 1960–2022*, https://www.macrotrends.net/countries/KOR/south-korea/military-spending-defense-budget [https://perma.cc/H6NP-L8QD].

438 See Emanuel Pastreich, "The Balancer: Roh Moo-hyun's Vision of Korean Politics and the Future of Northeast Asia" (2005) 3(8) *Asian-Pacific Journal* 1–14.

439 Jina Kim, *China and Regional Security Dynamics on the Korean Peninsula* (March 18, 2020), https://carnegieendowment.org/2020/03/18/china-and-regional-security-dynamics-on-korean-peninsula-pub-81235 [https://perma.cc/F7J3-4UEF].

440 World Bank, *Exports of Goods and Services (% of GDP) – Korea, Rep.*, https://data.worldbank.org/indicator/NE.EXP.GNFS.ZS?locations=KR [https://perma.cc/779N-HQVA].

441 International Trade Administration, *South Korea - Country Commercial Guide*, https://www.trade.gov/country-commercial-guides/south-korea-market-overview [https://perma.cc/RZ39-MXQF].

442 Sam Kim, "South Korea Posts Longest Run of Trade Deficits Since 1997," *Bloomberg*, September 30, 2022, https://www.bloomberg.com/news/articles/2022-10-01/south-korea-posts-longest-string-of-trade-deficits-since-1997?leadSource=uverify%20wall [https://perma.cc/FH9W-P3CV].

443 Lee (2022), *supra* note 56.

444 Lee Seung-hoon, Kwon Han-wool, and Lee Eun-joo, "U.S. Pressure Mounts on Korea to Join Chip 4 Amid Pelosi Visit to Taipei and Seoul," *Pulse*, August 4, 2022, https://pulsenews.co.kr/view.php?year=2022&no=686003 (accessed December 30, 2022).

445 Lind and Press (2021), *supra* note 94.

446 See, *e.g.*, Heung-Gil Koh, "South-North Diplomatic Warfare in Africa," *The JoongAng*, February 26, 1977, https://www.joongang.co.kr/article/1457070#home [https://perma.cc/L5ND-HW8K].

447 Sebastien Roblin, "The Rangoon Bombing: North Korea's 1983 Attempt to Destroy South Korea's Government," *National Interest*, July 29, 2021, https://nationalinterest.org/blog/reboot/rangoon-bombing-north-korea%E2%80%99s-1983-attempt

-destroy-south-korea%E2%80%99s-government-190689   [https://perma.cc/9JPJ
-XE74].
448 Pastreich (2005), *supra* note 438.
449 *Ibid.*
450 *Ibid.*
451 *Ibid.*, at 10–11.
452 *Ibid.*, at 10.
453 *Ibid.* See also Choong-Nam Kim, "Changing Northeast Asia and Korea-US Relations" (2000) 14(1) *Journal of East Asian Affairs* 1–36.
454 Gilbert Rozman, "Regionalism in Northeast Asia: Korea's Return to Center Stage," in Charles K. Armstrong *et al.* (eds.), *Korea at the Center: Dynamics of Regionalism in Northeast Asia* (Routledge, 2006), at 151–166.
455 *Ibid.*
456 See also Jong Kun Choi and Chung-in Moon, "Understanding Northeast Asian Regional Dynamics: Inventory Checking and New Discourses on Power, Interest, and Identity" (2010) 10 *International Relations of the Asia-Pacific* 343–372.
457 See "What does Xi Jinping's China Dream mean?" *BBC News*, June 6, 2013, *supra* note 369.
458 McCurry (2022), *supra* note 96.
459 See Eunjung Irene Oh, "Ambitions Are Not Opportunities: South Korean President Moon Jae-in's Failed North Korea Policy," *Yale Journal of International Affairs* (January 14, 2022), https://www.yalejournal.org/publications/ambitions-are-not-opportuni-ties-south-korean-president-moon-jae-ins-failed-north-korea-policy [https://perma.cc/A8W8-XHYL].
460 *Ibid.*
461 *Ibid.*
462 Yosuke Onchi, "Kim Jong Un's Fury Stems from His Blaming Moon for Hanoi Debacle," *NikkeiAsia*, July 5, 2020, https://asia.nikkei.com/Spotlight/N-Korea-at-crossroads/Kim-Jong-Un-s-fury-stems-from-his-blaming-Moon-for-Hanoi-debacle [https://perma.cc/335C-EBJR].
463 See Esme Howard, "British Policy and the Balance of Power" (1925) 19(2) *American Political Science Review* 261–267.
464 Michael Sheehan, "The Sincerity of the British Commitment to the Maintenance of the Balance of Power 1714-1763" (2004) 15(3) *Diplomacy and Statecraft* 489–506.
465 As of 2021, the GDPs of South Korea, Japan, and China were US$ 1.81 trillion, 4.94 trillion, and 17.73 trillion, respectively. World Bank, *GDP (current US$) – Japan, Korea, Rep., China*, https://data.worldbank.org/indicator/NY.GDP.MKTP.CD?locations=JP-KR-CN [https://perma.cc/Z6PL-KGEF].
466 For further discussion on the balance of power in 19th-century Europe, see Paul W. Schroeder, "The 'Balance of Power' System in Europe, 1815–1871" (1975) 27(5) *Naval War College Review* 18–31.
467 See Seth (2011), *supra* note 32.
468 *Ibid.*
469 *Ibid.*
470 *Ibid.*
471 See also Bae-ho Han and Young Ick Lew, "Korea under Japanese Rule," *Encyclopaedia Britannica*, https://www.britannica.com/place/Korea/Korea-under-Japanese-rule [https://perma.cc/2N65-UTZ2].

472 *Ibid.*
473 *Ibid.*
474 *Ibid.*
475 Andrea Matles Savada and William Shaw (eds.), *South Korea: A Country Study* (1990), http://countrystudies.us/south-korea/7.htm#:~:text=Japan's%20initial%20coloni al%20policy%20was,self%2Dsufficiency%20and%20war%20preparation [https:// perma.cc/J6GX-9HJ9].
476 *Ibid.*
477 *Ibid.*
478 *Ibid.*
479 *Ibid.*
480 *Ibid.*
481 Han and Lew, *supra* note 471.
482 Lee, Saito, and Todres (2021), *supra* note 40.
483 Savada and Shaw (1990), *supra* note 475.
484 Benjamin R. Young, "When the Lights Went Out: Electricity in North Korea and Dependency on Moscow" (2020) 29(1) *International Journal of Korean Unification Studies* 107–134.
485 Millett (2021), *supra* note 20. See also Lee (2001), *supra* note 178.
486 Dae-Keun Lee, *The South Economy in the 1950s after Liberation: A Study of the Historical Background of Industrialization* (in Korean) (Samsung Economic Research Institute, 2002).
487 *Ibid.*
488 *Ibid.*
489 Seth (2011), *supra* note 32.
490 Lee (2018), *supra* note 59.
491 *Ibid.*
492 *Ibid.*
493 *Ibid.*
494 Organisation for Economic Co-operation and Development, *Average wages* (2022), https://data.oecd.org/earnwage/average-wages.htm [https://perma.cc/478A -L47D].
495 Lee (2018), *supra* note 59 and Lee (2016), *supra* note 290.
496 Lee (2018), *supra* note 59.
497 *Ibid.*
498 For further discussion of the theory, see Lee (2017), *supra* note 387.
499 Lee (2018), *supra* note 59.
500 *Ibid.*
501 *Ibid.*
502 *Ibid.* In addition to this policy, other factors, such as prewar industrial experience, land reform, the rise of national firms, administrative quality, and precision in policy targeting contributed to successful economic development. See Alice H. Amsden, *Asia's Next Giant: Korea and Late Industrialization* (New York: Oxford University Press, 1992).
503 Lee (2018), *supra* note 59.
504 *Ibid.*
505 World Bank, *The World Bank in Republic of Korea*, https://www.worldbank.org/en/ country/korea [https://perma.cc/WJY8-4BJT].

506 World Bank, *GNI Per Capita, Atlas Method (Current US$)* – *Korea, Rep.*, https://data
.worldbank.org/indicator/NY.GNP.PCAP.CD?locations=KR [https://perma.cc/
J6YW-QNUC].

507 Lee (2018), *supra* note 59.

508 *Ibid.*

509 Korea's Gini coefficient, which shows income distribution, was 0.28–0.29 in the
1990s, based on disposable income, which was lower (*i.e.*, a better income distribution) than most other countries including the United States (0.34).

510 See also United Nations Research Institute for Social Development, *Economic and
Social Development in the Republic of Korea: Processes, Institutions and Actors*, Research and
Policy Brief 14 (October 2012).

511 Seth (2011), *supra* note 32.

512 *Ibid.*

513 Han and Lew, *supra* note 471. See also Frederick Arthur McKenzie, *Korea's Fight for
Freedom* (Pinnacle Press, 2017).

514 Seth (2011), *supra* note 32.

515 *Ibid.*

516 See also Sang-Gu Shin, "The Cause, Progress, and Impact of the April Revolution
and Historical Assessment" (in Korean), *Dae Jeon Munwha Newspaper*, April 20, 2021,
http://djmunhwa.kr/news/view.php?no=8574 [https://perma.cc/SX8J-848K].

517 Seth (2011), *supra* note 32.

518 *Ibid.*

519 *Ibid.*

520 See Martin Hart-Landsberg, *The Rush to Development: Economic Change and Political
Struggle in Korea* (Monthly Review Press, 1993).

521 *Ibid.*

522 William Chapman, "S. Korean Dissidents Praise Carter for Pressing Rights Issue
With Park," *Washington Press*, July 2, 1979, https://www.washingtonpost.com/
archive/politics/1979/07/02/s-korean-dissidents-praise-carter-for-pressing-rights
-issue-with-park/b3f3d383-0bad-4b60-b109-69ef28e0cbf5/ [https://perma.cc/
K8VG-ECYK].

523 For further discussion of the Kwangju Massacre, see Tim Warnberg, "The Kwangju
Uprising: An Inside View" (1987) 11 *Korean Studies* 33–57.

524 Han Sung-Joo, "South Korea in 1987: The Politics of Democratization" (1988) 28(1)
A Survey of Asia in 1987: Part 1, 52–61.

525 *Ibid.*

526 Ministry of Public Administration and Security (South Korea), *Regional Self-
Governance* (in Korean), https://www.pa.go.kr/research/contents/policy/index10.jsp
[https://perma.cc/F9RA-V8BQ].

527 See, *e.g.*, Hagen Koo, "Civil Society and Democracy in South Korea" (2002) 11(2) *The
Good Society* 40-45 and Sunhyuk Kim and Jong-Ho Jeong, "Historical Development
of Civil Society in Korea since 1987" (2017) 24(2) *Journal of International and Area
Studies* 1–14.

528 Lee (2018), *supra* note 59.

529 World Population Review, *Democracy Countries 2022* (2022), https://worldpopula
tionreview.com/country-rankings/democracy-countries [https://perma.cc/W843
-BJ3P].

530 World Justice Project, *Rule of Law Index 2022* (2022), https://worldjusticeproject.org/
rule-of-law-index/global/2022 [https://perma.cc/E4D5-SKTE].

531 For further discussion of the oil crisis, see Charles Issawi, "The 1973 Oil Crisis and After" (1978) 1(2) *Journal of Post Keynesian Economics* 3–26.
532 For further discussion of the financial crisis, see Hider A. Khan, *Global Markets and Financial Crises in Asia* (New York: Palgrave Macmillan, 2004).
533 *Ibid.*
534 *Ibid.*
535 Korean Statistical Information Service, *Amounts of Foreign Exchange Reserve* (in Korean), https://kosis.kr/statHtml/statHtml.do?orgId=301&tblId=DT_038Y001&vw_cd=&list_id=&scrId=&seqNo=&lang_mode=ko&obj_var_id=&itm_id=&conn_path=E1 (accessed December 30, 2022).
536 Khan (2004), *supra* note 532.
537 See Jahyeong Koo and Sherry L. Kiser, "Recovery from a Financial Crisis: The Case of South Korea," *Economic and Financial Review* (Fourth Quarter, 2001), 24–36.
538 Yong-Shik Lee, "South Korean Economy at the Crossroads: Structure Issues under External Pressure–An Essay from a Law and Development Perspective" (2019) 12(3) *Law and Development Review* 865–885.
539 Khan (2004), *supra* note 532.
540 Jeong-Hoon Lee, "Samsung Flies and the Economic Concentration by Other Chaebols Has Increased" (in Korean), *Hankyurye*, June 27, 2022, https://www.hani.co.kr/arti/economy/marketing/1048550.html [https://perma.cc/AB4Q-C5QE].
541 *Ibid.*
542 Korea Statistical Office, *Gini Coefficient* (in Korean), https://www.index.go.kr/unity/potal/main/EachDtlPageDetail.do?idx_cd=1407 [https://perma.cc/SYD6-TGD2].
543 Organisation for Economic Co-operation and Development, "Economy," *Korea Policy Brief* (October 2016), https://www.oecd.org/policy-briefs/korea-productivity-through-innovation-and-structural-reform_EN.pdf [https://perma.cc/G5ZH-DSBG]. See also Kyung-Jin Min, "SMEs' Labor Productivity Is 27 Percent of Large Companies" (in Korean), *Hankyung*, July 11, 2021, https://www.hankyung.com/economy/article/2021071122481 [https://perma.cc/5RL4-6MHV].
544 Ministry of SMEs and Startups (South Korea), *The Status of SMEs*, https://www.mss.go.kr/site/smba/foffice/ex/statDB/MainSubStat.do [https://perma.cc/4P38-UXZZ].
545 Lee (2019), *supra* note 538.
546 See Randall S. Jones and Jae Wan Lee, *Enhancing Dynamism in SMEs and Entrepreneurship in Korea*, OECD Economic Development Working Papers, no. 1510, ECO/WKP(2018)58 (October 5, 2018).
547 Lee (2019), *supra* note 538.
548 *Ibid.*
549 *Ibid.*
550 *Ibid.*
551 See Lee, Kwon, and Lee (2022), *supra* note 444.
552 See Patsy Widakuswara, "Biden Pushes Expansion of Domestic Semiconductor Manufacturing," *Voice of America*, January 21, 2022, https://www.voanews.com/a/biden-pushes-expansion-of-domestic-semiconductor-manufacturing/6407527.html [https://perma.cc/63BL-PSRA].
553 Moon Chung-In, "S Korea 'all in' on US Economic Security Alliance," *Asia Times*, November 10, 2022, https://asiatimes.com/2022/11/s-korea-all-in-on-us-economic-security-alliance/ [https://perma.cc/63BB-XA8U].

554 John Chalmers and Hyunjoo Lin, "EU, South Korea Say U.S. Plan for EV Tax Breaks May Breach WTO Rules," *Reuters*, August 11, 2022, https://www.reuters .com/business/autos-transportation/eu-says-us-plan-ev-tax-breaks-discriminatory -may-breach-wto-rules-2022-08-11/ (accessed December 30, 2022).

555 "United States Continues to Block New Appellate Body Members for the World Trade Organization, Risking the Collapse of the Appellate Process" (2019) 113(4) *American Journal of International Law* 822–831.

556 For further discussion of this confrontation, see Sook-Jong Lee, "Democratization and Polarization in Korean Society" (2005) 29(3) *Asian Perspective* 99–125.

557 On a related topic, see Asher Arian and Michal Shamir, "The Primarily Political Functions of the Left-Right Continuum" (1983) 15(2) *Comparative Politics* 139-158.

558 See Shin Ji-hye, "Why Does Korea Have Such a Deep Political Divide?" *Korea Herald*, November 6, 2021, https://www.koreaherald.com/view.php?ud=20211108000739 [https://perma.cc/CNW5-YSLL].

559 In the United States, for example, confrontation between Republicans and Democrats have undermined each party's initiatives. See Christopher Hare and Keith T. Poole, "The Polarization of Contemporary American Politics" (2014) 46(3) *Polity* 411–429.

560 For further discussion on the pro-Japan and pro-China debate, see Sang-Cheol Kim, "Hallow Debate on Pro-China v. Pro-Japan" (in Korean), *Aju Kyeongje*, August 23, 2020, https://www.ajunews.com/view/20200823130640749 [https://perma.cc /K539-CPU6].

561 Shin Ji-hye, "36-Year-Old Lee Jun-Seok Becomes New Leader of People Power Party," *Korea Herald*, June 11, 2021, https://www.koreaherald.com/view.php?ud =20210611000445 [https://perma.cc/R8BL-FMVK].

562 Jung Da-min, "Young leader's nomination exam plan raises question," *Korea Times*, June 16, 2021, https://www.koreatimes.co.kr/www/nation/2021/06/356_310594 .html [https://perma.cc/F2A8-45WV].

563 Soo-Hyang Choi, "South Korea's Ruling Party Cements Presidential Win with Local Vote Success," *Reuters*, June 1, 2022, https://www.reuters.com/world/asia -pacific/south-koreas-ruling-party-cements-presidential-win-with-local-vote-suc- cess-2022-06-02/ (accessed December 30, 2022).

564 For an account of political attacks on Lee Jun-Seok, see Konstantin Asmolov, "Lee Jun-seok Under Attack," *New Eastern Outlook*, July 13, 2022, https://journal-neo.org /2022/07/13/lee-jun-seok-under-attack/ [https://perma.cc/5X3D-ESYE].

565 Jung Da-min, "Lee Jun-Seok's Victory Ushers Korean Politics into New Era," *Korea Times*, June 14, 2021, https://www.koreatimes.co.kr/www/nation/2021/06/356 _310361.html [https://perma.cc/KFC5-JBMC].

566 Asmolov (2022), *supra* note 564.

567 Michael Lee, "Joo Ho-Young Picked to Lead PPP Temporarily," *Korea JoongAng Daily*, August 9, 2022, https://koreajoongangdaily.joins.com/2022/08/09/national /politics/Korea-PPP-People-Power-Party/20220809181854797.html   [https:// perma.cc/LA9P-2FA8].

568 For further discussion of Confucian values, see Cawley (2021), *supra* note 417.

569 United Nations, The International Covenant on Civil and Political Rights, G.A. Res. 2200A (XXI) (Dec. 16, 1966).

570 World Population Review (2022), *supra* note 529. For example, the interim head of South Korea's ruling party, Jeong Jin-Seok, voiced discontent with some conservative

panelists who criticized his party and sent a formal request to eleven media agencies to recruit panelists who represent "true" conservative views. Kyung-Soek Kang, "Jung Jin Seok Says, 'Please Recruit the Current Affairs Panelists Fairly,'" *Dong-A Ilbo*, https://www.donga.com/news/Politics/article/all/20221223/117127188/1 [https://perma.cc/8LC8-JKCU]. His position does not appreciate the importance of viewpoint diversity (including differing views on who are legitimate conservative panelists) in a democratic society and could also be viewed as unduly exerting pressure on the press.

571 For further discussion of the generational divide in South Korea, see Sook Jong Lee, *Generational Divides and the Future of South Korean Democracy* (Carnegie Endowment for International Peace, 2021), https://carnegieendowment.org/2021/06/29/generational-divides-and-future-of-south-korean-democracy-pub-84818 [https://perma.cc/PK9X-MZJV].

572 The president's approval rate fell to 24 percent in September 2022. Park Jin-Yong, "President Yoon Seok-Yeol Approval Rate 24%...Again the Lowest [Gallup]" (in Korean), *Seoul Kyeongje*, September 30, 2022, https://www.sedaily.com/NewsView/26B9WC9VMD [https://perma.cc/EH6T-6DK4].

573 "Yoon's Approval Rating Rises to 38.9%: Poll," *The Korea Herald*, December 5, 2022, https://www.koreaherald.com/view.php?ud=20221205000142 [https://perma.cc/7MM2-VZ3P].

574 Sarah Kim, "PPP's Rule Change to Elect Next Leader Causes Divide within Party," *Korea JoongAng Daily*, December 20, 2022, https://koreajoongangdaily.joins.com/2022/12/20/national/politics/Korea-People-Power-Party-chairman/20221220161103412.html [https://perma.cc/L2QT-DKQM].

575 David Harrison, "How High Is Inflation and What Causes It? What to Know," *Wall Street Journal*, September 13, 2022, https://www.wsj.com/articles/inflation-definition-cause-what-is-it-11644353564 [https://perma.cc/TH3B-DJAW].

576 Choi Jae-hee, "Ruling Party Mulls Universal Cash Relief Before Chuseok," *Korea Herald*, June 2, 2021, https://www.koreaherald.com/view.php?ud=20210602000792 [https://perma.cc/L2W4-HR4Z].

577 See, *e.g.*, Amanda Hess, "How Fan Culture Is Swallowing Democracy," *New York Times*, September 11, 2019, https://www.nytimes.com/interactive/2019/09/11/arts/how-fan-culture-is-swallowing-democracy.html [https://perma.cc/MK5L-KR6M].

578 For further discussion of populism in the context of democracy in South Korea, see Sangjin Han and Younghee Shim, "The Two Driving Forces of Populism and Democracy in South Korea: A Conceptual, Historical, and Empirical Analysis" (2021) 50(2) *Journal of Asian Sociology* 371–400.

579 According to reports, South Korea also has a plan to assassinate Kim Jong-Un if the country feels threatened by North Korean nuclear weapons. See, *e.g.*, Paula Hancocks, "South Korea Reveals It Has a Plan to Assassinate Kim Jong Un," *CNN*, September 23, 2016, https://www.cnn.com/2016/09/23/asia/south-korea-plan-to-assassinate-kim-jong-un/index.html [https://perma.cc/6TC7-CRTH].

580 Young-Seok Park, "470 Provocations by North Korea after the War, 4,119 People Killed or Kidnapped" (in Korean), *The JoonAng*, December 6, 2010, https://www.joongang.co.kr/article/4754445#home [https://perma.cc/B45X-XGMG].

581 *U.S. Army Garrison Humphreys*, supra note 434.

582 Chang Gyu Ahn, "North Korean Air Force Launches 150 Planes in Rare Large-Scale Drill," *RFA*, October 12, 2022, https://www.rfa.org/english/news/korea/

strike-drill-10122022142956.html [https://perma.cc/C45Q-L39J]. Another report observed that the actual number of planes launched were about 40 and some even crashed. Myeong-Seong Kim, "North Korea Advertised the Launch of 150 Planes… But Old Planes Crashed" (in Korean), *Chosun Ilbo*, October 15, 2022, https://www.chosun.com/politics/north_korea/2022/10/15/NJEVJVV6WFF37AU7YHM M6VEIA4/ [https://perma.cc/5J42-EBPC].

583 Carlotta Dotto, Brad Lendon, and Jessie Yeung, "North Korea's Record Year of Missile Testing Is Putting the World on Edge," *CNN*, December 26, 2022, https://www.cnn.com/2022/12/26/asia/north-korea-missile-testing-year-end-intl-hnk/index.html#:~:text=In%202022%2C%20the%20isolated%20nation,nuclear%20test%20on%20the%20horizon [https://perma.cc/J9Q2-WV32].

584 "In 1991, South and North Korea Join the U.N. Simultaneously" (in Korean), *KBC World*, April 26, 2018, http://world.kbs.co.kr/service/contents_view.htm?lang=k&board_seq=275292 (accessed December 30, 2022).

585 Sang-Mi Han, "North Korea Kim Il Sung Prepared for the Second Invasion of South Korea in 1965…Requested Reinforcement to China" (in Korean), *Voice of America*, October 24, 2013, https://www.voakorea.com/a/1775964.html [https://perma.cc/24S8-DE8F].

586 Lankov (2021), *supra* note 65.

587 Sung Man Kim, "Analysis on Kim Jung Un's 2015 Grand War for Reunification" (in Korean), *NK Chosun*, September 15, 2014.

588 Calingaert (1988), *supra* note 21.

589 Article 4 of the South Korean Constitution provides: "The Republic of Korea shall seek unification and shall formulate and carry out a policy of peaceful unification based on the basic free and democratic order." Article 4, Constitution of the Republic of Korea, https://www.law.go.kr/LSW/lsInfoP.do?lsiSeq=61603&viewCls=engLsInfoR&urlMode=engLsInfoR#0000 (accessed December 30, 2022). Article 9 of the North Korean Constitution also stipulates the unification of Korea as a national objective.

590 The July 4 South-North Joint Communiqué, July 4, 1972, https://peacemaker.un.org/sites/peacemaker.un.org/files/KR%20KP_720704_The%20July%204%20South-North%20Joint%20Communiqu%C3%A9.pdf [https://perma.cc/C572-T8NF].

591 *Ibid.*

592 Agreement on Reconciliation, Non-Aggression and Exchanges and Cooperation between the South and North, December 13, 1991, DC/1147 (March 25, 1992), https://peacemaker.un.org/sites/peacemaker.un.org/files/KR%20KP_911213_Agreement%20on%20reconciliation%20non%20aggression%20and%20exchangespdf.pdf [https://perma.cc/GQQ2-44CV].

593 Park, Young Ho, *South and North Korea's Views on the Unification of the Korean Peninsula and Inter-Korean Relations* (2014), https://www.brookings.edu/wp-content/uploads/2014/04/park-young-ho-paper.pdf [https://perma.cc/3SUL-6BJA].

594 *Ibid.*

595 *Ibid.*

596 This excludes over 33,000 North Korean defectors who escaped North Korea and entered South Korea in search of better lives. However the number of defectors has decreased in recent years due to reinforced control over the North Korean border.

597 Laura Bicker, "North Korea Blows Up Joint Liaison Office with South in Kaesong," *BBC News*, June 16, 2020, https://www.bbc.com/news/world-asia-53060620 (accessed December 30, 2022).

598 See, *e.g.*, Marcus Noland, Sherman Robinson, and Li-gang Liu, "The Costs and Benefits of Korean Unification: Alternate Scenarios" (1998) 38(8) *Asian Survey* 801–814.

599 Joon Seok Hong, "The Economic Costs of Korean Reunification," *Spice Digest*, Fall 2011, https://fsi9-prod.s3.us-west-1.amazonaws.com/s3fs-public/Korean_Reunification.pdf [https://perma.cc/YDA3-TL3J].

600 See Norbert Eschborn, "North Korean Refugees in South Korea" (2014) 292 *ISPSW Strategy Series* 1-17, https://www.files.ethz.ch/isn/184307/292_Eschborn_Apel%20(2).pdf [https://perma.cc/JY9K-XMXP].

601 Josh Rogin, "Trump Still Holds Jimmy Carter's View on Withdrawing U.S. Troops from South Korea," *Washington Post*, June 7, 2018, https://www.washingtonpost.com/news/josh-rogin/wp/2018/06/07/trump-still-holds-jimmy-carters-view-on-with-drawing-u-s-troops-from-south-korea/ [https://perma.cc/8YZT-ENZ8].

602 See discussion *supra* Section 4.1.1. See also Seth (2011), *supra* note 32.

603 Cartwright (2019), *supra* note 408.

604 United Nations Human Rights Council (2014), *supra* note 210.

Chapter 5. A Power with Rising Concerns: Escalation of Tensions between Japan and Its Neighbors

605 Economic Stabilization Board (Japan), *A Comprehensive Report on the War Damage of Japan Caused by the Pacific War* (1949).

606 Marius B. Jansen and Fed G. Notehelfer, "Japan: World War II and Defeat," *Encyclopaedia Britannica* (last updated January 27, 2022), https://www.britannica.com/place/Japan/World-War-II-and-defeat#ref23207 [https://perma.cc/QNX2-S4R6].

607 SCAP denotes the supreme commander's office as well as the supreme commander himself (General Douglas MacArthur).

608 Kozo Yamamura, *Economic Policy in Postwar Japan: Growth versus Economic Democracy* (University of California Press, 1967), at 18.

609 G. C. Allen, *Japan's Economic Expansion* (Oxford University Press, 1965), at 85.

610 Toshihiko Kawagoe, *Agricultural Land Reform in Postwar Japan: Experiences and Issues*, World Bank Policy Research Working Papers (June 25, 2013).

611 Jerome B. Cohen, *Japan's Postwar Economy* (Indiana University Press, 1958), at 49.

612 Marius B. Jansen and Fred G. Notehelfer, "Japan: Japan Since 1945," *Encyclopaedia Britannica* (last updated January 27, 2022), https://www.britannica.com/place/Japan/Japan-since-1945 [https://perma.cc/6U65-44T6].

613 World Bank, *GDP Per Capita (Current US$) – Japan, United States*, https://data.worldbank.org/indicator/NY.GDP.PCAP.CD?end=1995&locations=JP-US&start=1960 [https://perma.cc/FF3Z-TLFY]. See also "Global 500 1995," *Fortune*, https://fortune.com/ranking/global500/1995/ (accessed December 30, 2022).

614 Dylan Gerstel and Matthew P. Goodman, *From Industrial Policy to Innovation Strategy: Lessons from Japan, Europe, and the United States* (Center for Strategic and International Studies, 2020).

615 As a consequence, exports, as a share of Japan's GDP, have decreased from 14.4 percent in 1984 to 8.8 percent in 1995. World Bank, *Exports of Goods and Services (% of GDP) – Japan*, https://data.worldbank.org/indicator/NE.EXP.GNFS.ZS?locations =JP [https://perma.cc/7LZH-3JYS].

616 Gerstel and Goodman (2020), *supra* note 614.

617 *Ibid.*

618 *Ibid.*

619 *Ibid.*

620 For further discussion of the stagnation of the Japanese economy, see Takeo Hoshi and Anil K. Kashyap, "Japan's Financial Crisis and Economic Stagnation" (2004) 18(1) *Journal of Economic Perspectives* 3–26.

621 *Ibid.*, See also Daniel I. Okimoto, *Causes of Japan's Economic Stagnation*, https://aparc .fsi.stanford.edu/research/causes_of_japans_economic_stagnation [https://perma .cc/G4ZX-ALNK].

622 Hoshi and Kashyap (2004), *supra* note 620.

623 See James Mayger, "Cash-Rich Japanese Companies Aren't Investing at Home," *Bloomberg*, March 9, 2015, https://www.bloomberg.com/news/articles/2015-03 -09/cash-rich-japanese-companies-aren-t-investing-at-home#xj4y7vzkg (accessed December 30, 2022).

624 See Brad W. Setser, *Meanwhile, in Japan, Household Consumption Continues to Fall* (July 7, 2016), https://www.cfr.org/blog/meanwhile-japan-household-consumption-contin- ues-fall [https://perma.cc/23V6-M7PV].

625 World Bank, *GNI Per Capita, Atlas Method (Current US$) – Japan*, https://data.world- bank.org/indicator/NY.GNP.PCAP.CD?locations=JP [https://perma.cc/Z32Z -NLMS].

626 Michael A. Panton, "Politics, Practice and Pacifism: Revising Article 9 of the Japanese Constitution" (2010) 11(2) *Asian Pacific Law & Policy Journal* 163–218.

627 For further discussion of the Meiji Empire and its influence on Japanese society, see Masaru Tamamoto, "Reflections on Japan's Postwar State" (1995) 124(2) *Daedalus* 1–22.

628 Tomoyuki Sasaki, *Japan's Postwar Military and Civil Society: Contesting a Better Life* (Bloomsbury, 2015). See also Masaru Tamamoto, "Reflections on Japan's Postwar State" (1995) 124(2) *Daedalus* 1–22 and Panton (2010), *supra* note 626.

629 Jansen and Notehelfer (2022), *supra* note 612.

630 Panton (2010), *supra* note 626.

631 *Ibid.*

632 Constitution of Japan, Article 9, https://japan.kantei.go.jp/constitution_and_gov- ernment_of_japan/constitution_e.html [https://perma.cc/R5ZY-9L4J].

633 Theodore McNelly, "American Political Traditions and Japan's Postwar Constitution" (1977) 140(1) *World Affairs* 58–66.

634 *Ibid.*

635 Jansen and Notehelfer (2022), *supra* note 612.

636 *Ibid.*

637 *Ibid.*

638 McNelly (1977), *supra* note 633.

639 Jansen and Notehelfer (2022), *supra* note 612.

640 *Ibid.*

641 *Ibid.*

642 *Ibid.*

643 Panton (2010), *supra* note 626.

644 Tamamoto (1995), *supra* note 627.

645 Panton (2010), *supra* note 626.

646 *Ibid.*

647 World Bank, *Armed Forces Personnel, Total – Japan*, https://data.worldbank.org/indi-cator/MS.MIL.TOTL.P1?most_recent_value_desc=true&locations=JP [https://perma.cc/5DUG-R68S].

648 World Bank, *Military Expenditure (Current US$) – Japan*, https://data.worldbank.org/indicator/MS.MIL.XPND.CD?most_recent_value_desc=true&locations=JP [https://perma.cc/6XKB-RZVF].

649 World Bank, *Military Expenditure (% of GDP) – Japan*, https://data.worldbank.org/indicator/MS.MIL.XPND.GD.ZS?most_recent_value_desc=true&locations=JP [https://perma.cc/QU4L-UCRM]. See also Keita Nakamura, "Japan OKs Enemy Base Strike Capability in Major Defense Policy Shift," *Kyodo News*, December 16, 2022, https://english.kyodonews.net/news/2022/12/02fc9015409c-japan-to-vow -to-obtain-enemy-base-strike-capability-amid-threats.html [https://perma.cc/SX6T-7FQU].

650 James R. Homes, "Japan's Cold War Navy," *The Diplomat*, October 12, 2012, https://thediplomat.com/2012/10/japans-cold-war-navy/ [https://perma.cc/93SE -B25N].

651 Panton (2010), *supra* note 626.

652 See Tomoyuki Sasaki, "Whose Peace? Anti-Military Litigation and the Right to Live in Peace in Postwar Japan" (2012) 10(29) *Asia-Pacific Journal* 1–19.

653 Jo He-rim, "US Support for Japan's Military Ambitions May Spell Concerns for Korea," *Korea Herald*, May 24, 2022, https://www.koreaherald.com/view.php?ud =20220524000833 [https://perma.cc/6M2X-7FHB].

654 For further discussion on this subject, see Thomas L. Wilborn, *Japan's Self-Defense Forces: What Dangers to Northeast Asia?* (Strategic Studies Institute, US Army War College, 1994).

655 For further discussion on Japanese character traits, see Douglas Gilbert Haring, "Japanese Character in the Twentieth Century" (1967) 370 *The Annals of the American Academy of Political and Social Science* 133–142.

656 Global Firepower (2022), *supra* note 428.

657 See also Roger W. Bowen, "Japan's Foreign Policy" (1992) 25(1) *Political Science and Politics* 57–73.

658 The Treaty of San Francisco, which was signed in 1951 and enacted in 1952, restored Japan's sovereignty after World War II. For further discussion, see Jennifer R. Miller, *Cold War Democracy: The United States and Japan* (Harvard University Press, 2019).

659 Hiroko Yamane, "Japan as an Asian/Pacific Power" (1987) 27(12) *Asian Survey* 1302–1308.

660 *Ibid.*

661 *Ibid.*

662 See also Ryutaro Komiya and Ryuhei Wakasugi, "Japan's Foreign Direct Investment" (1991) 513 *The Annals of the American Academy of Political Social Science* 48–61.

663 Yamane (1987), *supra* note 659.

664 Bowen (1992), *supra* note 657, at 57.

665 See Masahiko Fukada, "How Socialism and the Left Wing Failed in Japan," *Japan Times*, December 30, 2019, https://www.japantimes.co.jp/news/2019/12/30/national/politics-diplomacy/socialism-japan/ [https://perma.cc/PTL8-NHQH].

666 See, *e.g.*, Edward Kwon and Liza Abram Benham, "Shinzo's Abe's Scheme of Staking Territorial Claims to Korea's Dokdo" (2016) 3(1) *Journal of Territorial and Maritime Studies* 47–64.

667 *Ibid.*

668 See also Willem van Kemenade, *China and Japan: Partners or Permanent Rivals?* (Clingendael Institute, 2006).

669 Greg Rienzi, "Other Nations Could Learn from Germany's Efforts to Reconcile after WWII," *Johns Hopkins Magazine* (Summer 2015), https://hub.jhu.edu/magazine/2015/summer/germany-japan-reconciliation/ [https://perma.cc/D9DQ-3C6Y].

670 In Taiwan, for example, there was an explosion in the demand for products relating to Japanese popular culture in the 1990s. I-yun Lee and Christine Han, "Politics, Popular Culture and Images of Japan in Taiwan," *in* Paul Morris, Naoko Shimazu, and Edward Victors (eds.), *Imagining Japan in Postwar East Asia* (Routledge, 2013).

671 For example, Japan owns 10.5 metric tons of weapons-grade plutonium. Alan J. Kuperman and Hina Acharya, *Japan's Misguided Plutonium Policy* (October 2018), https://www.armscontrol.org/act/2018-10/features/japan%E2%80%99s-misguided-plutonium-policy [https://perma.cc/E8HM-3Z36].

672 See, *e.g.*, John Feffer, "An Arms Race in Northeast Asia?" (2009) 33(4) *Asian Perspective* 5–15.

673 See, *e.g.*, Kirk Spitzer, "Why Japan Is Still Not Sorry Enough," *Time*, December 11, 2012, https://nation.time.com/2012/12/11/why-japan-is-still-not-sorry-enough/ [https://perma.cc/3XP5-WSL6].

674 Articles I and II, Agreement on the settlement of problems concerning property and claims and on economic co-operation (1965), *supra* note 84.

675 See James Claxton, Luke Nottage, and Brett Williams, "Litigating, Arbitrating and Mediating Japan–Korea Trade and Investment Tensions" 54(4) *Journal of World Trade* 591–614 (2020). See also Kevin J. Cooney and Alex Scarbrough, "Japan and South Korea: Can These Two Nations Work Together?" (2008) 35(3) *Asian Affairs* 173–192.

676 Lee (2020), *supra* note 86.

677 *Ibid.*

678 Korea relies on the supply of materials from Japan for the production of its key products such as semiconductors (*e.g.*, 90 percent of photo resists, 43.9 percent of hydrogen fluoride [etching gas], and 93.7 percent of fluorinated polyimides). Chang Sung Ku, "Japan's Three Items Subject to Export Restraint Measures, Import Dependency up to the Maximum of 94 Percent," *MK News*, July 1, 2019, https://www.mk.co.kr/news/business/view/2019/07/476728/ [https://perma.cc/5FSN-8PKF].

679 Lee (2020), *supra* note 86.

680 *Ibid.*

681 Kim Tong-Hyung, "S Korean Business Owners Call for Boycott of Japanese Goods," *Japan Today*, July 15, 2019, https://japantoday.com/category/politics/s.-korean-business-owners-call-for-boycott-of-japanese-goods [https://perma.cc/JRK9-67XK].

682 World Bank, *GNI Per Capita, Atlas Method (Current US$) – Korea, Rep., Japan*, https://data.worldbank.org/indicator/NY.GNP.PCAP.CD?locations=KR-JP [https://perma.cc/B3DL-972X].

683 *Ibid.*

684 Organisation for Economic Co-operation and Development (2022), *supra* note 494.

685 Hwang Jae Ha, "Japan's Export Restraints – Could Have Been Implemented to Keep Korea's Semiconductor Industry in Check" (in Korean), *Yonhap News*, July 12, 2019, https://www.yna.co.kr/view/AKR20190712026700008 [https://perma.cc /9UGP-R5CS].

686 *Ibid.*

687 Ku (2019), *supra* note 678.

688 Lee Jaeha, "The Problems of Dokdo's Development Policy and an Alternative for Future Development" (2013) 19(2) *Korea Journal of Regional Geography* 282–300.

689 *Ibid.*

690 *Ibid.*

691 Mark Valencia, "Japan's New Assertiveness Re-energizes Its Territorial Disputes," *Asia Times*, August 17, 2021, https://asiatimes.com/2021/08/japans-new-assertive- ness-re-energizes-its-territorial-disputes/ [https://perma.cc/DYK6-56J6].

692 See Clint Richards, "Japan's New Remote Island Defense Plan," *The Diplomat*, August 13, 2014, https://thediplomat.com/2014/08/japans-new-remote-island -defense-plan/ [https://perma.cc/7PHD-PA3X].

693 Before the pandemic, for the first eight months of 2019, as many as 2.3 million Japanese and 4.7 million South Koreans crossed each other's borders. Seung-Mok Yoo, "Koreans Stop Going to Japan, but Japanese Still Come to Korea," *Money Today*, September 23, 2019, https://news.mt.co.kr/mtview.php?no=2019092314261312525 [https://perma.cc/88QT-49DW].

694 For an overview of the tense relationship between China and Japan, see Tsuneo Nishida, "China and Japan: Managing a Complex Relationship" (2015) 4 *Horizons: Journal of International Relations and Sustainable Development* 62–73.

695 For a detailed account of the normalization of the Sino-Japanese relationship in 1972, see Lee W. Farnsworth, "Japan 1972: New Faces and New Friends" (1972) 13(1) *Asian Survey* 113–125.

696 See, *e.g.*, Mari Yamaguchi, "What's Behind Strained China-Japan Relations," *AP News*, September 28, 2022, https://apnews.com/article/taiwan-china-japan-asia -tokyo-44df15b19e710fb8da38e69deae85b53 [https://perma.cc/76RG-L3CC]. See also David M. Gordon, "Historiographical Essay: The China-Japan War, 1931- 1945" (2006) 70(1) *Journal of Military History* 137–182.

697 For further discussion on the subject, see James L. Schoff and Li Bin, *A Precarious Triangle: U.S.-China Strategic Stability and Japan* (Carnegie Endowment for International Peace, 2017).

698 World Bank, *GDP (Current US$) – China, Japan*, https://data.worldbank.org/indica- tor/NY.GDP.MKTP.CD?locations=CN-JP [https://perma.cc/5EX9-2VRC].

699 Alicia García-Herrero, *Japan Must Boost R&D to Keep Rising Chinese Rivals at Bay* (September 20, 2018), https://www.bruegel.org/comment/japan-must-boost-rd -keep-rising-chinese-rivals-bay [https://perma.cc/CHR6-2GWE].

700 A. Patalano, "Japan as a Maritime Power: Deterrence, Diplomacy, and Maritime Security," *in* Mary McCarthy (ed.), *Routledge Handbook of Japanese Foreign Policy* (Routledge, 2018), at 155–172.

701 Yamaguchi (2022), *supra* note 696.

702 *Ibid.*

703 For further discussion of the dispute, see Tseng (2014), *supra* note 93. See also Paul J. Smith, "The Senkaku/Diaoyu Island Controversy: A Crisis Postponed" (2013) 66(2) *Naval War College Review* 27–44.

704 Smith (2013), *ibid.*

705 "John H. Holdridge to the President's Assistant for National Security Affairs" [Kissinger], memorandum, FRUS, doc. 115, *cited in* Smith (2013), *supra* note 703, at 33.

706 Tsuyoshi Nagasawa and Masaya Kato, "US Supports Japan's Sovereignty over Senkakus: Pentagon," *Nikkei Asia*, February 25, 2021, https://asia.nikkei.com/Politics/International-relations/Biden-s-Asia-policy/US-supports-Japan-s-sovereignty-over-Senkakus-Pentagon [https://perma.cc/ZP8L-7JAY].

707 Smith (2013), *supra* note 703.

708 Unryu Suganuma, *Sovereign Rights and Territorial Space in Sino-Japanese Relations: Irredentism and the Diaoyu/Senkaku Islands* (University of Hawaii Press, 2000).

709 *Ibid.*

710 *Ibid.*

711 Smith (2013), *supra* note 703.

712 *Ibid.*

713 *Ibid.*

714 For a related discussion, see Thomas J. Christensen, "China, the U.S.-Japan Alliance, and the Security Dilemma in East Asia" (1999) 23(4) *International Security* 49–80.

715 *Ibid.*

716 See, *e.g.*, Amber Wang, "China Warns Japan against Joining Forces with US, *South China Morning Post*," May 18, 2022, https://www.scmp.com/news/china/diplomacy/article/3178259/china-warns-japan-against-joining-forces-us [https://perma.cc/P76R-WSSP].

717 For further discussion of the Russo-Japanese War, see Martin (1967), *supra* note 35.

718 Article II, Treaty of Portsmouth (1905), https://portsmouthpeacetreaty.org/process/peace/TreatyText.pdf [https://perma.cc/U675-AW2Q].

719 *Ibid.*

720 Amy Tikkanen, "Sakhalin Island," *Encyclopaedia Britannica*, https://www.britannica.com/place/Sakhalin-Island [https://perma.cc/JA7X-T5JG].

721 *Ibid.*

722 John J. Stephan, "Sakhalin Island: Soviet Outpost in Northeast Asia" (1970) 12(12) *Asian Survey* 1090–1100.

723 *Ibid.*

724 *Ibid.*

725 *Ibid.*

726 *Ibid.*

727 *Ibid.*

728 *Ibid.*

729 Kimie Hara, "50 Years from San Francisco: Re-Examining the Peace Treaty and Japan's Territorial Disputes" (2001) 74(3) *Pacific Affairs* 361–382.

730 Article 2(c), Treaty of Peace with Japan (1951), https://treaties.un.org/doc/Publication/UNTS/Volume%20136/volume-136-I-1832-English.pdf [https://perma.cc/DNX3-CMD8].

731 *Ibid.*

732 James D. J. Brown, *Japan, Russia, and Their Territorial Dispute: The Northern Delusion* (Routledge, 2016).

733 "Kuril Islands Dispute between Russia and Japan," *BBC News*, April 29, 2013, https://www.bbc.com/news/world-asia-pacific-11664434 (accessed December 30, 2022).

734 See "Russia scraps visa-free visits to islands claimed by Japan," *Japan Times*, September 6, 2022, https://www.japantimes.co.jp/news/2022/09/06/national/politics-diplomacy/islands-visa-agreement/ [https://perma.cc/5MSV-X6FX]. See also "Russia Suspends Fisheries Agreement with Japan," *Nippon.com*, June 7, 2022, https://www.nippon.com/en/news/yjj2022060701155/ [https://perma.cc/M3HP-ZBJT].

735 Hiroyuki Akiyama, Takuya Mizogori, and Miki Okuyama, "Ukraine Crisis Roils Waters for Japan's Bid to Reclaim Islands from Russia," *Nikkei Asia*, February 8, 2022, https://asia.nikkei.com/Politics/International-relations/Ukraine-crisis-roils-waters-for-Japan-s-bid-to-reclaim-islands-from-Russia [https://perma.cc/98U9-NNAH].

736 "Japan Protests Russia-China Military Drills, Moscow Scraps Kuril Islands Visa Deal," *South China Morning Post*, September 6, 2022, https://www.scmp.com/news/asia/east-asia/article/3191470/japan-protests-russia-china-military-drills-moscow-scraps-visa [https://perma.cc/9S3K-W66H].

737 Ike Barrash, *Russia's Militarization of the Kuril Islands* (September 27, 2022), https://www.csis.org/blogs/new-perspectives-asia/russias-militarization-kuril-islands [https://perma.cc/L8BJ-DJFH].

738 *Ibid.*

739 *Ibid.*

740 See Articles I and II, Agreement on the settlement of problems concerning property and claims and on economic co-operation (1965), *supra* note 84.

741 See David Hundt and Roland Bleiker, "Reconciling Colonial Memories in Korea and Japan" (2007) 31(1) *Asian Perspective* 61–91.

742 See, *e.g.*, "Korea Strongly Protests Japan Diplomat's Comments on Comfort Women," *Korea Herald*, June 29, 2017, https://www.koreaherald.com/view.php?ud=20170629000790 [https://perma.cc/U23E-QZRX].

743 *Ibid.*

744 Rienzi (2015), *supra* note 669.

745 For further discussion, see Samuel Guex, "Legality or Legitimacy: Revisiting Debates on the Korea-Japan Annexation Treaties," *in* Marie Seong-Hak Kim (ed.), *The Spirit of Korean Law* (Brill, 2016), at 155–173.

746 See, *e.g.*, Mark Brown, "Colonial States, Colonial Rule, Colonial Governmentalities: Implications for the Study of Historical State Crime" (2018) 7(2) *State Crime and Colonialism* 173–198.

747 See also Hundt and Bleiker (2007), *supra* note 741.

748 *Ibid.*, at 65–66.

749 Ahn Byung-jik, *The History of Korean Economic Growth* (in Korean) (Seoul National University Press, 2001).

750 Savada and Shaw (eds.) (1990), *supra* note 475.

751 See, *e.g.*, Lee, Saito, and Todres (2021), *supra* note 40.

752 *Ibid.*

753 "Japan's PM Denies 'comfort women' Coerced," *NBC News*, March 1, 2007, https://www.nbcnews.com/id/wbna10625961 [https://perma.cc/W95U-9CYA]. Japan had been more willing to admit to the occurrence of the atrocities in the 1990s as demonstrated by the Kono Statement issued in 1993. Ministry of Foreign Affairs of Japan, *Statement by the Chief Cabinet Secretary* (August 4, 1993), https://www.mofa.go.jp/a_o/rp/page25e_000343.html [https://perma.cc/78V7-K4VP].

754 Zheng Wang, "History Education: The Source of Conflict Between China and Japan," *The Diplomat*, April 23, 2014, https://thediplomat.com/2014/04/history-education-the-source-of-conflict-between-china-and-japan/ [https://perma.cc/NJ8L-Y7UF].

755 Raleigh Morgan, "Chinese, Japanese, and United States Views of the Nanking Massacre: The Supreme Court Trial of Shiro Azuma" (2002) 9(2) *American Journal of Chinese Studies* 235–246. See also Mark Seldon, "Japanese and American War Atrocities, Historical Memory and Reconciliation: World War II to Today" (2008) 6(4) *Japan Focus* 1–19.

756 See, *e.g.*, Paul Armstrong, "Fury over Japanese Politician's Nanjing Massacre Denial," *CNN*, February 23, 2012, https://www.cnn.com/2012/02/23/world/asia/china-nanjing-row [https://perma.cc/8C33-AM6B].

757 Se-Won Lee, "The Japanese Government Submitted an Opinion to UNESCO Citing the Denialists" (in Korean), *Yonhap News*, November 6, 2015, https://www.yna.co.kr/view/AKR20151106088700073 [https://perma.cc/WQF2-HS8A].

758 *Ibid.*

759 *Ibid.*

760 See "Japan's PM Denies 'comfort women' Coerced," *NBC News*, March 1, 2007, *supra* note 753.

761 Article 9, Constitution of Japan, *cited in* Institute for Security and Development Policy, *Amending Japan's Pacifist Diet* (April 2018), https://isdp.eu/content/uploads/2018/04/Amending-Japan%E2%80%99s-Pacifist-Constitution.pdf [https://perma.cc/5XME-TUZV].

762 Jansen and Notehelfer (2022), *supra* note 612.

763 Institute for Security and Development Policy, *Amending Japan's Pacifist Diet* (April 2018), https://isdp.eu/wp-content/uploads/2018/04/Amending-Japan%E2%80%99s-Pacifist-Constitution-2.pdf [https://perma.cc/5B35-EDC5].

764 *Ibid.*

765 *Ibid.* Japan has also increased military activities in space and abandoned the "three principles of arms control" (no arms export to communist bloc countries, countries subject to arms embargo under U.N. Security Council Resolutions, and countries involved or likely to be involved in international conflicts).

766 Nakamura (2022), *supra* note 649.

767 See, *e.g.*, Grace Cheng, *China's Response to a Post-Pacifist Japan* (September 14, 2014), https://www.e-ir.info/2014/09/14/chinas-response-to-a-post-pacificist-japan/ [https://perma.cc/6YNQ-N6RK] and E. J. R. Cho and Ki-young Shin, "South Korean Views on Japan's Constitutional Reform Under the Abe Government" (2018) 31(2) *Pacific Review* 256–266.

768 *Ibid.*

769 Global Firepower (2022), *supra* note 428. Professor Hiroyuki Hoshiro notes, however, that an armed conflict is possible between China and Japan and between Russia and Japan, although it is "unthinkable" between South Korea and China as they are both allies of the United States. Correspondence on file with the author.

770 "Japan Still Divided on Revising War-Renouncing Constitution: Survey," *Kyodo News*, May 2, 2022, https://english.kyodonews.net/news/2022/05/a8faf66fd209 -japan-still-divided-on-revising-war-renouncing-constitution-survey.html?phrase =nhk&words= [https://perma.cc/783G-2CPP].

771 *Ibid.*

772 See, *e.g.*, H. D. P. Envall, "Japan: From Passive Partner to Active Ally," *in* Michel Wesley (ed.), *Global Allies* (Australian National University Press, 2017), at 15–30.

773 "In the Midst of Provocations from North Korea, Kishida Emphasizes on His Desire to Amend Constitution During His Tenure" (in Korean), *Newsis*, October 6, 2022, https://mobile.newsis.com/view.html?ar_id=NISX20221006_0002039740 [https://perma.cc/6J85-RHPD].

774 Nam-Gu Jeong, "America Supports Constitutional Amendment Citing 'Japan's Constitutional Amendment is Japan's Business'" (in Korean), *Hankyoreh*, May 3, 2013, https://www.hani.co.kr/arti/international/international_general/585883 .html [https://perma.cc/QA87-U4VT].

775 See, *e.g.*, Bruce W. Bennett, *Why Japan's Military Shift Is Necessary for South Korea* (July 7, 2014), https://www.rand.org/blog/2014/07/why-japans-military-shift-is-necessary -for-south-korea.html [https://perma.cc/PKQ9-AH8E].

776 Jesse Johnson, "Trump's Push for South Korea to Pay More for U.S. Troops Puts Japan on Notice," *Japan Times*, August 8, 2019, https://www.japantimes.co.jp/ news/2019/08/08/asia-pacific/trumps-push-south-korea-pay-u-s-troops-puts-japan -notice/ [https://perma.cc/EM88-3BAS].

777 See, *e.g.*, Mark Toth and Jonathan Sweet, "Why Japan Must Rescind Article 9," *The Hill*, May 11, 2022, https://thehill.com/opinion/international/3480598-why-japan -must-rescind-article-9/ [https://perma.cc/RXB8-TH45].

778 Adam N. Sterling, "Implicit Limits on Amending the Japanese Constitution" (2019) 28(1) *Washington International Law Journal* 243–309.

779 Nakamura (2022), *supra* note 649.

780 Rienzi (2015), *supra* note 669.

781 *Ibid.*

782 *Ibid.*

783 *Ibid.*

784 *Ibid.*

785 See "Japan's PM Denies 'comfort women' Coerced," *NBC News*, March 1, 2007, *supra* note 753.

786 J. Mark Ramseyer, "Contracting for Sex in the Pacific War" (2021) 65 *International Review of Law and Economics* 1–8. Ramseyer's controversial argument has provoked public outcry, and thousands of scholars, including Nobel laureates, have criticized his paper and denounced it. Michael Chwe, *Letter by Concerned Economists Regarding "Contracting for Sex in the Pacific War" in the International Review of Law and Economics*, http://chwe.net/irle/letter [https://perma.cc/FLQ2-YMEC].

787 Alexis Dudden (ed.), "Supplement to Special Issue: Academic Integrity at Stake: The Ramseyer Article - Four Letters (Table of Contents)" (2021) 19(5) *Asian-Pacific Journal* 1–2.

788 Lee, Saito, and Todres (2021), *supra* note 40. See also Yong-Shik Lee, "On Ramseyer's Response to the Critics of 'Contracting for Sex in the Pacific War'" (2022) 15(1) *Law and Development Review* 201–214. See also Radhika Coomaraswamy (Special Rapporteur on Violence against Women, Its Causes and Consequences), *Report on the Mission to the Democratic People's Republic of Korea, the Republic of Korea and*

222 SUSTAINABLE PEACE IN NORTHEAST ASIA

Japan on the Issue of Military Sexual Slavery in Wartime, U.N. Doc. E/CN.4/1996/53/ Add.1 (January 4, 1996).

789 Silence could be construed as indirect encouragement; for example, J. Mark Ramseyer, after receiving worldwide criticism, changed his tactics and began to dilute the issue by alleging "the North Korean connection" to the comfort women. Tetsuo Arima and J. Mark Ramseyer, *Comfort Women: The North Korean Connection*, The Harvard John M. Olin Discussion Paper Series, no. 1084 (August 2022).

790 Rienzi (2015), *supra* note 669.

791 *Ibid.*

792 *Ibid.*

793 *Ibid.*

794 See Stephen D. Wrage, "Germany and Japan Handle History Very Differently," *New York Times*, August 17, 1995, https://www.nytimes.com/1995/08/17/opinion/IHT-germany -and-japan-handle-history-very-differently.html [https://perma.cc/U47K-QXL4]. See also Park Byong-su, "Germany Offers Lessons for Remembering Atrocities - Japan Should Take Them," *Hankyoreh*, September 24, 2022, https://english.hani.co.kr/arti/ english_edition/e_international/1059951.html [https://perma.cc/JKV8-74PD].

795 Ministry of Foreign Affairs of Japan (1993), *supra* note 753.

796 Ministry of Foreign Affairs of Japan, *Japan's Position on the United Nations Security Council for the 21st Century* (March 2011), https://www.mofa.go.jp/policy/un/sc/pdfs/ pamph_unsc21c_en.pdf [https://perma.cc/BKU6-5Q3B].

797 See also Chen Yang, "Japan's Dream for UN Security Council Seat Crushed by Its Historical Mirages," *Global Times*, September 26, 2020, https://www.globaltimes.cn /content/1202114.shtml [https://perma.cc/9BBP-KJT4].

798 Benjamin K. Sibbett, "Tokdo or Takeshima? The Territorial Dispute Between Japan and the Republic of Korea" (1998) 21(4) *Fordham International Law Journal* 1606–1646. The article notes that South Korea has a stronger claim because it has "manifested greater affirmative acts of sovereignty." *Id.*, at 1631.

799 "S. Korea Expresses Strong Protest over Japan's Renewed Dokdo Claims in Defense White Paper," *Korea Herald*, July 13, 2021, https://www.koreaherald.com/view.php ?ud=20210713000503 [https://perma.cc/RSR4-9MZT].

800 "Kuril Islands Dispute between Russia and Japan," *BBC News*, April 29, 2013, https://www.bbc.com/news/world-asia-pacific-11664434 (accessed December 30, 2022).

801 "46% of Japanese Favor Initial Return of 2 Islands from Russia," Nikkei Asia, November 26, 2018, https://asia.nikkei.com/Politics/46-of-Japanese-favor-initial -return-of-2-islands-from-Russia [https://perma.cc/4QTP-MTRR].

802 Ministry of Foreign Affairs of Japan (2011), *supra* note 796.

803 Barrash (2022), *supra* note 737.

Chapter 6. Insiders from the Outside: The United States and Russia

804 Robert G. Sutter, *US-China Relations: Perilous Past, Uncertain Present* (3d ed., Rowman & Littlefield, 2018).

805 Warren I. Cohen, *America's Response to China: A History of Sino-American Relations* (6th ed., Columbia University Press, 2019).

806 Sutter (2018), *supra* note 804.

807 *Ibid.*

808 *Ibid.*

809 Cohen (2019), *supra* note 805.

810 Tosh Minohara and Kaoru Iokibe. "America Encounters Japan, 1836–94," *in* Makoto Iokibe and Tosh Minohara (eds.), *The History of US-Japan Relations: From Perry to Present* (Palgrave Macmillan, 2017), at 3–22.

811 *Ibid.*

812 *Ibid.*

813 Treaty of Peace, Amity, Commerce and Navigation between the United States and the Kingdom of Korea (1882), https://www.degruyter.com/document/doi/10.1515/9780824885380-020/pdf (accessed December 30, 2022).

814 *Ibid.*

815 Edward B. Parsons, "Roosevelt's Containment of the Russo-Japanese War" (1969) 38(1) *Pacific Historical Review* 21–44.

816 *Ibid.*

817 Article I of the treaty provides in relevant part, "If other Powers deal unjustly or oppressively with either Government, the other will exert their good offices, on being informed of the case, to bring about an amicable arrangement, thus showing their friendly feelings." Article I, Treaty of Peace, Amity, Commerce and Navigation between the United States and the Kingdom of Korea (1882), *supra* note 813.

818 Larsen and Seeley (2014), *supra* note 36.

819 R. Veatch, "Japan, the United States, and Manchuria" (1932) 1 *Editorial Research Reports 1932*, https://library.cqpress.com/cqresearcher/document.php?id=cqres-rre1932062000 [https://perma.cc/GT7J-M62K].

820 See U.S. Department of State, *Japan, China, the United States and the Road to Pearl Harbor, 1937–41*, https://history.state.gov/milestones/1937-1945/pearl-harbor [https://perma.cc/7RLH-6QN4].

821 *Ibid.*

822 *Ibid.*

823 *Ibid.*

824 Alan Wood, *Russia's Frozen Frontier: A History of Siberia and the Russian Far East, 1581–1991* (Bloomsbury, 2011).

825 *Ibid.*

826 Peter C. Purdue, *China Marches West: The Qing Conquest of Central Eurasia* (Belknap Press, 2005).

827 *Ibid.*

828 *Ibid.*

829 *Ibid.*

830 *Ibid.*

831 Victor Zatsepine, *Beyond the Amur: Frontier Encounters between Russia and China, 1850–1930* (University of British Columbia Press, 2017).

832 Wood (2011), *supra* note 824.

833 *Ibid.*

834 See Purdue (2005), *supra* note 826.

835 Mikhail Nosov, "Russia between Europe and Asia" (2014) 81(1) *Rivista di Studi Politici Internazionali* 15–34.

836 Zatsepine (2017), *supra* note 831.

837 *Ibid.*

838 *Ibid.*

839 *Ibid.*

840 Martin (1967), *supra* note 35.

841 *Ibid.* See also Geoffrey Jukes, *The Russo-Japanese War 1904–1905* (Osprey Publishing, 2002).

842 Seth (2011), *supra* note 32.

843 Martin (1967), *supra* note 35 and Jukes (2002), *supra* note 841.

844 See David Wolff, Yokote Shinji, and Willard Sunderland (eds.), *Russia's Great War and Revolution in the Far East: Re-imagining the Northeast Asian Theater, 1914–22* (Slavica, 2018).

845 See Quincy Wright, "The Manchurian Crisis" (1932) 26(1) *American Political Science Review* 45–76.

846 See Amnon Sella, "Khalkhin-Gol: The Forgotten War" (1983) 18(4) *Journal of Contemporary History* 651–687.

847 Pact of Neutrality between Union of Soviet Socialist Republics and Japan (1941), https://avalon.law.yale.edu/wwii/s1.asp [https://perma.cc/V2NQ-SG92].

848 David M. Glant, *August Storm: The Soviet 1945 Strategic Offensive in Manchuria*, Leavenworth Papers, no. 7 (February 1983).

849 *Ibid.*

850 Seth (2011), *supra* note 32.

851 *Ibid.*

852 For further discussion of the American military government in South Korea (1945-1948), see Hakjoon Kim, "The American Military Government in South Korea, 1945-1948: Its Formation, Policies, and Legacies" (1988) 12(1) *Asian Perspective* 51–83.

853 For further discussion of the American occupation of Japan, see Makoto Iokibe, *The Occupation of Japan* (Congressional Information Service, 1987).

854 Both countries pursued export-oriented economic development policies. For a discussion of the export-oriented development policies, see Lee (2016), *supra* note 290.

855 See Michael Beckley, Yusaku Horiuchi, and Jennifer M. Miller, "America's Role in the Making of Japan's Economic Miracle" (2018) 18(1) *Journal of East Asian Studies* 1–21. See also Michael J. Seth, *South Korea's Economic Development, 1948–1996* (December 19, 2017), https://oxfordre.com/asianhistory/view/10.1093/acrefore/9780190277727.001.0001/acrefore-9780190277727-e-271 [https://perma.cc/7PH4-GPQK].

856 See Khan (2004), *supra* note 532.

857 See Kent Calder and Min Ye, *The Making of Northeast Asia* (Stanford University Press, 2010).

858 Mutual Defense Treaty Between the United States and the Republic of Korea (1953), https://www.usfk.mil/Portals/105/Documents/SOFA/H_Mutual%20Defense%20Treaty_1953.pdf [https://perma.cc/MZD6-BKGC].

859 Sutter (2018), *supra* note 804.

860 See, *e.g.*, Center for Strategic and International Studies, *A Speech by Assistant Secretary of State for East Asian and Pacific Affairs David R. Stilwell* (December 13, 2019), https://www.csis.org/analysis/speech-assistant-secretary-state-east-asian-and-pacific-affairs-david-r-stilwell [https://perma.cc/7F89-B3CD].

861 See Office of Strategic Industries and Economic Security Bureau of Export Administration and DFI International, *U.S. Commercial Technology Transfers to the*

People's Republic of China (January 1999), https://www.bis.doc.gov/index.php/
documents/technology-evaluation/71-u-s-commercial-technology-transfers-to-the
-people-s-republic-of-china-1999/file [https://perma.cc/6A3N-N6LY]. The United
States also provides the largest export market for China. World Bank, *China Trade*,
https://wits.worldbank.org/CountrySnapshot/en/CHN (accessed December 30,
2022).

862 See Kimitaka Matsuzato (ed.), *Russia and Its Northeast Asian Neighbors: China, Japan, and
Korea, 1858–1945* (Lexington Books, 2017). See also Ulyana Shipitko, "Rediscovering
Russia in Northeast Asia" (2010) 9 *Ritsumeikan Annual Review of International Studies*
205–229.

863 Max Mark, "Chinese Communism" (1951) 13(2) *Journal of Politics* 232–252.

864 See discussion *supra* Section 1.2.1.

865 *Ibid.*

866 *Ibid.*

867 For a related discussion, see Manwoo Lee, "Some Reflections on Soviet Influence in
East Asia" (1986) 10(2) *Asian Perspective* 255–271.

868 Yaroslav Trofimov, "The New Beijing-Moscow Axis," *Wall Street Journal*, February
2, 2019.

869 Kenneth G. Lieberthal, *Mao Tse-Tung's Perception of the Soviet Union as Communicated in
the Mao Tse-tung Ssu-Hsiang Wan Sui*, Rand Paper Series (1976).

870 *Ibid.*

871 Donald S. Zagora, "Mao's Role in the Sino-Soviet Conflict" (1974) 47(2) *Pacific Affairs*
139–153.

872 *Ibid.*

873 Gerson (2010), *supra* note 346. See also discussion *supra* Section 3.2.3.

874 See Vladislav Zubok, "The Soviet Union and China in the 1980s: Reconciliation
and Divorce" (2017) 17 *Cold War History* 121–141.

875 For further discussion on the subject, see Georgy Toloraya, "The Six Party Talks: A
Russian Perspective" (2008) 32(4) *Asian Perspective* 45–69.

876 See also Gilbert Rozman (ed.). *U.S. Leadership, History, and Bilateral Relations in Northeast
Asia* (Cambridge University Press, 2011).

877 Mutual Defense Treaty Between the United States and the Republic of Korea (1953),
supra note 858 and the Security Treaty between the United States and Japan (1951),
replaced with the Treaty of Mutual Cooperation and Security between Japan and
the United States of America (1960), https://www.mofa.go.jp/region/n-america/us
/q&a/ref/1.html [https://perma.cc/CDQ9-RUAR].

878 For a related discussion, see Leif-Eric Easley, "Defense Ownership or Nationalist
Security: Autonomy and Reputation in South Korean and Japanese Security
Policies" (2007) 27(2) *The SAIS Review of International Affairs* 153–166.

879 See discussion *supra* Section 2.1.2.

880 See Joel Gehrke, "Chinese Military to 'prepare for war' as Xi Jinping Menaces
Taiwan," *Washington Examiner*, October 19, 2022, https://www.washingtonexaminer
.com/policy/defense-national-security/china-military-prepare-war-xi-jinping-men-
aces-taiwan [https://perma.cc/DKW3-KWPQ].

881 Eric Johnston, "How Russia Quietly Built Up Its Military Presence in Asia," *Japan
Times*, March 9, 2022, https://www.japantimes.co.jp/news/2022/03/09/national/
russia-asia-presence-ukraine-invasion/ [https://perma.cc/G5V4-DGYG].

882 Timothy S. Rich and Mallory Hardesty, *Americans Largely Reject Closing Bases in Germany, South Korea and Japan* (July 26, 2022), https://www.e-ir.info/2022/07/26/americans-largely-reject-closing-bases-in-germany-south-korea-and-japan/ [https://perma.cc/3FHJ-N2VV].

883 Commander, U.S. 7th Fleet, *The United States Seventh Fleet*, https://www.c7f.navy.mil/About-Us/Facts-Sheet/ [https://perma.cc/6URB-ZDDY].

884 However, commentators warn of China's naval challenge in the region. See, *e.g.*, Phelim Kine and Lara Seligman, "Why the U.S. Isn't Ready for a Fight in the Indo-Pacific," *Politico*, December 27, 2022, https://www.politico.com/news/2022/12/27/united-states-china-taiwan-pacific-00075555 [https://perma.cc/Z4AE-TY5Y].

885 *Ibid.*

886 U.S. Indo-Pacific Command, *About USINDOPACOM*, https://www.pacom.mil/About-USINDOPACOM/ [https://perma.cc/F8GS-3JBA].

887 *Ibid.*

888 Mari Yamaguchi, "US Vows Full Military Defense of Allies against North Korea," *AP News*, October 25, 2022, https://apnews.com/article/technology-japan-united-states-tokyo-south-korea-7397d3c81ecc6ceff76a4f0ffe25ec24 [https://perma.cc/L3AM-XYZP].

889 See, *e.g.*, G. John Ikenberry, "American Hegemony and East Asian Order" (2004) 58(3) *American Journal of International Affairs* 353–367.

890 Hyug Baeg Im, "The US Role in Korean Democracy and Security Since Cold War Era" (2006) 6(2) *International Relations of Asia-Pacific* 157–187.

891 Cho Ah Ra, "The U.S. Role in Korea-Japan Normalization Talks: Focusing on the Claim Negotiations under the Kennedy Administration" (in Korean) (2014) 4 *Korean Journal of Japanese Studies* 270–307.

892 *Ibid.*

893 Lee, Kwon, and Lee (2022), *supra* note 444. See also Jae Chang, *The United States Looks to Form Semiconductor Alliance with Indo-Pacific Partners* (June 1, 2022), https://asiamattersforamerica.org/articles/the-united-states-looks-to-form-semiconductor-alliance-with-indo-pacific-partners [https://perma.cc/W46V-4LXX] and Robyn Klingler-Vidra and Yu-Ching Kuo, *Washington Shores-up Friends in the Semiconductor Industry* (September 28, 2022), https://www.eastasiaforum.org/2022/09/28/washington-shores-up-friends-in-the-semiconductor-industry/ [https://perma.cc/ARL7-PM6P].

894 Louisa Lim, *The People's Republic of Amnesia: Tiananmen Revisited* (Oxford University Press, 2014).

895 For protests in Hong Kong, see Anthony Dapiran, *City of Protest: A Recent History of Dissent in Hong Kong* (Penguin Books, 2017) and Loong Yu Au, *Hong Kong in Revolt: The Protest Movement and the Future of China* (Pluto Press, 2020).

896 According to a report, some demonstrators echoed the following slogans: "We want to eat, not do coronavirus tests; reform, not the Cultural Revolution. We want freedom, not lockdowns; elections, not rulers. We want dignity, not lies. Be citizens, not enslaved people." See "What the Chinese People Are Revealing About Themselves," *New York Times*, December 3, 2022, https://www.nytimes.com/2022/12/03/opinion/china-covid-protests.html (accessed December 30, 2022).

897 Lee (2016), *supra* note 290.

898 See, *e.g.*, Min-Hua Chiang, *China More Dependent on U.S. and Our Technology Than You Think* (July 7, 2022), https://www.heritage.org/asia/commentary/china-more-dependent-us-and-our-technology-you-think [https://perma.cc/SH92-V8QK].

899   Bureau of Economic Analysis (U.S. Department of Commerce), *U.S. Direct Investment Abroad: Balance of Payments and Direct Investment Position Data*, https://apps.bea.gov/international/xls/usdia-current/usdia-detailedcountry-2020-2021.xlsx (accessed December 30, 2022).

900   For further discussion on the Plaza accord, see C. Randall Henning and I. M. Destler, "From Neglect to Activism: American Politics and the 1985 Plaza Accord" (1988) 8(3) *Journal of Public Policy* 317–333 and Youn-Suk Kim, "Prospects of Japanese-U.S. Trade and Industrial Competition" (1990) 30(5) *Asian Survey* 493–504.

901   Yong-Shik Lee, Jaemin Lee, and Kyung Han Sohn, "The United States – Korea Free Trade Agreement: Path to Common Economic Prosperity or False Promise?" (2011) 7 *University of Pennsylvania East Asia Law Review* 111–162, at 154.

902   United States Census Bureau, *Top Trading Partners—September 2022*, https://www.census.gov/foreign-trade/statistics/highlights/top/top2209yr.html [https://perma.cc/GK26-WWXH].

903   *Ibid.*

904   *Ibid.*

905   See Kenneth G. Lieberthal, *The American Pivot to Asia* (December 21, 2011), https://www.brookings.edu/articles/the-american-pivot-to-asia/ [https://perma.cc/D87F-H8GZ].

906   For further discussion, see Lee (2016), *supra* note 24.

907   Center for Strategic and International Studies (2019), *supra* note 860.

908   See Lieberthal (2011), *supra* note 905.

909   See Lee (2020), *supra* note 296.

910   *Ibid.*

911   Lee (2017), *supra* note 383.

912   Lee (2022), *supra* note 56.

913   United States Trade Representative, "Notice of Modification of s. 301 Action: China's Acts, Policies, and Practices Related to Technology Transfer, Intellectual Property, and Innovation," 83 *Federal Register* (September 21, 2018).

914   *Ibid.*

915   Lee (2022), *supra* note 56.

916   See "What does Xi Jinping's China Dream Mean?" *BBC News*, June 6, 2013, *supra* note 369.

917   For a discussion of China's peaceful rise, see Zheng Bijian, "China's 'Peaceful Rise' to Great-Power Status," *Foreign Affairs*, September/October 2005, https://www.foreignaffairs.com/articles/asia/2005-09-01/chinas-peaceful-rise-great-power-status [https://perma.cc/5RRT-Y8MJ].

918   See also Valerie Hernandez, "Have the Huawei Bans Achieved the US' Intended Goals?" *International Banker*, September 7, 2022, https://internationalbanker.com/technology/have-the-huawei-bans-achieved-the-us-intended-goals/ [https://perma.cc/VND3-9SX3].

919   World Trade Organization, *United States – Tariff Measures on Certain Goods from China*, Report of the Panel, WT/DS543/R (September 15, 2020), at 65.

920   Lee (2022), *supra* note 56.

921   Hernandez (2022), *supra* note 918.

922   See Lee, Kwon, and Lee (2022), *supra* note 444.

923   Bureau of Industry and Security (U.S. Department of Commerce), *Commerce Implements New Export Controls on Advanced Computing and Semiconductor Manufacturing Items to the People's Republic of China (PRC)* (October 7, 2022), https://www.bis.doc

.gov/index.php/documents/about-bis/newsroom/press-releases/3158-2022-10-07 -bis-press-release-advanced-computing-and-semiconductor-manufacturing-controls -final/file [https://perma.cc/C9LH-TZYL]. See also Michael Schuman, "Why Biden's Block on Chips to China Is a Big Deal," *The Atlantic*, October 25, 2022, https://www.theatlantic.com/international/archive/2022/10/biden-export-con-trol-microchips-china/671848/ [https://perma.cc/9FHF-2XWV].

924 Rintaro Tobita, "U.S. Calls Out Japan and Netherlands over China Chip Curbs," *Nikkei Asia*, November 6, 2022, https://asia.nikkei.com/Business/Electronics/U .S.-calls-out-Japan-and-Netherlands-over-China-chip-curbs [https://perma.cc /5HDM-GD6U].

925 Public Law 117–167 (2022).

926 Arjun Gargeyas, "The Chip 4 Alliance Might Work on Paper, But Problems Will Persist," *The Diplomat*, August 25, 2022, https://thediplomat.com/2022/08/the -chip4-alliance-might-work-on-paper-but-problems-will-persist/ [https://perma.cc /44FA-27WA].

927 *Ibid.* See also Kuancheng Huang *et al.*, "East Asian Firms Are Critical to America's Semiconductor Success," *The Diplomat*, May 4, 2022, https://thediplomat.com/2022 /05/east-asian-firms-are-critical-to-americas-semiconductor-success/ [https:// perma.cc/PUH6-RB44].

928 Hernandez (2022), *supra* note 918.

929 For further discussion of Russia's post-cold war decline, see Thomas E. Graham, *Russia's Decline and Uncertain Recovery* (Carnegie Endowment for International Peace, 2002), https://carnegieendowment.org/pdf/files/Decline.pdf [https://perma.cc/ FK8F-DLJG].

930 *Ibid.*

931 *Ibid.*

932 Leszek Busnyski, "Russia and Northeast Asia: Facing a Rising China" (2002) 3(1) *Georgetown Journal of International Affairs* 69–76.

933 *Ibid.*

934 World Bank, *GDP (current US$) – China, Russian Federation*, https://data.worldbank .org/indicator/NY.GDP.MKTP.CD?locations=CN-RU [https://perma.cc/93Z4 -3SFY].

935 *Ibid.*

936 Sara Su Jones, "Embarked on a New Path: US Assistance to Russia After the Cold War" (1994) 17(1) *Harvard International Review* 56–57, at 55.

937 See discussion *supra* Section 5.2.3.

938 Busnyski (2002), *supra* note 932.

939 *Ibid.*

940 *Ibid.*

941 Anastasia Barannikova, *United States-DPRK Relations* (Center for Strategic and International Studies, 2019), at 48–51.

942 See Sergey Guriyev, "20 Years of Vladimir Putin: The Transformation of the Economy," *The Moscow Times*, August 16, 2019, https://www.themoscowtimes .com/2019/08/16/20-years-of-vladimir-putin-the-transformation-of-the-economy -a66854 [https://perma.cc/5W76-RJ2B].

943 Liudmila Zakharova, "Russia and Northeast Asia: Pursuing Strategic and Economic Goals" (2017) 12(4) *Global Asia* 57–61.

944 Emma Ashford, "Not-So-Smart Sanctions" (2016) 95(1) *Foreign Affairs* 114–123.

945 *Ibid.*

946 Dimitri Simes Jr. and Tatiana Simes, "Putin's Big Plans for Russia's Far East Aren't Panning Out," *World Politics Review*, October 5, 2021, https://www.worldpolitics-review.com/putin-s-big-plans-for-russia-s-far-east-aren-t-panning-out/ [https://perma.cc/QQL6-QYDF].

947 See Ellen Nakashima, John Hudson, Michelle Ye Hee Lee, and Cate Cadell, "Key Asian Nations Join Global Backlash Against Russia, with an Eye Toward China," *Washington Post*, March 3, 2022, https://www.washingtonpost.com/national-security/2022/03/03/ukraine-asia-sanctions/ [https://perma.cc/WL3D-R6NK].

948 Barannikova (2019), *supra* note 941.

949 *Ibid.*

950 For further discussion on the subject, see Robert S. Ross, *The Fate of the Pivot: U.S. Policy in East Asia* (S. Rajaratnam School of International Studies, 2014); Bruce Cumings, "Power and Plenty in Northeast Asia: The Evolution of U.S. Policy" (1987) 5(1) *World Policy Journal* 79–106; Ralph A. Cossa and Brad Glosserman, "Washington 'Pivots' to Asia" (2022) 24(2) *Pacific Forum Comparative Connections* 1–20.

951 *Ibid.*

952 See Peter Gibbon and Jakob Vestergaard, *US Trade Policy under Trump: Assessing the Unilateralist Turn* (Danish Institute for International Studies, 2017).

953 Lee (2020), *supra* note 296.

954 Lee (2017), *supra* note 383.

955 Gibbon and Vestergaard (2017), *supra* note 952.

956 Lee (2016), *supra* note 24.

957 *Ibid.*

958 *Ibid.*

959 Mireya Solís, *China Moves to Join the CPTPP, But Don't Expect a Fast Pass* (September 23, 2021), https://www.brookings.edu/blog/order-from-chaos/2021/09/23/china-moves-to-join-the-cptpp-but-dont-expect-a-fast-pass/ [https://perma.cc/X2XG-ZH2D].

960 For further discussion on the subject, see Bernard Hoekman and Petros C. Mavroidis, "Burning Down the House?: The Appellate Body at the Center of the WTO Crisis," in Bernard Hoekman and Ernesto Zedillo (eds.), *Trade in the 21st Century: Back to the Past?* (Brookings Institution, 2021), at 243–272.

961 World Trade Organization, *Members Continue Push to Commence Appellate Body Appointment Process* (March 28, 2022), https://www.wto.org/english/news_e/news22_e/dsb_28mar22_e.htm [https://perma.cc/N68E-WTWP].

962 World Trade Organization (2020), *supra* note 919.

963 Yong-Shik Lee, "Three Wrongs Do Not Make a Right: The Conundrum of the U.S. Steel and Aluminum Tariffs" (2019) 18(3) *World Trade Review* 481–501.

964 Article 11(b) of the Agreement on Safeguards stipulates, ". . . furthermore, a Member shall not seek, take or maintain any voluntary export restraints, orderly marketing arrangements or any other similar measures on the export or the import side. These include actions taken by a single Member as well as actions under agreements, arrangements and understandings entered into by two or more Members . . ." (footnote omitted). See also Yong-Shik Lee, "The Steel and Aluminum Quota Agreements: A Question of Compatibility with WTO Disciplines and Their Impact on the World Trading System" (2019) 52(5) *Journal of World Trade* 811–832.

965 David Lawder, "USTR Tai Calls U.S. Tariffs on Chinese Goods 'significant' Leverage," *Reuters*, June 22, 2022, https://www.reuters.com/business/ustr-tai-says -us-tariffs-chinese-goods-are-significant-leverage-2022-06-22/ (accessed December 30, 2022).

966 Bruce Klingner, Jung H. Pak, and Sue Mi Terry, *Trump Shakedowns Are Threatening Two Key US Alliances in Asia* (December 18, 2019), https://www.brookings.edu/blog /order-from-chaos/2019/12/18/trump-shakedowns-are-threatening-two-key-u-s -alliances-in-asia/ [https://perma.cc/YH9J-KXS3].

967 *Ibid.*

968 See, *e.g.*, Kuperman and Acharya (2018), *supra* note 671.

969 U.S. Department of State, *Nuclear Non-Proliferation Treaty*, https://www.state.gov/ nuclear-nonproliferation-treaty/ [https://perma.cc/KF5E-V6TV].

970 Rebecca Falconer, "U.S. and South Korean Militaries Launch Biggest-Ever Air Drills," *Axios*, October 31. 2022, https://www.axios.com/2022/10/31/us-south -korea-largest-warplane-air-drills# [https://perma.cc/WD5C-E8BX].

971 White House, *National Security Strategy* (October 2022), at 38, https://www.white- house.gov/wp-content/uploads/2022/10/Biden-Harris-Administrations-National -Security-Strategy-10.2022.pdf [https://perma.cc/HH24-B83N]. See also Ryan Neuhard, *The New US National Security Strategy: Four Takeaways for Asia Policy* (October 21, 2022), https://www.fpri.org/article/2022/10/the-new-us-national-security-strat egy-four-takeaways-for-asia-policy/ [https://perma.cc/FQ95-4BDX].

972 See Gargeyas (2022), *supra* note 926.

973 United States Trade Representative, *Indo-Pacific Economic Framework for Prosperity (IPEF)*, https://ustr.gov/trade-agreements/agreements-under-negotiation/indo -pacific-economic-framework-prosperity-ipef [https://perma.cc/Y2DE-QXNM].

974 These countries include Australia, Brunei, Fiji, India, Indonesia, Japan, South Korea, Malaysia, New Zealand, Philippines, Singapore, Thailand, and Vietnam. See also "In Tokyo, Biden set to launch new Indo-Pacific trade pact to replace TPP," *Associated Press*, May 22, 2022, https://www.marketwatch.com/story/bidens-indo -pacific-trade-pact-wont-include-taiwan-at-launch-01653261066 [https://perma.cc /BV43-7549].

975 National Archive, *Marshall Plan* (1948), https://www.archives.gov/milestone-docu- ments/marshall-plan [https://perma.cc/ZQH3-RE6Y].

976 *Ibid.*

977 Center for Strategic and International Studies (2019), *supra* note 860.

978 Gibbon and Vestergaard (2017), *supra* note 952.

979 Laura Silver, *Some Americans' Views of China Turned More Negative after 2020, But Others Became More Positive* (September 28, 2022), https://www.pewresearch.org/fact-tank /2022/09/28/some-americans-views-of-china-turned-more-negative-after-2020 -but-others-became-more-positive/ [https://perma.cc/54PB-SEXS].

980 White House, *Indo-Pacific Strategy of the United States* (February 2022), https://www .whitehouse.gov/wp-content/uploads/2022/02/U.S.-Indo-Pacific-Strategy.pdf [https://perma.cc/8ZJL-RXK4].

981 *Ibid.*

982 *Ibid.*

983 *Ibid.*, at 5.

984 See discussion *supra* Sections 5.2.1 and 5.3.1.

985 *Ibid.*

986 Lee (2020), *supra* note 86.
987 U.S. Department of State, *Resolution of the Comfort Woman Issue*, https://2009-2017.state
     .gov/secretary/remarks/2015/12/250874.htm [https://perma.cc/TA4P-362F].
988 *Ibid.*
989 Public Law 117–167 (Chips and Science Act of 2022) and Public Law 117–169
     (Inflation Reduction Act of 2022). See also White House, *Building Resilient Supply
     Chains, Revitalizing American Manufacturing, and Fostering Broad-Based Growth* (June
     2021), https://www.whitehouse.gov/wp-content/uploads/2021/06/100-day-sup-
     ply-chain-review-report.pdf [https://perma.cc/VXX9-QSLQ].
990 Public Law 117–167 (2022).
991 Public Law 117–169 (2022).
992 See also Alan Sykes, *Stanford's Al Sykes on the $280 Billion Chips and Science Act,
     Government Intervention, and Trade* (August 2, 2022), https://law.stanford.edu/2022
     /08/02/stanfords-al-sykes-on-the-280-billion-chips-and-science-act-government
     -intervention-and-trade/ [https://perma.cc/27MX-A9SK].
993 White House (2021), *supra* note 989.
994 See, *e.g.*, Lee (2022), *supra* note 297.
995 United Nations, Memorandum on security assurances in connection with Ukraine's
     accession to the Treaty on the Non-Proliferation of Nuclear Weapons, UNTS, vol.
     3007, I-52241 (December 5, 1994), https://treaties.un.org/doc/Publication/UNTS/
     Volume%203007/Part/volume-3007-I-52241.pdf [https://perma.cc/S289-6SZK].
996 Steven Pifer, *Why Care about Ukraine and the Budapest Memorandum* (December 5, 2019),
     https://www.brookings.edu/blog/order-from-chaos/2019/12/05/why-care-about
     -ukraine-and-the-budapest-memorandum/ [https://perma.cc/74XB-85GD].
997 See also "Why Did Russia Invade Ukraine and Has Putin's War Failed?" *BBC
     News*, November 16, 2022, https://www.bbc.com/news/world-europe-56720589
     (accessed December 30, 2022).
998 United Nations, *Aggression against Ukraine*, A/ES-11/L.1 (March 1, 2022), https://
     digitallibrary.un.org/record/3958976?ln=en (assessed December 22, 2022).
999 Nectar Gan, "Putin concedes China has 'questions and concerns' over Russia's fal-
     tering invasion of Ukraine," *CNN*, September 16, 2022, https://www.cnn.com/2022
     /09/15/asia/xi-putin-meeting-main-bar-intl-hnk (accessed December 30, 2022).
1000 See Nakashima, Hudson, Lee, and Cadell (2022), *supra* note 947.
1001 "Ukraine war: US estimates 200,000 military casualties on all sides," *BBC
     News*, November 10, 2022, https://www.bbc.com/news/world-europe-63580372
     (accessed December 30, 2022).
1002 Jim Garamone, *Russia Continues Attacks on Ukraine Civilian Targets* (October 31, 2022),
     https://www.defense.gov/News/News-Stories/Article/Article/3205450/russia
     -continues-attacks-on-ukraine-civilian-targets/ [https://perma.cc/N6XJ-N6K6].
1003 Nick Schifrin and Zaba Warsi, "UN Investigator Outlines Evidence of Russian
     War Crimes in Liberated Areas of Ukraine," *PBS News Hour*, September 28,
     2022, https://www.pbs.org/newshour/show/un-investigator-outlines-evidence-
     of-russian-war-crimes-in-liberated-areas-of-ukraine#:~:text=Ukraine's%20p
     rosecutor%20general%20also%20said,the%20beginning%20of%20the%20war
     [https://perma.cc/JE42-DHLZ].
1004 See Andrew MacLeod, *Ukraine Invasion: Should Russia Lose Its Seat on the UN Security
     Council?* (February 25, 2022), https://www.kcl.ac.uk/ukraine-invasion-should
     -russia-lose-its-seat-on-the-un-security-council [https://perma.cc/KU75-PYSD].

1005 United Nations, "UN General Assembly Votes to Suspend Russia from the Human Rights Council," *UN News*, April 7, 2022, https://news.un.org/en/story/2022/04 /1115782 [https://perma.cc/XX6W-HEPW].

1006 See, *e.g.*, Yong-Chool Ha and Beom-Shik Shin, "The Impact of the Ukraine War on Russian–North Korean Relations" (2022) 62(5) *Asian Survey* 1–27.

1007 "Losses of Russia for the Period from Feb 24 to Nov 18," *Odessa Journal*, November 24, 2022, https://odessa-journal.com/losses-of-russia-for-the-period-from-feb-24 -to-nov-18/ [https://perma.cc/33W9-M9LD].

1008 Alberto Nardelli, "Russia Turns to Old Tanks as It Burns Through Weapons in Ukraine," *Bloomberg*, June 14, 2022, https://www.bloomberg.com/news/articles /2022-06-14/russia-turns-to-old-tanks-as-it-burns-through-weapons-in-ukraine [https://perma.cc/LT88-VGHY].

1009 Marc Santora, Andrew E. Kramer, Dan Bilefsky, Ivan Nechepurenko, and Anton Troianovski, "Russia Orders Retreat from Kherson, a Serious Reversal in the Ukraine War," *New York Times*, November 9, 2022, https://www.nytimes.com /2022/11/09/world/europe/ukraine-russia-kherson-retreat.html [https://perma .cc/7AJN-ES7D].

1010 Alexander Marrow, "Russia Announces Troop Build-Up in Far East," *Reuters*, September 17, 2020, https://www.reuters.com/article/us-russia-military/russia-announces-troop -build-up-in-far-east-idUSKBN2682JM (accessed December 30, 2022).

1011 Warren P. Strobel, Michael R. Gordon, and Nancy A. Youssef, "Russia Moves More Weaponry Toward Ukraine, Keeps the West Guessing," *Wall Street Journal*, January 14, 2022, https://www.wsj.com/articles/russia-moves-more-weaponry-toward -ukraine-keeps-the-west-guessing-11642161605 [https://perma.cc/G66K-PGBK].

1012 Karen Freifeld, "U.S. Official Says Export Curbs on Russia Hit Car Production and Tank Building," *Reuters*, March 30, 2022, https://www.reuters.com/business/ us-official-says-export-curbs-russia-hit-car-production-tank-building-2022-03-30/ (accessed December 30, 2022).

1013 International Energy Agency, *Energy Fact Sheet: Why Does Russian Oil and Gas Matter?* (March 21, 2022), https://www.iea.org/articles/energy-fact-sheet-why-does-rus- sian-oil-and-gas-matter [https://perma.cc/H64C-3GY4].

1014 White House, *Background Press Call by a Senior Administration Official on Announcement of U.S. Ban on Imports of Russian Oil, Liquefied Natural Gas, and Coal* (March 8, 2022), https:// www.whitehouse.gov/briefing-room/press-briefings/2022/03/08/background -press-call-on-announcement-of-u-s-ban-on-imports-of-russian-oil-liquefied-natural -gas-and-coal/#:~:text=Today%2C%20President%20Biden%20signed%20an,his %20needless%20war%20of%20choice [https://perma.cc/D29N-P7ZN].

1015 Takeo Kumagai, "Japan's Russian Crude Oil Imports Fall to Zero in June," *S&P Global*, July 22, 2022, https://www.spglobal.com/commodityinsights/en/market -insights/latest-news/oil/072222-japans-russian-crude-oil-imports-fall-to-zero-in -june#:~:text=%22Considering%20the%20risk%20involved%20in,Gas%20and %20Metals%20National%20Corp [https://perma.cc/6DRU-YTTB]; Alexandre Kinche, "South Korea: Seoul Disengages from Russian Oil," *Energynews*, June 22, 2022, https://energynews.pro/en/south-korea-seoul-disengages-from-russian-oil/ [https://perma.cc/XM5Y-5A7W].

1016 Anna Cooban and Uliana Pavlova, "Russia Threatens to Cut Supply of Gas through Ukraine," *CNN*, November 23, 2022, https://www.cnn.com/2022/11/23/ energy/russia-gas-ukraine-moldova [https://perma.cc/H6PQ-VBQM].

1017 Francesco Sassim, "Russia's Energy Game in Asia," *The Diplomat*, September 27, 2022, https://thediplomat.com/2022/09/russias-energy-game-in-asia/ [https://perma.cc/93B7-TYTJ].

1018 Chris Devonshire-Ellis, *China's Relations with Russia in a New Age* (September 8, 2022), https://www.china-briefing.com/news/chinas-relations-with-russia-in-a-new-age [https://perma.cc/XC5G-Y45C].

1019 See Andrea Kendall-Taylor and Michael Kofman, "Russia's Dangerous Decline: The Kremlin Won't Go Down Without a Fight" (2022) 101(6) *Foreign Affairs* 22–35.

1020 Hyonhee Shin, "N.Korea Backs Russia's Proclaimed Annexations, Criticises U.S. 'double standards,'" *Reuters*, October 3, 2022, https://www.reuters.com/world/asia-pacific/nkorea-backs-russias-proclaimed-annexations-criticises-us-double-standards-2022-10-03/ (accessed December 30, 2022). See also Steve Holland, "US says Russia's Wagner Group Bought North Korean Weapons for Ukraine War," *Reuters*, December 22, 2022, https://www.reuters.com/world/us-says-russias-wagner-group-bought-north-korean-weapons-ukraine-war-2022-12-22/ [https://perma.cc/N33M-KK5P].

1021 Matthew Luxmoore, "In Russia's Far East, a Rare Protest Movement Refuses to Be Cowed," *RadioFreeEurope/RadioLiberty*, September 11, 2020, https://www.rferl.org/a/in-russia-far-east-a-rare-protest-movement-refuses-to-be-cowed/30833806.html [https://perma.cc/5MTF-UAVP].

1022 "In Rare Display of Dissent, Lawmakers in Russia's Far East Urge Putin to Stop Ukraine War," *RadioFreeEurope/RadioLiberty*, March 27, 2022, https://www.rferl.org/a/russia-primorye-parliament-war-dissent/31871358.html [https://perma.cc/8Z4D-CJEF].

Chapter 7. A Hidden Player: Mongolia and Its Role in the Power Dynamics of Northeast Asia

1023 World Bank, *supra* note 25.

1024 For a comprehensive account of the Mongol Empire, see Timothy May and Michael Hope (eds.), *The Mongol World* (Routledge, 2022). See also Prajakti Kalra, *The Silk Road and the Political Economy of the Mongol Empire* (Routledge, 2018).

1025 May and Hope (eds.) (2022), *ibid.*

1026 *Ibid.*

1027 *Ibid.*, at 382.

1028 *Ibid.*

1029 *Ibid.*

1030 *Ibid.*, at 693.

1031 *Ibid.*, at 25.

1032 *Ibid.*, at 850.

1033 Bawden (1989), *supra* note 31, at 39.

1034 *Ibid.*, at 188.

1035 Cyril E. Black, Louis Dupree, Elizabeth Endicott-West, Daniel C. Matuszewski, Eden Naby, and Arthur N. Waldron, *The Modernization of Inner Asia* (Routledge, 1991), at 47.

1036 *Ibid.*

1037 Franck Billé, Grégory Delaplace, and Caroline Humphrey, *Frontier Encounters: Knowledge and Practice at the Russian, Chinese and Mongolian Border* (Open Book Publishers, 2012), at 41.

1038 James Reardon-Anderson, "Land Use and Society in Manchuria and Inner Mongolia during the Qing Dynasty" (2000) 5(4) *Environmental History* 503–530, at 506.

1039 Thomas E. Ewing, "Revolution of the Chinese Frontier: Outer Mongolia in 1911" (1978) 12(2) *Journal of Asian History* 101–119, at 101.

1040 Bawden (1989), *supra* note 31, at 200.

1041 *Ibid.*, at 201.

1042 U.S. Library of Congress, *Modern Mongolia, 1911-84*, http://countrystudies.us/mongolia/26.htm [https://perma.cc/54F4-8E5B].

1043 *Ibid.*

1044 Alan J. K. Sanders, "Mongolia: Independence and Revolution," *Encyclopaedia Britannica*, https://www.britannica.com/place/Mongolia/Independence-and-revolution [https://perma.cc/D6YF-B7A6].

1045 *Ibid.*

1046 Bawden (1989), *supra* note 31, at 188.

1047 Alan J. K. Sanders, "Mongolia since 1990: Constitutional Change," *Encyclopaedia Britannica*, https://www.britannica.com/place/Mongolia/Reform-and-the-birth-of-democracy [https://perma.cc/G9L3-5EWU].

1048 See May and Hope (eds.) (2022), *supra* note 1024.

1049 See, *e.g.*, Rob Gill, "Balancing Mongolia's Growth and Sovereignty: Up, Down, or Out?" (2017) 14 *New Perspectives in Foreign Policy*, 28–33.

1050 Mongolia has reportedly been keen to distance itself from Moscow and Beijing since the outbreak of the Ukraine War. Julian Dierkes, "Mongolia Is Keen to Distance Itself From Moscow and Beijing," *Foreign Policy*, October 27, 2022, https://foreignpolicy.com/2022/10/27/mongolia-independence-russia-china-relations-ukraine/ [https://perma.cc/N6UB-QBTB].

1051 U.S. Department of State, *Integrated Country Strategy: Mongolia* (March 8, 2022), https://www.state.gov/wp-content/uploads/2022/05/ICS_EAP_Mongolia_Public-1.pdf [https://perma.cc/L2CU-ZD5M].

1052 *Ibid.*

1053 Gill (2017), *supra* note 1049, at 29.

1054 Giulia Interesse, *China-Mongolia: Bilateral Trade, Investment, and Future Prospects* (December 2, 2022), https://www.china-briefing.com/news/china-mongolia-bilateral-trade-investment-and-future-prospects/ [https://perma.cc/L96M-QUJG].

1055 U.S. Department of State (2022), *supra* note 1051.

1056 See Antonio Graceffo, "Mongolia Suffers under China's Zero Covid Policy," *The Interpreter*, January 19, 2022, https://www.lowyinstitute.org/the-interpreter/mongolia-suffers-under-china-s-zero-covid-policy [https://perma.cc/5RNT-5HCW].

1057 See Lee (2022), *supra* note 56 and U.S. Department of State (2022), *supra* note 1051.

1058 For further discussion of the third neighbor policy, see Bayasgalan Sanallkhundev, "Third Neighbor Policy Concept in Mongolia's Geopolitics" (2021) 22 *Mongolian Journal of International Affairs* 81–98.

1059 Daniel Workman, *Mongolia's Top 10 Exports*, https://www.worldstopexports.com/mongolias-top-10-exports/ [https://perma.cc/3X28-6HN7].

1060 World Bank, *Manufacturing, Value Added (% of GDP)*, https://databank.worldbank.org /reports.aspx?source=2&series=NV.IND.MANF.ZS&country=MNG (accessed December 30, 2022).

1061 U.S. Department of State (2022), *supra* note 1051.

1062 Korean Statistical Information Service, *Status of Resident Foreigners by Nationality and Age*, https://kosis.kr/statHtml/statHtml.do?orgId=111&tblId=DT_1B040A6 (accessed December 30, 2022). See also Je-Seong Hong, "Korea-Mongolia Cooperation" (in Korean), *Yonhap News*, July 10, 2016, https://www.yna.co.kr/view /AKR20160709031400083 [https://perma.cc/77CA-JZNU].

1063 World Bank, *GDP Growth (Annual %) – Mongolia*, https://data.worldbank.org/indi-cator/NY.GDP.MKTP.Kd.zg?end=2021&locations=MN&start=1982 [https:// perma.cc/W5WH-CJ92].

1064 Tsolmon Baatarzorig, Ragchaasuren Galindev, and Hélène Maisonnave, "Effects of Ups and Downs of the Mongolian Mining Sector" (2018) 23 *Environment and Development Economics* 527–542.

1065 Jaewon Chung, "The Mineral Industry of Mongolia," *in* USGS, *2017–2018 Minerals Yearbook* (U.S. Department of the Interior, 2022), at 19.1–19.7.

1066 World Bank, *Exports of Goods and Services (Current US$) – Mongolia*, https://data .worldbank.org/indicator/NE.EXP.GNFS.CD?locations=MN [https://perma.cc /AFU7-XJ2Y].

1067 World Bank, *GDP (Current US$) – Mongolia*, *supra* note 25.

1068 World Bank, *GNI Per Capita, Atlas Method (Current US$) – Mongolia*, https://data .worldbank.org/indicator/NY.GNP.PCAP.CD?locations=MN [https://perma.cc /HAQ4-DVCP].

1069 World Bank, *The World Bank in Mongolia* (updated October 6, 2022), https://www .worldbank.org/en/country/mongolia/overview#1 [https://perma.cc/P4XJ -PHBE].

1070 World Population Review, *Mongolian Population 2022*, https://worldpopulation review.com/countries/mongolia-population [https://perma.cc/TU48-PEY4].

1071 World Bank (2022), *supra* note 1069.

1072 *Ibid.*

1073 U.S. Department of State (2022), *supra* note 1051.

1074 World Bank, *GDP (Current US$) – Mongolia*, *supra* note 25.

1075 Emily Kwong, "Mongolia's Long Road to Mining Wealth, Changing Mongolia," *National Public Radio*, July 31, 2019, https://www.npr.org/2019/07/31/741798613/ mongolias-long-road-to-mining-wealth [https://perma.cc/PA4A-8X52].

1076 See, *e.g.*, Jae-Yong Lee and Ka-Woen Gwon "Measures to Expand the Economic Cooperation between South Korea and Mongolia" (in Korean) (2016) 16(15) *World Economy Today* 1–22.

1077 Trading Economics, *Mongolia Foreign Direct Investment* (2022), https://tradingeco-nomics.com/mongolia/foreign-direct-investment#:~:text=Foreign%20Direct %20Investment%20in%20Mongolia%20averaged%2019380.19%20USD %20Million%20from,the%20fourth%20quarter%20of%202010. [https://perma .cc/7YKN-F3VC].

1078 Pranay Varada, "Mongolia: On the Verge of a Mineral Miracle," *Harvard International Review*, February 11, 2022, https://hir.harvard.edu/mongolia-on-the -verge-of-a-mineral-miracle/ [https://perma.cc/8Z3B-PEYD].

1079 *Ibid.*

1080 *Ibid.*
1081 In 2017, the IMF approved a US$ 5.5 billion bailout package. Varada (2022), *supra* note 1078.
1082 See Lee Jae Young, "Korea-Mongolia Economic Relations: Current Status and Cooperation Measures" (2021) 31 *Korea's Economy* 31–37.
1083 *Ibid.*
1084 World Bank (2022), *supra* note 1069.
1085 Sophie Boehm, Elizabeth Moses and Carole Excell, *Left in the Dark on Pollution, Mongolia's Poorest Communities Must Use Contaminated Water* (September 6, 2017), https://www.wri.org/insights/left-dark-pollution-mongolias-poorest-communities -must-use-contaminated-water [https://perma.cc/W6XU-CK8C].
1086 Sergelen Bayarbat, *What Is Desertification and How Does It Impact Mongolia?* (July 23, 2021), https://breathemongolia.org/en/news-article/desertification-impact-mon-golia [https://perma.cc/63V5-36J4].
1087 Unicef Mongolia, *Environment & Air Pollution*, https://www.unicef.org/mongolia /environment-air-pollution#:~:text=Ulaanbaatar%20%E2%80%93%20home %20to%20half%20of,level%20WHO%20recommends%20as%20safe. [https:// perma.cc/7RPK-RMPB].
1088 Korea International Cooperation Agency, *Ex-post Evaluation Report on the Pilot Project to Reduce Air Pollution by Improving Heating Culture in Ulaanbaatar, Mongolia* (December 2013), https://www.oecd.org/derec/korea/Ex-post-Evaluation-Report -on-the-Pilot-Project-to-Reduce-Air-Pollution-by-Improving-Heating-Culture-in -Ulaanbaatar-Mongolia.pdf [https://perma.cc/6D8Y-DD6U].
1089 Elena Gordiollo Fuertes, "Toxic Winter: The 'Slow Violence' of Air Pollution in Mongolia," *The Diplomat*, December 8, 2022, https://thediplomat.com/2022/12 /toxic-winter-the-slow-violence-of-air-pollution-in-mongolia/ [https://perma.cc /7ET6-AYCF].
1090 For further discussion on the subject, see Burmaa Tsogtochir and Soyoung Park, "Natural Resource Curse Exists in Mongolia? Focusing on Budget Transparency in Local Governments" (2021) *Journal of the Asia Pacific Economy*, https://doi.org/10 .1080/13547860.2021.1892566 (accessed December 30, 2022). See also Bin Grace Li, Pranav Gupta, and Jiangyan Yu, "From Natural Resource Boom to Sustainable Economic Growth: Lessons from Mongolia" (2017) 151 *International Economics* 7–25 (discussing how a country like Mongolia could invest in its mining industry in a way that would benefit its local economies).
1091 Julian Dierkes, "Mass Protests in Mongolia Decry 'Coal Mafia,' Corruption," *The Diplomat*, December 6, 2022, https://thediplomat.com/2022/12/mass-protests-in -mongolia-decry-coal-mafia-corruption/ [https://perma.cc/A7Z5-5JPY].
1092 Francesca Fiaschetti, "Diplomacy in the Age of Mongol Globalization: An Introduction" (2019) 17 *European Studies* 175–181, at 175.
1093 Global Firepower, *2022 Mongolia Military Strength* (May 2, 2022), https:// www.globalfirepower.com/country-military-strength-detail.php?country_id =mongolia#:~:text=For%202022%2C%20Mongolia%20is%20ranked,for%20the %20annual%20GFP%20review [https://perma.cc/MQC3-BZVM].
1094 Mongolia's former president, Tsakhiagiin Elbegdorj, justified the proposal by stating that Mongolia "is the most suitable, neutral territory" and "facilitated important meetings, including between Japan and NK (North Korea) and Mongolia's continuing legacy-UB (Ulaanbaatar) dialogue on NEA (Northeast

Asia)" (explanation added). Julian Dierkes and Mendee Jargalsaikhan, "8 Reasons Why Mongolia's Capital Ulaanbaatar Might Be The Place for a Trump-Kim Summit," *The Diplomat*, March 10, 2018, https://thediplomat.com/2018/03/8 -reasons-why-mongolias-capital-ulaanbaatar-might-be-the-place-for-a-trump-kim -summit/ [https://perma.cc/3RSS-P6N8].

1095 Elizabeth Wishnick, "Mongolia: Bridge or Buffer in Northeast Asia?" *The Diplomat*, June 19, 2019, https://thediplomat.com/2019/06/mongolia-bridge-or-buffer-in -northeast-asia/ [https://perma.cc/WML5-TLJ5].

1096 *Ibid.*

1097 Kyodo, "Japan Seeks Cooperation from Mongolia in North Korean Abduction Issue, Denuclearization," *Japan Times*, June 16, 2019, https://www.japantimes.co .jp/news/2019/06/16/national/politics-diplomacy/japan-seeks-cooperation-mon golia-north-korean-abduction-issue-denuclearization/ [https://perma.cc/6RDU -NVFX].

1098 David L. Caprara, Katharine H. S. Moon, and Paul Park, *Mongolia: Potential Mediator between the Koreas and Proponent of Peace in Northeast Asia* (January 20, 2015), https://www.brookings.edu/opinions/mongolia-potential-mediator-between-the -koreas-and-proponent-of-peace-in-northeast-asia/ [https://perma.cc/T5KD -3VDG].

1099 *Ibid.*

1100 Bolor Lkhaajav, "Mongolia Hosts 7th Ulaanbaatar Dialogue on Northeast Asian Security," *The Diplomat*, June 28, 2022, https://thediplomat.com/2022/06/mongo lia-hosts-7th-ulaanbaatar-dialogue-on-northeast-asian-security/ [https://perma.cc /BH8P-AKLA].

1101 Caprara *et al.* (2015), *supra* note 1098.

1102 *Ibid.*

1103 Permanent Mission of Mongolia to the United Nations, *Mongolia-Neutrality* (September 10, 2015), https://www.un.int/mongolia/news/mongolia-neutrality [https://perma.cc/KCV5-DGKR].

1104 U.S. Department of State, *U.S. Relations with Mongolia* (June 24, 2021), https://www .state.gov/u-s-relations-with-mongolia/ [https://perma.cc/V4GQ-C97T].

1105 *Ibid.*

1106 Jargalsaikhan Mendee, *Mongolia's Military Diplomacy and Geopolitical Balance* (March 18, 2021), https://www.eastasiaforum.org/2021/03/18/mongolias-military-diplo macy-and-geopolitical-balance/ [https://perma.cc/FZH7-PAVB].

1107 "Russia and Mongolia Held Military Exercises 'Selenga-2020,'" *VPK*, November 3, 2020, https://vpk.name/en/459716_russia-and-mongolia-held-military-exer cises-selenga-2020.html [https://perma.cc/8R92-7S69]. For further discussion on Mongolian-Russian relations, see also Tsedendamba Batbayar, "Mongolian-Russian Relations in the Past Decade" (2003) 43(6) *Asian Survey* 951–970.

1108 Sinclaire Prowse, *Mongolia - Neutrality and Anxiety* (2022), https://asiasociety.org/aus tralia/mongolia-neutrality-and-anxiety [https://perma.cc/V7BH-NBS4].

1109 See discussion *supra* Section 4.1.3.

1110 Soyolgerel Nyamjav and Mendee Jargalsaikhan, *Why Is the UB Dialogue Important?* (July 25, 2022), https://blogs.ubc.ca/mongolia/2022/ubdialogue-neasia-security/ [https://perma.cc/HR22-4CJG].

1111 In recognition of Mongolia's role, Russia has acknowledged that Mongolia is a con tributor to stability in the region. Batbayar (2003), *supra* note 1107.

1112 See U.S. Department of State (2021), *supra* note 1104.
1113 Constitution of Mongolia, https://www.constituteproject.org/constitution/ Mongolia_2001.pdf?lang=en [https://perma.cc/EBH8-3ANV].
1114 *Ibid.*
1115 *Ibid.*
1116 *Ibid.*
1117 See Paula L. W. Sabloff, "Why Mongolia? The Political Culture of an Emerging Democracy" (2010) 21(1) Central Asian Survey 19–36. See also M. Steven Fish, "Mongolia: Democracy Without Prerequisites" (1998) 9(3) *Journal of Democracy* 127–141.
1118 Alessandra Tamponi, *The Start of a Generational Turn in Mongolian Politics: What Can We Expect from L. Oyun-Erdene's New Cabinet?* (February 8, 2021), https://eias.org/publications/op-ed/the-start-of-a-generational-turn-in-the-mongolian-politics-what-can-we-expect-from-l-oyun-erdenes-new-cabinet/ [https://perma.cc/8W3P-UDS4].
1119 "Mongolian Prime Minister Submits Resignation after COVID-19 Protests," *Reuters*, January 21, 2021, https://www.reuters.com/article/us-health-coronavirus-mongolia/mongolian-prime-minister-submits-resignation-after-covid-19-protests-idUSKBN29Q1GT [https://perma.cc/6ZH3-NK6K].
1120 Tamponi (2021), *supra* note 1118.
1121 *Ibid.*
1122 Munkhnaran Bayarlkhagva, "Mongolia Edges Towards Autocracy," *Aljajeera*, July 18, 2021, https://www.aljazeera.com/opinions/2021/7/18/mongolia-edges-towards-autocracy [https://perma.cc/2QRG-PZBW].
1123 *Ibid.*
1124 *Ibid.*
1125 *Ibid.*
1126 *Ibid.*
1127 *Ibid.*
1128 "Xi Calls for Closer Cooperation between Chinese, Mongolian Ruling Parties," *Xinhuanet*, July 4, 2020, http://www.xinhuanet.com/english/2020-07/04/c_139187996.htm [https://perma.cc/5T5B-ZS58].
1129 Bayarlkhagva (2021), *supra* note 1122.
1130 *Ibid.*
1131 *Ibid.*
1132 *Ibid.*
1133 Lee (2022), *supra* note 284.
1134 For example, the Democratic Republic of Congo is known to have mineral deposits worth US$ 24 trillion, but it remains one of the poorest countries in the world. Oluwole Ojewale, *What Coltan Mining in the DRC Costs People and the Environment* (May 29, 2022), https://theconversation.com/what-coltan-mining-in-the-drc-costs-people-and-the-environment-183159 [https://perma.cc/4RZN-HTT7].
1135 Ji-Youn Suh, "Mongolian Leader to N. Korea: 'No tyranny lasts forever.'" *Korean Herald*, November 15, 2013, http://www.koreaherald.com/view.php?ud=20131115000897 [https://perma.cc/2UGH-5RSE].
1136 "Seminar on Korea-Mongolia National Union" (in Korean) (2007) *Shin-Dong-A*, no. 573, 334–337.

1137 For further discussion on a national union between Korea and Mongolia, see Choi
      Jung Il, "A New Search on Cooperation Methods between Korea and Mongolia-
      based on the Political and Economic Consideration" (in Korean) (2018) 2(1) *Journal
      of Social Convergence Studies* 29–36.

1138 The interviewees included Ms. Lkhagva Yesu, Ms. Saruul Khaliun, and Mr. Bill Guudei.

1139 Joon-Beom Jeon, "Commodity Imports Over \$30 Billion per Month for the First
      Time" (in Korean), *Chosun Biz*, March 10, 2022. Recently a major Korean telecom-
      munication company ("KT") concluded an agreement (MOU) with the Mongolian
      government to supply eighty mineral items, including rare earth minerals, to
      Korean companies.

1140 Korean Statistical Information Service, *supra* note 1062 and Hong (2016), *supra* note
      1062.

1141 "Ethnic Mongolians in China Protest Removal of Traditional Language in
      Schools," *Reuters*, September 2, 2020, https://www.reuters.com/article/us-china
      -education-mongolian-protests/ethnic-mongolians-in-china-protest-removal-of-tra-
      ditional-language-in-schools-idUSKBN25T0YP [https://perma.cc/CA33-SCS4].

1142 Hong (2016), *supra* note 1062.

1143 Thus, Korea (Goryeo), with its own government and dynasty, did not become a part
      of the Mongol Empire. See *supra* Figure 7.1.

1144 See "Seminar on Korea-Mongolia National Union" (in Korean) (2007), *supra* note
      1136.

1145 *Ibid.*

1146 *Ibid.*

1147 Choi (2018), *supra* note 1137.

1148 *Ibid.*

1149 See discussion *supra* Sections 4.2.2 and 4.2.3.

1150 Bayarlkhagva (2021), *supra* note 1122.

1151 See Yi Whan-woo, "South Korea's Population to Shrink to 38 Million by 2070 Amid
      Rising World Population," *Korea Herald*, December 26, 2022, https://www.korea-
      times.co.kr/www/biz/2022/09/602_335593.html [https://perma.cc/67NM-
      RMGY].

1152 See discussion *supra* Section 4.3.3.

1153 *Ibid.*

1154 See Choi (2018), *supra* note 1137.

1155 *Ibid.*

1156 See discussion *supra* Section 7.2.

Chapter 8. Pathway to Peace and Stability in Northeast Asia

1157 See, *e.g.*, Constitution of the Republic of Korea, *supra* note 589; Constitution of
      Japan, *supra* note 632.

1158 See discussion *supra* Section 5.2.1.

1159 Eun-Joon Kim, "China's Wang Yi Calls the United States a Rule Breaker Citing
      IRA to Park Jin," *Chosun Ilbo*, December 13, 2022, https://www.chosun.com/poli-
      tics/diplomacy-defense/2022/12/12/KR5O2NUZNBAKVPFY7672MSLDOA/
      [https://perma.cc/8UBE-KUX2].

1160 For further discussion on the subject, see Ernest Gellner, *Nations and Nationalism* (Cornell University Press, 1983).

1161 See discussion *supra* Section 7.3.3.

1162 See discussion *supra* Section 7.1.

1163 See discussion *supra* Section 3.1.2.

1164 See Beasley (1972), *supra* note 33.

1165 For further discussion on a related subject, see Nathan Park, "Abe Ruined the Most Important Democratic Relationship in Asia," *Foreign Policy*, September 4, 2020, https://foreignpolicy.com/2020/09/04/shinzo-abe-japan-south-korea-war-nation-alism/ [https://perma.cc/82DW-UP7K].

1166 See "Seminar on Korea-Mongolia National Union" (in Korean) (2007), *supra* note 1136.

1167 See discussion *supra* Section 7.2.

1168 See "What Does Xi Jinping's China Dream Mean?" *BBC News*, June 6, 2013, *supra* note 369.

1169 See discussion *supra* Section 3.2.

1170 Lee (2022), *supra* note 284.

1171 *Ibid.*

1172 *Ibid.*

1173 In 2019, a quarter of the Chinese population lived on less than US$ 6.85 per day (2017 PPP). World Bank, *Poverty headcount ratio at $6.85 a day (2017 PPP) (% of population) – China*, https://data.worldbank.org/indicator/SI.POV.UMIC?locations=CN [https://perma.cc/WBX4-J2D3].

1174 Bureau of Industry and Security (2022), *supra* note 923. The United States argues that there is also an important security dimension to the control. *Id.*

1175 Kim (2011), *supra* note 357.

1176 See discussion *supra* Section 3.3.1.

1177 Kim (2022), *supra* note 1159.

1178 See discussion *supra* Section 2.3.3.

1179 See discussion *supra* Section 4.3.2.

1180 See, *e.g.*, Shaun O'Dwyer (ed.), *Handbook of Confucianism in Modern Japan* (MHN Limited, 2021).

1181 See, *e.g.*, Insook Han Park and Lee-Jay Cho, "Confucianism and the Korean Family" (1995) 26(1) *Journal of Comparative Family Studies* 117–134.

1182 See Brooke A. Ackerly, "Is Liberalism the Only Way toward Democracy? Confucianism and Democracy" (2005) 33(4) *Political Theory* 547–576.

1183 See discussion *supra* Sections 4.2.3 and 6.2.1.

1184 See discussion *supra* Section 7.1.

1185 "China Protests Spread as Demonstrators Call for Xi to Step Down over COVID Policies," *CBS News*, November 27, 2022, https://www.cbsnews.com/news/china-protests-shanghai-beijing-covid-lockdown/ [https://perma.cc/S8NA-FD87].

1186 Luxmoore (2020), *supra* note 1021.

1187 Waltz (1979), *supra* note 393, at 118.

1188 See Waltz (1979), *supra* note 393; Hans Morgenthau, *Politics Among Nations: The Struggle for Power and Peace* (Alfred A. Knopf, 1948); Hedley Bull, *The Anarchical Society: A Study of Order in World Politics* (4th ed., Palgrave Macmillan, 2012); Robert Gilpin, War and Change in World Politics (Cambridge University Press, 1981); Stephen M. Walt, *The Origins of Alliances* (Cornell University Press, 1987); Robert

Jervis, "Cooperation Under the Security Dilemma" (1987) 30(2) *World Politics* 167–214; John J. Mearsheimer, *The Tragedy of Great Power Politics* (W. W. Norton & Company, 2001); Emerson N. S. Niou, Peter C. Ordeshook, and Gregory F. Rose, *The Balance of Power: Stability in International Systems* (Cambridge University Press, 1989). In contrast, Stephen Haggard opined that there are limits to applying major international relations theories in the Northeast Asian context.

1189 See Stephan Haggard, "The Balance of Power, Globalization, and Democracy: International Relations Theory in Northeast Asia" (2004) 4(1) *Journal of East Asian Studies* 1–38.

1190 See Maoz and Russett (1993), *supra* note 394.

1191 According to Professor Haggard, the differences among the authoritarian regimes (China, Russia, and North Korea) and the democracies (United States, South Korea, and Japan) would prove more consequential for the politics of the region. Haggard (2004), *supra* note 1189, at 31.

1192 See discussion *supra* Section 3.3.3.

1193 See discussion *supra* Section 1.2.

1194 *Ibid.*

1195 See Hyeok Hweon Kang, "Big Heads and Buddhist Demons: The Korean Musketry Revolution and the Northern Expeditions of 1654 and 1658" (2014) 2(2) *Journal of Chinese Military History* 127–189.

1196 Mihajio Kopanja discusses the strategic approaches of Northeast Asian states in terms of both the balance of power and domestic cultural considerations. Kopanja is concerned with South Korea and Japan and seeks to explain how they make strategic decisions vis-à-vis China's power in the region and their relationships with the United States. See Mihajlo Kopanja, "The Curious Case of Northeast Asia: External Balancing Meets Strategic Culture" (2019) 70 (1176) *Review of International Affairs* 67–83.

1197 Lee, Kwon, and Lee (2022), *supra* note 444.

1198 See, *e.g.*, Kim (2022), *supra* note 1159. See also John J. Mearsheimer, "The Gathering Storm: China's Challenge to US Power in Asia" (2010) 3(4) *Chinese Journal of International Politics* 381–396.

1199 Grieco (2020), *supra* note 73.

1200 Dotto, Lendon and Yeung (2022), *supra* note 583.

1201 Choe (2022), *supra* note 124.

1202 *Ibid.*

1203 *Ibid.*

1204 *Ibid.*

1205 U.S. Department of Defense (2022), *supra* note 232.

1206 *Ibid.*

1207 Mitch Shin, "US Warns North Korea: Nuclear Attack Will End Kim Regime," *The Diplomat*, October 28, 2022, https://thediplomat.com/2022/10/us-warns-north -korea-nuclear-attack-will-end-kim-regime/ [https://perma.cc/SP5U-MHQR].

1208 *Ibid.*

1209 Choe Sang-Hun and Motoko Rich, "North Korea Fires 6 More Missiles Toward Japan, Including an ICBM," *New York Times*, November 2, 2022, https://www .nytimes.com/2022/11/02/world/asia/north-korea-missile-japan.html [https:// perma.cc/GDF9-D25A].

1210 "US Confronts China, Russia at UN over N Korean Missile Launches," *Aljazeera*, November 5, 2022, https://www.aljazeera.com/news/2022/11/5/us-confronts-china-russia-at-un-over-n-korean-missile-launches [https://perma.cc/J6KB-N8Y5].

1211 U.S. Department of Defense, *Military and Security Developments Involving the People's Republic of China 2021* (2021), at 1, https://media.defense.gov/2021/Nov/03/2002885874/-1/-1/0/2021-CMPR-FINAL.PDF [https://perma.cc/88FK-5MQV].

1212 *Ibid.*

1213 U.S. Government Accountability Office, *Burden Sharing: Benefits and Costs Associated with the U.S. Military Presence in Japan and South Korea*, GAO-21-270 (March 17, 2021), https://www.gao.gov/products/gao-21-270 [https://perma.cc/CQ9T-G4AE]. See also Andrew S. Erickson, "U.S. China Military-to-Military Relations Policy Considerations in a Changing Environment" (2019) 14(3) *Asia Policy* 123–144 (articulating the tensions between the United States and China as China's military continues to undergo rapid modernization and become increasingly assertive under Xi Jinping). For a contrasting view, see Phillip C. Saunders and Julia G. Bowie, "US-China military relations: competition and cooperation" (2016) 39 *Journal of Strategic Studies* 662–684 (contending that it is not the increase in China's military capabilities that is causing tension/restricting military-to-military relations between China and the United States, but rather political relations between the two, which has set limits on military cooperation).

1214 See discussion *supra* Section 3.2.2. See also Shu-Mei Huang and Hyun-Kyung Lee, "Difficult Heritage Diplomacy? Re-articulating Places of Pain and Shame as World Heritage in Northeast Asia" (2019) 25(2) *International Journal of Heritage Studies* 143–159. U.S. Congress passed a resolution calling on China to cease its retaliatory trade measures against South Korea. See U.S. Congress, *Calling on the People's Republic of China (PRC) to Cease Its Retaliatory Measures against the Republic of Korea in Response to the Deployment of the U.S. Terminal High Altitude Area Defense (THAAD) to U.S. Forces Korea (USFK), and for Other Purposes*, H. Res. 223, 115th Congress (2017).

1215 See, *e.g.*, Paul Haenle and Lucas Tcheyan, *How the World Is Responding to a Changing China* (June 10, 2020), https://carnegieendowment.org/2020/06/10/how-world-is-responding-to-changing-china-pub-82039 [https://perma.cc/WT7B-LLUD].

1216 Fang Jin, *The Belt and Road Initiative: Progress, Problems and Prospects* (2017), https://www.csis.org/belt-and-road-initiative-progress-problems-and-prospects [https://perma.cc/YHG5-24H7].

1217 John Hurley, Scott Morris, and Gailyn Portelance, "China's Belt and Road Initiative May Bankrupt 8 Nations While Financing Infrastructure," *The Print*, March 6, 2018, https://theprint.in/opinion/chinas-belt-and-road-initiative-bankrupt-nations-financing-infrastructure/39561/ [https://perma.cc/EK7X-3Q3A].

1218 Haenle and Tcheyan (2020), *supra* note 1215.

1219 Lee (2020), *supra* note 296.

1220 Yulmaz Akyuz, "Export Dependence and Sustainability of Growth in China" (2011) 1(23) *China and World Economy* 1–23.

1221 Lee (2020), *supra* note 296.

1222 See Dan Steinbock, "U.S.-China Trade War and Its Global Impacts" (2018) 4(4) *China Quarterly of International Strategic Studies* 515–542.

1223 See discussion *supra* Section 1.3.2.

1224 Keane (2021), *supra* note 331.

1225 See discussion *supra* Section 6.3.2.

1226 White House (2021), *supra* note 989; White House, *Fact Sheet: CHIPS and Science Act Will Lower Costs, Create Jobs, Strengthen Supply Chains, and Counter China* (August 9, 2022), https://www.whitehouse.gov/briefing-room/statements-releases/2022/08/09/fact-sheet-chips-and-science-act-will-lower-costs-create-jobs-strengthen-supply-chains-and-counter-china/ [https://perma.cc/74RA-4KHW].

1227 *Ibid.*

1228 Lee (2022), *supra* note 56.

1229 *Ibid.*

1230 Trend Economy, *Mongolia's Exports 2021 by Country*, https://trendeconomy.com/data/h2/Mongolia/TOTAL [https://perma.cc/Y2MT-9WL7]; Daniel Workman, *North Korea's Top Trading Partners* (2022), https://www.worldstopexports.com/north-koreas-top-import-partners/ [https://perma.cc/5YJK-6GY5]; Trading Economics, *South Korea Exports By Country* (2022), https://tradingeconomics.com/south-korea/exports-by-country [https://perma.cc/LGH4-CB7E]; Trading Economics, *Japan Exports By Country* (2022), https://tradingeconomics.com/japan/exports-by-country [https://perma.cc/4BM2-HHL7].

1231 Joe McDonald, "China's Economy Shrinks 2.6% During Virus Shutdowns," *U.S. News and World Report*, July 15, 2022, https://www.usnews.com/news/business/articles/2022-07-14/chinas-economic-growth-falls-to-0-4-amid-virus-shutdowns (accessed December 30, 2022).

1232 See Lee, Kwon, and Lee (2022), *supra* note 444.

1233 See, *e.g.*, Naoki Abe, *Japan's Shrinking Economy* (February 12, 2010), https://www.brookings.edu/opinions/japans-shrinking-economy/ [https://perma.cc/A34Y-N4AY].

1234 See Richard Katz, "Voodoo Abenomics: Japan's Failed Comeback Plan" (2014) 93(4) *Foreign Affairs* 133–141.

1235 Jong-Gu Lee, "Japan Becomes Conservative as a Whole, Due to the Decline of the Progressive Power and Economic Recession" (in Korean), *Pressian*, March 28, 2005, https://www.pressian.com/pages/articles/46252 (accessed December 30, 2022). See also Ian Bremmer, "In 2012, the Year of Politics, What Really Hit Japan?" (in Japanese), *Reuters*, December 20, 2012, https://www.reuters.com/article/tk0578637-column-ian-bremmer-japan-idJPTYE8BK01720121221 [https://perma.cc/YV9T-UPE4].

1236 Bayarlkhagva (2021), *supra* note 1122.

1237 Laura He, "China's Economy Is 'in deep trouble' as Xi Heads for Next Decade in Power," *CNN Business*, October 15, 2022, https://www.cnn.com/2022/10/14/economy/china-party-congress-economy-trouble-xi-intl-hnk/index.html [https://perma.cc/9ZCB-KTHK].

1238 See Startfor, *What Could Push China to Invade Taiwan* (September 20, 2022), https://worldview.stratfor.com/article/what-could-push-china-invade-taiwan [https://perma.cc/386F-U4EQ].

1239 Morgenthau (1948), *supra* note 1188, at 150.

1240 *Ibid.*, at 152.

1241 White House, *Phnom Penh Statement on US – Japan – Republic of Korea Trilateral Partnership for the Indo-Pacific* (November 13, 2022), https://www.whitehouse.gov/briefing-room/statements-releases/2022/11/13/phnom-penh-statement-on-trilateral-partnership-for-the-indo-pacific/ [https://perma.cc/T78M-8ERE].

1242 Bayarlkhagva (2021), *supra* note 1122.

1243 See, *e.g.*, Jude Blanchette, *Strengthening the CCP's "Ideological Work"* (Center for Strategic and International Studies, August 2020).

1244 Mutual Defense Treaty Between the United States and the Republic of Korea (1953), *supra* note 858 and the Security Treaty between the United States and Japan (1951), replaced by the Treaty of Mutual Cooperation and Security between Japan and the United States of America (1960), *supra* note 877.

1245 "China's top diplomat renews strong objection to THAAD deployment," *Korea Herald*, March 8, 2017, http://www.koreaherald.com/view.php?ud =20170308000730 [https://perma.cc/2TL2-EFZA].

1246 Yong-Shik Lee and Kwangkug Kim, "Tripartite Free Trade Agreement among China, Korea, and Japan: A Step Towards Economic Integration in Northeast Asia?" *in* Jiaxiang Hu and Matthias Vanhullebusch (eds.), *Regional Cooperation and Free Trade Agreements in Asia* (Leiden: Brill Publishers, 2014), at 123–145.

1247 Lee (2022), *supra* note 56.

1248 *Ibid.*

1249 For further discussion on the United States-South Korea Free Trade Agreement, see Lee *et al.* (2011), *supra* note 901.

1250 Lee (2017), *supra* note 383.

1251 United States Trade Representative, *supra* note 973.

1252 See World Bank, *GDP (current US$) – Japan, Korea, Rep., China, supra* note 465.

1253 See discussion *supra* Section 6.1.3.

1254 See discussion *supra* Section 3.3.3.

1255 Sarah Kirchberger, *Who Is Encircling Whom?: Security Policy Aspects of China's Relationship with Japan* (Federal Academy for Security Policy, January 2017), at 1.

1256 Edward Wong and Ana Swanson, "U.S. Aims to Constrain China by Shaping Its Environment, Blinken Says," *New York Times*, May 26, 2022, https://www.nytimes .com/2022/05/26/us/politics/china-policy-biden.html [https://perma.cc/9JEM -LEBR].

1257 See, *e.g.*, Center for Prevention Action, Territorial Disputes in the South China Sea (May 4, 2022), https://www.cfr.org/global-conflict-tracker/conflict/territorial -disputes-south-china-sea [https://perma.cc/QE5D-5GER].

1258 Wong and Swanson (2022), *supra* note 1256.

1259 Antonio Graceffo, "China's Crackdown on Mongolian Culture," *The Diplomat*, September 4, 2020, https://thediplomat.com/2020/09/chinas-crackdown-on -mongolian-culture/ [https://perma.cc/YZ6W-WPR7].

1260 Wong and Swanson (2022), *supra* note 1256.

1261 See "China Protests Spread as Demonstrators Call for Xi to Step Down over COVID Policies," *CBS News*, November 27, 2022, *supra* note 1185.

1262 See discussion *supra* Section 3.3.2.

1263 See discussion *supra* Section 3.3.3.

1264 Wong and Swanson (2022), *supra* note 1256.

1265 *Ibid.*

1266 See Lee (2020), *supra* note 296.

1267 Lee (2022), *supra* note 56.

1268 *Ibid.*

1269 See "What Does Xi Jinping's China Dream Mean?" *BBC News*, June 6, 2013, *supra* note 369.

1270 See discussion *supra* Section 8.2.

1271 Dong Wang and Friso M. S. Stevens, "Why Is There No Northeast Asian Security Architecture? – Assessing the Strategic Impediments to a Stable East Asia" (2021) 34(4) *Pacific Review* 577–604, at 578. See also Megan DuBois, Ankit Panda, and Toby Dalton (eds.), *Enhancing the Northeast Asia Regional Security Eco-System: Issues and Approaches* (Carnegie Endowment for International Peace, 2022) and Kyung Hwan Cho, "Feasibility of Regional Security Framework in Northeast Asia" (2020) 3(1) *Journal for Peace and Nuclear Disarmament* 129–143.

1272 Wang and Stevens (2021), *ibid.*, at 577–578.

1273 "Moon: Japan's not S. Korea's Ally," *KBS World*, November 15, 2017, http://world .kbs.co.kr/service/news_view.htm?lang=e&Seq_Code=131394 [https://perma.cc /S2CW-PMDP].

1274 Wang and Stevens (2021), *supra* note 1271.

1275 Wong and Swanson (2022), *supra* note 1256.

1276 *Ibid.*

1277 See discussion *supra* note Section 3.3.3.

1278 See United Nations Human Rights Council (2014), *supra* note 210.

1279 See discussion *supra* Section 5.3.1.

1280 Heajin Kim, "Northeast Asia, Trust and the NAPCI," *The Diplomat*, December 18, 2015, https://thediplomat.com/2015/12/northeast-asia-trust-and-the-napci/ [https://perma.cc/2824-9PSH].

1281 *Ibid.*

1282 *Ibid.*

1283 Eunmi Choi, "Where is NAPCI?: The Challenges and Limitations of the (Neo-) Functionalist Approach for Multilateral Cooperation in Northeast Asia" (in Korean) (2020) 26(3) *National Strategy* 181–208.

1284 Caprara *et al.* (2015), *supra* note 1098.

1285 See discussion *supra* Section 6.3.1. See also Wong and Swanson (2022), *supra* note 1256.

1286 For further discussion on the development of the European Union, see Giuliano Amato, Enzo Moavero-Milanesi, Gianfranco Pasquino, and Lucrezia Reichlin, *The History of the European Union* (Hart, 2018).

1287 Choe (2022), *supra* note 124.

1288 Global Firepower, *supra* note 428.

1289 "Hu Jintao Escorted Out of Party Congress," *Reuters*, October 22, 2022, https:// www.reuters.com/world/china/former-chinese-president-hu-jintao-escorted-out -party-congress-2022-10-22/ [https://perma.cc/YQ2B-LX5T].

1290 Choe (2022), *supra* note 124.

1291 "China-Taiwan Tensions: Xi Jinping Says 'reunification' Must Be Fulfilled," *BBC News*, October 9, 2021, https://www.bbc.com/news/world-asia-china-58854081 (accessed December 30, 2022).

1292 "Taiwan Rejects China's 'one country, two systems' Plan for the Island," *Reuters*, August 6, 2022, https://www.reuters.com/world/asia-pacific/taiwan-rejects-chi nas-one-country-two-systems-plan-island-2022-08-11/ [https://perma.cc/Z6XG -VEXB].

1293 Peter Gries and Tao Wang, "Taiwan's Perilous Futures: Chinese Nationalism, the 2020 Presidential Elections, and U.S.-China Tensions Spell Trouble for Cross-strait Relations" (2020) 183(1) *World Affairs* 40–61.

1294 For further discussion, see Lyman P. van Slyke, "The United Front in China" (1970) 5(3) *Popular Fronts* 119–135.

1295 See discussion *supra* Section 8.2.3.

1296 Choe (2022), *supra* note 124.

1297 See discussion *supra* Section 6.3.1.

1298 World Trade Organization (2020), *supra* note 919.

1299 Chalmers and Lin (2022), *supra* note 554.

1300 Nakamura (2022), *supra* note 649.

1301 *Ibid.*

1302 "U.S. Hails Japan's New Security Strategy as 'bold and historic,'" *Kyodo News*, December 17, 2022, https://english.kyodonews.net/news/2022/12/5ee1f51910f0 -us-hails-japans-new-security-policy-as-bold-and-historic.html [https://perma.cc/ UT89-R6M6].

1303 See, *e.g.,* Kim Jong-dae, "Korea Shouldn't Be Welcoming Japan's Pursuit of Counterstrike Capabilities," *Hankyoreh*, December 9, 2022, https://english.hani .co.kr/arti/english_edition/english_editorials/1070978.html [https://perma.cc/ S4P5-SMMS].

1304 See "Japan 'To Exercise Counterattack Capability to North Korea, No South Korean Permission Needed'" (in Korean), *Yonhap News*, December 17, 2022, https://www.yna.co.kr/view/AKR20221217031400704 [https://perma.cc/3RNX -TU5P]. See also Kim (2022), *supra* note 1303.

1305 Rienzi (2015), *supra* note 669.

1306 Ministry of Foreign Affairs of Japan (1993), *supra* note 753.

1307 "Seminar on Korea-Mongolia National Union" (in Korean) (2007), *supra* note 1136. See also Byunghun Baek, "Kim Jong-un's Fireworks and the Korean-Mongolian National Union" (in Korean), *Financial Review*, June 7, 2022, http://www.finan-cialreview.co.kr/news/articleView.html?idxno=22239 [https://perma.cc/3JMV -8TFD].

1308 *Ibid.*

1309 The United States and Russia may participate in a common security arrangement and economic integration, but with all or most of their territory located outside Northeast Asia, these countries are unlikely to participate in political integration. The specific form and extent of political integration is beyond the scope of this book and will be a subject of further studies.

BIBLIOGRAPHY

"46% of Japanese Favor Initial Return of 2 Islands from Russia," *Nikkei Asia*, November 26, 2018, https://asia.nikkei.com/Politics/46-of-Japanese-favor-initial-return-of-2 -islands-from-Russia [https://perma.cc/4QTP-MTRR].

Abe, Naoki, *Japan's Shrinking Economy* (February 12, 2010), https://www.brookings.edu/ opinions/japans-shrinking-economy/ [https://perma.cc/A34Y-N4AY].

Ackerly, Brooke A., "Is Liberalism the Only Way toward Democracy? Confucianism and Democracy" (2005) 33(4) *Political Theory* 547–576.

Agov, Avram, "North Korea's Alliances and the Unfinished Korean War" (1979) 18(2) *Journal of Korean Studies* 225–262.

Agreement on Reconciliation, Non-aggression and Exchanges and Cooperation between the South and North, December 13, 1991, DC/1147 (March 25, 1992), https://peacemaker.un.org/sites/peacemaker.un.org/files/KR%20KP_911213_ Agreement%20on%20reconciliation%20non%20aggression%20and%20 exchangespdf.pdf [https://perma.cc/GQQ2-44CV].

Agreement on the Settlement of Problems Concerning Property and Claims and on Economic Co-operation (1965), https://treaties.un.org/doc/Publication/UNTS/ Volume%20583/volume-583-I-8473-English.pdf [https://perma.cc/F6Y3-QGNU].

Ahn, Byung-jik, *The History of Korean Economic Growth* (in Korean) (Seoul National University Press, 2001).

Ahn, Chang Gyu, "North Korean Air Force Launches 150 Planes in Rare Large-Scale Drill," *RFA*, October 12, 2022, https://www.rfa.org/english/news/korea/strike-drill -10122022142956.html [https://perma.cc/C45Q-L39J].

Ahn, Mun Suk, "What Is the Root Cause of the North Korean Nuclear Program?" (2011) 38(4) *Asian Affairs* 175–187.

Ahn, Young-Joon, "North Korea's Kim Jong Un Threatens to Use Nuclear Weapons in Potential Conflicts with South Korea and United States," *CBS News*, July 28, 2022, https://www.cbsnews.com/news/kim-jong-un-threatens-to-use-nukes-amid-tensions -with-us-south-korea/ [https://perma.cc/7Q7B-PTVT].

Akiyama, Hiroyuki, Takuya Mizogori, and Miki Okuyama, "Ukraine Crisis Roils Waters for Japan's Bid to Reclaim Islands from Russia," *Nikkei Asia*, February 8, 2022, https://asia.nikkei.com/Politics/International-relations/Ukraine-crisis-roils-waters -for-Japan-s-bid-to-reclaim-islands-from-Russia [https://perma.cc/98U9-NNAH].

Akyuz, Yulmaz, "Export Dependence and Sustainability of Growth in China" (2011) 1(23) *China and World Economy* 1–23.

Albert, Eleanor Albert, *The China–North Korea Relationship* (June 25, 2019), https://www .cfr.org/backgrounder/china-north-korea-relationship [https://perma.cc/BBB5 -4UXM].

"Alibaba And Tencent Fined in China Tech Crackdown," *Forbes*, July 13, 2022, https://www.forbes.com/sites/qai/2022/07/13/alibaba-and-tencent-fined-in-china-tech-crackdown/?sh=71737b083dac (accessed December 30, 2022).

Allen, G. C., *Japan's Economic Expansion* (Oxford University Press, 1965).

Alsop, Thomas, *DRAM Manufacturers Revenue Share Worldwide from 2011 to 2021, by Quarter* (May 12, 2021), https://www.statista.com/statistics/271726/global-market-share-held-by-dram-chip-vendors-since-2010/ [https://perma.cc/8SYC-F64M].

Amato, Giuliano, Enzo Moavero-Milanesi, Gianfranco Pasquino, and Lucrezia Reichlin, *The History of the European Union* (Hart, 2018).

"America's Top Brass Responds to the Threat of China in the Pacific," *The Economist*, March 11, 2021, https://www.economist.com/asia/2021/03/11/americas-top-brass-responds-to-the-threat-of-china-in-the-pacific [https://perma.cc/2G52-QEFT].

Amsden, Alice H., *Asia's Next Giant: Korea and Late Industrialization* (New York: Oxford University Press, 1992).

Arian, Asher and Michal Shamir, "The Primarily Political Functions of the Left-Right Continuum" (1983) 15(2) *Comparative Politics* 139–158.

Armstrong, Charles K., *The North Korean Revolution, 1945-1950* (Cornell University, 2003).

Armstrong, Paul, "Fury over Japanese Politician's Nanjing Massacre Denial," *CNN*, February 23, 2012, https://www.cnn.com/2012/02/23/world/asia/china-nanjing-row [https://perma.cc/8C33-AM6B].

Ashford, Emma, "Not-So-Smart Sanctions" (2016) 95(1) *Foreign Affairs* 114–123.

Asmolov, Konstantin, "Lee Jun-seok Under Attack," *New Eastern Outlook*, July 13, 2022, https://journal-neo.org/2022/07/13/lee-jun-seok-under-attack/ [https://perma.cc/5X3D-ESYE].

Au, Loong Yu, *Hong Kong in Revolt: The Protest Movement and the Future of China* (Pluto Press, 2020).

Baatarzorig, Tsolmon, Ragchaasuren Galindev, and Hélène Maisonnave, "Effects of Ups and Downs of the Mongolian Mining Sector" (2018) 23 *Environment and Development Economics* 527–542.

Bae, Chinsoo, "Territorial Issue in the Context of Colonial History and International Politics: The Dokdo Issue Between Korea and Japan" (2012) 26(1) *Journal of East Asian Affairs* 19–51.

Bae, Gawon and Jessie Yeung, "North Korea Rejects South's Aid Offer, Calls President Yoon 'Really Simple,'" *CNN*, August 19, 2022, https://www.cnn.com/2022/08/19/asia/north-korea-south-korea-aid-denuclearization-intl-hnk/index.html [https://perma.cc/ZXP9-CYFV].

Baek, Byunghun, "Kim Jong-un's Fireworks and the Korean-Mongolian National Union" (in Korean), *Financial Review*, June 7, 2022, http://www.financialreview.co.kr/news/articleView.html?idxno=22239 [https://perma.cc/3JMV-8TFD].

Bajoria, Jayshree and Beina Xu, *The Six Party Talks on North Korea's Nuclear Program* (September 30, 2013), https://www.cfr.org/backgrounder/six-party-talks-north-koreas-nuclear-program [https://perma.cc/8WPR-BKR7].

Bank of Korea, *Gross Domestic Product Estimates for South and North Korea*, https://knoema.com/KPKRGDPE2017/gross-domestic-product-estimates-for-north-and-south-korea (accessed December 30, 2022).

Bank of Korea, *North Korea's GDP Estimation Result in 1996* (December 2, 1997) (in Korean), https://www.bok.or.kr/portal/bbs/P0000559/view.do?nttId=1023&menuNo=2&pageIndex=1131 (accessed December 22, 2022).

Bank of Korea, *Korea's Major Industrial Production Map* (in Korean) (June 2021), https://www.bok.or.kr/viewer/skin/doc.html?fn=202106080424430000.pdf&rs=/webview/result/P0002125/202106 [https://perma.cc/4DZ3-LHS4].

Barannikova, Anastasia, *United States-DPRK Relations* (Center for Strategic and International Studies, 2019).

Barrash, Ike, *Russia's Militarization of the Kuril Islands* (September 27, 2022), https://www.csis.org/blogs/new-perspectives-asia/russias-militarization-kuril-islands [https://perma.cc/L8BJ-DJFH].

Batbayar, Tsedendamba, "Mongolian-Russian Relations in the Past Decade" (2003) 43(6) *Asian Survey* 951–970.

Bawden, Charles R., *The Modern History of Mongolia* (Kegan Paul International, 1989).

Bayarbat, Sergelen, *What Is Desertification and How Does It Impact Mongolia?* (July 23, 2021), https://web.archive.org/web/20221020123005/ [https://perma.cc/63V5-36J4].

Bayarlkhagva, Munkhnaran, "Mongolia Edges Towards Autocracy" *Aljajeera*, July 18, 2021, https://www.aljazeera.com/opinions/2021/7/18/mongolia-edges-towards-autocracy [https://perma.cc/2QRG-PZBW].

Beasley, W. G., *The Meiji Restoration* (Stanford University Press, 1972).

Beckley, Michael, Yusaku Horiuchi, and Jennifer M. Miller, "America's Role in the Making of Japan's Economic Miracle" (2018) 18(1) *Journal of East Asian Studies* 1–21.

Bennett, Bruce W., *Why Japan's Military Shift Is Necessary for South Korea* (July 7, 2014), https://www.rand.org/blog/2014/07/why-japans-military-shift-is-necessary-for-south-korea.html [https://perma.cc/PKQ9-AH8E].

Berger, Carl, *The Korea knot: A Military-Political History* (University of Pennsylvania Press, 1965).

Bicker, Laura, "North Korea Blows Up Joint Liaison Office with South in Kaesong," *BBC News*, June 16, 2020, https://www.bbc.com/news/world-asia-53060620 (accessed, December 20, 2022).

"Biden Says US will Defend Taiwan If China Attacks," *BBC News*, October 22, 2021, https://www.bbc.com/news/world-asia-59005300 (accessed, December 20, 2022).

Billé, Frank, Grégory Delaplace, and Caroline Humphrey, *Frontier Encounters: Knowledge and Practice at the Russian, Chinese and Mongolian Border* (Open Book Publishers, 2012).

Black, Cyril E., Louis Dupree, Elizabeth Endicott-West, Daniel C. Matuszewski, Eden Naby, and Arthur N. Waldron, *The Modernization of Inner Asia* (Routledge, 1991).

Blanchette, Jude, *Strengthening the CCP's "Ideological Work"* (Center for Strategic and International Studies, August 2020).

Boehm, Sophie, Elizabeth Moses and Carole Excell, *Left in the Dark on Pollution, Mongolia's Poorest Communities Must Use Contaminated Water* (September 6, 2017), https://www.wri.org/insights/left-dark-pollution-mongolias-poorest-communities-must-use-contaminated-water [https://perma.cc/W6XU-CK8C].

Bowen, Roger W., "Japan's Foreign Policy" (1992) 25(1) *Political Science and Politics* 57–73.

Bremmer, Ian, "In 2012, the Year of Politics, What Really Hit Japan?" (in Japanese), *Reuters*, December 20, 2012, https://www.reuters.com/article/tk0578637-column-ian-bremmer-japan-idJPTYE8BK01720121221 [https://perma.cc/YV9T-UPE4].

Brennan, Peter, *Push to Reshore US Manufacturing Challenged by Reliance on Global Supply Chain* (April 14, 2022), https://www.spglobal.com/marketintelligence/en/news-insights/latest-news-headlines/push-to-reshore-us-manufacturing-challenged-by-reliance-on-global-supply-chain-69752018 [https://perma.cc/L39K-BD3W].

Bridges, Brian, "North Korea after Kim Il-Sung" (1995) 51(6) *The World Today* 103–107.

"Britain's Queen Elizabeth Aircraft Carrier to Visit Japan, S Korea on Maiden Deployment," *Reuters*, April 26, 2021, https://www.reuters.com/world/uk/britain -says-queen-elizabeth-aircraft-carrier-visit-japan-s-korea-maiden-2021-04-26/ (accessed December 22, 2022).

Brown, James D. J., *Japan, Russia, and Their Territorial Dispute: The Northern Delusion* (Routledge, 2016).

Brown, Mark, "Colonial States, Colonial Rule, Colonial Governmentalities: Implications for the Study of Historical State Crime" (2018) 7(2) *State Crime and Colonialism* 173–198.

Buchholz, Katharina, *Who Is North Korea Trading With?* (September 6, 2019), https:// www.statista.com/chart/10683/north-korea-trading-partners/ [https://perma.cc/ MD4U-RUZ2].

Bull, Hedley, *The Anarchical Society: A Study of Order in World Politics* (4th ed., Palgrave Macmillan, 2012).

Bureau of Economic Analysis (U.S. Department of Commerce), *U.S. Direct Investment Abroad: Balance of Payments and Direct Investment Position Data*, https://apps.bea.gov/ international/xls/usdia-current/usdia-detailedcountry-2020-2021.xlsx (accessed December 22, 2022).

Bureau of Industry and Security (U.S. Department of Commerce), *Commerce Implements New Export Controls on Advanced Computing and Semiconductor Manufacturing Items to the People's Republic of China (PRC)* (October 7, 2022), https://www.bis.doc.gov/index .php/documents/about-bis/newsroom/press-releases/3158-2022-10-07-bis-press -release-advanced-computing-and-semiconductor-manufacturing-controls-final/file [https://perma.cc/C9LH-TZYL].

Busnyski, Leszek, "Russia and Northeast Asia: Facing a Rising China" (2002) 3(1) *Georgetown Journal of International Affairs* 69–76.

Calder, Kent and Min Ye, *The Making of Northeast Asia* (Stanford University Press, 2010).

Calingaert, Daniel, "Nuclear Weapons and the Korean War" (1988) 11(2) *Journal of Strategic Studies* 177–202.

Campbell, Joel R., "The Wrong War: The Soviets and the Korean War, 1945–1953" (2014) 88(3) *International Social Science Review* 1–29.

Caprara, David L., Katharine H. S. Moon, and Paul Park, *Mongolia: Potential Mediator between the Koreas and Proponent of Peace in Northeast Asia* (January 20, 2015), https:// www.brookings.edu/opinions/mongolia-potential-mediator-between-the-koreas-and -proponent-of-peace-in-northeast-asia/ [https://perma.cc/T5KD-3VDG].

Cartwright, Mark, "The Japanese Invasion of Korea, 1592-8 CE," *World History Encyclopedia* (June 11, 2019), https://www.worldhistory.org/article/1398/the-japanese -invasion-of-korea-1592-8-ce/ [https://perma.cc/2F3E-L8TM].

Cawley, Kevin N., "Korean Confucianism," *Stanford Encyclopedia of Philosophy* (November 24, 2021), https://plato.stanford.edu/entries/korean-confucianism/ [https://perma .cc/K8VX-JL9C].

CEIC, *China Exports: ICT Goods*, https://www.ceicdata.com/en/indicator/china/exports -ict-goods [https://perma.cc/5837-6WAP].

Center for Prevention Action, *Territorial Disputes in the South China Sea* (May 4, 2022), https://www.cfr.org/global-conflict-tracker/conflict/territorial-disputes-south-china -sea [https://perma.cc/QE5D-5GER].

Center for Strategic and International Studies, *A Speech by Assistant Secretary of State for East Asian and Pacific Affairs David R. Stilwell* (December 13, 2019), https://www.csis

.org/analysis/speech-assistant-secretary-state-east-asian-and-pacific-affairs-david-r
-stilwell [https://perma.cc/7F89-B3CD].

Centre for Economics and Business Research, *World Economic League Table* (December 2020), https://cebr.com/wp-content/uploads/2020/12/WELT-2021-final-29.12.pdf [https://perma.cc/7UFK-WE89].

Cha, Victor, "The North Korean Question" (2016) 56(2) *Asian Survey* 243–269.

Cha, Victor, *Assessment of the Singapore Summit* (June 12, 2018), https://www.csis.org/analysis/assessment-singapore-summit [https://perma.cc/4GF4-LY8J].

Chalmers, John and Hyunjoo Lin, "EU, South Korea Say U.S. Plan for EV Tax Breaks may Breach WTO Rules," *Reuters*, August 11, 2022, https://www.reuters.com/business/autos-transportation/eu-says-us-plan-ev-tax-breaks-discriminatory-may-breach-wto-rules-2022-08-11/ (accessed December 22, 2022).

Chan, Steve, "Human Rights in China and the United States: Competing Visions and Discrepant Performances" (2002) 24(4) *Human Rights Quarterly* 1035–1053.

Chang, Gordon, *China's Conception of the World and Model of Global Governance*, https://www.hoover.org/sites/default/files/gordon_chang_paper.pdf (accessed December 22, 2022).

Chang, Jae, *The United States Looks to Form Semiconductor Alliance with Indo-Pacific Partners* (June 1, 2022), https://asiamattersforamerica.org/articles/the-united-states-looks-to-form-semiconductor-alliance-with-indo-pacific-partners [https://perma.cc/W46V-4LXX].

Chang, Semoon, "The Saga of U.S Economic Sanctions Against North Korea" (2006) 20(2) *Journal of East Asian Affairs* 109–139.

Chang, Semoon, "Economic Cooperation Between the Two Koreas" (2012) 8(2) *North Korean Review* 6–16.

Chapman, William, "S. Korean Dissidents Praise Carter for Pressing Rights Issue with Park," *Washington Press*, July 2, 1979, https://www.washingtonpost.com/archive/politics/1979/07/02/s-korean-dissidents-praise-carter-for-pressing-rights-issue-with-park/b3f3d383-0bad-4b60-b109-69ef28e0cbf5/ [https://perma.cc/K8VG-ECYK].

Cheng, Grace, *China's Response to a Post-Pacifist Japan* (September 14, 2014), https://www.e-ir.info/2014/09/14/chinas-response-to-a-post-pacificist-japan/ [https://perma.cc/6YNQ-N6RK].

Cheng, Hung-ta and Evelyn Kao, "U.S.-Led Chip Alliance Aimed at Curbing China Influence: Analyst," *Focus Taiwan*, August 21, 2022, https://focustaiwan.tw/business/202208210007 [https://perma.cc/JTS8-4U46].

Cheng, Jonathan, "How Seoul Would Defend Itself Against a North Korean Attack," *Wall Street Journal*, August 11, 2017, https://www.wsj.com/articles/how-seoul-would-defend-itself-against-a-north-korean-attack-1502466710 [https://perma.cc/G4WL-BZSS].

Chiang, Min-Hua, *China More Dependent on U.S. and Our Technology Than You Think* (July 7, 2022), https://www.heritage.org/asia/commentary/china-more-dependent-us-and-our-technology-you-think [https://perma.cc/SH92-V8QK].

"China is the World's Factory, More Than Ever," *The Economist*, June 23, 2020, https://www.economist.com/finance-and-economics/2021/09/08/china-is-the-worlds-factory-more-than-ever [https://perma.cc/9PB2-YFTT].

"China Protests Spread as Demonstrators Call for Xi to Step down over COVID Policies," *CBS News*, November 27, 2022, https://www.cbsnews.com/news/china-protests-shanghai-beijing-covid-lockdown/ [https://perma.cc/S8NA-FD87].

"China Reaffirms Threat of Military Force to Annex Taiwan," *Voice of America*, August 10, 2022, https://www.voanews.com/a/china-reaffirms-threat-of-military-force-to-annex-taiwan-/6695555.html [https://perma.cc/LY7A-4H6N].

"China Says 2021 Fiscal Revenues Rise 10.7% y/y, Boosted by Economic Recovery," *Reuters*, January 25, 2022, https://www.reuters.com/markets/rates-bonds/china-says-2021-fiscal-revenues-rise-107-yryr-2022-01-25/ (accessed December 22, 2022).

"China to Enforce UN Sanctions Against North Korea," *The Guardian*, September 23, 2017, https://www.theguardian.com/world/2017/sep/23/china-to-enforce-un-sanctions-against-north-korea [https://perma.cc/6XX3-FQPQ].

"China will Stop Reporting Asymptomatic COVID Cases After Dropping Mass Testing Requirements," *PBS*, December 14, https://www.pbs.org/newshour/world/china-will-stop-reporting-asymptomatic-covid-cases-after-dropping-mass-testing-requirements [https://perma.cc/8CRF-YTBT].

"China-Taiwan Tensions: Xi Jinping Says 'Reunification' must be Fulfilled," *BBC News*, October 9, 2021, https://www.bbc.com/news/world-asia-china-58854081 (accessed December 22, 2022).

"China's Top Diplomat Renews Strong Objection to THAAD Deployment," *Korea Herald*, March 8, 2017, http://www.koreaherald.com/view.php?ud=20170308000730 [https://perma.cc/2TL2-EFZA].

Cho, Ah Ra, "The U.S. Role in Korea-Japan Normalization Talks: Focusing on the Claim Negotiations under the Kennedy Administration" (in Korean) (2014) 4 *Korean Journal of Japanese Studies* 270–307.

Cho, E. J. R. and Ki-young Shin, "South Korean Views on Japan's Constitutional Reform Under the Abe Government" (2018) 31(2) *Pacific Review* 256–266.

Cho, Kyung Hwan, "Feasibility of Regional Security Framework in Northeast Asia" (2020) 3(1) *Journal for Peace and Nuclear Disarmament* 129–143.

Choe, Sang-Hun, "Kim Jong-un Calls K-Pop a 'Vicious Cancer' in the New Culture War," *New York Times*, June 10, 2021, https://www.nytimes.com/2021/06/11/world/asia/kim-jong-un-k-pop.html [https://perma.cc/44GY-YDGX].

Choe, Sang-Hun, "North Korea Adopts New Law Hardening Its Nuclear Doctrine," *New York Times*, September 9, 2022, https://www.nytimes.com/2022/09/09/world/asia/north-korea-kim-weapons-law.html [https://perma.cc/FX4K-KNBY].

Choe, Sang-Hun and David E. Sanger, "Kim Jong-il, North Korean Dictator, Dies," *New York Times*, December 19, 2011, https://www.nytimes.com/2011/12/19/world/asia/kim-jong-il-is-dead.html [https://perma.cc/2RCH-PWJG].

Choe, Sang-Hun and Motoko Rich, "North Korea Fires 6 More Missiles Toward Japan, Including an ICBM," *New York Times*, November 2, 2022, https://www.nytimes.com/2022/11/02/world/asia/north-korea-missile-japan.html [https://perma.cc/GDF9-D25A].

Choi, Eunmi, "Where is NAPCI?: The Challenges and Limitations of the (Neo-) Functionalist Approach for Multilateral Cooperation in Northeast Asia" (in Korean) (2020) 26(3) *National Strategy* 181–208.

Choi, Jae-hee, "Ruling Party Mulls Universal Cash Relief Before Chuseok," *Korea Herald*, June 2, 2021, https://www.koreaherald.com/view.php?ud=20210602000792 [https://perma.cc/L2W4-HR4Z].

Choi, Jong Kun and Chung-in Moon, "Understanding Northeast Asian Regional Dynamics: Inventory Checking and New Discourses on Power, Interest, and Identity" (2010) 10 *International Relations of the Asia-Pacific* 343–372.

Choi, Jung Il, "A New Search on Cooperation Methods between Korea and Mongolia-based on the Political and Economic Consideration" (in Korean) (2018) 2(1) *Journal of Social Convergence Studies* 29–36.

Choi, Soo-Hyang, "South Korea's Ruling Party Cements Presidential Win with Local Vote Success," *Reuters*, June 1, 2022, https://www.reuters.com/world/asia-pacific/south-koreas-ruling-party-cements-presidential-win-with-local-vote-success-2022-06-02/ (accessed December 22, 2022).

Choi, Tae-Ho, "Trade," *Encyclopedia of Korean Culture* (1995), http://encykorea.aks.ac.kr/Contents/Item/E0019151 [https://perma.cc/9YZE-JBLV].

Christensen, Thomas J., "China, the U.S.-Japan Alliance, and the Security Dilemma in East Asia" (1999) 23(4) *International Security* 49–80.

Chu, Sinan, *Whither Chinese IR? The Sinocentric Subject and the Paradox of Tianxia-ism* (Cambridge University Press, 2020).

Chung, Jae Ho, "Korean Views of Korea-China Relations: Evolving Perceptions and Upcoming Challenges" (2012) 36(2) *Asian Perspective* 219–236.

Chwe, Michael, *Letter by Concerned Economists Regarding "Contracting for Sex in the Pacific War"* in the *International Review of Law and Economics*, http://chwe.net/irle/letter [https://perma.cc/FLQ2-YMEC].

Claxton, James, Luke Nottage, and Brett Williams, "Litigating, Arbitrating and Mediating Japan–Korea Trade and Investment Tensions" (2020) 54(4) *Journal of World Trade* 591–614.

Clemens, W. C., "North Korea's Quest for Nuclear Weapons" (2010) 10(1) *Journal of East Asian Studies* 127–154.

Cohen, Jerome B., *Japan's Postwar Economy* (Indiana University Press, 1958).

Cohen, Warren I., *America's Response to China: A History of Sino-American Relations* (6th ed., Columbia University Press, 2019).

Commander, U.S. 7th Fleet, *The United States Seventh Fleet*, https://www.c7f.navy.mil/About-Us/Facts-Sheet/ [https://perma.cc/6URB-ZDDY].

Congressional Research Service, *China Naval Modernization: Implications for U.S. Navy Capabilities—Background and Issues for Congress*, RL33153 (March 8, 2022), https://sgp.fas.org/crs/row/RL33153.pdf [https://perma.cc/X3PL-74ZA].

Congressional Research Service, *China's Military: The People's Liberation Army (PLA)* (June 4, 2021), https://crsreports.congress.gov/product/pdf/R/R46808 (assessed December 20, 2022).

Congressional-Executive Commission on China, *Judicial Independence in the RPC*, https://www.cecc.gov/judicial-independence-in-the-prc (assessed September 19, 2022).

Constitution of Japan, https://japan.kantei.go.jp/constitution_and_government_of_japan/constitution_e.html [https://perma.cc/R5ZY-9L4J].

Constitution of Mongolia, https://www.constituteproject.org/constitution/Mongolia_2001.pdf?lang=en [https://perma.cc/EBH8-3ANV].

Constitution of the People's Republic of China, http://www.npc.gov.cn/zgrdw/englishnpc/Constitution/node_2825.htm [https://perma.cc/M8NG-ZKXF].

Constitution of the Republic of Korea, https://www.law.go.kr/LSW/lsInfoP.do?lsiSeq=61603&viewCls=engLsInfoR&urlMode=engLsInfoR#0000 (accessed December 22, 2022).

Cooban, Anna and Uliana Pavlova, "Russia Threatens to Cut Supply of Gas Through Ukraine,"*CNN*, November 23, 2022, https://www.cnn.com/2022/11/23/energy/russia-gas-ukraine-moldova [https://perma.cc/H6PQ-VBQM].

Coomaraswamy, Radhika (Special Rapporteur on Violence against Women, Its Causes and Consequences), *Report on the Mission to the Democratic People's Republic of Korea, the Republic of Korea and Japan on the Issue of Military Sexual Slavery in Wartime*, U.N. Doc. E/CN.4/1996/53/Add.1 (January 4, 1996).

Cooney, Kevin J. and Alex Scarbrough, "Japan and South Korea: Can These Two Nations Work Together?" (2008) 35(3) *Asian Affairs* 173–192.

Cordesman, Anthony H., *The Korean Civil-Military Balance*, Center for Strategic and International Studies Report (May 24, 2018), https://www.csis.org/analysis/korean-civil-military-balance [https://perma.cc/969N-AJT8].

Corradini, Piero, "The Legitimization of the Qing Dynasty" (2002) 46(1) *Central Asiatic Journal* 112–127.

Cossa, Ralph A. and Brad Glosserman, "Washington 'Pivots' to Asia" (2022) 24(2) *Pacific Forum Comparative Connections* 1–20.

Cumings, Bruce, *The Origins of the Korean War* (Princeton University Press, 1981).

Cumings, Bruce, "Power and Plenty in Northeast Asia: The Evolution of U.S. Policy" (1987) 5(1) *World Policy Journal* 79–106.

"Current Status of Support for North Korea" (in Korean), *National Index* (July 11, 2022), https://web.archive.org/web/20221008235217/https://www.index.go.kr/potal/main/EachDtlPageDetail.do?idx_cd=2784 (accessed December 22, 2022).

Dapiran, Anthony, *City of Protest: A Recent History of Dissent in Hong Kong* (Penguin Books, 2017).

Dardess, John W., "From Mongol Empire to Yuan Dynasty: Changing Forms of Imperial Rule in Mongolia and Central Asia" 30 *Monumenta Serica* 117–165.

Das, Santosh, *Top 10 Consumer Electronics Companies in the World* (October 4, 2021), http://www.electronicsandyou.com/blog/top-10-consumer-electronics-companies-in-the-world.html [https://perma.cc/E53R-YFMW].

Denyer, Simon, "Japan Effectively Bans China's Huawei and ZTE from Government Contracts, Joining U.S.," *Washington Post*, December 10, 2018, https://www.washingtonpost.com/world/asia_pacific/japan-effectively-bans-chinas-huawei-zte-from-government-contracts-joining-us/2018/12/10/748fe98a-fc69-11e8-ba87-8c7facdf6739_story.html [https://perma.cc/WLF3-HDS2].

Devonshire-Ellis, Chris, *China's Relations with Russia in a New Age* (September 8, 2022), https://www.china-briefing.com/news/chinas-relations-with-russia-in-a-new-age [https://perma.cc/XC5G-Y45C].

Diaz, Daniella, "Top General Says He'd Push Back Against 'Illegal' Nuclear Strike Order," *CNN*, November 20, 2017, https://www.cnn.com/2017/11/18/politics/air-force-general-john-hyten-nuclear-strike-donald-trump [https://perma.cc/MS3F-S548].

Dierkes, James and Mendee Jargalsaikhan, "8 Reasons Why Mongolia's Capital Ulaanbaatar might be the Place for a Trump-Kim Summit," *The Diplomat*, March 10, 2018, https://thediplomat.com/2018/03/8-reasons-why-mongolias-capital-ulaanbaatar-might-be-the-place-for-a-trump-kim-summit/ [https://perma.cc/3RSS-P6N8].

Dierkes, Julian, "Mongolia is Keen to Distance Itself from Moscow and Beijing," *Foreign Policy*, October 27, 2022, https://foreignpolicy.com/2022/10/27/mongolia-independence-russia-china-relations-ukraine/ [https://perma.cc/N6UB-QBTB].

Dierkes, Julian, "Mass Protests in Mongolia Decry 'Coal Mafia,' Corruption," *The Diplomat*, December 6, 2022, https://thediplomat.com/2022/12/mass-protests-in -mongolia-decry-coal-mafia-corruption/ [https://perma.cc/A7Z5-5JPY].

Dikötter, Frank, *The Cultural Revolution: A People's History*, 1962–1976 (Bloomsbury Press, 2017).

Ding, Xiaoqin, "The Socialist Market Economy: China and the World" (2009) 73(2) *Science and Society* 235–241.

Dollar, David and Ryan Hass, *Getting the China Challenge Right* (January 25, 2021), https:// www.brookings.edu/research/getting-the-china-challenge-right/ [https://perma.cc /JGL2-NYTF].

Donnan, S., "Trump Trade Tsar Warns Against China 'Market Economy' Status," *Financial Times*, June 22, 2017, https://www.ft.com/content/4d6ba03e-56b0-11e7 -9fed-c19e2700005f (accessed December 22, 2022).

Donnan, S., L. Hornby, and A. Beesley, "China Challenges EU and US over Market Economy Status," *Financial Times*, December 13, 2016, https://www.ft.com/content /6af8da62-bf5d-11e6-9bca-2b93a6856354?mhq5j=e2 (accessed December 22, 2022).

Dotto, Carlotta, Brad Lendon, and Jessie Yeung, "North Korea's Record Year of Missile Testing is Putting the World on Edge," *CNN*, December 26, 2022, https://www .cnn.com/2022/12/26/asia/north-korea-missile-testing-year-end-intl-hnk/index .html#:~:text=In%202022%2C%20the%20isolated%20nation,nuclear%20test %20on%20the%20horizon [https://perma.cc/J9Q2-WV32].

DuBois, Megan, Ankit Panda, and Toby Dalton (eds.), *Enhancing the Northeast Asia Regional Security Eco-System: Issues and Approaches* (Carnegie Endowment for International Peace, 2022).

Dudden, Alexis (ed.), "Supplement to Special Issue: Academic Integrity at Stake: The Ramseyer Article - Four Letters (Table of Contents)" (2021) 19(5) *Asian-Pacific Journal* 1–2.

Easley, Leif-Eric, "Defense Ownership or Nationalist Security: Autonomy and Reputation in South Korean and Japanese Security Policies" (2007) 27(2) *The SAIS Review of International Affairs* 153–166.

Envall, H. D. P., "Japan: From Passive Partner to Active Ally," *in* Michel Wesley (ed.), *Global Allies* (Australian National University Press, 2017).

Erickson, Andrew S., "U.S. China Military-to-Military Relations Policy Considerations in a Changing Environment" (2019) 14(3) *Asia Policy* 123–144.

Eschborn, Norbert, "North Korean Refugees in South Korea" (2014) 292 *ISPSW Strategy Series* 1–17, https://www.files.ethz.ch/isn/184307/292_Eschborn_Apel%20(2).pdf [https://perma.cc/JY9K-XMXP].

"Ethnic Mongolians in China Protest Removal of Traditional Language in Schools," *Reuters*, September 2, 2020, https://www.reuters.com/article/us-china-education -mongolian-protests/ethnic-mongolians-in-china-protest-removal-of-traditional -language-in-schools-idUSKBN25T0YP [https://perma.cc/CA33-SCS4].

Ewing, Thomas E., "Revolution of the Chinese Frontier: Outer Mongolia in 1911" (1978) 12(2) *Journal of Asian History* 101–119.

Fairbank, John King (ed.), *The Chinese World Order* (Harvard University Press, 1968).

Falconer, Rebecca, "U.S. and South Korean Militaries Launch Biggest-Ever Air Drills," *Axios*, October 31. 2022, https://www.axios.com/2022/10/31/us-south-korea-largest -warplane-air-drills# [https://perma.cc/WD5C-E8BX].

Farnsworth, Lee, W., "Japan 1972: New Faces and New Friends" (1972) 13(1) *Asian Survey* 113–125.

Feffer, John, "An Arms Race in Northeast Asia?" (2009) 33(4) *Asian Perspective* 5–15.

Fenby, Jonathan, *Modern China: The Fall and Rise of a Great Power, 1850 to the Present* (HarperCollins, 2008).

Feng, Li, "'Feudalism' and Western Zhou China: A Criticism" (2003) 63(1) *Harvard Journal of Asiatic Studies* 115–144.

Fiaschetti, Francesca, "Diplomacy in the Age of Mongol Globalization: An Introduction" (2019) 17 *European Studies* 175–181.

Fischer, Hanah, *North Korean Provocative Actions, 1950 – 2007*, CRS Report for Congress (April 20, 2007), https://sgp.fas.org/crs/row/RL30004.pdf [https://perma.cc/WR8Z-PJTQ].

Fish, M. Steven, "Mongolia: Democracy Without Prerequisites" (1998) 9(3) *Journal of Democracy* 127–141.

"Forced Laborers Seeking Justice 70 Years On," *Korea Herald*, August 9, 2013, http://www.koreaherald.com/view.php?ud=20130809000689 [https://perma.cc/V3XM-2WQM].

Frank, Rüdiger, "Economic Sanctions against North Korea" (2018) 13(3) *Asia Policy* 5–12.

Freifeld, Karen, "U.S. Official Says Export Curbs on Russia Hit Car Production and Tank Building," *Reuters*, March 30, 2022, https://www.reuters.com/business/us-official-says-export-curbs-russia-hit-car-production-tank-building-2022-03-30/ (accessed December 22, 2022).

Frohman, Ben, Emma Rafaelof, and Alexis Dale-Huang, *The China-North Korea Strategic Rift: Background and Implications for the United States* (January 24, 2022), https://www.uscc.gov/sites/default/files/2022-01/China-North_Korea_Strategic_Rift.pdf [https://perma.cc/45FZ-EYCM].

Fuertes, Elena Gordiollo, "Toxic Winter: The 'Slow Violence' of Air Pollution in Mongolia," *The Diplomat*, December 8, 2022, https://thediplomat.com/2022/12/toxic-winter-the-slow-violence-of-air-pollution-in-mongolia/ [https://perma.cc/7ET6-AYCF].

Fukada, Masahiko, "How Socialism and the Left Wing Failed in Japan," *Japan Times*, December 30, 2019, https://www.japantimes.co.jp/news/2019/12/30/national/politics-diplomacy/socialism-japan/ [https://perma.cc/PTL8-NHQH].

Gaddis, John Lewis, *The Cold War: A New History* (Penguin Books, 2006).

Gan, Nectar, "'Stop Asking Why': Shanghai Intensifies Covid Lockdown Despite Falling Cases," *CNN*, May 9, 2022, https://www.cnn.com/2022/05/09/china/china-covid-shanghai-restrictions-escalate-intl-hnk/index.html [https://perma.cc/AQJ6-QXAS].

Gan, Nectar, "Putin Concedes China has 'Questions and Concerns' over Russia's Faltering Invasion of Ukraine," *CNN*, September 16, 2022, https://www.cnn.com/2022/09/15/asia/xi-putin-meeting-main-bar-intl-hnk (accessed December 22, 2022).

Gang, Fan and Nicholas Hope, *The Role of State-Owned Enterprises in the Chinese Economy*, https://www.chinausfocus.com/2022/wp-content/uploads/Part+02-Chapter+16.pdf (accessed December 22, 2022).

Garamone, Jim, *Russia Continues Attacks on Ukraine Civilian Targets* (October 31, 2022), https://www.defense.gov/News/News-Stories/Article/Article/3205450/russia-continues-attacks-on-ukraine-civilian-targets/ [https://perma.cc/N6XJ-N6K6].

Garcia, Manuel Perez, "From Eurocentrism to Sinocentrism: The New Challenges in Global History" (2014) 119(3) *European Journal of Scientific Research* 337–352.

García-Herrero, Alicia, *Japan must Boost R&D to Keep Rising Chinese Rivals at Bay* (September 20, 2018), https://www.bruegel.org/comment/japan-must-boost-rd-keep-rising-chinese-rivals-bay [https://perma.cc/CHR6-2GWE].

Gargeyas, Arjun, "The Chip 4 Alliance Might Work on Paper, But Problems Will Persist," *The Diplomat*, August 25, 2022, https://thediplomat.com/2022/08/the-chip4-alliance-might-work-on-paper-but-problems-will-persist/ [https://perma.cc/44FA-27WA].

"GDP, 1000 to 2018," *Our World in Data* (2020), https://ourworldindata.org/grapher/gdp-world-regions-stacked-area?country=CHN~OWID_WRL [https://perma.cc/T2X3-3H2J].

Gehrke, Joel, "Chinese Military to 'Prepare for War' as Xi Jinping Menaces Taiwan," *Washington Examiner*, October 19, 2022, https://www.washingtonexaminer.com/policy/defense-national-security/china-military-prepare-war-xi-jinping-menaces-taiwan [https://perma.cc/DKW3-KWPQ].

Gellner, Ernest, *Nations and Nationalism* (Cornell University Press, 1983).

Gerson, Michael S., *The Sino-Soviet Border Conflict (November 2010)*, https://www.cna.org/archive/CNA_Files/pdf/d0022974.a2.pdf [https://perma.cc/3GQ2-X6RZ].

Gerstel, Dylan and Matthew P. Goodman, *From Industrial Policy to Innovation Strategy: Lessons from Japan, Europe, and the United States* (Center for Strategic and International Studies, 2020).

Gewirtz, Julian, *Chinese Reformers, Western Economists, and the Making of Global China* (Harvard University Press, 2017).

Gibbon, Peter and Jakob Vestergaard, *US Trade Policy under Trump: Assessing the Unilateralist Turn* (Danish Institute for International Studies, 2017).

Gill, Rob, "Balancing Mongolia's Growth and Sovereignty: Up, Down, or Out?" (2017) 14 *New Perspectives in Foreign Policy* 28–33.

Gilpin, Robert, *War and Change in World Politics* (Cambridge University Press, 1981).

Gladstone, Rick, "U.N. Security Council Imposes Punishing New Sanctions on North Korea," *New York Times*, August 5, 2017, https://www.nytimes.com/2017/08/05/world/asia/north-korea-sanctions-united-nations.html [https://perma.cc/4EBQ-F98E].

Glant, David M., *August Storm: The Soviet 1945 Strategic Offensive in Manchuria*, Leavenworth Papers, no. 7 (February 1983).

"Global 500 1995," *Fortune*, https://fortune.com/ranking/global500/1995/ (accessed December 30, 2022).

Global Edge, *South Korea: Trade Statistics*, https://globaledge.msu.edu/countries/south-korea/tradestats [https://perma.cc/Z9U5-7ZNW].

Global Firepower, *2022 Mongolia Military Strength* (May 2, 2022), https://www.globalfirepower.com/country-military-strength-detail.php?country_id=mongolia#:~:text=For%202022%2C%20Mongolia%20is%20ranked,for%20the%20annual%20GFP%20review [https://perma.cc/MQC3-BZVM].

Global Firepower, *2022 Military Strength Ranking*, https://www.globalfirepower.com/countries-listing.php [https://perma.cc/B78N-DN23].

Gordon, David M., "Historiographical Essay: The China-Japan War, 1931-1945" (2006) 70(1) *Journal of Military History* 137–182.

Graceffo, Antonio, "China's Crackdown on Mongolian Culture," *The Diplomat*, September 4, 2020, https://thediplomat.com/2020/09/chinas-crackdown-on-mongolian-culture/ [https://perma.cc/YZ6W-WPR7].

Graceffo, Antonio, "Mongolia suffers under China's zero Covid policy," *The Interpreter*, January 19, 2022, https://www.lowyinstitute.org/the-interpreter/mongolia-suffers -under-china-s-zero-covid-policy [https://perma.cc/5RNT-5HCW].

Graham, Thomas E., *Russia's Decline and Uncertain Recovery* (Carnegie Endowment for International Peace, 2002), https://carnegieendowment.org/pdf/files/Decline.pdf [https://perma.cc/FK8F-DLJG].

Gregor, A. James and Maria Hsia Chang, "Anti-Confucianism: Mao's Last Campaign" (1979) 19(11) *Asian Survey* 1073–1092.

Grieco, Kelly A., "Assessing the Singapore Summit—Two Years Later" (2020) 14(3) *Strategic Studies Quarterly* 12–21.

Gries, Peter and Tao Wang, "Taiwan's Perilous Futures: Chinese Nationalism, the 2020 Presidential Elections, and U.S.-China Tensions Spell Trouble for Cross-strait Relations" (2020) 183(1) *World Affairs* 40–61.

Guex, Samuel, "Legality or Legitimacy: Revisiting Debates on the Korea-Japan Annexation Treaties," *in* Marie Seong-Hak Kim (ed.), *The Spirit of Korean Law* (Brill, 2016).

Guluzade, Amir, "How Reform has made China's State-Owned Enterprises Stronger," *World Economic Forum* (May 21, 2020), https://www.weforum.org/agenda/2020/05/ how-reform-has-made-chinas-state-owned-enterprises-stronger/ [https://perma.cc/ KGK8-YDW3].

Gunderson, Gerald, "The Origin of the American Civil War" (1974) 34(4) *Journal of Economic History* 915–950.

Guriyev, Sergey, "20 Years of Vladimir Putin: The Transformation of the Economy," *The Moscow Times*, August 16, 2019, https://www.themoscowtimes.com/2019/08/16 /20-years-of-vladimir-putin-the-transformation-of-the-economy-a66854 [https:// perma.cc/5W76-RJ2B].

Ha, Eunyoung and Christopher Hwang, "The U.S.-North Korea Geneva Agreed Framework: Strategic Choices and Credible Commitments" (2015) 11(1) *North Korea Review* 7–23.

Ha, Yong-Chool and Beom-Shik Shin, "The Impact of the Ukraine War on Russian– North Korean Relations" (2022) 62(5) *Asian Survey* 1–27.

Haenle, Paul and Lucas Tcheyan, *How the World is Responding to a Changing China* (June 10, 2020), https://carnegieendowment.org/2020/06/10/how-world-is-responding-to -changing-china-pub-82039 [https://perma.cc/WT7B-LLUD].

Haggard, Stephen, "The Balance of Power, Globalization, and Democracy: International Relations Theory in Northeast Asia" (2004) 4(1) *Journal of East Asian Studies* 1–38.

Han, Bae-ho and Young Ick Lew, "Korea under Japanese Rule," *Encyclopaedia Britannica*, https://www.britannica.com/place/Korea/Korea-under-Japanese-rule (accessed December 22, 2022).

"Han Chinese," *New World Encyclopedia* (2022), https://www.newworldencyclopedia.org/ entry/Han_Chinese [https://perma.cc/RD7V-93SB].

Han, Sang-Mi, *"North Korea Kim Il Sung Prepared for the Second Invasion of South Korea in 1965...Requested Reinforcement to China"* (in Korean), Voice of America, October 24, 2013, https://www.voakorea.com/a/1775964.html [https://perma.cc/24S8-DE8F].

Han, Sangjin and Younghee Shim, "The Two Driving Forces of Populism and Democracy in South Korea: A Conceptual, Historical, and Empirical Analysis" (2021) 50(2) *Journal of Asian Sociology* 371–400.

Han, Sung-Joo, "South Korea in 1987: The Politics of Democratization" (1988) 28(1) *A Survey of Asia in 1987*: Part 1, 52–61.

Hancocks, Paula, "South Korea Reveals It has a Plan to Assassinate Kim Jong Un," *CNN*, September 23, 2016, https://www.cnn.com/2016/09/23/asia/south-korea -plan-to-assassinate-kim-jong-un/index.html [https://perma.cc/6TC7-CRTH].

Hara, Kimie, "50 Years from San Francisco: Re-Examining the Peace Treaty and Japan's Territorial Disputes" (2001) 74(3) *Pacific Affairs* 361–382.

Hare, Christopher and Keith T. Poole, "The Polarization of Contemporary American Politics" (2014) 46(3) *Polity* 411–429.

Haring, Douglas Gilbert, "Japanese Character in the Twentieth Century" (1967) 370 *The Annals of the American Academy of Political and Social Science* 133–142.

Harrison, David, "How High Is Inflation and What Causes It? What to Know," *Wall Street Journal*, September 13, 2022, https://www.wsj.com/articles/inflation-definition -cause-what-is-it-11644353564 [https://perma.cc/TH3B-DJAW].

Hart-Landsberg, Martin, *The Rush to Development: Economic Change and Political Struggle in Korea* (Monthly Review Press, 1993).

Hastings, Max, *The Korean War* (Simon and Schuster, 1987).

He, Laura, "China's Economy is 'in Deep Trouble' as Xi Heads for Next Decade in Power," *CNN Business*, October 15, 2022, https://www.cnn.com/2022/10/14/ economy/china-party-congress-economy-trouble-xi-intl-hnk/index.html [https:// perma.cc/9ZCB-KTHK].

Helgesen, Geir, "Political Revolution in a Cultural Continuum: Preliminary Observations on the North Korean 'Juche' Ideology with Its Intrinsic Cult of Personality" (1991) 15(1) *Asian Perspective* 187–213.

Hellman, Gregory, "U.S. Prepared to Launch Preemptive Strike on North Korea," *Politico*, April 14, 2017, https://www.politico.com/tipsheets/morning-defense/2017 /04/officials-warn-us-could-launch-preemptive-strike-on-north-korea-219774 [https://perma.cc/3WV6-PU2Z].

Henning, C. Randall and I. M. Destler, "From Neglect to Activism: American Politics and the 1985 Plaza Accord" (1988) 8(3) *Journal of Public Policy* 317–333.

Herman, Steve, "White House Ordered to Return Press Pass to CNN Reporter," *Voice of America*, November 17, 2018, https://www.voanews.com/a/white-house-ordered-to -return-press-pass-to-cnn-reporter/4661693.html [https://perma.cc/6GGJ-ETY9].

Hernandez, Valerie, "Have the Huawei Bans Achieved the US' Intended Goals?" *International Banker*, September 7, 2022, https://internationalbanker.com/technology /have-the-huawei-bans-achieved-the-us-intended-goals/ [https://perma.cc/VND3 -9SX3].

Hess, Amanda, "How Fan Culture is Swallowing Democracy," *New York Times*, September 11, 2019, https://www.nytimes.com/interactive/2019/09/11/arts/how-fan-culture-is -swallowing-democracy.html [https://perma.cc/MK5L-KR6M].

Hicks, George, *The Comfort Women: Japan's Brutal Regime of Enforced Prostitution in the Second World War* (W. W. Norton & Company, 1997).

Hoekman, Bernard, and Petros C. Mavroidis, "Burning Down the House?: The Appellate Body at the Center of the WTO Crisis," *in* Bernard Hoekman and Ernesto Zedillo (eds.), *Trade in the 21st Century: Back to the Past?* (Brookings Institution, 2021).

Holland, Steve, "US Says Russia's Wagner Group Bought North Korean Weapons for Ukraine War," *Reuters*, December 22, 2022, https://www.reuters.com/world/us

-says-russias-wagner-group-bought-north-korean-weapons-ukraine-war-2022-12-22/ [https://perma.cc/N33M-KK5P].

Holodny, Elena, "The Rise, Fall, and Comeback of the Chinese Economy Over the Past 800 Years," *Business Insider,* January 8, 2017, https://www.businessinsider.com/history-of-chinese-economy-1200-2017-2017-1 [https://perma.cc/S2VN-8CLV].

Homes, James R., "Japan's Cold War Navy," *The Diplomat,* October 12, 2012, https://thediplomat.com/2012/10/japans-cold-war-navy/ [https://perma.cc/93SE-B25N].

Hong, Je-Seong, "Korea-Mongolia Cooperation" (in Korean), *Yonhap News,* July 10, 2016, https://www.yna.co.kr/view/AKR20160709031400083 [https://perma.cc/77CA-JZNU].

Hong, Joon Seok, "The Economic Costs of Korean Reunification," *Spice Digest,* Fall 2011, https://fsi9-prod.s3.us-west-1.amazonaws.com/s3fs-public/Korean_Reunification.pdf [https://perma.cc/YDA3-TL3J].

Hoshi, Takeo and Anil K. Kashyap, "Japan's Financial Crisis and Economic Stagnation" (2004) 18(1) *Journal of Economic Perspectives* 3–26.

"How many Foreign Companies in China?" *RegistrationChina* (November 2, 2021), https://www.registrationchina.com/articles/how-many-foreign-companies-in-china/ [https://perma.cc/R683-EKK6].

Howard, Esme, "British Policy and the Balance of Power" (1925) 19(2) *American Political Science Review* 261–267.

Howell, Edward, "The juche H-bomb? North Korea, Nuclear Weapons and Regime-State Survival" (2020) 96(4) *International Affairs* 1051–1068.

"Hu Jintao Escorted Out of Party Congress," *Reuters,* October 22, 2022, https://www.reuters.com/world/china/former-chinese-president-hu-jintao-escorted-out-party-congress-2022-10-22/ [https://perma.cc/YQ2B-LX5T].

Huang, Kuancheng *et al.,* "East Asian Firms Are Critical to America's Semiconductor Success," *The Diplomat,* May 4, 2022, https://thediplomat.com/2022/05/east-asian-firms-are-critical-to-americas-semiconductor-success/ [https://perma.cc/PUH6-RB44].

Huang, Shu-Mei and Hyun-Kyung Lee, "Difficult Heritage Diplomacy? Re-Articulating Places of Pain and Shame as World Heritage in northeast Asia" (2019) 25(2) *International Journal of Heritage Studies* 143–159.

Hundt, David and Roland Bleiker, "Reconciling Colonial Memories in Korea and Japan" (2007) 31(1) *Asian Perspective* 61–91.

Hurley, John, Scott Morris, and Gailyn Portelance, "China's Belt and Road Initiative may Bankrupt 8 Nations While Financing Infrastructure," *The Print,* March 6, 2018, https://theprint.in/opinion/chinas-belt-and-road-initiative-bankrupt-nations-financing-infrastructure/39561/ [https://perma.cc/EK7X-3Q3A].

Hwang, In-Chan, "Xi Jinping Says Korea was a Part of China," *Dong-A Ilbo,* April 20, 2017, https://www.donga.com/en/article/all/20170420/902176/1 [https://perma.cc/R38F-DZFG].

Hwang, Jae Ha, "Japan's Export Restraints – Could Have Been Implemented to Keep Korea's Semiconductor Industry in Check" (in Korean), *Yonhap News,* July 12, 2019, https://www.yna.co.kr/view/AKR20190712026700008 [https://perma.cc/9UGP-R5CS].

Hymans, Jacques E. C., "Assessing North Korean Intentions and Capacities: A New Approach" (2008) 8 *Journal of East Asian Studies* 259–292.

Ikenberry, G. John, "American Hegemony and East Asian Order" (2004) 58(3) *American Journal of International Affairs* 353–367.

Im, Byung Do, "Japanese Patrol Boats Appear 440 Times Near Dokdo Islands for the Last Five Years" (in Korean), *IMPeterNews*, October 5, 2021, http://www.impeternews .com/news/articleView.html?idxno=60398 [https://perma.cc/JUZ6-PV2L].

Im, Hyug Baeg, "The US Role in Korean Democracy and Security Since Cold War Era" (2006) 6(2) *International Relations of Asia-Pacific* 157–187.

"In 1991, South and North Korea Join the U.N. Simultaneously" (in Korean), *KBC World*, April 26, 2018, http://world.kbs.co.kr/service/contents_view.htm?lang=k&board _seq=275292 (accessed December 22, 2022).

"In Rare Display of Dissent, Lawmakers In Russia's Far East Urge Putin To Stop Ukraine War," *RadioFreeEurope/RadioLiberty*, March 27, 2022, https://www.rferl.org/a/russia -primorye-parliament-war-dissent/31871358.html [https://perma.cc/8Z4D-CJEF].

"In the Midst of Provocations from North Korea, Kishida Emphasizes on His Desire to Amend Constitution During His Tenure" (in Korean), *Newsis*, October 6, 2022, https://mobile.newsis.com/view.html?ar_id=NISX20221006_0002039740 [https:// perma.cc/6J85-RHPD].

"In Tokyo, Biden Set to Launch New Indo-Pacific Trade Pact to Replace TPP," *Associated Press*, May 22, 2022, https://www.marketwatch.com/story/bidens-indo-pacific-trade -pact-wont-include-taiwan-at-launch-01653261066 [https://perma.cc/BV43-7549].

Interesse, Giulia,*China-Mongolia: Bilateral Trade, Investment, and Future Prospects* (December 2, 2022), https://www.china-briefing.com/news/china-mongolia-bilateral-trade -investment-and-future-prospects/ [https://perma.cc/L96M-QUJG].

International Energy Agency, *Energy Fact Sheet: Why does Russian Oil and Gas Matter?* (March 21, 2022), https://www.iea.org/articles/energy-fact-sheet-why-does-russian -oil-and-gas-matter [https://perma.cc/H64C-3GY4].

International Trade Administration, *U.S. Trade in 2021: U.S. Exporters on Road to Recovery* (February 11, 2022), https://blog.trade.gov/2022/02/11/u-s-trade-in-2021-u-s -exporters-on-road-to-recovery/#:~:text=The%20top%20four%20U.S.%20goods ,followed%20by%20China%20and%20Japan [https://perma.cc/3F52-735G].

International Trade Administration, *South Korea - Country Commercial Guide*, https://www .trade.gov/country-commercial-guides/south-korea-market-overview [https://perma .cc/RZ39-MXQF].

Iokibe, Makoto, *The Occupation of Japan* (Congressional Information Service, 1987).

Issawi, Charles, "The 1973 Oil Crisis and After" (1978) 1(2) *Journal of Post Keynesian Economics* 3–26.

Jackson, Brianna, "Confucianism and Korean Dramas: How Cultural and Social Proximity, Hybridization of Modernity and Tradition, and Dissimilar Confucian Trajectories Affect Importation Rates of Korean Broadcasting Programs between Japan and China," *Virginia Commonwealth University Scholars Compass* (2017), https:// scholarscompass.vcu.edu/cgi/viewcontent.cgi?article=1041&context=auctus (accessed December 22, 2022).

James, David H., *The Rise and Fall of the Japanese Empire* (Routledge, 2011).

Jansen, Marius B. and Fed G. Notehelfer, "Japan: World War II and Defeat," *Encyclopaedia Britannica* (last updated January 27, 2022), https://www.britannica.com/place/Japan /World-War-II-and-defeat#ref23207 [https://perma.cc/QNX2-S4R6].

"Japan Protests Russia-China Military Drills, Moscow Scraps Kuril Islands Visa Deal," *South China Morning Post*, September 6, 2022, https://www.scmp.com/news/asia/east

-asia/article/3191470/japan-protests-russia-china-military-drills-moscow-scraps-visa [https://perma.cc/9S3K-W66H].

"Japan Still Divided on Revising War-Renouncing Constitution: Survey," *Kyodo News*, May 2, 2022, https://english.kyodonews.net/news/2022/05/a8faf66fd209-japan-still -divided-on-revising-war-renouncing-constitution-survey.html?phrase=nhk&words= [https://perma.cc/783G-2CPP].

"Japan 'To Exercise Counterattack Capability to North Korea, No South Korean Permission Needed'" (in Korean), *Yonhap News*, December 17, 2022, https://www.yna .co.kr/view/AKR20221217031400704 [https://perma.cc/3RNX-TU5P].

"Japan's PM Denies 'Comfort Women' Coerced," *NBC News*, March 1, 2007, https:// www.nbcnews.com/id/wbna10625961 [https://perma.cc/W95U-9CYA].

Jeon, Hong Taek, "Economic Growth of North Korea: 1945– 1995" (in Korean) (1995) 1 *Journal of Economic Development* 77–105.

Jeon, Joon-Beom, "Commodity Imports Over $30 Billion per Month for the First Time" (in Korean), *Chosun Biz*, March 10, 2022.

Jeong, Nam-Gu, "America Supports Constitutional Amendment Citing 'Japan's Constitutional Amendment is Japan's business'" (in Korean), *Hankyoreh*, May 3, 2013, https://www.hani.co.kr/arti/international/international_general/585883.html [https://perma.cc/QA87-U4VT].

Jeong, Yong-Hwan and Eun-Jee Park, "18 Percent of North Koreans Now Thought to Own Mobile Phones," *JoongAng Daily*, August 11, 2020, https://koreajoongangdaily.joins .com/2020/08/11/business/tech/North-Korea-smartphone/20200811180400430 .html [https://perma.cc/6H7N-9P8U].

Jervis, Robert, "The Impact of the Korean War on the Cold War" (1980) 24(4) *Journal of Conflict Resolution* 563–592.

Jervis, Robert, "Cooperation under the Security Dilemma" (1987) 30(2) *World Politics* 167–214.

Jin, Fang, *The Belt and Road Initiative: Progress, Problems and Prospects* (2017), https://www .csis.org/belt-and-road-initiative-progress-problems-and-prospects [https://perma.cc /YHG5-24H7].

Jo, He-rim, "US Support for Japan's Military Ambitions may Spell Concerns for Korea," *Korea Herald*, May 24, 2022, https://www.koreaherald.com/view.php?ud =20220524000833 [https://perma.cc/6M2X-7FHB].

Johnston, Eric, "How Russia Quietly Built up Its Military Presence in Asia," *Japan Times*, March 9, 2022, https://www.japantimes.co.jp/news/2022/03/09/national/russia -asia-presence-ukraine-invasion/ [https://perma.cc/G5V4-DGYG].

Johnson, Jesse, "Trump's Push for South Korea to Pay More for U.S. Troops Puts Japan on Notice," *Japan Times*, August 8, 2019, https://www.japantimes.co.jp/news/2019 /08/08/asia-pacific/trumps-push-south-korea-pay-u-s-troops-puts-japan-notice/ [https://perma.cc/EM88-3BAS].

Joint Declaration on the Question of Hong Kong (December 19, 1984), https://treaties .un.org/doc/Publication/UNTS/Volume%201399/v1399.pdf [https://perma.cc/ T8WC-UZ5A].

Jones, Randall S. and Jae Wan Lee, *Enhancing Dynamism in SMEs and Entrepreneurship in Korea*, OECD Economic Development Working Papers, no. 1510, ECO/WKP(2018)58 (October 5, 2018).

Jones, Sara Su, "Embarked on a New Path: US Assistance to Russia After the Cold War" (1994) 17(1) *Harvard International Review* 56–57, 87–88.

Jukes, Geoffrey, *The Russo-Japanese War 1904–1905* (Osprey Publishing, 2002).

Jung, Da-min, "Lee Jun-seok's Victory Ushers Korean Politics into New Era," *Korea Times*, June 14, 2021, https://www.koreatimes.co.kr/www/nation/2021/06/356 _310361.html [https://perma.cc/KFC5-JBMC].

Jung, Da-min, "Young Leader's Nomination Exam Plan Raises Question," *Korea Times*, June 16, 2021, https://www.koreatimes.co.kr/www/nation/2021/06/356_310594 .html [https://perma.cc/F2A8-45WV].

Kallander, George (trans.), *The Diary of 1636: The Second Manchu Invasion of Korea* (Columbia University Press, 2020).

Kalra, Prajakti, *The Silk Road and the Political Economy of the Mongol Empire* (Routledge, 2018).

Kang, Hyeok Hweon, "Big Heads and Buddhist Demons: The Korean Musketry Revolution and the Northern Expeditions of 1654 and 1658" (2014) 2(2) *Journal of Chinese Military History* 127–189.

Kang, Jin Woong, "Political Use of Confucianism in North Korea" (2011) 16(1) *Journal of Korean Studies* 63–87.

Kanno-Youngs, Zolan and Peter Baker, "Biden Pledges to Defend Taiwan if It Faces a Chinese Attack," *New York Times*, May 23, 2022, https://www.nytimes.com/2022/05 /23/world/asia/biden-taiwan-china.html [https://perma.cc/FM2H-2STW].

Katz, Richard, "Voodoo Abenomics: Japan's Failed Comeback Plan" (2014) 93(4) *Foreign Affairs* 133–141.

Kawagoe, Toshihiko, *Agricultural Land Reform in Postwar Japan: Experiences and Issues*, World Bank Policy Research Working Papers (June 25, 2013).

Keane, Sean, "Huawei Ban Timeline: Detained CFO Makes Deal with US Justice Department," *CNET* (September 30, 2021), https://www.cnet.com/news/privacy/ huawei-ban-timeline-detained-cfo-makes-deal-with-us-justice-department/ [https:// perma.cc/82C5-CNTV].

Kendall-Taylor, Andrea and Michael Kofman, "Russia's Dangerous Decline: The Kremlin Won't Go Down Without a Fight" (2022) 101(6) *Foreign Affairs* 22–35.

Khan, Hider A., *Global Markets and Financial Crises in Asia* (New York: Palgrave Macmillan, 2004).

Kim, Bo Kwang, "Diplomatic Issue between Goryeo-Song Relation in the Early 12th Century" (in Korean) (2016) 60 *Dongguk Journal of History* 43–84.

Kim, Choong-Nam, "Changing Northeast Asia and Korea-US Relations" (2000) 14(1) *Journal of East Asian Affairs* 1–36.

Kim, Eun-Joon, "China's Wang Yi Calls the United States a Rule Breaker Citing IRA to Park Jin," *Chosun Ilbo*, December 13, 2022, https://www.chosun.com/politics /diplomacy-defense/2022/12/12/KR5O2NUZNBAKVPFY7672MSLDOA/ [https://perma.cc/8UBE-KUX2].

Kim, Hakjoon, "The American Military Government in South Korea, 1945–1948: Its Formation, Policies, and Legacies" (1988) 12(1) *Asian Perspective* 51–83.

Kim, Heajin, "Northeast Asia, Trust and the NAPCI," *The Diplomat*, December 18, 2015, https://thediplomat.com/2015/12/northeast-asia-trust-and-the-napci/ [https:// perma.cc/2824-9PSH].

Kim, Hyun-Wook and Won K. Paik, "Alliance Cohesion in the Post-Cold War US– South Korea Security Relations" (2009) 23(2) *Journal of Asian Affairs* 1–40.

Kim, Hyung-Jin, "Kim Threatens to Use Nukes Amid Tensions with US, S. Korea," *AP News*, July 28, 2022, https://apnews.com/article/covid-health-seoul-south-korea

-nuclear-weapons-e285be60ef404092fe3324748fa60707 [https://perma.cc/9XJ5 -GHF6].

"Kim Il-Sung," *Encyclopaedia Britannica* (July 4, 2022), https://www.britannica.com/ biography/Kim-Il-Sung [https://perma.cc/9E75-HRZJ].

Kim, Ji Young, "Escaping the Vicious Cycle: Symbolic Politics and History Disputes Between South Korea and Japan" (2014) 38(1) *Asian Perspective* 31–60.

Kim, Jina, *China and Regional Security Dynamics on the Korean Peninsula* (March 18, 2020), https://carnegieendowment.org/2020/03/18/china-and-regional-security-dynamics -on-korean-peninsula-pub-81235 [https://perma.cc/F7J3-4UEF].

Kim, Jong-dae, "Korea shouldn't be Welcoming Japan's Pursuit of Counterstrike Capabilities," *Hankyoreh*, December 9, 2022, https://english.hani.co.kr/arti/english _edition/english_editorials/1070978.html [https://perma.cc/S4P5-SMMS].

Kim, Min-hyung, "Why Nuclear? Explaining North Korea's Strategic Choice of Going Nuclear and Its Implications for East Asian Security" (2021) 56(7) *Journal of Asian and African Studies* 1488–1502.

Kim, Myeong-Seong, "North Korea Advertised the Launch of 150 Planes...But Old Planes Crashed" (in Korean), *Chosun Ilbo*, October 15, 2022, https://www.chosun .com/politics/north_korea/2022/10/15/NJEVJVV6WFF37AU7YHMM6VEIA4/ [https://perma.cc/5J42-EBPC].

Kim, Sam, "South Korea Posts Longest Run of Trade Deficits Since 1997," *Bloomberg*, September 30, 2022, https://www.bloomberg.com/news/articles/2022-10-01/south -korea-posts-longest-string-of-trade-deficits-since-1997?leadSource=uverify%20wall [https://perma.cc/FH9W-P3CV].

Kim, Sang-Cheol, "Hallow Debate on Pro-China v. Pro-Japan" (in Korean), *Aju Kyeongje*, August 23, 2020, https://www.ajunews.com/view/20200823130640749 [https:// perma.cc/K539-CPU6].

Kim, Sarah, "PPP's Rule Change to Elect Next Leader Causes Divide within Party," *Korea JoongAng Daily*, December 20, 2022, https://koreajoongangdaily.joins.com/2022/12 /20/national/politics/Korea-People-Power-Party-chairman/20221220161103412 .html [https://perma.cc/L2QT-DKQM].

Kim, Suk Hi and Mario Martin-Hermosillo, "The Effectiveness of Economic Sanctions Against a Nuclear North Korea" (2013) 9(2) *North Korea Review* 99–110.

Kim, Sung Man, "Analysis on Kim Jung Un's 2015 Grand War for Reunification" (in Korean), *NK Chosun*, September 15, 2014.

Kim, Sunhyuk and Jong-Ho Jeong, "Historical Development of Civil Society in Korea since 1987" (2017) 24(2) *Journal of International and Area Studies* 1–14.

Kim, Tong-Hyung, "S Korean Business Owners Call for Boycott of Japanese Goods," *Japan Today*, July 15, 2019, https://japantoday.com/category/politics/s.-korean-business -owners-call-for-boycott-of-japanese-goods [https://perma.cc/JRK9-67XK].

Kim, Youn-Suk, "Prospects of Japanese-U.S. Trade and Industrial Competition" (1990) 30(5) *Asian Survey* 493–504.

Kim, Young-Hwan, "Confucianism as Sinocentrism" (in Korean) (2011) 40 *Journal of Philosophical Ideas* 3–33.

Kinche, Alexandre, "South Korea: Seoul Disengages from Russian oil," *Energynews*, June 22, 2022, https://energynews.pro/en/south-korea-seoul-disengages-from-russian -oil/ [https://perma.cc/XM5Y-5A7W].

Kine, Phelim and Lara Seligman, "Why the U.S. Isn't Ready for a Fight in the Indo-Pacific," *Politico*, December 27, 2022, https://www.politico.com/news/2022/12/27/ united-states-china-taiwan-pacific-00075555 [https://perma.cc/Z4AE-TY5Y].

Kirchberger, Sarah, *Who is Encircling Whom?: Security Policy Aspects of China's Relationship with Japan* (Federal Academy for Security Policy, 2017).

Klingler-Vidra, Robyn and Yu-Ching Kuo, Washington Shores-up Friends in the Semiconductor Industry (September 28, 2022), https://www.eastasiaforum.org/2022 /09/28/washington-shores-up-friends-in-the-semiconductor-industry/ [https:// perma.cc/ARL7-PM6P].

Klingner, Bruce, Jung H. Pak, and Sue Mi Terry, *Trump Shakedowns are Threatening Two Key US Alliances in Asia* (December 18, 2019), https://www.brookings.edu/blog/order -from-chaos/2019/12/18/trump-shakedowns-are-threatening-two-key-u-s-alliances -in-asia/ [https://perma.cc/YH9J-KXS3].

Koh, Heung-Gil, "South-North Diplomatic Warfare in Africa," *The JoongAng*, February 26, 1977, https://www.joongang.co.kr/article/1457070#home [https://perma.cc/ L5ND-HW8K].

Köllner, Patrick, "The Denuclearisation of North Korea: From Maximum Demands to Arms Control," *GIGA Focus*, no. 2 (February 2019).

Komiya, Ryutaro and Ryuhei Wakasugi, "Japan's Foreign Direct Investment" (1991) 513 *The Annals of the American Academy of Political Social Science* 48–61.

Koo, Hagen, "Civil Society and Democracy in South Korea" (2002) 11(2) *The Good Society* 40–45.

Koo, Jahyeong and Sherry L. Kiser, "Recovery from a Financial Crisis: The Case of South Korea," *Economic and Financial Review (Fourth Quarter*, 2001).

Kopanja, Mihajlo, "The Curious Case of Northeast Asia: External Balancing Meets Strategic Culture" (2019) 70 (1176) *Review of International Affairs* 67–83.

Korea Institute for National Unification, *Analysis on North Korea's 4th Plenary Meeting of the 8th Central Committee of the Workers' Party of Korea* (January 4, 2022), https://www.kinu .or.kr/pyxis-api/1/digital-files/b4062b0f-180d-4647-9c8b-96ba26380fdc [https:// perma.cc/Y5BL-HKPN].

Korea International Cooperation Agency, *Ex-post Evaluation Report on the Pilot Project to Reduce Air Pollution by Improving Heating Culture in Ulaanbaatar, Mongolia* (December 2013), https://www.oecd.org/derec/korea/Ex-post-Evaluation-Report-on-the-Pilot-Project -to-Reduce-Air-Pollution-by-Improving-Heating-Culture-in-Ulaanbaatar-Mongolia .pdf [https://perma.cc/6D8Y-DD6U].

Korea Statistical Office, *Gini Coefficient* (in Korean), https://www.index.go.kr/unity/potal /main/EachDtlPageDetail.do?idx_cd=1407 [https://perma.cc/SYD6-TGD2].

"Korea Strongly Protests Japan Diplomat's Comments on Comfort Women," *Korea Herald*, June 29, 2017, https://www.koreaherald.com/view.php?ud=20170629000790 [https://perma.cc/U23E-QZRX].

Korean Statistical Information Service, *Amounts of Foreign Exchange Reserve* (in Korean), https://kosis.kr/statHtml/statHtml.do?orgId=301&tblId=DT_038Y001&vw_cd= &list_id=&scrId=&seqNo=&lang_mode=ko&obj_var_id=&itm_id=&conn_path =E1 (accessed December 22, 2022).

Korean Statistical Information Service, *Status of Resident Foreigners by Nationality and Age*, https://kosis.kr/statHtml/statHtml.do?orgId=111&tblId=DT_1B040A6 (accessed December 22, 2022).

Ku, Chang Sung, "Japan's Three Items Subject to Export Restraint Measures, Import Dependency up to the Maximum of 94 Percent," *MK News*, July 1, 2019, https://www .mk.co.kr/news/business/view/2019/07/476728/ [https://perma.cc/5FSN-8PKF].

Kumagai, Takeo, "Japan's Russian Crude Oil Imports Fall to Zero in June," *S&P Global*, July 22, 2022, https://www.spglobal.com/commodityinsights/en/market-insights

/latest-news/oil/072222-japans-russian-crude-oil-imports-fall-to-zero-in-june#:~
:text=%22Considering%20the%20risk%20involved%20in,Gas%20and%20Metals
%20National%20Corp [https://perma.cc/6DRU-YTTB].

Kuperman, Alan J. and Hina Acharya, *Japan's Misguided Plutonium Policy* (October 2018),
https://www.armscontrol.org/act/2018-10/features/japan%E2%80%99s-misguided
-plutonium-policy [https://perma.cc/E8HM-3Z36].

"Kuril Islands Dispute Between Russia and Japan," *BBC News*, April 29, 2013, https://
www.bbc.com/news/world-asia-pacific-11664434 (accessed December 22, 2022).

Kwon, Edward and Liza Abram Benham, "Shinzo's Abe's Scheme of Staking Territorial
Claims to Korea's Dokdo" (2016) 3(1) *Journal of Territorial and Maritime Studies* 47–64.

Kwong, Emily, "Mongolia's Long Road to Mining Wealth, Changing Mongolia," *National
Public Radio*, July 31, 2019, https://www.npr.org/2019/07/31/741798613/mongolias
-long-road-to-mining-wealth [https://perma.cc/PA4A-8X52].

Kyodo, "Japan Seeks Cooperation from Mongolia in North Korean Abduction Issue,
Denuclearization," *Japan Times*, June 16, 2019, https://www.japantimes.co.jp/news
/2019/06/16/national/politics-diplomacy/japan-seeks-cooperation-mongolia-north
-korean-abduction-issue-denuclearization/ [https://perma.cc/6RDU-NVFX].

Lampton, David M., *Following the Leader: Ruling China, From Deng Xiaoping to Xi Zingping*
(University of California Press, 2014).

Lankov, Andrei, "Kim Takes Control: The 'Great Purge' in North Korea, 1956–1960"
(2002) 26(1) *Korean Studies* 87–119.

Lankov, Andrei, "'The Big Hunt': When North Korean Agents Almost Killed South
Korea's President," *NK News*, January 21, 2021, https://www.nknews.org/2021/01
/the-big-hunt-when-north-korean-agents-almost-killed-south-koreas-president/
[https://perma.cc/D9SK-T7JS].

Lankov, Andrei, "North Korea's Perfectly Logical Strategy of Missile Launches and
Dialogue," *NK News*, October 14, 2021, https://www.nknews.org/2021/10/north
-koreas-perfectly-logical-strategy-of-missile-launches-and-dialogue/ [https://perma
.cc/NR7E-DNDU].

Larkins, Christopher M., "Judicial Independence and Democratization: A Theoretical
and Conceptual Analysis" (1996) 44 *American Journal of Comparative Law* 605–626.

Larsen, Kirk W. and Joseph Seeley, "Simple Conversation or Secret Treaty? The Taft-
Katsura Memorandum in Korean Historical Memory" (2014) 19(1) *Journal of Korean
Studies* 59–92.

Lary, Diana, *China's Civil War: A Social History, 1945–1949* (Cambridge University Press,
2015).

Latourette, Kenneth Scott, *A History of Modern China* (Penguin Books, 1954).

Lawder, David, "USTR Tai Calls U.S. Tariffs on Chinese Goods 'Significant' Leverage,"
Reuters, June 22, 2022, https://www.reuters.com/business/ustr-tai-says-us-tariffs
-chinese-goods-are-significant-leverage-2022-06-22/ (accessed December 22, 2022).

Layne, Christopher, "China's Challenge to US Hegemony" (2008) 107 *Current History*
13–18.

Lee, Dae-Keun, *The South Economy in the 1950s after Liberation: A Study of the Historical
Background of Industrialization* (in Korean) (Samsung Economic Research Institute,
2002).

Lee, I-yun and Christine Han, "Politics, Popular Culture and Images of Japan in
Taiwan," *in* Paul Morris, Naoko Shimazu, and Edward Victors (eds.), *Imagining Japan
in Postwar East Asia* (Routledge, 2013).

Lee, Jae Young, "Korea-Mongolia Economic Relations: Current Status and Cooperation Measures" (2021) 31 *Korea's Economy* 31–37.

Lee, Jae-Yong and Ka-Woen Gwon, "Measures to Expand the Economic Cooperation between South Korea and Mongolia" (in Korean) (2016) 16(15) *World Economy Today* 1–22.

Lee, Jaeha, "The Problems of Dokdo's Development Policy and an Alternative for Future Development" (2013) 19(2) *Korea Journal of Regional Geography* 282–300.

Lee, Jeong-Hoon, "Samsung Flies and the Economic Concentration by Other Chaebols has Increased" (in Korean), *Hankyurye*, June 27, 2022, https://www.hani.co.kr/arti/economy/marketing/1048550.html [https://perma.cc/AB4Q-C5QE].

Lee, Jong-Gu, "Japan Becomes Conservative as a Whole, Due to the Decline of the Progressive Power and Economic Recession" (in Korean), *Pressian*, March 28, 2005, https://www.pressian.com/pages/articles/46252 (accessed December 22, 2022).

Lee, Jong Won, "The Impact of the Korean War on the Korean Economy" (2001) 5(1) *International Journal of Korean Studies* 97–118.

Lee, Manwoo, "Some Reflections on Soviet Influence in East Asia" (1986) 10(2) *Asian Perspective* 255–271.

Lee, Michael, "Joo Ho-Young Picked to Lead PPP Temporarily," *Korea JoongAng Daily*, August 9, 2022, https://koreajoongangdaily.joins.com/2022/08/09/national/politics/Korea-PPP-People-Power-Party/20220809181854797.html [https://perma.cc/LA9P-2FA8].

Lee, Sangsoo, *North Korea's Economy is Recentralised and China-Reliant*, East Asia Forum (April 10, 2021), https://www.eastasiaforum.org/2021/04/10/north-koreas-economy-is-recentralised-and-china-reliant/ [https://perma.cc/2HLM-7XTC].

Lee, Se-Won, "The Japanese Government Submitted an Opinion to UNESCO Citing the Denialists" (in Korean), *Yonhap News*, November 6, 2015, https://www.yna.co.kr/view/AKR20151106088700073 [https://perma.cc/WQF2-HS8A].

Lee, Seung-hoon, Kwon Han-wool, and Lee Eun-joo, "U.S. Pressure Mounts on Korea to Join Chip 4 Amid Pelosi Visit to Taipei and Seoul," *Pulse*, August 4, 2022, https://pulsenews.co.kr/view.php?year=2022&no=686003 (accessed December 22, 2022).

Lee, Sook Jong, *Generational Divides and the Future of South Korean Democracy* (Carnegie Endowment for International Peace, 2021), https://carnegieendowment.org/2021/06/29/generational-divides-and-future-of-south-korean-democracy-pub-84818 [https://perma.cc/PK9X-MZJV].

Lee, Sook-Jong, "Democratization and Polarization in Korean Society" (2005) 29(3) *Asian Perspective* 99–125.

Lee, Steven Hugh, *The Korean War* (Longman, 2001).

Lee, Yong-Shik, *Reclaiming Development in the World Trading System* (2d ed., Cambridge University Press, 2016).

Lee, Yong-Shik, "The Eagle Meets the Dragon – Two Superpowers, Two Mega RTAs, and So Many In Between: Reflections on TPP and RCEP" (2016) 50(3) *Journal of World Trade* 479–500.

Lee, Yong-Shik, "General Theory of Law and Development" (2017) 50(3) *Cornell International Law Journal* 415–471.

Lee, Yong-Shik, "Future of Trans–Pacific Partnership Agreement: Just a Dead Trade Initiative or a Meaningful Model for the North-South Economic and Trade Integration?" (2017) 51(5) *Journal of World Trade* 1–26.

Lee, Yong-Shik, "Should China be Granted Market Economy Status?: In View of Recent Development" (2017) 3(2) *China and WTO Review* 319–341.

Lee, Yong-Shik, "Law and Development: Lessons from South Korea" (2018) 11(2) *Law and Development Review* 433–465.

Lee, Yong-Shik, "South Korean Economy at the Crossroads: Structure Issues under External Pressure–An Essay from a Law and Development Perspective" (2019) 12(3) *Law and Development Review* 865–885.

Lee, Yong-Shik, "Three Wrongs Do Not Make a Right: The Conundrum of the U.S. Steel and Aluminum Tariffs" (2019) 18(3) *World Trade Review* 481–501.

Lee, Yong-Shik, "The Steel and Aluminum Quota Agreements: A Question of Compatibility with WTO Disciplines and Their Impact on the World Trading System" (2019) 52(5) *Journal of World Trade* 811–832.

Lee, Yong-Shik, "International Trade Law Post Neoliberalism" (2020) 68(2) *Buffalo Law Review* 413–478.

Lee, Yong-Shik, "Mimicking President Trump? – Trade and Politics in Japan's Recent Export Measure" (2020) 14(1) *Review of Institution and Economics* 1–5.

Lee, Yong-Shik, "New General Theory of Economic Development" (2020) 24(2) *Review of Development Economics* 402–423.

Lee, Yong- *Shik, Law and Development: Theory and Practice* (2d ed., Routledge, 2022).

Lee, Yong-Shik, "National Security as a Means to a Commercial End—Call for a New Approach," *SSRN* (May 27, 2022), https://papers.ssrn.com/sol3/papers.cfm?abstract _id=4117777.

Lee, Yong-Shik, "On Ramseyer's Response to the Critics of 'Contracting for Sex in the Pacific War'" (2022) 15(1) *Law and Development Review* 201–214.

Lee, Yong-Shik, "Weaponizing International Trade in Political Disputes: Issues under International Economic Law and Systemic Risks" (2022) 56(3) *Journal of World Trade* 405–428.

Lee, Yong-Shik, Jaemin Lee, and Kyung Han Sohn, "The United States – Korea Free Trade Agreement: Path to Common Economic Prosperity or False Promise?" (2011) 7 *University of Pennsylvania East Asia Law Review* 111–162.

Lee, Yong-Shik and Kwangkug Kim, "Tripartite Free Trade Agreement among China, Korea, and Japan: A Step Towards Economic Integration in Northeast Asia?" *in* Jiaxiang Hu and Matthias Vanhullebusch (eds.), *Regional Cooperation and Free Trade Agreements in Asia* (Leiden: Brill Publishers, 2014).

Lee, Yong-Shik, Natsu Taylor Saito, and Jonathan Todres, "The Fallacy of Contract in Sexual Slavery" (2021) 42(2) *Michigan Journal of International Law* 291–319.

Lee, Yong-Shik and Xiaojie Lu, "China's Trade and Development Policy under the WTO: An Evaluation of Law and Economics Aspect" (2016) 2(2) *China and WTO Review* 339–360.

Lee, Y.S., Young-Ok Kim, and Hye Seong Mun, "Economic Development of North Korea: International Trade Based Development Policy and Legal Reform" (2010) 3(1) *Law and Development Review* 136–156.

Lei, Cui, "Why It's Nearly Impossible to Denuclearize North Korea," *The Diplomat*, June 22, 2018, https://thediplomat.com/2018/06/why-its-nearly-impossible-to -denuclearize-north-korea/ [https://perma.cc/CM87-GM7G].

Li, Bin Grace, Pranav Gupta, and Jiangyan Yu, "From Natural Resource Boom to Sustainable Economic Growth: Lessons from Mongolia" (2017) 151 *International Economics* 7–25.

Li, Lianshui and Zhanyuan Du (eds.), *A Research Report on the Development of China's Manufacturing Sector (2016)* (Springer, 2017).

Li, Wei and Dennis Tao Yang, "The Great Leap Forward: Anatomy of a Central Planning Disaster" (2005) 113(4) *Journal of Political Economy* 840–877.

Lieberthal, Kenneth G., *Mao Tse-Tung's Perception of the Soviet Union as Communicated in the Mao Tse-tung Ssu-Hsiang Wan Sui*, Rand Paper Series (1976).

Lieberthal, Kenneth G., *The American Pivot to Asia* (December 21, 2011), https://www.brookings.edu/articles/the-american-pivot-to-asia/ [https://perma.cc/D87F-H8GZ].

Lim, Jae-Cheon, "North Korea's Hereditary Succession, Comparing Two Key Transitions in DPRK" (2012) 52(3) *Asian Survey* 550–570.

Lim, Louisa, *The People's Republic of Amnesia: Tiananmen Revisited* (Oxford University Press, 2014).

Lin, Karen Jingrong, Xiaoyan Lu, Junsheng Zhang, and Ying Zheng, "State-Owned Enterprises in China: A Review of 40 Years of Research and Practice" (2020) 13(1) *China Journal of Accounting Research* 31–55.

Lind, Jennifer and Daryl G. Press, "Should South Korea Build Its Own Nuclear Bomb?" *Washington Post*, October 7, 2021, https://www.washingtonpost.com/outlook/should-south-korea-go-nuclear/2021/10/07/a40bb400-2628-11ec-8d53-67cfb452aa60_story.html [https://perma.cc/3KKR-EB23].

Lkhaajav, Bolor, "Mongolia Hosts 7th Ulaanbaatar Dialogue on Northeast Asian Security," *The Diplomat*, June 28, 2022, https://thediplomat.com/2022/06/mongolia-hosts-7th-ulaanbaatar-dialogue-on-northeast-asian-security/ [https://perma.cc/BH8P-AKLA].

"Losses of Russia for the Period from Feb 24 to Nov 18," *Odessa Journal*, November 24, 2022, https://odessa-journal.com/losses-of-russia-for-the-period-from-feb-24-to-nov-18/ [https://perma.cc/33W9-M9LD].

Lowenthal, Richard, "Russia and China: Controlled Conflict" (1971) 49(3) *Foreign Affairs* 507–518.

Luxmoore, Matthew, "In Russia's Far East, a Rare Protest Movement Refuses To Be Cowed," *RadioFreeEurope/RadioLiberty*, September 11, 2020, https://www.rferl.org/a/in-russia-far-east-a-rare-protest-movement-refuses-to-be-cowed/30833806.html [https://perma.cc/5MTF-UAVP].

Macdonald, Roderick A. and Hoi Kong, "Judicial Independence as a Constitutional Virtue," *in* Carles Boix and Susan C. Stokers (eds.), *Oxford Handbook of Comparative Politics* (New York, 2012).

MacFarquhar, Roderick and Michael Schoenhals, *Mao's Last Revolution* (Harvard University Press, 2006).

MacLeod, Andrew, *Ukraine Invasion: Should Russia Lose Its Seat on the UN Security Council?* (February 25, 2022), https://www.kcl.ac.uk/ukraine-invasion-should-russia-lose-its-seat-on-the-un-security-council [https://perma.cc/KU75-PYSD].

Mah, Jai S., "Patterns of International Trade and the Industrial-Led Economic Development of North Korea" (2018) 30(6) *Post-Communist Economies* 830–832.

Maizland, Lindsay, *Hong Kong's Freedoms: What China Promised and How It's Cracking Down* (May 19, 2022), https://www.cfr.org/backgrounder/hong-kong-freedoms-democracy-protests-china-crackdown [https://perma.cc/9HTZ-CBH4].

Maizland, Lindsay, *China's Repression of Uyghurs in Xinjiang* (September 22, 2022), https://www.cfr.org/backgrounder/china-xinjiang-uyghurs-muslims-repression-genocide-human-rights [https://perma.cc/A9LB-KZ6Z].

Makinen, Julie, "North Korean Leader Unveils 5-Year Plan for Economy, But No Radical Reforms," *Los Angeles Times*, May 8, 2016, https://www.latimes.com/world/asia/la-fg -north-korea-economy-20160508-story.html [https://perma.cc/UVY4-TRQX].

Mark, Max, "Chinese Communism" (1951) 13(2) *Journal of Politics* 232–252.

Marrow, Alexander, "Russia Announces Troop Build-Up in Far East," *Reuters*, September 17, 2020, https://www.reuters.com/article/us-russia-military/russia-announces -troop-build-up-in-far-east-idUSKBN2682JM (accessed December 22, 2022).

Martin, Christopher, *The Russo-Japanese War* (Abelard-Schuman, 1967).

Master, Farah and David Stanway, "China Lacked a 'Zero COVID' Exit Plan. Its People are Paying the Price," *Reuters*, December 22, 2022, https://www.reuters.com/world /china/china-lacked-zero-covid-exit-plan-its-people-are-paying-price-2022-12-23/ [https://perma.cc/2PMT-XA7R].

Matsuzato, Kimitaka (ed.), *Russia and Its Northeast Asian Neighbors: China, Japan, and Korea, 1858–1945* (Lexington Books, 2017).

May, Ernest R., "The United States, the Soviet Union, and the Far Eastern War, 1941– 1945" (1955) 24(2) *Pacific Historical Review* 153–174.

May, Timothy and Michael Hope (eds.), *The Mongol World* (Routledge, 2022).

Mayger, James "Cash-Rich Japanese Companies Aren't Investing at Home," *Bloomberg*, March 9, 2015, https://www.bloomberg.com/news/articles/2015-03-09/cash-rich -japanese-companies-aren-t-investing-at-home#xj4y7vzkg (accessed December 30, 2022).

McAleavy, Henry, *The Modern History of China* (Praeger, 1967).

McBride, James and Andrew Chatzky, "Is 'Made in China 2025' a Threat to Global Trade?" *Council on Foreign Relations* (May 13, 2019), https://www.cfr.org/backgrounder /made-china-2025-threat-global-trade [https://perma.cc/J3RN-QKDU].

McCurry, Justin, "North Korea Confirms Test of Its Largest Intercontinental Ballistic Missile Yet," *The Guardian*, March 25, 2022, https://www.theguardian.com/world /2022/mar/24/n-korea-confirms-missile-testing-ahead-of-long-confrontation-with -us [https://perma.cc/JY2J-YDAY].

McDonald, Joe, "China Criticizes US Action Against Huawei," *AP News*, May 16, 2019, https://apnews.com/article/china-technology-united-states-ap-top-news-beijing-6df fae234a3e45a8b1e7ede17480839d [https://perma.cc/WLF3-HDS2].

McDonald, Joe, "China's Economy Shrinks 2.6% During Virus Shutdowns," *U.S. News and World Report*, July 15, 2022, https://www.usnews.com/news/business/articles /2022-07-14/chinas-economic-growth-falls-to-0-4-amid-virus-shutdowns (accessed December 22, 2022).

McDonald, Scott, "NY Governor Cuomo Says a Federal Quarantine by Trump Would be a 'Declaration of War,' Trump Renegotiates," *Newsweek*, March 28, 2020, https:// www.newsweek.com/ny-governor-cuomo-says-federal-quarantine-ordered-trump -would-declaration-war-states-1494857 [https://perma.cc/7DLL-4BPC].

McGregor, Grady, "China's Lockdowns to Contain Omicron Snarled the Global Economy. Lockdowns to Contain Subvariant BA.5 could be Even Worse," *Fortune* (July 11, 2022), https://fortune.com/2022/07/11/china-covid-lockdowns-omicron-ba -5-subvariant-economy-shanghai/ [https://perma.cc/EJN9-YTRY].

McKenzie, Frederick Arthur, *Korea's Fight for Freedom* (Pinnacle Press, 2017).

McNelly, Theodore, "American Political Traditions and Japan's Postwar Constitution" (1977) 140(1) *World Affairs* 58–66.

Mearsheimer, John J., *The Tragedy of Great Power Politics* (W. W. Norton & Company, 2001).

Mearsheimer, John J., "The Gathering Storm: China's Challenge to US Power in Asia" (2010) 3(4) *Chinese Journal of International Politics* 381–396.

Meltzer, Joshua P. and Neena Shenai, *The US-China Economic Relationship: A Comprehensive Approach* (February 28, 2019), https://www.brookings.edu/research/the-us-china-economic-relationship-a-comprehensive-approach/ [https://perma.cc/FR8S-VAZS].

Meserve, Walter J. and Ruth I. Meserve, "Theatre for Assimilation: China's National Minorities" (1979) 13(2) *Journal of Asian History* 95–120.

Microtrends, *South Korea Military Spending/Defense Budget 1960–2022*, https://www.macrotrends.net/countries/KOR/south-korea/military-spending-defense-budget [https://perma.cc/H6NP-L8QD].

Miller, Jennifer R., *Cold War Democracy: The United States and Japan* (Harvard University Press, 2019).

Millett, Allan R., "Korean War," *Encyclopaedia Britannica* (June 18, 2021), https://www.britannica.com/event/Korean-War [https://perma.cc/8TA8-SPRF].

Min, Kyung-Jin, "SMEs' Labor Productivity is 27 Percent of Large Companies" (in Korean), *Hankyung*, July 11, 2021, https://www.hankyung.com/economy/article/2021071122481 [https://perma.cc/5RL4-6MHV].

Min, W-J and S. Han, "Economic Sanctions Against North Korea: The Pivotal Role of US–China Cooperation" (2020) 23(2) *International Area Studies Review* 177–193.

Ministry of Foreign Affairs of Japan, *Japan's Position on the United Nations Security Council for the 21st Century* (March 2011), https://www.mofa.go.jp/policy/un/sc/pdfs/pamph_unsc21c_en.pdf [https://perma.cc/BKU6-5Q3B].

Ministry of Foreign Affairs of the People's Republic of China, *Wang Yi: Promote Sound and Steady Growth of China-ROK Strategic Cooperative Partnership with a Five-point Commitment* (August 9, 2022), https://www.fmprc.gov.cn/mfa_eng/wjdt_665385/wshd_665389/202208/t20220810_10740381.html [https://perma.cc/PYZ7-GPGM].

Ministry of Public Administration and Security (South Korea), *Regional Self-Governance* (in Korean), https://www.pa.go.kr/research/contents/policy/index10.jsp [https://perma.cc/F9RA-V8BQ].

Ministry of SMEs and Startups (South Korea), *The Status of SMEs*, https://www.mss.go.kr/site/smba/foffice/ex/statDB/MainSubStat.do [https://perma.cc/4P38-UXZZ].

Ministry of Trade, Industry and Energy (South Korea), *Exports and Trade in 2011: The Largest in History* (in Korean) (January 4, 2022), https://www.korea.kr/news/visualNewsView.do?newsId=148897615 [https://perma.cc/3P55-EXGK].

Ministry of Unification (South Korea), *Current Status* (in Korean), https://www.unikorea.go.kr/unikorea/business/NKDefectorsPolicy/status/lately/ [https://perma.cc/FXJ4-K4TS].

Minohara, Tosh and Kaoru Iokibe, "America Encounters Japan, 1836–94," *in* Makoto Iokibe and Tosh Minohara (eds.), *The History of US-Japan Relations: From Perry to Present* (Palgrave Macmillan, 2017).

Mishra, Rohan, "Toward A Nuclear Recognition Threshold" (2020) 120(4) *Columbia Law Review* 1035–1076.

Mitter, Rana, "1911: The Unanchored Chinese Revolution" (2011) 208 *China Quarterly* 1009–1020.

Mizokami, Kyle, "Surprise: Japan Could Quickly Build Nuclear Weapons in a Crisis," *National Interest*, July 21, 2021, https://nationalinterest.org/blog/reboot/surprise

-japan-could-quickly-build-nuclear-weapons-crisis-190089 [https://perma.cc/S665 -LBET].

"Mongolia Under Pressure to Align with Russia and China," *The Guardian*, May 31, 2022, https://www.theguardian.com/world/2022/may/31/mongolia-under-pressure-to -align-with-russia-and-china [https://perma.cc/FV7H-V9XR].

"Mongolian Prime Minister Submits Resignation After COVID-19 Protests," *Reuters*, January 21, 2021, https://www.reuters.com/article/us-health-coronavirus -mongolia/mongolian-prime-minister-submits-resignation-after-covid-19-protests -idUSKBN29Q1GT [https://perma.cc/6ZH3-NK6K].

Moon, Chung-In, "S Korea 'all in' on US Economic Security Alliance," *Asia Times*, November 10, 2022, https://asiatimes.com/2022/11/s-korea-all-in-on-us-economic -security-alliance/ [https://perma.cc/63BB-XA8U].

"Moon: Japan's Not S. Korea's Ally," *KBS World*, November 15, 2017, http://world.kbs.co .kr/service/news_view.htm?lang=e&Seq_Code=131394 [https://perma.cc/S2CW -PMDP].

Morgan, Raleigh, "Chinese, Japanese, and United States Views of the Nanking Massacre: The Supreme Court Trial of Shiro Azuma" (2002) 9(2) *American Journal of Chinese Studies* 235–246.

Morgenthau, Hans, *Politics Among Nations: The Struggle for Power and Peace* (Alfred A. Knopf, 1948).

Morrison, Wayne M., *China's Economic Rise: History, Trends, Challenges, and Implications for the United States*, Congressional Research Service, RL33534 (2019).

Mutual Defense Treaty Between the United States and the Republic of Korea (1953), https://www.usfk.mil/Portals/105/Documents/SOFA/H_Mutual%20Defense %20Treaty_1953.pdf [https://perma.cc/MZD6-BKGC].

Nagasawa, Tsuyoshi and Masaya Kato, "US Supports Japan's Sovereignty over Senkakus: Pentagon," *Nikkei Asia*, February 25, 2021, https://asia.nikkei.com/Politics /International-relations/Biden-s-Asia-policy/US-supports-Japan-s-sovereignty-over -Senkakus-Pentagon [https://perma.cc/ZP8L-7JAY].

Nakamura, Keita, "Japan OKs Enemy Base Strike Capability in Major Defense Policy Shift," *Kyodo News*, December 16, 2022, https://english.kyodonews.net/news/2022/12 /02fc9015409c-japan-to-vow-to-obtain-enemy-base-strike-capability-amid-threats .html [https://perma.cc/SX6T-7FQU].

Nakashima, Ellen, John Hudson, Michelle Ye Hee Lee, and Cate Cadell, "Key Asian Nations Join Global Backlash Against Russia, with An Eye Toward China," *Washington Post*, March 3, 2022, https://www.washingtonpost.com/national-security/2022/03 /03/ukraine-asia-sanctions/ [https://perma.cc/WL3D-R6NK].

Nardelli, Alberto, "Russia Turns to Old Tanks as It Burns Through Weapons in Ukraine," *Bloomberg*, June 14, 2022, https://www.bloomberg.com/news/articles/2022-06-14/ russia-turns-to-old-tanks-as-it-burns-through-weapons-in-ukraine [https://perma.cc /LT88-VGHY].

National Archive, *Marshall Plan* (1948), https://www.archives.gov/milestone-documents/ marshall-plan [https://perma.cc/ZQH3-RE6Y].

Naughton, Barry, "Is China Socialist?" (2017) 31(1) *Journal of Economic Perspectives* 3–24.

Neuhard, Ryan, *The New US National Security Strategy: Four Takeaways for Asia Policy* (October 21, 2022), https://www.fpri.org/article/2022/10/the-new-us-national-security -strategy-four-takeaways-for-asia-policy/ [https://perma.cc/FQ95-4BDX].

Nikitin, Mary Beth D. and Samuel D. Ryder, "North Korea's Nuclear Weapons and Missile Programs," *CRS Report, IF10472* (January 5, 2021), https://crsreports.congress.gov/product/pdf/IF/IF10472/19 (accessed December 22, 2022).

Niou, Emerson N. S., Peter C. Ordeshook, and Gregory F. Rose, *The Balance of Power: Stability in International Systems* (Cambridge University Press, 1989).

Nishida, Tsuneo, "China and Japan: Managing a Complex Relationship" (2015) 4 *Horizons: Journal of International Relations and Sustainable Development* 62–73.

No, Jae-Whan, "A Russian Report Says, 'South Korea Will Absorb North Korea into Reunification'" (in Korean), *Radio Free Asia*, November 4, 2011, https://www.rfa.org/korean/in_focus/russiareport-11042011114933.html [https://perma.cc/TW5A-PHPJ].

"No to Three No's," *Korea Herald* (August 12, 2022), https://www.koreaherald.com/view.php?ud=20220811000838 [https://perma.cc/B4JF-DL3J].

Noland, Marcus, Sherman Robinson, and Li-gang Liu, "The Costs and Benefits of Korean Unification: Alternate Scenarios" (1998) 38(8) *Asian Survey* 801–814.

"North Korea Says New Missile Puts All of US in Striking Range," *BBC News*, November 29, 2017, https://www.bbc.com/news/world-asia-42162462 (accessed December 22, 2022).

"North Korean Artillery Hits South Korean Island," *BBC News*, November 23, 2010, https://www.bbc.com/news/world-asia-pacific-11818005 (accessed December 22, 2022).

"North Korea's Kim Jong un Threatens to Use Nuclear Weapons Preemptively 'If Necessary," *CBS News*, April 30, 2022, https://www.cbsnews.com/news/north-korea-nuclear-weapons-kim-jong-un-preemptively/ [https://perma.cc/UGM3-35YB].

"North Korea's Military Capabilities," *Council on Foreign Relations*, December 22, 2021, https://www.cfr.org/backgrounder/north-korea-nuclear-weapons-missile-tests-military-capabilities [https://perma.cc/WJ2H-ZEMH].

Northeast Asian History Network, *Korea-China History Awareness*, http://contents.nahf.or.kr/english/item/level.do?itemId=iscd [https://perma.cc/G2B5-Y5ST].

Nosov, Mikhail, "Russia between Europe and Asia" (2014) 81(1) *Rivista di Studi Politici Internazionali* 15–34.

Nyamjav, Soyolgerel and Mendee Jargalsaikhan, *Why Is the UB Dialogue Important?* (July 25, 2022), https://blogs.ubc.ca/mongolia/2022/ubdialogue-neasia-security/ [https://perma.cc/HR22-4CJG].

O'Dwyer, Shuan (ed.), *Handbook of Confucianism in Modern Japan* (MHN Limited, 2021).

O'Neill, Mar, "Soviet Involvement in the Korean War: A New View from the Soviet-era Archives" (2000) 14(3) *OAH Magazine of History* 20–24.

Office of Strategic Industries and Economic Security Bureau of Export Administration and DFI International, *U.S. Commercial Technology Transfers to the People's Republic of China* (January 1999), https://www.bis.doc.gov/index.php/documents/technology-evaluation/71-u-s-commercial-technology-transfers-to-the-people-s-republic-of-china-1999/file [https://perma.cc/6A3N-N6LY].

Oh, Eunjung Irene, "Ambitions are not Opportunities: South Korean President Moon Jae-in's Failed North Korea Policy," *Yale Journal of International Affairs* (January 14, 2022), https://www.yalejournal.org/publications/ambitions-are-not-opportunities-south-korean-president-moon-jae-ins-failed-north-korea-policy [https://perma.cc/A8W8-XHYL].

Ohn, Chang-Il, "The Causes of the Korean War 1950-1953" (2010) 14(2) *International Journal of Korean Studies* 19–44.

Ojewale, Oluwole, *What Coltan Mining in the DRC Costs People and the Environment* (May 29, 2022), https://theconversation.com/what-coltan-mining-in-the-drc-costs-people-and -the-environment-183159 [https://perma.cc/4RZN-HTT7].

Okimoto, Daniel I., *Causes of Japan's Economic Stagnation*, https://aparc.fsi.stanford.edu /research/causes_of_japans_economic_stagnation [https://perma.cc/G4ZX -ALNK].

Okuyama, Yutaka, "The Dispute Over the Kurile Islands between Russia and Japan in the 1990s" (2003) 76(1) *Pacific Affairs* 37–53.

Olsen, Edward A., "U.S.–North Korean Relations: Foreign Policy Dilemmas" (2005) 1 *North Korean Review* 63–75.

Onchi, Yosuke, "Kim Jong Un's Fury Stems from His Blaming Moon for Hanoi Debacle," *NikkeiAsia*, July 5, 2020, https://asia.nikkei.com/Spotlight/N-Korea-at-crossroads /Kim-Jong-Un-s-fury-stems-from-his-blaming-Moon-for-Hanoi-debacle   [https:// perma.cc/335C-EBJR].

Organisation for Economic Co-operation and Development, "Economy," *Korea Policy Brief* (October 2016), https://www.oecd.org/policy-briefs/korea-productivity-through -innovation-and-structural-reform_EN.pdf [https://perma.cc/G5ZH-DSBG].

Organisation for Economic Co-operation and Development, *Average Wages* (2022), https:// data.oecd.org/earnwage/average-wages.htm [https://perma.cc/478A-L47D].

Pact of Neutrality between Union of Soviet Socialist Republics and Japan (1941), https:// avalon.law.yale.edu/wwii/s1.asp [https://perma.cc/V2NQ-SG92].

Paine, S. C. M., *The Sino-Japanese War of 1894-1895: Perceptions, Power, and Primacy* (University Press, 2003).

Palmer, Brandon, "Imperial Japan's Preparations to Conscript Koreans as Soldiers, 1942—1945" (2007) 31 *Korean Studies* 63–78.

Pamuk, Humeyra and David Brunnstrom, "U.S. Criticises China's Hong Kong Move, Set to Raise Xinjiang Genocide Charge in Talks," *Reuters*, March 11, 2021, https:// www.reuters.com/article/us-usa-china-hongkong/u-s-criticises-chinas-hong-kong -move-set-to-raise-xinjiang-genocide-charge-in-talks-idUSKBN2B32TC   (accessed December 22, 2022).

Panton, Michael A., "Politics, Practice and Pacifism: Revising Article 9 of the Japanese Constitution" (2010) 11(2) *Asian Pacific Law & Policy Journal* 163–218.

Park, Byong-su, "Germany Offers Lessons for Remembering Atrocities - Japan should Take Them," *Hankyoreh*, September 24, 2022, https://english.hani.co.kr/arti/english _edition/e_international/1059951.html [https://perma.cc/JKV8-74PD].

Park, H.-K., "American Involvement in the Korean War" (1983) 16(4) *The History Teacher* 249–263.

Park, Insook Han and Lee-Jay Cho, "Confucianism and the Korean Family" (1995) 26(1) *Journal of Comparative Family Studies* 117–134.

Park, Jin-Yong, "President Yoon Seok-Yeol Approval Rate 24%...Again the Lowest [Gallup]" (in Korean), *Seoul Kyeongje*, September 30, 2022, https://www.sedaily.com/ NewsView/26B9WC9VMD [https://perma.cc/EH6T-6DK4].

Park, Nathan, "Abe Ruined the Most Important Democratic Relationship in Asia," *Foreign Policy*, September 4, 2020, https://foreignpolicy.com/2020/09/04/shinzo-abe -japan-south-korea-war-nationalism/ [https://perma.cc/82DW-UP7K].

Park, Soo-Bin, *The North Korean Economy: Current Issues and Prospects, Association of Korean Studies* (2003), https://carleton.ca/economics/wp-content/uploads/cep04-05.pdf ?origin=publication_detail [https://perma.cc/H5EB-FNUU].

Park, Young Ho, *South and North Korea's Views on the Unification of the Korean Peninsula and Inter-Korean Relations* (2014), https://www.brookings.edu/wp-content/uploads/2014 /04/park-young-ho-paper.pdf [https://perma.cc/3SUL-6BJA].

Park, Young-Seok, "470 Provocations by North Korea after the War, 4,119 People Killed or Kidnapped" (in Korean), *The JoonAng*, December 6, 2010, https://www.joongang .co.kr/article/4754445#home [https://perma.cc/B45X-XGMG].

Parsons, Edward B., "Roosevelt's Containment of the Russo-Japanese War" (1969) 38(1) *Pacific Historical Review* 21–44.

Pastreich, Emanuel, "The Balancer: Roh Moo-hyun's Vision of Korean Politics and the Future of Northeast Asia" (2005) 3(8) *Asian-Pacific Journal* 1–14.

Patalano, A., "Japan as a Maritime Power: Deterrence, Diplomacy, and Maritime Security," *in* Mary McCarthy (ed.), *Routledge Handbook of Japanese Foreign Policy* (Routledge, 2018).

Perdue, Peter C., "Boundaries and Trade in the Early Modern World: Negotiations at Nerchinsk and Beijing" (2010) 43(3) *Eighteen-Century Studies* 341–346.

Permanent Mission of Mongolia to the United Nations, *Mongolia-Neutrality* (September 10, 2015), https://www.un.int/mongolia/news/mongolia-neutrality [https://perma.cc/ KCV5-DGKR].

Person, James, "North Korea's Purges Past," *National Interest*, December 30, 2013, https:// nationalinterest.org/commentary/north-koreas-purges-past-9628 [https://perma.cc /U5ZM-YCKM].

Pifer, Steven, *Why Care About Ukraine and the Budapest Memorandum* (December 5, 2019), https://www.brookings.edu/blog/order-from-chaos/2019/12/05/why-care-about -ukraine-and-the-budapest-memorandum/ [https://perma.cc/74XB-85GD].

"Power," *The U.S. News and World Report*, https://www.usnews.com/news/best-countries/ rankings/power (accessed December 22, 2022).

Prowse, Sinclaire, *Mongolia - Neutrality and Anxiety* (2022), https://asiasociety.org/australia /mongolia-neutrality-and-anxiety [https://perma.cc/V7BH-NBS4].

Psarras, Sophia-Karin, "Han and Xiongnu: A Reexamination of Cultural and Political Relations (II)" (2004) 52 *Monumenta Serica* 37–93.

PSCORE, *Forced to Hate*, http://pscore.org/life-north-korea/forced-to-hate/ [https:// perma.cc/ABV3-TM6S].

Public Law 117–167 (Chips and Science Act of 2022, United States).

Public Law 117–169 (Inflation Reduction Act of 2022, United States).

Purdue, Peter C., *China Marches West: The Qing Conquest of Central Eurasia* (Belknap Press, 2005).

Ramburg, Bennett, "North Korea's Ongoing Nuclear Missile Tests Prove It's Time to Normalize Relations," *NBC News*, October 21, 2021, https://www.nbcnews.com/ think/opinion/north-korea-s-ongoing-nuclear-missile-tests-prove-it-s-ncna1282118 [https://perma.cc/8FT8-TE4V].

Ramseyer, J. Mark, "Contracting for Sex in the Pacific War" (2021) 65 *International Review of Law and Economics* 1–8.

Reardon-Anderson, James, "Land Use and Society in Manchuria and Inner Mongolia during the Qing Dynasty" (2000) 5(4) *Environmental History* 503–530.

Record, Jeffrey, *Japan's Decision for War in 1941: Some Enduring Lessons* (U.S. Army War College, Strategic Studies Institute, 2009).

Revere, Evans J. R., *Kim Jong-un will Not Give Up North Korea's Nuclear Weapons* (April 9, 2018), https://www.brookings.edu/blog/order-from-chaos/2018/04/09/kim-jong-un-will-not-give-up-north-koreas-nuclear-weapons/ [https://perma.cc/3BPF-FCGA].

Revere, Evans J. R., "North Korea's Economic Crisis: Last Chance for Denuclearization?" *Brookings Institute Report* (February 26, 2021), https://www.brookings.edu/research/north-koreas-economic-crisis-last-chance-for-denuclearization/ [https://perma.cc/TV6M-6W7Z].

Reynolds, Isabel and Emi Nobuhiro, "China Says Unfair Treatment of Huawei Could Damage Japan Ties," *Bloomberg*, March 29, 2019, https://www.bloomberg.com/news/articles/2019-03-29/china-says-unfair-treatment-of-huawei-could-damage-japan-ties [https://perma.cc/S3HZ-ZF46].

Rich, Timothy S. and Mallory Hardesty, *Americans Largely Reject Closing Bases in Germany, South Korea and Japan* (July 26, 2022), https://www.e-ir.info/2022/07/26/americans-largely-reject-closing-bases-in-germany-south-korea-and-japan/ [https://perma.cc/3FHJ-N2VV].

Richards, Clint, "Japan's New Remote Island Defense Plan," *The Diplomat*, August 13, 2014, https://thediplomat.com/2014/08/japans-new-remote-island-defense-plan/ [https://perma.cc/7PHD-PA3X].

Rienzi, Greg, "Other Nations Could Learn from Germany's Efforts to Reconcile After WWII," *Johns Hopkins Magazine* (Summer 2015), https://hub.jhu.edu/magazine/2015/summer/germany-japan-reconciliation/ [https://perma.cc/D9DQ-3C6Y].

Roberts, Priscilla, "New Light on a "Forgotten War": The Diplomacy of the Korean Conflict" (2000) 14(3) *OAH Magazine of History* 10–14.

Robinson, Joan, "Korean Miracle" (1965) 16(9) *Monthly Review* 541–549.

Roblin, Sebastien, "The Rangoon Bombing: North Korea's 1983 Attempt to Destroy South Korea's Government," *National Interest*, July 29, 2021, https://nationalinterest.org/blog/reboot/rangoon-bombing-north-korea%E2%80%99s-1983-attempt-destroy-south-korea%E2%80%99s-government-190689 [https://perma.cc/9JPJ-XE74].

Rogin, Josh, "Trump Still Holds Jimmy Carter's View on Withdrawing U.S. Troops from South Korea," *Washington Post*, June 7, 2018, https://www.washingtonpost.com/news/josh-rogin/wp/2018/06/07/trump-still-holds-jimmy-carters-view-on-withdrawing-u-s-troops-from-south-korea/ [https://perma.cc/8YZT-ENZ8].

Rosato, Sebastian, "The Flawed Logic of Democratic Peace Theory" (2003) 97(4) *American Political Science Review* 585–602.

Ross, Robert S., *The Fate of the Pivot: U.S. Policy in East Asia* (S. Rajaratnam School of International Studies, 2014).

Roth, Antoine and Andrea A. Fischetti, "Japan's Growing Reliance on the Chinese Market," *Tokyo Review* (2021), https://www.tokyoreview.net/2021/02/japans-growing-reliance-on-the-chinese-market/ [https://perma.cc/CF33-Z2HQ].

Roth, Kenneth, *World Report 2022: North Korea (2022)*, https://www.hrw.org/world-report/2022/country-chapters/north-korea [https://perma.cc/4FYE-6XZP].

Rowe, William T., *China's Last Empire: The Great Qing* (Belknap Press, 2012).

Rozman, Gilbert, "Regionalism in Northeast Asia: Korea's Return to Center Stage," *in* Charles K. Armstrong *et al.* (eds.), *Korea at the Center: Dynamics of Regionalism in Northeast Asia* (Routledge, 2006).

Rozman, Gilbert (ed.). *U.S. Leadership, History, and Bilateral Relations in Northeast Asia* (Cambridge University Press, 2011).

"Russia Says China will Start Paying for Gas in Rubles and Yuan," *CNN Business*, September 6, 2022, https://www.cnn.com/2022/09/06/energy/china-russian-gas-payments-ruble-yuan/index.html [https://perma.cc/L3U2-S6C7].

"Russia Scraps Visa-Free Visits to Islands Claimed by Japan," *Japan Times*, September 6, 2022, https://www.japantimes.co.jp/news/2022/09/06/national/politics-diplomacy/islands-visa-agreement/ [https://perma.cc/5MSV-X6FX].

"Russia Suspends Fisheries Agreement with Japan," *Nippon.com*, June 7, 2022, https://www.nippon.com/en/news/yjj2022060701155/ [https://perma.cc/M3HP-ZBJT].

"S. Korea Expresses Strong Protest Over Japan's Renewed Dokdo Claims in Defense White Paper," *Korea Herald*, July 13, 2021, https://www.koreaherald.com/view.php?ud=20210713000503 [https://perma.cc/RSR4-9MZT].

Sabloff, Paula L. W., "Why Mongolia? The Political Culture of an Emerging Democracy" (2010) 21(1) *Central Asian Survey* 19–36.

Saich, Tony, *From Rebel to Ruler: One Hundred Years of the Chinese Communist Party* (Harvard University Press, 2021).

Sanallkhundev, Bayasgalan, "Third Neighbor Policy Concept in Mongolia's Geopolitics" (2021) 22 *Mongolian Journal of International Affairs* 81–98.

Sanders, Alan J. K., "Mongolia: Independence and Revolution," *Encyclopaedia Britannica*, https://www.britannica.com/place/Mongolia/Independence-and-revolution [https://perma.cc/D6YF-B7A6].

Sanders, Alan J. K., "Mongolia Since 1990: Constitutional Change," *Encyclopaedia Britannica*, https://www.britannica.com/place/Mongolia/Reform-and-the-birth-of-democracy [https://perma.cc/G9L3-5EWU].

Sanger, David E., "North Korea Say They Tested Nuclear Device," *New York Times*, October 9, 2006, https://www.nytimes.com/2006/10/09/world/asia/09korea.html [https://perma.cc/8ENQ-EG7U].

Santora, Marc, Andrew E. Kramer, Dan Bilefsky, Ivan Nechepurenko, and Anton Troianovski, "Russia Orders Retreat From Kherson, a Serious Reversal in the Ukraine War," *New York Times*, November 9, 2022, https://www.nytimes.com/2022/11/09/world/europe/ukraine-russia-kherson-retreat.html [https://perma.cc/7AJN-ES7D].

Sasaki, Tomoyuki, "Whose Peace? Anti-Military Litigation and the Right to Live in Peace in Postwar Japan" (2012) 10(29) *Asia-Pacific Journal* 1–19.

Sassim, Francesco, "Russia's Energy Game in Asia," *The Diplomat*, September 27, 2022, https://thediplomat.com/2022/09/russias-energy-game-in-asia/ [https://perma.cc/93B7-TYTJ].

Saunders, Phillip C. and Julia G. Bowie, "US-China military relations: competition and cooperation" (2016) 39 *Journal of Strategic Studies* 662–684.

Savada, Andrea Matles and William Shaw (eds.), *South Korea: A Country Study* (1990), http://countrystudies.us/south-korea/7.htm#:~:text=Japan's%20initial%20colonial%20policy%20was,self%2Dsufficiency%20and%20war%20preparation [https://perma.cc/J6GX-9HJ9].

Schifrin, Nick and Zaba Warsi, "UN Investigator Outlines Evidence of Russian War Crimes in Liberated Areas of Ukraine," *PBS News Hour*, September 28, 2022, https://www.pbs.org/newshour/show/un-investigator-outlines-evidence-of-russian-war-crimes-in-liberated-areas-of-ukraine#:~:text=Ukraine's%20prosecutor%20gen

eral%20also%20said,the%20beginning%20of%20the%20war   [https://perma.cc/
JE42-DHLZ].

Schoff, James L. and Li Bin, *A Precarious Triangle: U.S.-China Strategic Stability and Japan* (Carnegie Endowment for International Peace, 2017).

Schroeder, Paul W., "The 'Balance of Power' System in Europe, 1815–1871" (1975) 27(5) *Naval War College Review* 18–31.

Schuman, Michael, "Why Biden's Block on Chips to China Is a Big Deal," *The Atlantic*, October 25, 2022, https://www.theatlantic.com/international/archive/2022/10/biden-export-control-microchips-china/671848/ [https://perma.cc/9FHF-2XWV].

Seldon, Mark, "Japanese and American War Atrocities, Historical Memory and Reconciliation: World War II to Today" (2008) 6(4) *Japan Focus* 1–19.

Sella, Amnon, "Khalkhin-Gol: The Forgotten War" (1983) 18(4) *Journal of Contemporary History* 651–687.

"Seminar on Korea-Mongolia National Union" (in Korean) (2007) *Shin-Dong-A*, no. 573, 334–337.

Seth, Michael J., *A History of Korea: From Antiquity to the Present* (Rowman & Littlefield, 2011).

Seth, Michael J., *South Korea's Economic Development*, 1948–1996 (December 19, 2017), https://oxfordre.com/asianhistory/view/10.1093/acrefore/9780190277727.001.0001/acrefore-9780190277727-e-271 [https://perma.cc/7PH4-GPQK].

Setser, Brad W., *Meanwhile, in Japan, Household Consumption Continues to Fall* (July 7, 2016), https://www.cfr.org/blog/meanwhile-japan-household-consumption-continues-fall [https://perma.cc/23V6-M7PV].

Sheehan, Michael, "The Sincerity of the British Commitment to the Maintenance of the Balance of Power 1714–1763" (2004) 15(3) *Diplomacy and Statecraft* 489–506.

Shin, David W., "North Korea's Post-Totalitarian State: The Rise of the Suryong (Supreme Leader) and the Transfer of Charismatic Leadership" (2016) 33(1) *American Intelligence Journal* 31–48.

Shin, Gi-Wook, "The Rise of Anti-Chinese Sentiments in South Korea: Political and Security Implications," *FSI News* (Stanford Freeman Spogli Institute for International Studies), October 7, 2021.

Shin, Hyonhee, "N. Korea Backs Russia's Proclaimed Annexations, Criticises U.S. 'Double Standards,'" *Reuters*, October 3, 2022, https://www.reuters.com/world/asia-pacific/nkorea-backs-russias-proclaimed-annexations-criticises-us-double-standards-2022-10-03/ (accessed December 22, 2022).

Shin, Ji-hye, "36-year-old Lee Jun-seok Becomes New Leader of People Power Party," *Korea Herald*, June 11, 2021, https://www.koreaherald.com/view.php?ud=20210611000445 [https://perma.cc/R8BL-FMVK].

Shin, Ji-hye, "Why does Korea have Such a Deep Political Divide?" *Korea Herald*, November 6, 2021, https://www.koreaherald.com/view.php?ud=20211108000739 [https://perma.cc/CNW5-YSLL].

Shin, Mitch, "North Korea Issues Warning Over South Korea-US Joint Military Exercises," *The Diplomat*, August 12, 2021, https://thediplomat.com/2021/08/north-korea-issues-warning-over-south-korea-us-joint-military-exercises/ [https://perma.cc/NM6V-2BKU].

Shin, Mitch, "US Warns North Korea: Nuclear Attack Will End Kim Regime," *The Diplomat*, October 28, 2022, https://thediplomat.com/2022/10/us-warns-north-korea-nuclear-attack-will-end-kim-regime/ [https://perma.cc/SP5U-MHQR].

Shin, Sang-Gu, "The Cause, Progress, and Impact of the April Revolution and Historical Assessment" (in Korean), *Dae Jeon Munwha Newspaper*, April 20, 2021, http://djmunhwa .kr/news/view.php?no=8574 [https://perma.cc/SX8J-848K].

Shin, Wook and Daniel Sneider, *Divergent Memories* (Stanford University Press, 2016).

Shinkman, Paul D., "North Korea Threatens U.S.: Nuclear Attack 'The Only Option Left,'" *U.S. News and World Report*, June 26, 2020, https://www.usnews.com/news/ world-report/articles/2020-06-26/north-korea-threatens-us-with-nuclear-attack (accessed December 22, 2022).

Shinkman, Paul D., "China Indicates to Biden it Won't Send Weapons to Russia," *The U.S. News and World Report*, March 18, 2022, https://www.usnews.com/news/world -report/articles/2022-03-18/china-indicates-to-biden-it-wont-send-weapons-to-russia -as-bloody-war-in-ukraine-grinds-on (accessed December 22, 2022).

Shipitko, Ulyana, "Rediscovering Russia in Northeast Asia" (2010) 9 *Ritsumeikan Annual Review of International Studies* 205–229.

Shirk, Susan L., "China in Xi's 'New Era': The Return to Personalistic Rule" (2018) 29(2) *Journal of Democracy* 22–36.

Sibbett, Benjamin K., "Tokdo or Takeshima? The Territorial Dispute Between Japan and the Republic of Korea" (1998) 21(4) *Fordham International Law Journal* 1606–1646.

Silver, Laura, *Some Americans' Views of China Turned More Negative After 2020, But Others Became More Positive* (September 28, 2022), https://www.pewresearch.org/fact-tank /2022/09/28/some-americans-views-of-china-turned-more-negative-after-2020-but -others-became-more-positive/ [https://perma.cc/54PB-SEXS].

Simes Jr., Dimitri and Tatiana Simes, "Putin's Big Plans for Russia's Far East Aren't Panning Out," *World Politics Review*, October 5, 2021, https://www.worldpoliticsreview .com/putin-s-big-plans-for-russia-s-far-east-aren-t-panning-out/ [https://perma.cc/ QQL6-QYDF].

Smith, Paul J., "The Senkaku/Diaoyu Island Controversy: A Crisis Postponed" (2013) 66(2) *Naval War College Review* 27–44.

Smith, Shane, *North Korea's Evolving Nuclear Strategy*, US-Korea Institute at SAIS (August 2015), https://www.38north.org/wp-content/uploads/2015/09/NKNF_Evolving -Nuclear-Strategy_Smith.pdf [https://perma.cc/4ALC-HA42].

Solís, Mireya, *China Moves to Join the CPTPP, But Don't Expect a Fast Pass* (September 23, 2021), https://www.brookings.edu/blog/order-from-chaos/2021/09/23/china -moves-to-join-the-cptpp-but-dont-expect-a-fast-pass/ [https://perma.cc/X2XG -ZH2D].

Somin, Ilya, "Remembering the Biggest Mass Murder in the History of the World," *Washington Post*, August 3, 2016, https://www.washingtonpost.com/news/volokh -conspiracy/wp/2016/08/03/giving-historys-greatest-mass-murderer-his-due/ [https://perma.cc/8NMN-ARKU].

Son, Ji-hyoung, "Chinese Envoy Warns Korea Against 'Interference' in Chip Supply Chain," *Korea Herald*, July 26, 2022, https://www.koreaherald.com/view.php?ud =20220726000627 [https://perma.cc/MV22-T83M].

Son, Seung-Chul, "Sa-Dae-Gyo-Rin" (in Korean), *Encyclopedia of Korean Culture* (1998), http://encykorea.aks.ac.kr/Contents/Index?contents_id=E0025448 [https://perma .cc/7H76-QLY6].

"South Korea and U.S. Begin Their Largest Military Drills," *CNBC*, August 22, 2022, https://www.cnbc.com/2022/08/22/s-korea-and-us-begin-largest-military-drills -amid-n-korea-backlash.html [https://perma.cc/V8HL-77DJ].

Spitzer, Kirk, "Why Japan Is Still Not Sorry Enough," *Time*, December 11, 2012, https://
nation.time.com/2012/12/11/why-japan-is-still-not-sorry-enough/ [https://perma
.cc/3XP5-WSL6].

Startfor, *What Could Push China to Invade Taiwan* (September 20, 2022), https://worldview
.stratfor.com/article/what-could-push-china-invade-taiwan [https://perma.cc/386F
-U4EQ].

Statista, *China Is the World's Manufacturing Superpower* (May 4, 2021), https://www.statista
.com/chart/20858/top-10-countries-by-share-of-global-manufacturing-output/
[https://perma.cc/98Z5-FMBB].

Statista, *Share of the Leading Merchandise Importers Worldwide in 2020, by Importing Nation*
(October 11, 2021), https://www.statista.com/statistics/252140/share-of-the-leading
-merchandise-importers-worldwide-by-importing-nation/ [https://perma.cc/U93A
-D6TT].

Stavridis, James, "A US-China War over Taiwan Isn't Happening Anytime Soon,"
Bloomberg, August 9, 2022, https://www.bloomberg.com/opinion/articles/2022-08
-09/a-us-china-war-over-taiwan-isn-t-happening-anytime-soon?leadSource=uverify
%20wall [https://perma.cc/7WCY-5W7T].

Steen, Bard Nikolas Vik, "Is Pacific Asia Returning to Sinocentrism?" *E-International
Relations* (September 14, 2014), https://www.e-ir.info/2014/09/14/is-pacific-asia
-returning-to-sinocentrism/ [https://perma.cc/FLV4-V9HC].

Steinbock, Dan, "U.S.-China Trade War and Its Global Impacts" (2018) 4(4) *China
Quarterly of International Strategic Studies* 515–542.

Stephen, John J., "Sakhalin Island: Soviet Outpost in Northeast Asia" (1970) 12(12) *Asian
Survey* 1090–1100.

Stokes, Bruce, *Hostile Neighbors: China vs. Japan* (September 13, 2016), https://www
.pewresearch.org/global/2016/09/13/hostile-neighbors-china-vs-japan/ [https://
perma.cc/A5CN-CKR8].

Strobel, Warren P., Michael R. Gordon, and Nancy A. Youssef, "Russia Moves More
Weaponry Toward Ukraine, Keeps the West Guessing," *Wall Street Journal*, January
14, 2022, https://www.wsj.com/articles/russia-moves-more-weaponry-toward
-ukraine-keeps-the-west-guessing-11642161605 [https://perma.cc/G66K-PGBK].

Suganuma, Unryu, *Sovereign Rights and Territorial Space in Sino-Japanese Relations: Irredentism
and the Diaoyu/Senkaku Islands* (University of Hawaii Press, 2000).

Suh, Dae-Sook, "Military-First Politics of Kim Jong Il" (2002) 26(3) *Asian Perspective*
145–167.

Suh, Ji-Youn, "Mongolian Leader to N. Korea: 'No Tyranny Lasts Forever'" *Korean Herald*,
November 15, 2013, http://www.koreaherald.com/view.php?ud=20131115000897
[https://perma.cc/2UGH-5RSE].

Sutter, Robert G., *US-China Relations: Perilous Past, Uncertain Present* (3d ed., Rowman &
Littlefield, 2018).

Sykes, Alan, *Stanford's Al Sykes on the $280 Billion Chips and Science Act, Government Intervention,
and Trade* (August 2, 2022), https://law.stanford.edu/2022/08/02/stanfords-al-sykes
-on-the-280-billion-chips-and-science-act-government-intervention-and-trade/
[https://perma.cc/27MX-A9SK].

Tachikawa, Tomoyuki, "FOCUS: Chinese Citizens Support Xi's Hard-Line Policy
Against Hong Kong," *Kyoto News*, March 6, 2021, https://english.kyodonews.net/
news/2021/03/39fe8d7e5ccd-focus-chinese-citizens-support-xis-hard-line-policy
-against-hong-kong.html [https://perma.cc/GLP5-73QT].

"Taiwan Rejects China's 'One Country, Two Systems' Plan for the Island," *Reuters*, August 6, 2022, https://www.reuters.com/world/asia-pacific/taiwan-rejects-chinas-one -country-two-systems-plan-island-2022-08-11/ [https://perma.cc/Z6XG-VEXB].

Tamamoto, Masaru, "Reflections on Japan's Postwar State" (1995) 124(2) *Daedalus* 1–22.

Tamponi, Alessandra, *The Start of a Generational Turn in Mongolian Politics: What Can We Expect from L. Oyun-Erdene's New Cabinet?* (February 8, 2021), https://eias.org/publications/op -ed/the-start-of-a-generational-turn-in-the-mongolian-politics-what-can-we-expect -from-l-oyun-erdenes-new-cabinet/ [https://perma.cc/8W3P-UDS4].

Tanner, Harold M., *China: A History: From the Great Qing Empire through The People's Republic of China (1644 - 2009)*, vol. 2 (Hackett Publishing Company, 2010).

The July 4 South-North Joint Communiqué, July 4, 1972, https://peacemaker.un.org/ sites/peacemaker.un.org/files/KR%20KP_720704_The%20July%204%20South-North%20Joint%20Communiqu%C3%A9.pdf [https://perma.cc/C572-T8NF].

Tikkanen, Amy, "Sakhalin Island," *Encyclopaedia Britannica*, https://www.britannica.com /place/Sakhalin-Island [https://perma.cc/JA7X-T5JG].

Tobita, Rintaro, "U.S. Calls Out Japan and Netherlands over China Chip Curbs," *Nikkei Asia*, November 6, 2022, https://asia.nikkei.com/Business/Electronics/U.S. -calls-out-Japan-and-Netherlands-over-China-chip-curbs [https://perma.cc/5HDM -GD6U].

Toloraya, Georgy, "The Six Party Talks: A Russian Perspective" (2008) 32(4) *Asian Perspective* 45–69.

Trading Economics, *Japan Exports by Country* (2022), https://tradingeconomics.com/ japan/exports-by-country [https://perma.cc/4BM2-HHL7].

Trading Economics, *Mongolia Foreign Direct Investment* (2022), https://tradingeconomics.com /mongolia/foreign-direct-investment#:~:text=Foreign%20Direct%20Investment %20in%20Mongolia%20averaged%2019380.19%20USD%20Million%20from,the %20fourth%20quarter%20of%202010. [https://perma.cc/7YKN-F3VC].

Trading Economics, *South Korea Exports by Country* (2022), https://tradingeconomics.com/ south-korea/exports-by-country [https://perma.cc/LGH4-CB7E].

Treaty of Mutual Cooperation and Security between Japan and the United States of America (1960), https://www.mofa.go.jp/region/n-america/us/q&a/ref/1.html [https://perma.cc/CDQ9-RUAR].

Treaty of Peace, Amity, Commerce and Navigation between the United States and the Kingdom of Korea (1882), https://www.degruyter.com/document/doi/10.1515 /9780824885380-020/pdf (accessed December 22, 2022).

Treaty of Peace with Japan (1951), https://treaties.un.org/doc/Publication/UNTS/ Volume%20136/volume-136-I-1832-English.pdf [https://perma.cc/DNX3-CMD8].

Treaty of Portsmouth (1905), https://portsmouthpeacetreaty.org/process/peace/ TreatyText.pdf [https://perma.cc/U675-AW2Q].

Treaty on Basic Relations Between Japan and the Republic of Korea (1965), https:// treaties.un.org/doc/Publication/UNTS/Volume%20583/volume-583-I-8471 -English.pdf [https://perma.cc/K2JH-RLTD].

Trend Economy, *Mongolia's Exports 2021 by Country*, https://trendeconomy.com/data/h2/ Mongolia/TOTAL [https://perma.cc/Y2MT-9WL7].

Trofimov, Yaroslav, "The New Beijing-Moscow Axis," *Wall Street Journal*, February 2, 2019.

Tseng, Hui-Yi Katherine, "China's Territorial Disputes with Japan: The Case of Senkaku/Diaoyu Islands" (2014) 1(2) *Journal of Territorial and Maritime Studies* 71–95.

Tsogtochir, Burmaa and Soyoung Park, "Natural Resource Curse Exists in Mongolia? Focusing on Budget Transparency in Local Governments" (2021) *Journal of the Asia Pacific Economy*, doi: 10.1080/13547860.2021.1892566 (accessed December 22, 2022).

"Ukraine War: US Estimates 200,000 Military Casualties on All Sides," *BBC News*, November 10, 2022, https://www.bbc.com/news/world-europe-63580372 (accessed December 22, 2022).

Unicef Mongolia, *Environment & Air Pollution*, https://www.unicef.org/mongolia/environment-air-pollution#:~:text=Ulaanbaatar%20%E2%80%93%20home%20to%20half%20of,level%20WHO%20recommends%20as%20safe. [https://perma.cc/7RPK-RMPB].

United Nations, The International Covenant on Civil and Political Rights, G.A. Res. 2200A (XXI) (Dec. 16, 1966).

United Nations, Memorandum on security assurances in connection with Ukraine's accession to the Treaty on the Non-Proliferation of Nuclear Weapons, UNTS, vol. 3007, I-52241 (December 5, 1994), https://treaties.un.org/doc/Publication/UNTS/Volume%203007/Part/volume-3007-I-52241.pdf [https://perma.cc/S289-6SZK].

United Nations, *Aggression against Ukraine*, A/ES-11/L.1 (March 1, 2022), https://digitallibrary.un.org/record/3958976?ln=en (assessed December 22, 2022).

United Nations, "UN General Assembly Votes to Suspend Russia from the Human Rights Council," *UN News*, April 7, 2022, https://news.un.org/en/story/2022/04/1115782 [https://perma.cc/XX6W-HEPW].

United Nations Conference on Trade and Development, *Evolution of the World's 25 Top Trading Nations*, https://unctad.org/topic/trade-analysis/chart-10-may-2021 (accessed December 22, 2022).

United Nations Human Rights Council, *Report of the Commission of Inquiry on Human Rights in the Democratic People's Republic of Korea*, A/HRC/25/63 (February 7, 2014).

United Nations Human Rights Office of the High Commissioner, *OHCHR Assessment of human rights concerns in the Xinjiang Uyghur Autonomous Region, People's Republic of China* (August 31, 2022), https://www.ohchr.org/sites/default/files/documents/countries/2022-08-31/22-08-31-final-assesment.pdf [https://perma.cc/M8VT-5PUL].

United Nations Research Institute for Social Development, *Economic and Social Development in the Republic of Korea: Processes, Institutions and Actors*, Research and Policy Brief 14 (October 2012).

United States Census Bureau, *Top Trading Partners—September 2022*, https://www.census.gov/foreign-trade/statistics/highlights/top/top2209yr.html [https://perma.cc/GK26-WWXH].

"United States Continues to Block New Appellate Body Members for the World Trade Organization, Risking the Collapse of the Appellate Process" (2019) 113(4) *American Journal of International Law* 822–831.

United States Statistics Division, *Value Added by Economic Activity, at Current Prices – US Dollars (Mining Manufacturing, and Utilities)*, https://unstats.un.org/unsd/snaama/Basic (accessed December 22, 2022).

United States Trade Representative, "Notice of Modification of s. 301 Action: China's Acts, Policies, and Practices Related to Technology Transfer, Intellectual Property, and Innovation," 83 *Federal Register* (September 21, 2018).

United States Trade Representative, *Indo-Pacific Economic Framework for Prosperity (IPEF)*, https://ustr.gov/trade-agreements/agreements-under-negotiation/indo-pacific-economic-framework-prosperity-ipef [https://perma.cc/Y2DE-QXNM].

U.S. Army Garrison Humphreys, https://home.army.mil/humphreys/index.php [https://perma.cc/EMV2-RB4Q].

"US Calls on China, Hong Kong to Release Stand News staff," *France* 24, December 30, 2021, https://www.france24.com/en/asia-pacific/20211230-us-calls-on-china-hong-kong-to-release-stand-news-staff [https://perma.cc/ZB8P-WEJR].

U.S. Chamber of Commerce, *Made in China 2025: Global Ambitions Built on Local Protections* (2017), https://www.uschamber.com/assets/archived/images/final_made_in_china_2025_report_full.pdf [https://perma.cc/YU48-CXW9].

"US Confronts China, Russia at UN over N Korean Missile Launches," *Aljazeera*, November 5, 2022, https://www.aljazeera.com/news/2022/11/5/us-confronts-china-russia-at-un-over-n-korean-missile-launches [https://perma.cc/J6KB-N8Y5].

U.S. Congress, *Calling on the People's Republic of China (PRC) to cease its retaliatory measures against the Republic of Korea in response to the deployment of the U.S. Terminal High Altitude Area Defense (THAAD) to U.S. Forces Korea (USFK), and for other purposes*, H. Res. 223, 115th Congress (2017).

U.S. Department of Defense, *Military and Security Developments Involving the People's Republic of China 2021* (2021), https://media.defense.gov/2021/Nov/03/2002885874/-1/-1/0/2021-CMPR-FINAL.PDF [https://perma.cc/88FK-5MQV].

U.S. Department of Defense, *2022 National Defense Strategy of the United States* (October 2022), https://media.defense.gov/2022/Oct/27/2003103845/-1/-1/1/2022-NATIONAL-DEFENSE-STRATEGY-NPR-MDR.PDF [https://perma.cc/57D6-HE2D].

U.S. Department of State, *U.S. Relations with Mongolia* (June 24, 2021), https://www.state.gov/u-s-relations-with-mongolia/ [https://perma.cc/V4GQ-C97T].

U.S. Department of State, *Integrated Country Strategy: Mongolia* (March 8, 2022), https://www.state.gov/wp-content/uploads/2022/05/ICS_EAP_Mongolia_Public-1.pdf [https://perma.cc/L2CU-ZD5M].

U.S. Department of State, 2021 *Country Reports on Human Rights Practices: China (Includes Hong Kong, Macau, and Tibet)*, https://www.state.gov/reports/2021-country-reports-on-human-rights-practices/china/ [https://perma.cc/GP97-597E].

U.S. Department of State, *Japan, China, the United States and the Road to Pearl Harbor, 1937-41*, https://history.state.gov/milestones/1937-1945/pearl-harbor [https://perma.cc/7RLH-6QN4].

U.S. Department of State, *Nuclear Non-Proliferation Treaty*, https://www.state.gov/nuclear-nonproliferation-treaty/ [https://perma.cc/KF5E-V6TV].

U.S. Department of State, *Resolution of the Comfort Woman Issue*, https://2009-2017.state.gov/secretary/remarks/2015/12/250874.htm [https://perma.cc/TA4P-362F].

U.S. Department of Transportation's Bureau of Transportation Statistics, *World Motor Vehicle Production, Selected Countries*, https://www.bts.gov/content/world-motor-vehicle-production-selected-countries [https://perma.cc/L653-ZVPC].

U.S. Energy Information Administration, *North Korea* (June 2018), https://www.eia.gov/international/analysis/country/PRK [https://perma.cc/7JKX-JGHE].

U.S. Government Accountability Office, *Burden Sharing: Benefits and Costs Associated with the U.S. Military Presence in Japan and South Korea*, GAO-21-270 (March 17, 2021), https://www.gao.gov/products/gao-21-270 [https://perma.cc/CQ9T-G4AE].

"U.S. Hails Japan's New Security Strategy as 'Bold and Historic'" *Kyodo News*, December 17, 2022, https://english.kyodonews.net/news/2022/12/5ee1f51910f0-us-hails

-japans-new-security-policy-as-bold-and-historic.html [https://perma.cc/UT89 -R6M6].

U.S. Indo-Pacific Command, *About USINDOPACOM*, https://www.pacom.mil/About -USINDOPACOM/ [https://perma.cc/F8GS-3JBA].

U.S. Library of Congress, *Modern Mongolia, 1911-84*, http://countrystudies.us/mongolia /26.htm [https://perma.cc/54F4-8E5B].

U.S. Senate Committee on Appropriations, *Hearings on appropriations for 1951* (U.S. Government Printing Office, 1950).

Valencia, Mark, "Japan's New Assertiveness Re-Energizes Its Territorial Disputes," *Asia Times*, August 17, 2021, https://asiatimes.com/2021/08/japans-new-assertiveness-re -energizes-its-territorial-disputes/ [https://perma.cc/DYK6-56J6].

Van Kemenade, Willem, *China and Japan: Partners or Permanent Rivals?* (Clingendael Institute, 2006).

Van Ree, Erik, "The limits of Juche: North Korea's dependence on Soviet industrial aid, 1953–76" (1989) 5(1) *Journal of Communist Studies* 50–73.

Van Slyke, Lyman P., "The United Front in China" (1970) 5(3) *Popular Fronts* 119–135.

Varada, Pranay, "Mongolia: On the Verge of a Mineral Miracle," *Harvard International Review*, February 11, 2022, https://hir.harvard.edu/mongolia-on-the-verge-of-a -mineral-miracle/ [https://perma.cc/8Z3B-PEYD].

Veatch, R., "Japan, the United States, and Manchuria" (1932) 1 Editorial Research Reports 1932. https://library.cqpress.com/cqresearcher/document.php?id=cqresrre19 32062000 [https://perma.cc/GT7J-M62K].

Walt, Stephen M., *The Origins of Alliances* (Cornell University Press, 1987).

Waltz, Kenneth N., *Theory of International Politics* (Addison-Wesley, 1979).

Wang, Amber, "China Warns Japan Against Joining Forces with US," *South China Morning Post*, May 18, 2022, https://www.scmp.com/news/china/diplomacy/article/3178259 /china-warns-japan-against-joining-forces-us [https://perma.cc/P76R-WSSP].

Wang, Dong and Friso M. S. Stevens, "Why Is There No Northeast Asian Security Architecture? – Assessing the Strategic Impediments to a Stable East Asia" (2021) 34(4) *Pacific Review* 577–604.

Wang, Orange, "How Much Is China's Foreign Direct Investment and Is It Still a Good Destination for Overseas Investors?" *South China Morning Post*, June 10, 2022, https:// www.scmp.com/economy/economic-indicators/article/3181037/how-much-chinas -foreign-direct-investment-and-it-still [https://perma.cc/8B9C-W4FA].

Wang, Yi, "The Backward Will Be Beaten: Historical Lesson, Security, and Nationalism in China" (2020) 29(126) *Journal of Contemporary China* 887–900.

Wang, Zheng, "History Education: The Source of Conflict Between China and Japan," *The Diplomat*, April 23, 2014, https://thediplomat.com/2014/04/history-education -the-source-of-conflict-between-china-and-japan/ [https://perma.cc/NJ8L-Y7UF].

Ward, Alexander and Quint Forgey, "North Korea Tested Its First ICBM since 2017," *Politico*, March 10, 2022, https://www.politico.com/newsletters/national-security -daily/2022/03/10/north-korea-tested-its-first-icbm-since-2017-00016206 [https:// perma.cc/WAD3-FGGY].

Warnberg, Tim, "The Kwangju Uprising: An Inside View" (1987) 11 *Korean Studies* 33–57.

Weber, Isabella M., *How China Escaped Shock Therapy: The Market Reform Debate* (Routledge, 2021).

Wertz, Daniel, Matthew McGrath, and Scott Lafoy, "North Korea's Nuclear Weapons Program," *Issue Brief*, The National Committee on North Korea (April 2018), https://www.ncnk.org/sites/default/files/issue-briefs/NCNK_IssueBrief_NorthKoreaN uclearWeapons_April2018.pdf [https://perma.cc/3RGU-2Z3R].

Westad, Odd Arne, *The Cold War: A World History* (Basic Books, 2019).

Westcott, Ben, "Kim Jong Un 'Ordered' Half Brother's Killing, South Korean Intelligence Says," *CNN*, February 28, 2017, https://www.cnn.com/2017/02/27/asia /kim-jong-nam-north-korea-killed [https://perma.cc/WS5J-K57B].

"What Does Xi Jinping's China Dream Mean?" *BBC News*, June 6, 2013, https://www .bbc.com/news/world-asia-china-22726375 (accessed December 22, 2022).

"What the Chinese People are Revealing about Themselves," *New York Times*, December 3, 2022, https://www.nytimes.com/2022/12/03/opinion/china-covid-protests.html (accessed December 30, 2022).

White, Edward, Song Jung-a, and Kang Buseong, "Lotte's China Woes a Harbinger of South Korean Exodus," *Financial Times*, June 20, 2019, https://www.ft.com/content /3a2eaeb2-9330-11e9-aea1-2b1d33ac3271 [https://perma.cc/7U22-J4ZM].

White House, *Building Resilient Supply Chains, Revitalizing American Manufacturing, and Fostering Broad-Based Growth* (June 2021), https://www.whitehouse.gov/wp-content /uploads/2021/06/100-day-supply-chain-review-report.pdf   [https://perma.cc/ VXX9-QSLQ].

White House, *Indo-Pacific Strategy of the United States* (February 2022), https://www .whitehouse.gov/wp-content/uploads/2022/02/U.S.-Indo-Pacific-Strategy.pdf [https://perma.cc/8ZJL-RXK4].

White House, *Background Press Call by a Senior Administration Official on Announcement of U.S. Ban on Imports of Russian Oil, Liquefied Natural Gas, and Coal* (March 8, 2022), https:// www.whitehouse.gov/briefing-room/press-briefings/2022/03/08/background -press-call-on-announcement-of-u-s-ban-on-imports-of-russian-oil-liquefied-natural -gas-and-coal/#:~:text=Today%2C%20President%20Biden%20signed%20an,his %20needless%20war%20of%20choice [https://perma.cc/D29N-P7ZN].

White House, *Fact Sheet: CHIPS and Science Act Will Lower Costs, Create Jobs, Strengthen Supply Chains, and Counter China* (August 9, 2022), https://www.whitehouse.gov/briefing -room/statements-releases/2022/08/09/fact-sheet-chips-and-science-act-will-lower -costs-create-jobs-strengthen-supply-chains-and-counter-china/   [https://perma.cc /74RA-4KHW].

White House, *National Security Strategy* (October 2022), https://www.whitehouse.gov/ wp-content/uploads/2022/10/Biden-Harris-Administrations-National-Security -Strategy-10.2022.pdf [https://perma.cc/HH24-B83N].

White House, *Phnom Penh Statement on US – Japan – Republic of Korea Trilateral Partnership for the Indo-Pacific* (November 13, 2022), https://www.whitehouse.gov/briefing-room /statements-releases/2022/11/13/phnom-penh-statement-on-trilateral-partnership -for-the-indo-pacific/ [https://perma.cc/T78M-8ERE].

"Why did Russia Invade Ukraine and Has Putin's War Failed?" *BBC News*, November 16, 2022, https://www.bbc.com/news/world-europe-56720589 (accessed December 22, 2022).

Widakuswara, Patsy, "Biden Pushes Expansion of Domestic Semiconductor Manufacturing," *Voice of America*, January 21, 2022, https://www.voanews.com/a/ biden-pushes-expansion-of-domestic-semiconductor-manufacturing/6407527.html [https://perma.cc/63BL-PSRA].

Wilborn, Thomas L., *Japan's Self-Defense Forces: What Dangers to Northeast Asia?* (Strategic Studies Institute, US Army War College, 1994).

Wishnick, Elizabeth, "The Sino-Russian Partnership and the North Korean Nuclear Crisis," *The National Bureau of Asian Research* (June 14, 2019), https://www.nbr.org/publication/the-sino-russian-partnership-and-the-north-korean-nuclear-crisis/ [https://perma.cc/8CDA-8M2V].

Wishnick, Elizabeth, "Mongolia: Bridge or Buffer in Northeast Asia?" *The Diplomat*, June 19, 2019, https://thediplomat.com/2019/06/mongolia-bridge-or-buffer-in-northeast-asia/ [https://perma.cc/3R8E-GBZY].

Wolff, David, Yokote Shinji, and Willard Sunderland (eds.), *Russia's Great War and Revolution in the Far East: Re-imagining the Northeast Asian Theater, 1914–22* (Slavica, 2018).

Wong, Chun Han, "Is China's Communist Party Still Communist?" *Wall Street Journal*, June 30, 2021, https://www.wsj.com/articles/is-chinas-communist-party-still-communist-11625090401 [https://perma.cc/D2HB-84CC].

Wong, Edward and Ana Swanson, "U.S. Aims to Constrain China by Shaping Its Environment, Blinken Says," *New York Times*, May 26, 2022, https://www.nytimes.com/2022/05/26/us/politics/china-policy-biden.html [https://perma.cc/9JEM-LEBR].

Wood, Alan, *Russia's Frozen Frontier: A History of Siberia and the Russian Far East, 1581–1991* (Bloomsbury, 2011).

Workman, Daniel, *North Korea's Top Trading Partners* (2022), https://www.worldstopexports.com/north-koreas-top-import-partners/ [https://perma.cc/5YJK-6GY5].

Workman, Daniel, *Mongolia's Top 10 Exports*, https://www.worldstopexports.com/mongolias-top-10-exports/ [https://perma.cc/3X28-6HN7].

World Bank, *Armed Forces Personnel, Total - Japan*, https://data.worldbank.org/indicator/MS.MIL.TOTL.P1?most_recent_value_desc=true&locations=JP [https://perma.cc/5DUG-R68S].

World Bank, *China Trade*, https://wits.worldbank.org/CountrySnapshot/en/CHN (accessed December 22, 2022).

World Bank, *Exports of Goods and Services (% of GDP) – Korea, Rep.*, https://data.worldbank.org/indicator/NE.EXP.GNFS.ZS?locations=KR [https://perma.cc/779N-HQVA].

World Bank, *Exports of Goods and Services (Current US$) – Mongolia*, https://data.worldbank.org/indicator/NE.EXP.GNFS.CD?locations=MN [https://perma.cc/AFU7-XJ2Y].

World Bank, *GDP (Current US$)*, https://data.worldbank.org/indicator/NY.GDP.MKTP.CD [https://perma.cc/UJ53-S2T9].

World Bank, *GDP (Current US$) – China, Japan*, https://data.worldbank.org/indicator/NY.GDP.MKTP.CD?locations=CN-JP [https://perma.cc/5EX9-2VRC].

World Bank, *GDP (Current US$) – China, Russian Federation*, https://data.worldbank.org/indicator/NY.GDP.MKTP.CD?locations=CN-RU [https://perma.cc/93Z4-3SFY].

World Bank, *GDP (Current US$) – Japan*, https://data.worldbank.org/indicator/NY.GDP.MKTP.CD?locations=JP [https://perma.cc/NQK5-7EVK].

World Bank, *GDP (Current US$) – Japan, Korea, Rep., China*, https://data.worldbank.org/indicator/NY.GDP.MKTP.CD?locations=JP-KR-CN [https://perma.cc/Z6PL-KGEF].

World Bank, *GDP (Current US$) – Korea, Rep.*, https://data.worldbank.org/indicator/NY.GDP.MKTP.CD?locations=KR [https://perma.cc/254J-FEYA].

World Bank, *GDP (current US$) – Mongolia*, https://data.worldbank.org/indicator/NY
.GDP.MKTP.CD?locations=MN [https://perma.cc/QQ66-DHD4].

World Bank, *GDP Per Capita (Current US$) – China*, https://data.worldbank.org/indicator/
NY.GDP.PCAP.CD?locations=CN [https://perma.cc/AH9M-BMC5].

World Bank, *GDP Per Capita (Current US$) – Japan, United States*, https://data.worldbank
.org/indicator/NY.GDP.PCAP.CD?end=1995&locations=JP-US&start=1960
[https://perma.cc/FF3Z-TLFY].

World Bank, *GDP Growth (Annual %) – Mongolia*, https://data.worldbank.org/indicator/
NY.GDP.MKTP.Kd.zg?end=2021&locations=MN&start=1982 [https://perma.cc/
W5WH-CJ92].

World Bank, *GNI Per Capita, Atlas Method (Current US$) – Japan*, https://data.worldbank
.org/indicator/NY.GNP.PCAP.CD?locations=JP [https://perma.cc/Z32Z-NLMS].

World Bank, *GNI Per Capita, Atlas Method (Current US$) – Korea, Rep.*, https://data
.worldbank.org/indicator/NY.GNP.PCAP.CD?locations=KR   [https://perma.cc/
J6YW-QNUC].

World Bank, *GNI Per Capita, Atlas Method (Current US$) – Korea, Rep., Japan*, https://data
.worldbank.org/indicator/NY.GNP.PCAP.CD?locations=KR-JP [https://perma.cc
/B3DL-972X].

World Bank, *GNI Per Capita, Atlas Method (Current US$) – Mongolia*, https://data.worldbank
.org/indicator/NY.GNP.PCAP.CD?locations=MN   [https://perma.cc/HAQ4
-DVCP].

World Bank, *Gross Domestic Product 2021*, https://databankfiles.worldbank.org/data/
download/GDP.pdf [https://perma.cc/ZH97-G9JB].

World Bank, *Manufacturing, Value-Added (Current US$) – China*, https://data.worldbank.org
/indicator/NV.IND.MANF.CD?locations=CN [https://perma.cc/4N25-9AEK].

World Bank, *Manufacturing, Value Added (% of GDP)*, https://databank.worldbank.org
/reports.aspx?source=2&series=NV.IND.MANF.ZS&country=MNG   (accessed
December 25, 2022).

World Bank, *Military Expenditure (% of GDP) – Japan*, https://data.worldbank.org/indicator
/MS.MIL.XPND.GD.ZS?most_recent_value_desc=true&locations=JP   [https://
perma.cc/QU4L-UCRM].

World Bank, *Military Expenditure (Current US$) – Japan*, https://data.worldbank.org
/indicator/MS.MIL.XPND.CD?most_recent_value_desc=true&locations=JP
[https://perma.cc/6XKB-RZVF].

World Bank, *Poverty Headcount Ratio at $6.85 a Day (2017 PPP) (% of Population) – China*,
https://data.worldbank.org/indicator/SI.POV.UMIC?locations=CN [https://
perma.cc/WBX4-J2D3].

World Bank, *The Global Economic Outlook During the COVID-19 Pandemic: A Changed World*,
https://www.worldbank.org/en/news/feature/2020/06/08/the-global-economic
-outlook-during-the-covid-19-pandemic-a-changed-world [https://perma.cc/MZ29
-JJ7J].

World Bank, *The World Bank in Mongolia* https://www.worldbank.org/en/country/
mongolia/overview#1 [https://perma.cc/P4XJ-PHBE].

World Bank, *The World Bank in Republic of Korea*, https://www.worldbank.org/en/country
/korea [https://perma.cc/WJY8-4BJT].

World Justice Project, *Rule of Law Index 2022* (2022), https://worldjusticeproject.org/rule
-of-law-index/global/2022 [https://perma.cc/E4D5-SKTE].

World Population Review, *Democracy Countries 2022* (2022), https://worldpopulationreview .com/country-rankings/democracy-countries [https://perma.cc/W843-BJ3P].

World Population Review, *Largest Countries in the World 2022* (2022), https://worldpopula tionreview.com/country-rankings/largest-countries-in-the-world [https://perma.cc/ MT79-LNZC].

World Population Review, *Mongolian Population 2022* (2022) https://worldpopulation review.com/countries/mongolia-population [https://perma.cc/TU48-PEY4].

World Steel Association, *World Steel in Figures 2022* (2022), https://worldsteel.org/steel -topics/statistics/world-steel-in-figures-2022/ [https://perma.cc/S9WQ-A2LB].

World Trade Organization, *United States – Tariff Measures on Certain Goods from China*, Report of the Panel, WT/DS543/R (September 15, 2020).

World Trade Organization, *Members Continue Push To Commence Appellate Body Appointment Process* (March 28, 2022), https://www.wto.org/english/news_e/news22_e/dsb _28mar22_e.htm [https://perma.cc/N68E-WTWP].

World Trade Organization, *Regional Trade Agreements Database* (September 16, 2022), http://rtais.wto.org/UI/PublicMaintainRTAHome.aspx [https://perma.cc/D22X -6LVR].

World Trade Organization, *World Trade Statistical Review 2022*, Table A6, https://www.wto .org/english/res_e/booksp_e/wtsr_2022_e.pdf [https://perma.cc/UYJ7-DDAS].

Wrage, Stephen D., "Germany and Japan Handle History Very Differently," *New York Times*, August 17, 1995, https://www.nytimes.com/1995/08/17/opinion/IHT -germany-and-japan-handle-history-very-differently.html [https://perma.cc/U47K -QXL4].

Wright, Quincy, "The Manchurian Crisis" (1932) 26(1) *American Political Science Review* 45–76.

"Xi Calls for Closer Cooperation Between Chinese, Mongolian Ruling Parties," *Xinhuanet*, July 4, 2020, http://www.xinhuanet.com/english/2020-07/04/c_139187996.htm [https://perma.cc/5T5B-ZS58].

Yamaguchi, Mari, "What's Behind Strained China-Japan Relations," *AP News*, September 28, 2022, https://apnews.com/article/taiwan-china-japan-asia-tokyo-44d f15b19e710fb8da38e69deae85b53 [https://perma.cc/76RG-L3CC].

Yamaguchi, Mari, "US Vows Full Military Defense of Allies Against North Korea," *AP News*, October 25, 2022, https://apnews.com/article/technology-japan-united-states -tokyo-south-korea-7397d3c81ecc6ceff76a4f0ffe25ec24 [https://perma.cc/L3AM -XYZP].

Yamamura, Kozo, *Economic Policy in Postwar Japan: Growth versus Economic Democracy* (University of California Press, 1967).

Yamane, Hiroko, "Japan as an Asian/Pacific Power" (1987) 27(12) *Asian Survey* 1302–1308.

Yang, Chen, "Japan's dream for UN Security Council seat crushed by its historical mirages," *Global Times*, September 26, 2020, https://www.globaltimes.cn/content /1202114.shtml [https://perma.cc/9BBP-KJT4].

Yeo, Hokyu, "China's Northeast Project and Trends in the Study of Koguryŏ History" (2006) 10 *International Journal of Korean History* 121–155.

Yi, Myonggu and William A. Douglas, "Korean Confucianism Today" (1967) 40 *Pacific Affairs* 43–59.

Yi, Whan-woo, "South Korea's Population to Shrink to 38 Million by 2070 Amid Rising World Population," *Korea Herald*, December 26, 2022, https://www.koreatimes.co.kr/ www/biz/2022/09/602_335593.html [https://perma.cc/67NM-RMGY].

Yoo, Sangchul, "Xi's Power is at Climax…Why Voices Missing Hu Jintao?" (in Korean), *The JoongAng*, October 27, 2019, https://www.joongang.co.kr/article/23616322 #home [https://perma.cc/AU59-EL2R].

Yoo, Seung-Mok, "Koreans Stop Going to Japan, but Japanese Still Come to Korea," *Money Today*, September 23, 2019, https://news.mt.co.kr/mtview.php?no =2019092314261312525 [https://perma.cc/88QT-49DW].

Yoon, Jong-Ju, "People Who Left Home" (in Korean), *Encyclopedia of Korean Culture* (1995), http://encykorea.aks.ac.kr/Contents/Item/E0033696 [https://perma.cc/5HXN -PFVJ].

"Yoon's Approval Rating Rises to 38.9%: Poll," *The Korea Herald*, December 5, 2022, https://www.koreaherald.com/view.php?ud=20221205000142 [https://perma.cc /7MM2-VZ3P].

Yoshimi, Yoshiaki, *Comfort Women* (Columbia University Press, 2002).

Young, Benjamin R., "When the Lights Went Out: Electricity in North Korea and Dependency on Moscow" (2020) 29(1) *International Journal of Korean Unification Studies* 107–134.

Zagora, Donald S., "Mao's Role in the Sino-Soviet Conflict" (1974) 47(2) *Pacific Affairs* 139–153.

Zakharova, Liudmila, "Russia and Northeast Asia: Pursuing Strategic and Economic Goals" (2017) 12(4) *Global Asia* 57–61.

Zatsepine, Victor, *Beyond the Amur: Frontier Encounters between Russia and China, 1850–1930* (University of British Columbia Press, 2017).

Zhang, Feng, "Chinas Rise Will be Peaceful," *in* Robert S. Ross and Zhu Feng (eds.), *China's Ascent-Power, Security, and the Future of International Politics* (Cornell University Press, 2008).

Zhao, Suisheng, "Rethinking the Chinese World Order: the imperial cycle and the rise of China" (2015) 24(96) *Journal of Contemporary China* 961–982.

Zheng, Bijan, "China's 'Peaceful Rise' to Great-Power Status," *Foreign Affairs*, September/ October 2005, https://www.foreignaffairs.com/articles/asia/2005-09-01/chinas -peaceful-rise-great-power-status [https://perma.cc/5RRT-Y8MJ].

Zheng, Sara, "Three reasons China will not accept a nuclear armed North Korea," *South China Morning Post*, September 19, 2017, https://www.scmp.com/news/china /diplomacy-defence/article/2111788/three-reasons-china-will-not-accept-nuclear -armed-north [https://perma.cc/X3Q8-86XD].

Zheng, William, "China's Communist Party Backs Xi Jinping's Firm Hand on Hong Kong and Taiwan," *South China Morning Post*, November 12, 2021, https://www .scmp.com/news/china/politics/article/3155755/chinas-communist-party-backs-xi -jinpings-firm-hand-hong-kong [https://perma.cc/3K88-NYP4].

Zubok, Vladislav, "The Soviet Union and China in the 1980s: reconciliation and divorce" (2017) 17 *Cold War History* 121–141.

INDEX

Note: Page numbers in **bold** indicate figures and tables.

www.ingramcontent.com/pod-product-compliance
Lightning Source LLC
Chambersburg PA
CBHW030640270326
41929CB00007B/151